Where the wild thyme blew

GROWING UP WITH NATURE
IN THE FIFTIES AND SIXTIES

First published in 2016 by Pisces Publications.
www.naturebureau.co.uk

Copyright © Peter Marren (2016)

All rights reserved. No part of this publication may be reproduced, stored in a retrieval system or transmitted, in any form or by any means electronic, mechanical, photocopying, recording or otherwise, without the prior permission of the publishers.

First published 2016.

Design and layout by Pisces Publications
Pisces is Publications is the imprint of NatureBureau

NatureBureau, 36 Kingfisher Court, Hambridge Road, Newbury, Berkshire RG14 5SJ
www.naturebureau.co.uk

Printed and bound in Britain by Gomer Press Ltd.

ISBN 978 1 874357 76 6

*To my nephews
Ben and George:
the latest Marrens*

Where the wild thyme blew

GROWING UP WITH NATURE IN THE FIFTIES AND SIXTIES

by Peter Marren

*'I know a bank where the wild thyme blows,
Where oxlips and the nodding violet grows,
Quite over-canopied with luscious woodbine,
With sweet musk-roses and with eglantine:
There sleeps Titania sometime of the night.'*

A Midsummer Night's Dream, 2.1

Contents

Introduction ix

Part 1 1
1. Under Faint Starlight 2
2. The Orphan and the Village Girl 12
3. Dad's War 25
4. Remlap 34
5. Snapshots from the Pram 44
6. Dad's Songs 56
7. A Little Learning 65
8. Childworld 74
9. Harpur Hill 87
10. Games we Played 96
11. Wet Holidays and Cold Playgrounds 104
12. Singapore 111
13. Manners Makyth Man 120
14. 14, Adam Drive 126
15. Songs of the Island 139
16. Back to Blighty 148
17. High Noon 154
18. Golden Afternoons at the House on the Hill 163
19. At the Crossroads 171

Part 2 177
1. Loughborough College School 178
2. A Hole and its Rules 185
3. Arrival 192
4. *Veritate, scientia, labore* 198
5. Alarums and Excursions 206
6. End of Term Report 212
7. Figures of Authority 220
8. Last Summer at The Mount 227

9. Clarence Knows the Ropes	233
10. Third Form	238
11. The Visible Man	244
12. Charlie and Other Hole-dwellers	250
13. Escaping from Kenmore Avenue	260
14. The Black Blazer	267
15. Butting in the Alps	273
16. The Ice Box	280
17. *Pater in filium*	285
18. Discovering Girls	292
19. Dorms in the Attic	298
20. Mr Henderson	303
21. A Vast Teenage Shrug	311
22. Farewell to the Hole	317
Part 3	**325**
1. A Trail of Flowers	326
2. Not the Place's Fault	336
3. Failing to Impress	345
4. Wordplay	353
5. Finding a Direction	360
6. Falling for a Welsh Girl	368
7. As a Moth to a Flame	375
8. On the Anvil	381
9. Finals	387
10. In Which Our Hero Sets Forth	394
Acknowledgements	400

Introduction

Wondering how to introduce this memoir of youth in bygone decades, I came across this quote by the Canadian writer Margaret Atwood in her 2000 novel, *The Blind Assassin*: 'When you are young you think everything is disposable. You move from now to now, crumpling up time in your hands, throwing it away.' It is only as you grow older that you realise that time has a habit of coming back. 'You can never get away from where you've been', concludes Atwood. Those distant days, you realise now, have been with you all the time, crumpled up, maybe, but not erased. We tuck away memories without being aware of it.

Whether you remember a little or a lot, all childhood memories are personal. They may or may not mean anything to other people. Why did I decide to share mine, to commit childhood moments to the public gaze, with all the attendant risk of embarrassing both of us? Initially I didn't. I had reached the age of sixty and, with a pension in the bank from my days in the Nature Conservancy, I decided to take a break from routine and to write down my memories while I still had them. I wrote it all out in longhand in one of those big 'Black n' Red' planners you can buy in Smiths. And then I typed it all up and saved it. A few friends read the text and said they liked it; that it had brought back nostalgic memories for them too. So next I decided to self-publish *Where the Wild Thyme Blew* with the help of a small legacy, intending to give away most of the copies to family and friends. I put the substantial remainder on sale (clearly I'd overestimated the number of my friends), advertised them not very prominently in a wildlife journal I write for, and, to my surprise, the memoir soon sold out.

I had not anticipated this. Encouraged by the many kind remarks I received, I considered a reprint. Certain obstacles in the way of this were removed and I decided to go for it. This revised edition has enabled me to correct the many typos that had crept in thanks to my rubbish proofreading. And to make other small changes to the text. I also belatedly sought an ISBN number so the book could be reviewed and ordered.

Since *Where the Wild Thyme Blew* may now be read by people who do not know me or my writing, the question that could be asked, perfectly legitimately, is why anyone should want to read about the young life of a complete stranger, someone who hardly ever appears on the telly and isn't well-known outside the small world of natural history enthusiasts. Why indeed? I suppose one answer I can give is that it all happened a long time ago and that the Fifties and Sixties have become 'history'. To anyone under forty those decades seem as remote from modern living as Queen Victoria. There may be some curiosity in what life was like back then, especially in an account that tries to capture the way a child saw the world at that time, and in words the child might have used had he had a grown-up's perception and vocabulary. And nature writing is popular at the moment, by which I mean the experience of nature as filtered through the mindset of a particular individual. I am a natural history writer by trade (defined roughly as a craft that takes a closer interest in the wildlife than in oneself). I have been passionate about nature throughout my life and it started in early boyhood. There was more of it about in the Fifties (perhaps 40 million more birds, for instance); the countryside was closer and less suburbanised – you seldom had to 'pay and display'. And you were much freer to enjoy it. I happily picked toadstools and wild flowers, and collected butterflies and moths, and I don't remember anyone trying to stop me; on the contrary, schools encouraged you to gather stuff for projects and for 'the nature table'. Nature was fun. So, if you like natural history, you might be interested in this book. If, like me, you suffer from late-middle-age nostalgia, you might also find it jogs your own memories of that distant golden age.

My childhood was a fairly ordinary one, at least in externals. As the son of a junior officer in the RAF, we never lived in any single place for more than three years together. I attended village schools, and, later, a boarding school, like most RAF boys did in those days. I did the usual things kids do. I watched the telly, and ate a lot of sweets, played games with friends and got into scraps with rival gangs. My family life was stable; no one died; the parents stayed together and kept us fed and clothed, and sufficiently loved. We were neither rich nor poor. We lived a middling sort of life really: middling income, a modest 3-bedroom RAF married quarter, an ordinary 4-door family saloon car made by Austin or Morris. We were right in the middle of the middle class. Even my school, in Loughborough, Leicestershire, was in the dead centre of England, the very middle of the Midlands.

My young nephews, Ben and George, would look down in pity at the sort of lives we led. We had no ipods or ipads for a start. The magical chip of silicon that changed lives forever had not yet been invented. The youngster's quad-bike on which Ben whizzes around the garden, or the electric swegway on which he glides around the house, would have looked like science fiction to us. We only had bikes, old-fashioned granny-cycles with no gears but a little bell you could jingle right next to the basket on the front. Where today's boys have remote-controlled toy helicopters, even drones, we built balsa-wood Jet-ex gliders and flew kites. They watch films at home on a screen eight feet across. We had to go to the RAF cinema, housed in some Nissen hut with a noisy projector and hard chairs to sit on. As for kiddy food, we had never heard of pizzas, and even hamburgers were regarded as pretty exotic. It was mostly jelly, ice cream and home-made cakes, that sort of thing.

All the same, we were one up, or rather, two up, on kids today. Firstly we had imagination. We needed it because, due to the lack of decent technology, we had to make our own entertainment. We could build play opportunities out of anything that came our way: a tree, for instance, or some rocks, or a river. We were not, I think, easily bored. And secondly we were much freer to wander. I had a country childhood thanks to the various RAF bases to which my father was posted. Parents were not then afraid for their children as they are today, and we children weren't afraid of anything. I wandered for miles and no one cared so long as I came home for tea. Most of our fun went unseen and unsupervised; we were, in that sense, wild kids, like Titty and Co, in *Swallows and Amazons*. It was out there, in the hills around Buxton, at the seaside, and in rustic farmyards, that I discovered nature for myself, without much adult guidance. Nature, I repeat, was fun. From nature you could fashion weapons and missiles, or collect stuff – bones, shells, dead bugs, shells – for your den. You could play endless games with it – those pinging plantain-guns and itching powder gouged out of rose-hips. Wherever there was water you could mess about with buckets and nets, or simply splash. Nature was free, both in the sense of costing nothing and also in the freedom it bought us, away from home and school and the suffocating presence of adults. We were the Fifties boys, inheritors of the new world, free of rationing, with free health care, and, mostly, free of care in general.

Most RAF boys were like miniature versions of their dads, whose main aim in life was to join the RAF, like him, or at least a job in aviation. My younger brother Chris was that sort of boy. I wasn't. I always had a sense of being on the edge of things. A career in flying was never going to be mine since I was short-sighted, and, when for a long time I disguised it, was indeed practically half-blind. Partly for the same reason I was also rubbish at most organised games. Even on the occasions I could see the ball coming, I usually ran the wrong way. At village schools I sounded too posh to be popular. I tended to get on well with the teacher, too, another black mark. I didn't want to be like this; I would much rather have been a hearty, but it did at least leave more room for nature in my life, and that mattered more in the long run. I have a feeling, encouraged by Chris Packham's candid revelations in his *Fingers in the Sparkle Jar*, that many lifelong naturalists are like this, quiet boys with their heads in a book, in a world of their own. We think we are unusual, even unique, but the world is in fact full of boys like us. The naturalist Trevor Beebee believes there are 'unfathomed biological bases' to our passions over which we have no control. We didn't choose to be naturalists. In some way beyond understanding, nature seemed to choose us.

Many people have told me they cannot remember much about their own childhoods; it is only when they reach their teens – girls, guitars, sport – that memories start to crowd in. Maybe it is due to approaching old age, but I find I remember my childhood fairly well although I would have difficulty telling you what I did last week. Of course a lot of it has gone beyond recall, especially in those first years in the cot and then as a toddler when adults are giants and your world is no bigger than the garden and the playpen. But even there you remember the odd moment, which must have come and gone in a twinkling, one that takes you back to some prehistoric moment in existence: a sand-bucket with a picture of Mickey Mouse; the smell of RAF-issue lavender polish; a butterfly caught in a sweaty fist; the strange ecstasy of slipping your mother's hand and running away: tiny, Proustian fragments of past time that, for whatever reason, have stuck when everything else has fallen away.

Perhaps I should explain the title of this book. In Shakespeare's *A Midsummer Night's Dream*, the Queen of the Fairies, Titania, makes her bower on the kind of flowery bank which is itself a dream of nature: a place crowned with scented honeysuckle and musk-roses, and carpeted with violets and thyme, a wonder-world of fragrances and colours. As for 'blew', it means gone to seed. The season was late and the wild thyme had nearly finished flowering. I probably don't need to say any more.

Where the Wild Thyme Blew is in three parts. The first is about the progress of my free-range boyhood. It is, on the whole, a sunny tale of young Bevis discovering the wild world around him, and is also about the boy's world of the Fifties. Part 2 is about my incarceration in a place I call The Hole, an experience shared by many boys from my background and, again, one utterly untypical of boyhood today. Inside those high walls I grew from a frightened small boy into a moody, quietly rebellious teenager. Nature, now experienced mainly during school holidays, offered the best form of escape. Part 3 is about university, in which I failed at nearly everything but did emerge knowing what I wanted to do with my life. You'd never guess, but it was about nature. That was my young life; as Dogberry says in *Much Ado About Nothing*, 'an ill-favoured thing, Sir, but mine own'.

The images I have assembled for these pages are mostly of poor quality, and worse reproduction, but I rather like that. What matters more than quality, I think, is tone. The images match our memories: distinct yet blurred, and perhaps sentimentalised by distance.

I hope my young life reminds you of yours.

Peter Marren
Ramsbury, Wiltshire
August 2016

PART ONE

Today was good. Today was fun.
Tomorrow is another one.

'Dr Suess' (Theodor Geisel)

CHAPTER ONE

Under Faint Starlight

It is not easy being born. Looking back, I think it might have been one of the toughest things I ever did. As Miriam Rothschild noted, 'the average man is squeezed out into the world with blood to lubricate his passage and wild shrieks of anguish to speed him on his way'. I emerged into this breathing world at half-past-four in the afternoon to find myself in the ward of an RAF hospital in Hamburg, Germany. I was a healthy baby, a little on the large side, weighing eight pounds, six ounces. But I had not been co-operative and my poor, exhausted mother was put on a drip while the orderly looked around for a blood donor. The story goes that a volunteer was sought from the officer's mess—no plebian blood for *this* birth!—but the bar was open and no one was sober. I don't suppose this is true.

The problem was mother's rare blood type. She is A-negative, known in the trade as 'monkey blood', and, thanks to her, so am I. Top-whack, alpha-blood but without those useful rhesus things. It is dangerous blood. My grandmother inherited the gene for pernicious anaemia which doubtless has bounced down the generations like a pinball, hitting this chap and sparing that. On my father's side there is chronic leukaemia to contend with; that carried off *his* mother at the age of forty. There seems to be a lick of TB in there too, the scourge that carried off his *Dad*. But, as I say, despite all this, I was a normal, healthy baby, and apart from the odd nervous breakdown at school, I have remained healthy and strong ever since. Now in my sixties, I can, for instance, walk up a modest-sized hill without losing my puff. Efficient digestion, all my own hair and teeth. There's a danger in saying so, at my age, but just now this silver-haired old bloke with his late-middle-age paunch, this decrepit fatso, is starting to look like a survivor. And, I like to think, a testament to the resilience of the human spirit too. Because it's going to get a bit traumatic later on, you see if it doesn't.

The reason I was born in Hamburg was the Berlin Airlift. My father was helping to ensure that Stalin didn't get his blood-stained claws on the erstwhile German capital. Dad was an expert in the loading of RAF transport planes. The trick is to get the balance right so that the shifting loads don't wobble the plane in mid-flight. Hamburg was then the headquarters of the British High Command. Most babies born in Hamburg are native Hamburgers, the sons and daughters of sailors and dockers and whores. But the RAF hospital where I was born was officially British, and so I was a British baby. Our chaps had taken over those parts of the city left standing after the war, including our spacious house, sequestered from its rightful owner by the same force that had bombed the place flat back in July 1943. I have always been rather proud of being an honorary Hamburger. More exotic than York, which is where my younger brother first surfaced, and much cooler than Loughborough, which is where they sent me to school. You can imagine babies born in Loughborough taking one look and trying to clamber back in again. I know I would.

They called me Peter, for no particular reason. It is not a family name. There are no known Peters on my mother's side or my father's. They just liked it. I don't know why they liked it. I don't. Peter is a sap's name and, besides, at infant school a name beginning with P ensured you a place near the back of the line. And another thing: the arrangement of its letters makes Peter a real struggle for a fancy signature, especially when conjoined with the even more anodyne 'Marren'. There's no music in my name. Peter *Marren*. It comes out sounding like you've had a tooth out and your gums are still frozen. And it lends itself to mockery. "What are you called young fella?" the large, uniformed man demanded when poor, nervous little Peter found himself travelling alone for the first time. "What's that? Marram? Speak up, did you say *Moron*? He *looks* like a moron, don't he, Fred?" Anyway, there it is and I'm stuck with it: Peter Marren: a fine moniker to get lumbered with when so young and helpless. Thanks a lot, *Mum*.

My middle name is Richard. I don't mind that so much, except that Richards tend to end up as Dicks. Richard, or rather, *Dick*, was my maternal great-grandfather's name, known to mother as Granddad

Keeling. I never met him—he died before I was born—but mother says that's where my love of nature came from. It *must* have. Granddad Dick stuffed animals and collected birds' eggs, and he also did arty things like painting pub signs and reproducing portraits on glass. I did think of changing my name to Richard, not because of Great Granddad Dick so much but simply because it's a better name. But I left it too late. I tend to leave things until it is too late to do anything about them. I should have made the correction as soon as I could walk.

I wasn't too keen about being born in October either. My birthday, on 8th October, comes around the time of the first frosty mornings, when the low sun gets in your eyes and makes you irritable. It's a time for brooding about the year past: so much time, so little done. For a child it is too close to Christmas to really cash in. While any Christmas between, say, the age of three and ten is an eagerly anticipated toy-fest, October birthdays are, despite the jelly and candles, usually a disappointment.

This is Richard Keeling, my mother's maternal grandfather and supposedly my mentor though he was dead before I was born.

Parenthetically, October boys and girls are stuck with a star sign, Libra, which is the dullest in the sky. Have you ever *seen* Libra? It's pathetic. Summer-born kids get the lion, the bull, the ram, feisty constellations with bright stars and notable galaxies. October kids get a pair of scales. And no bright stars (speaking as an astro-nerd, I should tell you that one of the stars of Libra is green; whether that was a portent I really don't know). Born under the balance, so to speak, Librans are supposed to possess a strong sense of right and wrong. We are, they say, basically amiable, easy-going souls, but are inclined to be lazy, self-indulgent and indecisive. We enjoy some critical faculty—those scales again; we supposedly weigh things before coming to judgment. But, by an unfortunate paradox, we also tend to be gullible; in other words, we believe any old rubbish. I have noticed some of these traits in me but I daresay it is only coincidence. Like Edmund in *King Lear*, I would be that I am had the brightest stars in the firmament shone on my cradle. All the same, everything considered, October is a crap month to get born into.

The next event in my life followed fast on the heels of my first gulp of air and my first slurp of warm mother's milk. I was circumcised. Oh, great. Another treat. Apparently this was routine at the time. Like a sausage machine. No sooner had you settled into your nice warm cot for a well-earned rest than some fiend of a surgeon leers down, scoops you up, and, with a terrible motion, clips the top bit off your willy. Of course I remember none of this and wasn't aware of anything missing until years later when my still-intact brother Christopher pointed out an intriguing difference between his tinkle and mine. Yours is a *poon-ya*, he informed me, with a small child's wisdom, but mine is a *ty-mee* (forgive these intimacies; we were both very young). The only Libran judgment I can make about that is that it proves I did not spend my early childhood staring at my willy. But maybe that was only because I am short-sighted.

As you might expect by now, 1950 was not an auspicious year to be born. It lies inside the seven-year limbo between the end of the war and the beginning of what they wishfully termed the New Elizabethan Age. Two of the six most comprehensive histories of our times (Andrew Marr and A.J.P. Taylor) end in 1945, and three more (Martin Gilbert, A. N.

Wilson and Marr again) don't start until 1952. See? No one seems to care what happened in 1950. Well, for the record, King George VI was still on his throne, coughing throatily between drags, and a tiny, bald man called Clement Attlee was Prime Minister. The Korean War was in full swing, and UN troops crossed the 38th parallel the day before I was born. Petrol rationing ended, so people could once again travel by car and block the roads. Petrol then cost three shillings (15p) a gallon. The average weekly wage was £7 10 shillings for men, £4 two shillings and 5d for women, and, no, that wasn't much even in 1950. There was nothing at the top of the pops because there were no pops to be top of; instead we had 'light music'—'Good Night, Irene', 'My Foolish Heart'—and jazz. There were no home computers, no motorways or bypasses, no supermarkets, no multi-storey carparks, no jumbo jets and hardly any television sets. Good grief, until I was eight we didn't even have a *phone*. Or a fridge. The parents went to the cinema at least once a week, for which they dressed up smartly, stood for the national anthem, and smoked throughout. At home, the huge wooden radiogram was on all the time, tuned either to Home or Light. Nearly everyone was poor and the country was well-nigh bankrupt. But, so mother used to claim, we at least were comfortable. We got by. We were all right.

So: to sum up. At birth I inherited a rotten name, an unpromising star-sign, a bankrupt economy and a mutilated willy. Not a great start, and during moments of introspection and self-pity I have sometimes considered myself a peculiarly luckless person, born under a malign

Still Prime Minister. *Still King.* *Newly invented.*

planet in the not-so-twinkly stars of The Scales. But then I remember that in many ways the 1950s were a terrific time to be a boy, quite possibly the best time in history. We children of the baby-boom missed the war and post-war rationing. We could absolutely stuff ourselves with sweets, and so we were always seeing the NHS dentist, who did his stuff for free. We enjoyed comics in which the boy hero ends up either with a beating (father with his slipper, teacher with his cane) or a feast. We were the proud owners of an electric train set, a chemistry set, a fleet of Dinkies, a paintbox, a Meccano set, a children's encyclopedia, and an armoury of toy guns. We had the countryside to play in when it was still green and beautiful, and relatively traffic-free. And by the time we reached our teens we were the inheritors of the world's best popular music. We believed, in our sweet innocence, that we were the generation that would change the world for the better, or what we considered was better (free love, long hair, 'peace man' etc.). The Golden Age might have unravelled a bit in the 70s but at least we were now of just the right age to enjoy that partying decade, the noontime of sex, drink and drugs, before the arrival of AIDS and the breathalyzer. We reached the age of Mrs Thatcher at a good time to make money, while the 90s, we now realise, was a period of quite extraordinary prosperity, even if it was all built on sand. For the rest, it seems a good enough time to cultivate the garden and read the paper. It's someone else's time now. The party's over. The younger generation can clear up the mess.

When mother finally got over bringing me into the world, she lay in her hospital bed watching the birch leaves turn gold. She was discharged in time for Christmas, and decided to spend it with her family, Dad having no family of his own, a point to which I will return. On page 10 is a picture of me, taken shortly before we left the hospital. I'm held by the smiling, adoring nurse; in another my young and pretty mother has me artily lit by the big window, dressed in my special Christening gown. She looks proud and happy, as is right and proper. My own expression is harder to read; I think I look rather thoughtful.

I was scarcely two months old when my smiling and gurgling form was ferried, swaddled in wool, across the sea to Hull, and thence by steam train to Leicester and double-decker bus to my grandmother's house in the village of Mountsorrel. Since their marriage, this modest Victorian semi on Linkfield Road had been my parents' alternate home. It was now Christmas Eve and they all thought it would be nice if I was christened there. The gramps—mother's parents—were Anglican church-goers, and Grampa Redvers—gang-gang as I called him when I was very little—was the church warden. So it was probably not difficult to get me booked in at St Peter's, dunked in the font and given some godparents, all in short order. No one asked me, of course. The point of an infant baptism is that God won't accept babies unless they are baptized first. Without your baptism ticket, you get sent to some dark, foggy place where the sun never shines. But in practice it was a good excuse for a big family get-together at Christmas.

The parents returned to Hamburg laden with loot. There was a music box featuring some *'gemutlich'* cherubs garlanded in plaster roses, and an enormous lidded *stein* that would serenade you with *Du kannst nicht trau sein* as you knocked back the Kronenburg. There were pram accessories, spoons and serviette rings, as well as yet more woollen baby clothes, mostly knitted by my godmother, great-grandma Grace Mary. There was also a little book in which to record my vital statistics, plus an album for family snaps as the toddler grew in size and awareness and started breaking the crockery. I was, it seemed, quite a popular baby. And so I should have been, for I was the first of my generation: the postwar inheritors, the babies of a better world.

This tale of childhood and youth which I offer you now is based on an imperfect, but in certain respects pretty good, memory. It begins with disconnected, seemingly random recollections, which is pretty well all we are left with from those lost days when we toddled about in the playpen and slurped gloopy mush from the high chair. Eventually flickers of remembrance turn into proper memories and then the childhood retrospective can begin: that sunlit pageant where there was fun to be had on every fallen log and in every sand pit, and summer lasts for about a year (and when it hardly ever rained). I was fortunate in many ways, though, God knows, life seemed ordinary enough at the time. I had loving parents who, though necessarily thrifty, were not poor and needy and dependent on the state. I was allowed to run free, to a most astonishing extent it seems now. I was free to wander about, chase gilded butterflies and take an eager interest in the natural world. Though doomed to wear specs, I was bright, reasonably happy most of the time, and with a sufficiency of friends.

And then it all came tumbling down the day they sent me away to school. It wasn't even a very good school, just an ordinary grammar in the Midlands—the very middle of the Midlands—with a small boarding school attached. I was a boarder; at first, a very bored boarder. The general idea was that boarding would allow me a stable education— for my parents were always moving around, posted by the RAF from place to place. But school imposed austerities that came as a considerable shock to this free-range boy. The discomforts I experienced there were doubtless no worse than those of many similar establishments in postwar England (I say England advisedly; most Scots very sensibly kept their children at home). Indeed, a few of my fellow boarders have claimed that those were the best days of their lives (Christ, what were *their* lives like?) For me it was closer to Betjeman's portrayal of 'shivering doom'; the only thing that held up during this purgatory was the survival of my childhood love of nature. By the time I went to university I knew more or less what I wanted to do with my life, and, a year or two after that, I had worked out a way of doing it. Perhaps if I had not suffered social isolation at boarding school it might have been different. Perhaps my relationship with the natural world would have been less intense if I had had a more normal life with, for example, a steady girlfriend to straighten me out. As it was, I temporarily lost the capacity for friendship that I think I possessed as a boy and came to know again as a grown-up. I preferred wildlife to having a wild life, so to speak. It took me a while to put that right and to realize that some things, including the pleasures of discovery, are better when they are shared. As Cicero put it (in perfect Latin of course), nature abhors solitude.

Life is a mess; so is memory. I now have to knead it into some sort of shape, an art I used to exercise fairly regularly when I wrote obituaries for the papers. The writer has an advantage the child did not have; he knows what is coming next. You can make sense of things that once made none. For children don't look for external meaning; by and large, they accept things as they are. They live from day to day, play and quarrel and make up, and rarely look back—or forwards. If any of my lost childhood friends should read this, it is possible they might recall an event differently, or see it from another perspective, or threaten to sue me. For example, one day at my school, a boy, for a dare, jumped out of an upstairs window on to a pile of coke. That much we are agreed on. There was a big pile of freshly delivered coke out there and he thought it would be a great idea to leap down on to it and slide to the ground. It is in what happened next where our memories diverge. Whether he was spotted by the housemaster and caned, which is what I remember, or whether the boy broke his leg and was carried off on a stretcher, as my mate Kosh insists, who knows? That the leaper ended in the shit one way or another is clear; the rest, like so much of history, is argument and conjecture. We will never have the independent testimony of the leaper for he is dead, alas.

My first photographic portrait, in the RAF hospital in Hamburg, some time late in 1950.

Truth, as Oscar Wilde reminded us, is a many-sided thing. He saw it as something so personal it can never be shared. This book is my truth. Look on life as clay; it is fluid and shapeless until shaped by art, and if my clay pipe is someone else's teapot, I can only say that I must have a pipe-shaped memory. This is the boy's world as I remember it. It is also a record of a time and of circumstances that seemed ordinary enough then, but less now in a world that has changed utterly. Yes, it's a far-off land, the place where I was born.

CHAPTER TWO

The Orphan and the Village Girl

I'll start with my mother and father. There were moments, especially when in company, that you wished… well, you wished they were a bit more flash, that they knew a bit more, that they didn't say such boring things. Given the choice, I might have elevated my Dad to a landed earl of ancient lineage and mother perhaps to an heiress from the Californian demi-monde who had been in and out of half the houses in Hollywood. When I was small, I used to lie about them, especially Dad. My old man, I put it about, had shot up Japs in Burma, had spied for England behind the Iron Curtain, was test-piloting jet planes. I used to resent the fact that some of our neighbours had more medals than he had, that they had superior furniture and pictures, and a better-looking cat (though, I'd have to concede, Dad usually had the best garden). I should have appreciated them more for what they were: modest, kind, intermittently generous, and honest as the day is long. They placed their lives at the service of little Peter and his younger brother Chris. So much so, in fact, that in later life it was hard to shake them off. They worked hard, did their best, avoided strong liquor, stayed out of prison and brought up a family. I should bow my head before their solid virtues. They were my parents and I ask you now to stay in their company for a few pages so that I can try to explain how, behind their apparent ordinariness, lies a subset of history: pre-war life in an English village, an orphan in South London, the impact of a world war on two English families, the meeting of a rural Protestant and an urban Catholic, the challenges of a wrecked, postwar world. It was the world I grew up in: a steady sort of place despite its austerities. Men wore jackets and ties, and women wore blouses and skirts. Men had jobs for life while their wives stayed at home and brought up the family. Most people had only a fairly basic education but they were church-going and self-reliant, and usually possessed a solid measure of good English common-sense.

My mother, Jean Margaret Palmer, was born on 9th August 1922 in Mountsorrel, a Leicestershire village strung out along the A6 between the river and a hill of red granite—the 'mount' in Mountsorrel. She was the latest in a long line of Palmers that had lived in this corner of the world since at least the eighteenth century and probably long before; their names were inscribed in sepia-faded ink in the ancient family Bible. Mum had a brother two years older called George, my Uncle George. Mountsorrel folk were homely and rooted, and spoke with a soft, breathy Leicestershire accent. The old folks called the young folks 'me dooks' (ducks, that is). Jean and George called their parents 'Mam' and 'Pop'. The patriarch of my particular line was my mother's father, Grampa Redvers. His first name was Horace but no one ever called him that. Redvers was his name, a name once born by a fiery Victorian general with an enormous moustache. But our Redvers scarcely lived up to that image. He was quiet and unambitious, and he had no moustache, big or small. As soon as he left the little granite school at the top of the village green, Redvers took his turn at the lathe in the Wholesale Shoe Company where his father had worked as a foreman, and no doubt his father before that. In due course Redvers worked his way up to foreman in his turn. That was the way it was. After some basic education—mainly reading, writing and adding up—you joined your Dad at work, and did what your Dad did. When he wasn't working in the shoe factory, Redvers could be seen pottering about in the garden or smoking his pipe in the corner arm-chair that no one else was allowed to sit in. "Redvers has green fingers", they said. He liked being out there on his own, planting and potting and weeding. Otherwise, his life tended to revolve around the church. He served as church warden and took his family on church outings. He sent in his pools coupon every week and was a loyal supporter of Leicester City. He read library books—"that was a good 'un' ", he'd grunt, as he finished it—and, on Sunday afternoons, he walked to Swithland Reservoir and back, usually on his own.

That was Pop. He was a fairly easy-going Pop. It was his wife Doris, or Mam—my 'Nanna'—who was supposed to be the disciplinarian, though I find that hard to believe. Married in 1919, they lived first in a rented cottage on the Green before buying 48, Linkfield Road, the brick semi on the long street with a half-acre of back-garden that led down to a flooded clay pit. The green-fingered Redvers had been attracted by the potential of a large garden which was also close to the shoe factory. Also on the lane, past wobbly pavements bordered with kerbstones of Mountsorrel granite, was a factory that made cardboard boxes, as well as a garage, two grocers' shops and a lunatic asylum. On the other side of the clay pit stood the old brickworks that were later taken over by Rolls Royce to build aircraft components. Villages were busy places in those days.

My mother attended the same village school as her Pop had done. To judge from her reports, she was a bright, well-behaved girl. "Well done, Jean!" wrote the headmistress. Her best subject was arithmetic. She could add, subtract and multiply very nimbly, a talent she nurtured after leaving school through evening classes in accountancy. She might have been not bad at English either. When she was about 12 she wrote a poem beginning:

Far away the spring is calling
To the sleeping flowers.

It fell away a bit after that promising start but it is much better, I dare say, than I could have managed at that age. And there were indeed many wild flowers on the common and she knew all their names. In pre-war Mountsorrel, before the place was smothered by housing estates, the countryside was never far away. The Soar valley ran through the village like a long green ribbon, with its brooks and meadows, and the track we called The March where she would stop and pick 'March marigolds'—probably corn marigolds. In the village, you could hire a canal boat, buy fishing tackle or a bike, get your hair cut, watch a black-and-white film in the smoky cinema, down a pint of mild at the working men's club or the Legion, or in one of a dozen pubs, and buy all your daily necessities from a shop just yards down the street. There was hardly any need to go anywhere else, especially when your dad grew all his own fruit and veg. But just in case, there was a bus service every twenty minutes to Loughborough or Leicester. When I was little, only a minority of Mountsorrel folk owned a car and the bus was nearly always full.

Jean kept a succession of cats, the last of which was a half-Burmese called Misty. She had a kid's library of books, including a row of wholesome volumes bound in embossed red cloth with titles like 'Tales of the Schoolroom' and 'Stories for Reading and Telling'. Since both her Mam and Pop came from large families, Jean and her brother George had relatives all over the village. She accompanied her parents to church and was duly confirmed in the Anglican religion. By her early teens she used to go out to the cinema and the weekly dances in the village hall, doubtless after a strict admonition from Doris to beware of boys. She learned to play the Palmer pianola well enough for a jolly sing-song in the cramped 'front room', smoke billowing from cigarettes and pipes, coals glowing in the tiled fireplace. As far as one can tell from this distance she was a happy, uncomplicated village girl, close to her family, with every expectation of marrying some local lad and living out her life in another terraced street, later perhaps moving to one of the new estates built in the 50s and 60s, just like her parents, and theirs before them. Perhaps she would have been happier if she had.

Like most village children from working families, Jean left school at 14. It was, she insists, her own decision. She could read and write, and knew a bit of music, geography and needlework, and that was enough. She wanted to start earning her keep for the independence it would bring her. By then she had become quite a nice looking young woman, inheriting the oblong Palmer face and tall forehead with soft expressive eyes and a good figure, good legs. She never lacked attention from the village boys, she insisted, with some pride, nor, during the war, from a queue of British and then American servicemen. The most likely lad was a Yankee paratrooper. Hence, an alternative scenario might have been a transatlantic alliance with mother bringing up her boys on some mid-western farm or small town in Connecticut. But the American boy was killed in action, and two years later she met my father.

At the time, early in 1947, my father was a sergeant in the RAF, based at Wymeswold. One cold, dark evening Jean was taking the bus home from Leicester, as usual, when she found herself surrounded by noisy uniformed airmen scribbling noughts-and-crosses on the steamy windows. Mother opened her bag for a cigarette, and instantly a blue-clothed arm swept forward with a lighter. No, it wasn't Dad who was still immersed in his noughts-and-crosses game. It was some other guy. But Jean had obviously noticed my father with his dark, saturnine looks, and remembered that he seemed "well spoken, not rough, like some of the others". A few days later they met again in the village club and Dad asked her for a dance. After a courtship lasting no more than a few months they got married in St Peter's Church in September 1947. By then Dad was an officer. The year 1947 was his *annus mirabilis*. But his upbringing had been nothing like mother's; nothing like so collective and cosy.

My mother, aged about 20.

Poor orphan boy

My father, though he would have denied it, vehemently, was an Irishman, albeit of the expatriate kind. To judge by the variant spelling of 'Marren'—it is more usually spelt 'Marron'—his ancestors came from County Sligo in what is now the Irish Republic, and where there are still plenty of Marrens in the telephone directory. At some point, possibly after the famine in the late 1840s, Dad's grandparents, or perhaps great-grandparents, escaped to England to join the growing Irish community in Leeds. As exiles do, the Leeds Irish clung to their Roman Catholic and Gaelic heritage. Most of them lived on grimy terraced streets in the city's east end. The locals disliked the 'Micks', seeing them as a threat to their jobs. Anti-Irish and, just to liven things up, anti-Jewish, riots were commonplace. The social hub of the Irish community was the church, notably St Patrick's Church on Quarry Hill, built around 1840, and also the Irish clubs on York Road where they drank Guinness and danced

Berking Terrace, Leeds, in the 1920s, where poor old Dad was brought up.

to Gaelic bands. In 1881 there were at least five Leeds families called Marren. They were all working men. My father's father was William Marren who, at the time of his marriage, was a gramophone packer. *His* father, Patrick Marren, was in the terracotta trade. Bill and Pat: the working Marrens, all moral, God-fearing Catlicks.

Their marriage certificate tells us that William Marren married Bridget McGourty, Dad's mother, in Leeds on first February 1908. Bridget preferred to be known as Beatrice. She was a baker's daughter, also Irish, also from Leeds, and before her marriage, and perhaps after it too, she worked as a 'tailoress'. The couple lived on a mean street of terraced houses at Berking Terrace. They were at unlucky number 13, having moved at some point from No.2, a few yards down the road. Their children were Constance, born in 1913, Ralph, born in 1916, and finally Leonard, my father, born on 21st October 1919. It is hard to imagine anyone calling a baby Leonard, and I suspect he was really 'Lenny'. Little Lenny. Later on, if not just yet, he would become Len. But, unfortunately for William and Beatrice, there was no later on. William had been in the army and served on the Western Front in the First World War, where, according to Dad, he had been gassed and then invalided home. As an army pensioner, he found a stock ex-NCOs job as a bailiff, or, more officially, the County Court Warrant Officer. Whether he ever fully recovered his health we do not know, but on 18th June 1927 he died at home of pulmonary tuberculosis, aged only 40. Beatrice was present at the death. Only four months later, on 19th October, she too was dead, of 'chronic myelocytic leukaemia'. So, two days before his eighth birthday, my father, along with his bro and big sis, found himself an orphan.

The family, perhaps including a cousin, 'C. Maher', living on the nearby Napoleon Street, and who had witnessed Beatrice's death, must have come together to decide what to do. Ralph and little Lenny went to live with an uncle (Maher senior?) for a few months, but, recalled Mum, "it didn't work out". At that point the church seems to have stepped in. Foster homes for the orphans were found with Catholic families in London. Father found himself part of a large family of Irish descent called Cowling who lived in a 3-bedroomed semi opposite a chip shop at 74, Marlow Road in Annerly, South London. The Cowlings were not blood relations and their small house was already overflowing with two sons and three daughters, all older than Dad. He had to sleep on a sort of trunk. Nor were they well off. Father Cowling was an ex-army sergeant-major who now worked as a docker. Mother Cowling, whose real name was Edith Alice, but was apparently known within the family as 'Mick', nagged her husband and looked down on poor little orphan Lenny. He was by no means the equal of foster-brothers, Hugh and Conal, nor his foster-sisters, Pat, Eve and Marjory. But even so a place was found for him at a good Catholic day school, St Joseph's.

I have pieced together the early years of father's life from records, principally marriage and death certificates. He never talked about it. If you asked him, he just changed the subject or said it was all in the past, "all that". According to Mum, his only memory of his real mother was of them paddling in the sea one day, perhaps on a church outing to Scarborough. He also once let slip that he, too, had had a brush with TB as a child. Did he catch it off his Dad, or, perhaps, and here's a thought, his father off him? Of his lost sister Constance, he never spoke at all. It was a shock to discover her in the Records Office. Even Mum had never heard of her. It seems that Constance was also orphaned out in London, or at least found work there, for, when she too died in 1930, aged only seventeen, and of pneumonia, she was living in Wandsworth. So there was big sis gone too. Dad was only seven, coming on eight, when his parents died, and ten when Constance followed them. He must have remembered something. But he never shared it with us. Maybe he had blotted it all from his consciousness. But the experience marked him for life.

He was less reticent about the Cowlings of 74, Marlow. They were shabby-genteel Anglo-Irish Catholics who thought of themselves as middle class. Mother recalls that they were well spoken and that the two Cowling boys in particular were always smartly turned out and well-mannered. Perhaps between them they ensured that Dad's presumed Leeds-Irish brogue was corrected into the neutral, faintly posh English he spoke for the rest of his life. Far more than in mother's case, the church dominated their lives. The family went to Mass daily, wherever possible, and twice on Sundays. Little orphan Lenny served as altar boy on the early shift on Sunday when his duties included ringing the Angelus ('three times three and one of nine'). He had a Gothic memory of keeping vigil one night in the cold, dark church, illuminated only by the light of the Sanctuary lamp, standing alone by the coffin on its trestle. To reach the choir steps, he needed to squeeze past it, shrinking from contact with the cold wood and the dead body inside. He was paid sixpence a week for his services but was obliged to hand it over to the foster-parents. For some reason, he was also required to pump the organ at a Protestant church ("that damned organ"). No doubt it was this religious zeal of the Cowlings that had commended them as foster parents in the eyes of the Church.

In all this, the foster-mother, Edith Alice Cowling, was the prime mover. Her greatest ambition was to get Hugh and Conal into the priesthood. Both were sent to Jesuit-run seminaries, and Dad remembers the older boy in particular as "a great show-off", poncing about in his biretta and cassock. Neither of them succeeded. Hugh apparently disgraced himself by seducing a servant girl and was expelled. Called up in 1939, and serving as an ambulance driver, he was captured at Dunkirk and spent the rest of the war in a prison-of-war camp. It was all downhill for poor old Hugh. After his release he worked as a chauffeur, then in some humble job in a factory. Dad's last memory of his older, superior foster-brother was of him trying to bum a pound or two off my father at the Beckenham swimming baths, and then tricking him into paying for tea. That had evidently rankled ever since.

Nor did the good-looking Conal live up to Edith's expectations. Like Dad, he joined the RAF as an airman, but (Dad says) he proved useless and ended up among "the barrage balloon lot—the lowest of the low". Later on, he served in the 14th Army in Burma as a gunner, where eventually he went down with malaria and was invalided home with heart trouble. Dad recalls Conal working in some menial capacity for a photographer where he was bossed about and humiliated in front of his family ("he didn't deserve that"). He died in the 1960s. Dad apparently kept in touch with Conal's widow. Muriel, and visited her at least once at her home in Bromley.

The three Cowling girls, Eve, Marjorie and Pat, all married. Marjorie worked for a while at the Chilean embassy in London and lived to a grand old age in Gravesend. But we never met any of them. Dad stayed in touch with at least one of the sisters, presumably Marjorie, but it was clear that he had no intention of sharing this part of his life with us. That was all over. Done and dusted, and written out of the script. Grown-up Len had a new life now. They might have been his foster-sisters but they were not family.

Unfortunately the same goes for Dad's elder brother, our lost Uncle Ralph, from whom we might have expected avuncular advice and fun, a regular present at Christmas and a pound note on birthdays. Ralph, we know, joined the merchant navy in 1939. In 1943, he married Vera Nightingale by whom he had a daughter, my lost cousin Barbara, born in 1946. It was Vera, thought Mum, who was the cause of the quarrel between the brothers. Ralph and Lenny had always got on well and continued to meet from time to time. But at some point, certainly before 1947, Vera had "told tales" (Mum's words), presumably claiming that Lenny had made a pass at her. Whatever the truth of the matter, Ralph took offence and Dad was mortified. They never made it up; indeed, as far as I know, they never spoke or wrote to one another ever again. We now know that Ralph retired to Wantage in the early 70s at about the same time as my parents moved to Hungerford. They had lived in neighbouring small towns, no more than ten miles apart, for more than thirty years, but neither of them knew it. Well, it's all spilt milk now. Ralph Marren died in 2005, aged 89. We never met him and Dad never even told us his name.

Towards the end of the war, Dad visited Conal, who was then living in the New Forest. Edith Cowling was there, and this was apparently the famous occasion when she voiced her expectation that Conal would soon get his commission, while Len, then a corporal, "might get another stripe". Dad never forgot nor forgave this slight. You might say he had been given an incentive to get on. He had not relished the prospect of demobbing and a consequent return to 74, Marlow, "back to the church, all that". On the whole he had enjoyed his five years of wartime service in the RAF. And by then he had met and wished to marry my mother.

Dad's greatest friend, Jack Crowther, who had given officer training a try but failed, urged Dad to give it a shot. "I hadn't really thought about it before", admitted (now Sergeant) Len. He was having such a good time with his mates just then, drinking and socializing, flirting with the local girls in Loughborough, Sileby, Barrow, Mountsorrel… "marvellous days!" But, thinking it over, Dad got himself admitted to the OCTU (Officer Cadet's Training Unit) at Cosford, Wolverhampton. My brother Christopher remembers two anecdotes from this time. The cadets were told to make a block of hinges, and the often dismal results were duly inspected by a corporal. 'MTM' was what this corporal wrote on Dad's form. "What does that mean, Corp? Marvellous Tool-Maker?" "No, it means *Menace To Metal*!" Dad thought that was ever so funny. The second story finds Dad leading a patrol. As they approached a bridge, two hidden bren-guns opened up—firing blanks in a realistic sort of way. They all took cover but found themselves pinned down. Now what? It seemed to Dad that their choice lay between getting picked off one by one or adopting aggressive counter-measures. War comics to the rescue! "Fix bayonets and charge!" was his order. Apparently that was the right thing to do, and as a reward, he was made bren-gunner the next day.

Through feats such as this, Sergeant Len was judged to be officer material. He had done well. The RAF was demobbing as fast as it could go and there were relatively few new commissions at that time, least of all from the ranks. Dad duly passed out of Cosford in a smart new uniform bearing the narrow lapel stripe of a Pilot Officer (Equipment Branch). His was initially a short-service commission; it was only made permanent five years later, after I was born. Flying Officer Leonard Marren was gazetted on 11th November 1948 with seniority back-dated to June 1947.

So that was the hinge on which Dad's life turned. At the start of the year he was an airman living in a barrack with no expectations beyond a return to Annerly and work at some garage. At the end of it, he was not only an officer, but a married one, and looking forward to a service career in the still highly prestigious Royal Air Force. I bet he could hardly believe his luck.

Long ago, Dad used to chat about the lighter moments at 74, Marlow, but I was only a boy with my own life to lead and wasn't really listening. Towards the end of his life he told me a couple of stories, labouring under great emotion as he did so, and this time I wrote them down verbatim. Since it is the closest we are going to get to the sort of boy my father was, I offer them here, more or less as he told them to me. Lenny—he must have been nine or ten—had longed to keep bees. He could hardly imagine anything better than being a beekeeper. He read up about beekeeping in a library book, and thought he might be able knock up a makeshift hive from a cardboard box and a bit of perforated zinc. He had noticed bees visiting the raspberry canes in the garden, and managed to catch a few of them with a fishing net. He released them inside the box and waited. He was too excited to sleep properly that night and as soon as it was morning, rushed out to inspect the 'hive', hoping to find the beginning of a comb. But the bees had all escaped and the box was empty.

Love the hats. The parents on their wedding day, Mountsorrel, step-mother Edith Cowling second from left, Redvers and Nanna on the right.

On another, probably later, occasion, he made a disastrous solo outing to the countryside beyond Bromley. Having spent all his money on the bus fare, he was forced to plod home on foot, and thought he would pick some blackberries on the way to please Edith Cowling. Unfortunately they squashed together in his jacket pocket with the juice soaking through the paper bag. Unwilling to throw the leaking burden away, he tramped homewards through the drizzle. By the time he reached Marlow Road he was soaking wet, and the lining of his jacket was all splotched with blackberry juice. Edith Cowling had a fit and yet another spanking was delivered to poor little Lenny, or so he claimed.

Poor old Dad. What a life! Both stories have, to my ear, a flavour that was characteristic of him, with their weird particularity—the raspberry canes, the paper bag—and sense of pathos. What kind of a childhood was it that he could barely recall, at least in old age, without weeping? My father's reaction was to disown his past. He left the Church and denied his Irish roots. He quarrelled with his brother and wrote him out of his life too. And, he never, ever, talked about his true family, the lost Marrens. It was as if they had never existed. As far as he was concerned, my Dad had never had a family. He was reborn in the war.

CHAPTER THREE

Dad's War

When Hitler invaded Poland Dad was just the right age—18, coming on 19—to join up. It had all (he once told me) come as a great surprise—evidently Dad was not a great reader of newspapers—but he was young, fit, and eager to leave home. He had left school at 15, reasonably well-educated in the basics, and with a keen love of poetry, but without qualifications. Since he was good with his hands, and technically-minded, he became a trainee electrician at Moorheads—who, among other things, manufactured cathode ray tubes and other components for the RAF. Like many teenagers of the 1930s, Dad dreamed of flying. Hitler provided the opportunity for a new generation of would-be Biggleses, roaring through the skies in a Hurricane on the tail of Jerry in a Messerschmitt—*da-da-da-da*, gotcha! None of them thought of dying. Boys of that age think themselves immortal.

Dad turned up with his best friend Willie at the recruiting depot at Uxbridge on 5th October 1939. He expected to start his pilot-training right away, perhaps that very day. They checked him out on motivation. That seemed all right, but then they tested his colour vision. "You're colour blind!" they exclaimed. He couldn't make out the dot-images in a standard colour test.

Dad couldn't believe it. "Look here", he protested, "I came down here on a motorbike and I could see the traffic lights!" Then, in the gathering silence, he asked, in a quieter tone, "Can I have another go?"

"We could test you a hundred times and it would be the same. I'm afraid that, as a pilot, you're washed up".

"So, what do I do now? Go home?"

"Yes. Wait there till you're called up". Then, as an afterthought, one of them asked, "Do you know anything about engineering?" Well, yes he did, and he told them about the cathode tubes.

The man scribbled a note. "Take it down the corridor". Dad found himself in another office and was asked what he knew about measuring instruments. He told them about his brief experience using micrometers and that was enough to get him signed up then and there as an RAF instrument fitter and repairer.

Willie was not so lucky. He was turned down by the RAF, joined the army instead, and was killed in his tank at Anzio.

Three weeks of 'bloody horrible' square bashing followed. The moment it ended, Dad joined the war effort. With scant training and nil experience, Aircraftsman Marren was posted to RAF Marham in Norfolk as an 'instrument basher' for Wellington bombers at 3/6 a day. Among other things this meant leaving your barrack bed before daylight and heading off down the peritrack in your trusty 'Acc-trolly' to start those mighty Rolls Royce Merlin engines. And then, and all part of the service, he would remove the chocks from the wheels and wave off the thundering monsters to Germany to deliver their loads of bombs, or, more likely then, leaflets. The roar of the engines eventually affected his hearing. Without realizing it, Dad was left partially deaf for the rest of his life, though he only qualified for a disability allowance long after retirement.

Dad was responsible for the correct running of the various flying instruments, and for the replacement of defective parts. He presumably picked it up as he went along. The pilots, he remembered, knew nothing about how the various dials on their instrument panel actually worked. One day, probably during the invasion scare of summer 1940, the squadron was ordered to disperse to other, smaller airfields. A flight-sergeant pilot had to ask Dad to start the plane, and then invited him up to the cockpit to explain which instrument did what. Then: "Will you come with me?" Like a shot, Dad agreed and together they sat side by side as the great bomber with its broad wooden wings left the ground at Marham and deposited itself not far away at Barton Bendish. It was the first time father had ever actually flown in an aeroplane.

As for the expected invasion, Dad's orders were to arm himself with a rifle and defend the airfield to the last of his 25 rounds. And then, if still alive, to stick his hands up and surrender.

Towards the end of 1940 his squadron was ordered off to Egypt to take part in the North Africa campaign. The Wellingtons and their crew were to fly there directly via Malta. But the airmen, including my father, had to go by sea, embarking on the cruiser HMS Berwick at Greenock, housed in the cramped quarters underneath 'B' turret (the very turret that was knocked out by a shell a month later). The troop convoy left Scotland on 30 October 1940 and arrived at Malta eleven days later. At that stage in the war there was no way of making that particular journey without getting shot at. Once past Gibraltar, and now with an aircraft carrier escort, they were duly attacked by Italian fighter planes. "Don't worry", he remembers hearing over the tannoy, "our Fulmar fighters are getting airborne". That caused a groan among the anxious squaddies for the Fulmar was notoriously useless. Fortunately even the Fulmar was enough to scare off the *Regia Aeronautica*. Dad was lucky. On its next round of duty, a few weeks later, while still in the Atlantic, the gallant Berwick had to defend the convoy against the powerful German heavy cruiser, Admiral Hipper, and, after being badly holed, was forced to limp home for repairs. As for the Wellington bombers on the Malta airfield, in their flimsy shelters of sandbags and empty petrol tins, they were themselves bombed by the Germans and most of them burned to a crisp.

Dad was there at the height of the Maltese blitz. He didn't like the natives. He remembers spotting some boys poking a dead pilot with sticks and telling them to bugger off, sharpish. But he admired the bravery of the pilots of two Eyetie CR-42s that came in low, ignoring the flak and strafing the airfield with all guns blazing before pulling round and then coming in for another go. "It was the bravest thing I ever saw", said Dad. His short time on Malta was enough to qualify him for a special medal issued more than forty years later. Malta itself, of course, was awarded the George Cross.

At length, Dad embarked on the bomb-damaged ack-ack cruiser HMS Bonaventure, soon to be sunk off Crete, and rejoined his squadron in Egypt. His progress through the desert with the Eighth Army across the Libyan border, and then back again to Alamein is part of World War history. At one point Dad was based at El Adam near Tobruk, then, after the retreat, at Mersa Matruh, and finally, by the time of the battle of El Alamein, he was far behind the lines at a place called El Arish in Gaza. In the do-it-yourself nature of the desert war, he often found himself detached to other airfields, fitting up Bostons and other planes. Every now and again an enemy plane would come over and they all jumped into the nearest slit trench—for there were no air-raid shelters in the desert.

On one occasion Dad was dispatched in a lorry with other aircrew to find a crashed Wellington and bury the bodies. He remembers the terrible stink and having to lift part of the wing to extract two or three dead men squashed underneath it. The bodies were wrapped in blankets and buried on the spot. Someone asked, "Shouldn't we fire a volley?" So they all picked up their rifles, loaded, and then—one, two, three—they fired into the air: "a pathetic little succession of bangs".

Leave was spent in Cairo and other fleshpots of Egypt. Once, Dad and an Australian chum went upriver to Luxor and visited the Valley of the Kings. "Distract the guard", hissed the Aussie, as, according to Dad, he removed a fair-sized chunk from the walling of Tutankhamen's tomb: "They'll love this, back home". On another occasion, he and a friend called 'Cap' Cole hitched a lift to Cairo in a pair of Beaufighters. According to Dad, as they neared the military airport at Heliopolis he spotted a plume of smoke on the ground. It was the other Beaufighter. Cap Cole's plane had hit the ground, killing him and the pilot. At least that is what Dad told my brother, or what Chris remembers of it. But there is some mystery about that because a note we found among Dad's papers recorded Cap Cole's fatal accident as occurring in summer 1944, long after Dad's recall to Blighty.

His time in the desert was among the most vivid experiences of his life. He liked the easy attitude to dress, the comradeship, the adventures, the sheer otherness of the war in the sand. It was a long way from 74, Marlow Road, and that was good too. But by early 1944 his tour of duty—a double one, earning him a rosette on his Africa Star—came to an end and he returned to Blighty in a troopship, uneventfully this time. By now he was a corporal. Like many another desert veteran he hated the return to formality and discipline; of having to put on a uniform and tie, and polish his boots, and submit to inspections and parades. He was now experienced enough to train others in the intricacies of flight instruments on Wellingtons, and later on Dakotas, where he specialised in gyroscopes and the 'Sperry' autopilot system. He didn't enjoy it.

That, essentially, was Dad's war. He kept no diary or records. I have pieced it together from the scraps he let slip and from what my brother can remember from their war talk. Unlike most of his mates, Dad was not demobbed after the war. Perhaps he was regarded as too useful with his technical expertise and ability to work without supervision. One of his first postings as an officer was to Northern Ireland where he was put in charge of the closing-down of RAF Toome in County Derry—a challenging enough assignment for a young man. Mother remembers him sending home parcels of meat, which was not rationed in Ireland, although as often as not it had gone off by the time it reached them. Then he closed-down a second airfield, at Husband's Bosworth in Leicestershire. And then they got married.

It was at this point that things nearly came unstuck. For some reason, father was obliged to leave the RAF for what was expected to be at most a few weeks while they sorted out his permanent commission.

Dad (left) and a pal somewhere in the North African desert, 1942.

When those weeks turned into months, the newlyweds bought a caravan, finding space for it in Nanna's front garden. While he waited, Dad took what local work he could find—grafting roses, driving a funeral hearse, acting as a builder's mate—while mother continued to work as a book-keeper, first at a stationers, and then at a betting shop (pools coupons) in Leicester. After a while, Dad began to wonder what had happened to his brilliant career and took the train to London and the Ministry of Defence to find out. They had mislaid the file. Ah, here it is! And, almost before he could draw breath, Dad found himself on the way to Osnabruck in Germany. The Soviets had recently blocked road and rail access to Berlin, and the Berlin Airlift was underway. It was winter and the RAF needed all the air-freight movement specialists it could find to fly coal into Berlin. Since Dad knew all about Dakotas and how to load them (the secret was to get the centre of gravity right) he was exactly the kind of chap who was needed.

It must have been a bit of a shock when mother, waiting in the caravan for her man to come home, got the telegram from Occupied Germany. At some point around New Year 1949 she rejoined her husband for two months at a hotel in Buckeburg, near Hanover. And, if the dates are right, that is where I was conceived. I was, mother once told me, an unintended baby, unintended in the sense that they were not planning a family just yet. No doubt things got a bit carried away one night. After this rapturous reunion on the North German plain, my pregnant mother returned to Mountsorrel and the betting shop, while the RAF sorted out a married quarter for them in Hamburg, the operational centre for the airlift.

Once a house had been found—and a very nice house it was too—the two of them, or rather the three of us, moved to Hamburg. The stickiest part of the airlift was over by then; the blockade had been lifted in May and the Federal Republic of West Germany had come into being. In the meantime, and slightly overdue, Mummy was admitted to the RAF hospital at Hamburg, where, after a villainous struggle, little Peter was born. Which brings us back to where we started, in the nativity ward of an RAF hospital one autumn afternoon in Germany.

Mum's War

Never let them say that war is always hell. Mum quite enjoyed hers. After the teenage Jean Palmer left school in 1936, she worked for a short time in a shoe factory in Sileby. Feeling, understandably, that her talents were wasted there, she took the bus to Loughborough to attend evening classes in typing, shorthand and book-keeping. With those qualifications she was able to land a better white-collar job at the Mountsorrel Co-op, collecting the money, paying the dividends and keeping the books. The Co-op might not sound very important now—just another High Street shop—but in those days it was the hub of commercial life in the village. Mother's boss, the enterprising Ken Shuttlewood, also ran a drapery, a baker and a butcher, two shops and a bank. Mum was regarded as a good little worker, maintaining the books in her unique handwriting, rolling, flattish, and leaning heavily to the right. At some point she decided to leave the Co-op to join a friend at a hosiery company in Quorn. Ken Shuttlewood was miffed. He could have got her a *much* better job.

In the meantime, the war effort had penetrated even to Mountsorrel. Jean joined the local fire service as a volunteer, turning up for duty wearing a uniform and carrying her gas mask and tin hat. She remembers the practice drills with hoses and ladders, the marches and parades on Armistice Day, and having to man (woman?) the phones in the evenings and at weekends. But she never ran up those ladders in earnest. The nearest the Germans came was one fiery night late in 1940 when they bombed the hosiery factories in Leicester. The southern horizon glowed red all night long but mother was safe in her bed at Remlap.

As I say, it seems that mother was seldom without a boyfriend, and latterly they included one or more American paratroopers stationed nearby. The American boys were always welcome at 'Remlap'. The family album has a photograph of one of them, a likely looking lad in a double-breasted tunic and jeans, posing as though about to reach for his six-gun. They must have seemed worldly and exotic to the Palmers, especially Redvers, and you can picture him sitting in his corner chair asking the boy about the army and life back home, and nodding knowingly. Redvers was in the local Home Guard. He had seen military service at the end of the First World War though he had joined the Leicesters too late to do any actual fighting (and that was just as well because if he had joined up the previous year he would most probably be dead, for the Leicesters took a pasting at Passchendaele). As it was, his only sight of a German soldier was of a dead one, found in the mud of a shell crater where they were refilling their water bottles.

Mother's sweet-natured brother George joined the Royal Navy as a rating, hoping to see a bit of the world. What he saw instead was quite a bit of war. For him action began promptly in September 1939 when, while serving on a destroyer, he witnessed the sinking of the aircraft carrier Courageous by a German submarine. He was also at Dunkirk, helping to embark exhausted soldiers from the stricken beach. Later, after some fairly perfunctory training, he became an asdic operator on

Reach for the sky. Mother's American boyfriend.

corvettes. His ship, HMS Saxifrage, was credited with the sinking of two U-boats, and had a very close shave itself when an enemy 'tinfish' passed under the ship. Like many other naval ratings, he crisscrossed the ocean in his little boat, including one ill-fated convoy in which nine out of twelve tankers were sunk in mid-Atlantic. Later on he took part in Arctic convoys and remembered the, in every sense, chilly reception in Murmansk. The Russians presented George and his crewmates with a workers' solidarity medal, but he wasn't allowed to wear it. After more than four years of more or less continuous service at sea, he left the navy and returned home to Mountsorrel.

Jean, too, continued to live at home, giving her parents a cut from her wages, going out most nights to dances and the cinema. And then, one day at a social in the Working Men's Club, my father asked my mother for a dance.

CHAPTER FOUR

Remlap

My grandmother, the dear Nanna of my toddlerdom with her gentle smile, was Doris Clara Palmer, born Doris Keeling on 6th June 1899. She was the eldest of five sisters, the others being Ida, Florence, Hilda and Phyllis. She also had two younger brothers, Roy and Dick. They all married locally and found homes in and around Mountsorrel. I was never quite sure who was who, apart from Flo, who married my favourite uncle, Rupert, a decent old boy who owned a shoe factory in Sileby and would slip me the odd pound note—something all the others failed to do for some reason.

Doris Keeling's future husband Redvers we have met already. *His* parents, known to us as the Great-Granddad Palmers, lived in retirement in a little bungalow on top of Rothley Hill next to the village cemetery.

The golden boy on the beach with his Mickey Mouse bucket in the days when the camera loved him.

Years before, Great-Grandad Palmer had bought this plot of land next to the cemetery purely in order to live next to the grave of his youngest son Donald, a sickly boy who died at the age of twelve. I suppose he'd decided he wasn't going to get over it. When the patriarch eventually died in his turn they simply passed his coffin over the hedge and laid him to rest in the plot he'd reserved, alongside his long-dead son, in death as in life.

His boys were Grampa Redvers and his three younger siblings, Fred, Cyril and Donald, the one who died. Cyril and Fred briefly joined big brother Redvers in the shoe factory but, unlike him, they soon got out and moved on and up. They had obviously found it sole-destroying. Fred went into business, shrewdly manufacturing emery boards for the motoring industry, and was successful enough to be able to buy, first Jamaica Inn in Cornwall and then a comfortable villa with a swimming pool in Torquay. Cyril also did all right. But not poor old Redvers who just carried on cobbling. He worked at his lathe year on year, decade after decade, until retirement at 65. Shortly after that he had his first heart attack and seemed to shrink inside his own skin. It was the third attack that killed him. While being helped, groaning, from couch to commode, he suffered one last, fatal seizure. 'His heart but once heaved, and forever grew still' (Byron). Not much of a life, really.

His wife, my dear Nanna, was a sweet, steady, uncomplicated soul. She had some stock expressions: "you cheeky monkey!"—"well, I never did!"—and her mock threat at some amusing naughtiness: "I'll cut your tail off!" Whenever she caught us stuffing ourselves with sweets five minutes before a meal, she'd squawk, "You'll spoil your dinner!" She looked exactly the same at 70 as she had at 50, that is, a cheerful old wrinkly with pink-framed bifocals and an interesting scar on the side of her nose, the legacy of some childhood accident. To me she epitomized cosy, if somewhat austere, domesticity. She was very much an apostle of make-do-and-mend and, at least in her later years, something of a miser. She rarely spent much on herself, and that was sensible because she had little to spend. They seldom went on holiday unless you count the church outings to Brighton or Bognor. She used old cider bottles to warm the beds. Once, when she managed to win £500 on a Spot the

Ball competition in the *Leicester Mercury*, she disappointed the reporter by claiming to have no great plans for a splurge, a holiday or a new sofa. The only quote he could get out of her was: "I'm sure it will come in useful". One Christmas she was given a big box of fancy chocolates. She let me have one, possibly two, as a treat when I dropped by from boarding school on Sunday afternoons. It's probably still around somewhere, still with chocolates in it.

She rose early, often from a couch if she had a house full, and the first thing you heard in the morning was the low drone as she hoovered the carpet downstairs before making the first of several hundred cups of tea. In one corner of the gassy kitchen came a regular whistling from the tin kettle; in the other a different whistle from Joey, the budgie. After a while, Grampa stumped downstairs in his striped cotton pyjamas and slippers to smother his big chin with shaving soap from the badger-hair brush he kept by the sink. Why he didn't use the bathroom like everyone else I have no idea; maybe it was a habit he had acquired in the days before they had a bathroom and never thought to change. The last thing he had done the previous night was to fold the pages of the *Leicester Mercury* into plaits and pile them in the hearth. Now he lit the

Mother and daughter, that is, my mother and grandmother circa 1964.

fire. Then he lit his pipe and had his first cup of tea in his corner chair, which had a brass ashtray on the arm held in place by a leather strap. Later on he would do the pools and maybe dig up some potatoes.

All these Idas and Flos and Cyrils and Freds were one big family to Mum, but the person who mattered to her most, apart from her mam and pop, was her brother George. George, they say, had been an energetic lad, taking part in the church activities and sports, and lending his sweet treble voice singing to the local choir. But, after his war was over and he was demobbed from the Navy, nothing seemed to go right for George. Perhaps his wartime experiences had knocked the stuffing out of him. The best he could manage, after cutting granite curbstones for a while in Sileby, was to join a hosiery firm in Leicester as some sort of clerk. And there, Redvers-like, he stayed.

George was a gentle, lovable man, a plump Bob Cratchett. In 1948, he married a fellow hosiery worker, Mary, who, after a childless decade, bore him my cousins Jeffrey and Jenny. Their home, a tiny semi not far from Remlap, became a 1950s timewarp. They never bought anything and they never threw anything away. George used to ride a motor scooter wearing a white crash helmet like a great boiled egg. This machine might have been all right for scooting around Mountsorrel but it was manifestly not intended for long journeys on busy roads. Nonetheless one day George took it into his head to scoot down to visit his sister, my Mum, at that time living a good hundred miles away. It was to be a surprise in the sense that he omitted to ring her to say he was on his way. He duly arrived, staggered at how long the journey had taken, and mother insisted he stayed the night, which he did, reluctantly. Early next morning, he was off again, only to get hopelessly lost somewhere between Kettering and Lutterworth. And then it poured with rain and he got a flat. Probably. He was, as I say, a lovely man, and gave me ten bob on each and every birthday until I was about fifty.

Remlap, which the alert reader might have noticed is Palmer backwards, and otherwise known as 48, Linkfield Road, was the fixed reference point in my itinerant early childhood. Though we never stayed there for more than a few days at a time, I remember it better than any of our RAF houses. With typical Midlands thrift, Remlap had been built from bricks baked from the clay dug from a great deep pit just beyond the garden fence. Later on the disused pit flooded with water and was stocked with carp (the other fish—roach, perch, tench, pike— probably came in naturally). We knew this deep lake as The Pit, which was short for Parker's Pit, named after a nearby shoe factory. It was about two hundred yards long by about fifty wide with steep, willow-grown banks all round. None of the inhabitants of Linkfield Road seemed to appreciate the Pit for the terrific natural asset it was. To them it was not so much a Pit as a tip, and they casually threw all their tins and household rubbish over the iron railings to roll down the steep banks into the clear water. There the tin cans rusted, releasing toxic metal ions, killing the water snails and disrupting the natural food webs of the lake. Somewhere among the tins lay Dad's pistol. He might have handed it in during an amnesty on ex-wartime weapons, but in the end he just chucked it into the Pit. The jumble of rubbish on the bank, perhaps containing live pistol ammunition or even the odd grenade, were soon buried beneath a jungle of nettles and the foaming cow parsleys that Nanna called keck.

At some point in the early 1950s, when everyone seemed to have more energy, Dad and George shored up our bit of the bank and cut steps down to it from the garden gate. They rigged up a sail on a canoe, and later Dad made a makeshift punt out of planks strapped to a raft of fuel cans. When I was little I wasn't allowed out on the water, but I did make friends with a fisherman who was obliged to put up with me, the son of the manor, in exchange for his bit of free coarse fishing. There he sat with his angling kit, a couple of rods in their Y-shaped holders, a keep-net pegged to the shallows, coloured floats bobbing. "What would you do if you caught a pike?" I would pipe. "I'd be pleased", he answered wearily. "What if you caught a carp?" "I'd be *very* pleased." "What if you caught a bream?" "I'd be very surprised." "What if you caught a *shark*?" "Fuck off", he must have longed to say. "Now moving on to the roach family," I went on, remorselessly.

While the poor man tried to attract the attentions of a passing tench, there were usually other attractions. A moorhen would sound the alert from the next bank. Randy toads would try to mate with the tennis ball I had provided for their ease. Pretty magpie moths flew over the currant bushes like live confetti. With a net, you could find water bugs and leeches among the weeds and bring them back in a jam-jar to show Nanna. Or you could just clamber about among the boughs of willow trees that jutted far out into the water. Just as life evolved in ponds, so my love of pond life sprang from dreamy afternoons at the Pit. It was wilderness on my doorstep, my infant Walden, my watery Selborne. I spent hours there even before I owned a boat or a fishing rod. The smell of pond water is in my nostrils still, that blood memory of methane and chlorophyll, the presence of something extraordinary at the bottom of the garden but which then felt so normal and natural.

The house built from the brick pit was a mid-Victorian semi, basically two up, two down, on which the gramps had at various times added a bathroom, a kitchen extension, a conservatory and an indoor loo; when my mother was a girl the only loo was outside, halfway down the garden path beyond the coal-shed and the zinc-lined meat safe. It was a scary journey in the dark for there was once a deep well nearby which Redvers had covered with paving stones. These had cracked and

Sailing on the Pit in the early Fifties.

we were always told never to tread there, just in case. In fact every inch of the narrow garden bore Grandad's imprint. There was a greenhouse at the bottom of the paved path, and beyond that his shoe-shed that smelt of leather and matting. There was a small, close-clipped lawn with a wooden seat, a miniature crab tree garlanded with creosote to keep the winter moths at bay, a flowering almond the shape of a lollipop frequented by bullfinches in early spring, and a box-bush clipped to the shape of a light-bulb and under which I once dug up the pupa of an Eyed Hawk-moth. There was a rose garden, a border of Canterbury Bells and Chinese Lanterns, and, beyond, some apple trees and a potato patch. Right at the bottom, almost out of sight, were Grandad's currant bushes and the brick hearth where he burnt the garden rubbish, and which would one day become the funeral pyre of my teddy bear.

The house was tiny but it didn't seem that way when I was a toddler. I found it totally engrossing and crammed full of interesting things. In the front lounge, for instance, was the upright honky-tonk pianola and the glass-fronted bookcase full of Mum's old story books. There was an old wind-up gramophone that played their collection of pre-war 78s.

Mother at Remlap, c.1947.

Among our favourites was The Yodelling Blacksmith ('*I bang-a-bing-bang at my yodel so gay*') sung in a strangled north-country accent, and another one about a cowboy singing to his horse ('*giddy-up old fella, for the moon is yella, to-nigh-yite*'). Upstairs, in a cupboard in the bathroom, was George's old clockwork train-set with a circle of track you could line up on the carpet in five minutes and a beautiful brass-and-green-enamel locomotive to go round it. In the corner by the window was the black-and-white TV, with a screen fractionally larger than a matchbox on which you could dimly discern Bill and Ben ascending chummily from their plant-pot or Andy Pandy returning eagerly to the hamper with his ambiguous friend Looby Loo. Under the stairs, lay the pantry where you could creep down the stone steps and crawl into the cool, musty interior while the ceiling grew thrillingly lower and lower. The stairs were hidden behind a door with a little brass knob, and, being straight and steep, as well as almost pitch-dark, you could bump or slither down, soft-landing among the coats and macs at the bottom. The dining room contained a built-in cupboard crammed with more good stuff: a cloth tape measure inside a brass and leather case, a box of old buttons, a dud camera, and some medical books with cut-out human figures with paper bones, arteries and guts, all of which spilled out of the page like a pop-up that hadn't quite popped up. Along one wall was a sideboard containing bottles of sweet sherry or Bells whisky (with a dimple in the bottle) for the times when Fred or Rupert dropped round. The sherry tasted all right, but as for the whisky—was it some kind of adult joke? We kids double-dared one another to swig the whisky.

Above the dark, narrow stairs lay two bedrooms, one with twin beds and the other with a monstrous double one on mighty springs. When I was very little I remember gazing up at it with awe. It was a bed for Brobdingnag giants but there was a good bouncing plateau up there out of sight, once you clambered up to it. The room smelt of grandad: a musty, grown-up scent of dust, sweat and pipe tobacco. The other, much brighter bedroom, smelt of lavender, but contained nothing of play value apart from Nanna's powder puff and a flaking pair of plaster elephants. But it was a good place to curl up with a comic and a stash of sweet cigarettes and, through the net curtains, watch the Walkers go by.

At night I sometimes used to lie awake for a bit and watch the shadows move across the ceiling while, one by one, the lights of a passing motor car slipped across the ceiling and down the wall.

Perhaps I should explain about the Walkers. At the bottom of Linkfield Road was the former workhouse, now a hospital for what were then called the 'mentally handicapped'. Every now and then, its more mobile inmates would be let out for a supervised walk. They tottered up the lane past Remlap, two by two, hand in hand, and there was always this little twisted guy trailing along behind. Most of them didn't seem to have the faintest idea what was going on, or where they were going, but they bumbled along obediently, rolling their eyes and wobbling their heads. When I was very little I supposed it was some kind of walking club for oldies. Nothing seemed unlikely then, and I suppose I would not have been much more surprised to see a row of bouncing green men led by Dan Dare. As I got slightly older, though, the Walkers started to make me feel a little uneasy. They were the stuff of dreams; the strangers who came at night and stared at you with their moist yellow eyes.

Beyond Linkfield Road there was a long dull street to negotiate before you reached the other good bit, the walled common pitted with granite blocks and crags. On the way there the footpath led down between a row of terraced houses and some sort of allotment raised up by a wall where the flowers sometimes wore coloured cellophane hats and which gave the place, for me, a dreamy, wonderland quality. The magic intensified when you took the lane, bordered by granite walls, to the great quarry. Said to be one of the largest granite quarries in Europe, it had little trucks of stone rattling overhead on wires with an impressive and slightly frightening clatter, leaving puffs of dust hanging in the air. These days they wouldn't let you anywhere near the place without a hard hat, but back then Granddad would often take me there in my push chair. Later on we would slide down what we called the tips— steep cliffs of quarry overspill—on sheets of cardboard.

More fun could be found at the top of the hill where, by the lofty war memorial, we sometimes flew kites. What is it about a kite that makes you happy? It is only a bit of paper bobbing in the air, but it's also 'throwing your dreams into space', according to the sex maniac

Anais Nin. For my part I came to see it as more like fishing, casting your lure in the air where it would float with an occasional tug and a twist as if seized by some incorporeal sky-fish, some cloud-carp. It was a coloured float in the sky, a little bit of sky that was under my control and yet seemed to have a life of its own, bobbing and looping on invisible currents in the air. All things considered it was very thoughtful of my gramps to live in such an interesting place. Needless to say, it is nothing like so special now. Most of the places where we once swam and clambered and slid have long since been built over, or smoothed and sanitized away, or, in the case of The Pit, placed out of reach behind a chainlink fence. Do today's children miss what we had? Probably not; they have Twitter now and mobile phones and Facebook. If I had had access to social media then, I dare say I too wouldn't have been very interested in flying a kite, or casting a rod, or in the imaginative possibilities of a box of old buttons. Mountsorrel Common is still there, but the little outcrops of granite on which I loved to climb have either been filled in or are overgrown by gorse, and gorse is no use for play. But children still go there. I'm told you can get a marvelous strong signal on your mobile phone from the hilltop. Heck, for all I know you can probably get *Facebook*.

My attention wanders as Nanna reads another story, Remlap 1952.

CHAPTER FIVE

Snapshots from the Pram

Tony Blair, or more likely his factotum Alastair Campbell, claimed that the greatest Wonder of the World was the mind of a child. Leaving aside the sickly New Labour whimsicality, the real wonder is that, if so, we remember so little about our early childhoods. How far does memory recede into infancy? Does anyone remember their birth or their first gulp at their mother's breast, or any subsequent gulps (not me, though I have a Freudian memory of a nipple). Do we consciously recall a second of those long hours in the cot and the pram, gurgling speechlessly while quietly processing the information filtering in through those big baby eyes and snub but perfectly functioning baby nose? Do smells and sounds lodge in the mind before they turn into memories? The sweetish whiff of cots and prams and babydom generally seem to take me back

The golden boy at Remlap when the world was young.

to some prehistoric moment in my existence. So does the smell of fresh paint, perhaps from one of father's spells of home-decorating. But it is just as likely that those baby smells were not from my time but from my younger brother's, born four years later. As for sounds, is it just my imagination or does the swirl of the tide and the keen wind of the Humber still echo in my ears after more than half a century?

We learn from my baby logbook that my eyes were deep blue with long lashes; that my complexion was 'rosy'; that I could sit up by myself at seven months, could stand without falling over before my first birthday and totter along on my chubby legs a few months after that. It seems that teeth began to burst through my gums when I was seven months old. Then came the big day when my 'light brown' hair was cut for the first time on 29 August 1951. It must be admitted that mother had no great talent with the scissors. My standard kid's haircut was a lop-sided fringe with a no-quarter charge of the clippers up the sides. The result looked like a shaggy beret worn at a rakish tilt. Fortunately I was not alone in having a permanent bad hair day. Most Fifties kids looked as though some ragged animal had crawled on top of their head and died. I doubt whether many parents of that era thought very hard about making their boys presentable. It was enough to keep their head cropped and their feet shod and their middle parts covered.

I'm doubtful whether I can recover anything that happened to me during the first three years of my life when we lived first in Hamburg, then at Remlap for a few months and finally in a rented house on Seaside Road at Easington in the East Riding of Yorkshire. Easington was a funny place to wash up. If anywhere lies at the scrag end of England it is Easington, a village on the road to nowhere. It has, as it were, turned its back on the rest of England to stare longingly across the grey North Sea to Denmark. But the parents liked it. Father had been posted there to dispose of another store of overkill wartime munitions. They got there just in time for the great flood on 31 January 1953 when the wind blew and the waves came crashing in over broken sea-walls. The *watersnoodramp* they called it, over in Holland, the day when the sea came to call. Father was away at the time but mother remembers the gale and millions of bits of hay swirling around in the blackness.

Fortunately our house was on a rise and although the water crept up from the bottom of the garden it did not reach the kitchen. Thousands of others living along the North Sea coast were less lucky.

Of course I have no memory of the great flood, having only just turned two at the time. Nor of the Coronation that followed next June although I know I watched it, uncomprehendingly, on TV from my vantage point in mother's lap. It wasn't our TV for, along with most people, we didn't have one. We watched the ceremony from the saloon bar of The Neptune, the pub next door. The Neptune was my first local. Mum took me there every Wednesday to watch my favourite programme, Bill and Ben. Apparently I was fascinated by the doings of that pair of rather unconvincing little marionettes in a pot. *"Flobberdebob weed?" "Gloop a woddle plop!" "Blabappleplap plobbledop?!"* I spoke the same kind of language myself, and so probably reckoned to get the gist of it. Bill and Ben must have made a great impression because they gave me my first erotic dream, involving a new character called Little Willy. After some awkward goings-on among the flowerpots I woke up and found I had wet the bed.

Our house at Seaside Road, Easington, c.1951.

Two more cot-memories are similarly lavatorial. I have a faint recollection of Dad wiping my arse after I had routinely performed what he called a 'woppies'. He took this gruesome chore in his stride, whistling a jaunty tune as he polished away. I don't suppose he would have been anything like so happy to wipe anyone else's arse and it was a lesson in the extraordinary unselfishness that takes hold of us when we become a parent. Sometime later, after I had mastered this Rabelaisian art for myself, I remember waking in the night and, obliged to use the potty kept for emergency purposes beneath my cot, too late realising there was no paper to hand. So, in a magnificent example of British make-do, I found a pack of Happy Families and used that. And you're right, the families had nothing to be happy about *that* night, as Mr Bun the Baker followed Master Plod the Policeman's Son into the pot. I hope Mummy praised my ingenuity the next morning. I have read that such things are important in a child's development. I have always been inordinately fond of praise. As uncritical as possible.

The aptly named Seaside Road ended in a strand of scrappy dunes facing the grey North Sea. After Remlap, this became my second playground. I packed cold, muddy Yorkshire sand into my Mickey Mouse bucket and upended it to make endless pudding-shaped castles. I stamped in the pools of seawater and paddled in the chilly ripples holding tight to Mummy's hand. I picked up bladder wrack and cockle shells to take home. Sometimes we received visitors from the world of Remlap. The family album shows a still reasonably spry Grampa Redvers cranking up the Blu-wits stove on the beach, to brew another of those cups of tea without which no adult could survive for long. On another Uncle Rupert stares thoughtfully out to sea, his trademark fag at a carefree droop, while Auntie Mary has turned to me with a look neatly poised between annoyance and concern.

On special days, little Peter was taken to the more elaborate seaside attractions at nearby Withernsea. It had a small funfair with gaily painted merry-go-rounds and helter-skelters. But toddlers have to work their way up to the good stuff. For ages I seemed to be stuck on a pitiful little tot's train that simply went round and round on a circle of track like the clockwork train on the carpet at Nanna's. Was I sufficiently self-conscious to feel, as well as look, a bit of a wally? On a snap taken of my circular journey my expression is inscrutable. Perhaps I was quietly enjoying the ride, or perhaps I knew that it would come to an end soon and was making the best of it. According to my parents I regarded these outings as a very big deal, but parents are apt to misread situations involving their nearest and dearest. For instance, they liked to describe baby Susan, who lived next door to Remlap and sometimes shared my pram, as 'my girlfriend'. Well, excuse me, but I don't remember inviting her in. She was dumped on me, perhaps while I was having a pleasant and private daydream of my own. There was nothing going on there, believe me. No really.

The day was long delayed before one was at last permitted to mount the glitzy carousel and the challenging helter-skelter—looking immense to a small boy—which you ascended on internal wooden ladders with Dad close behind, and then descended at thrilling speed, round and round, on a smelly Hessian doormat. At the funfair you could eat things you never saw anywhere else: crisp apples covered in hot, sticky toffee and pink candyfloss on a stick which was like eating a cloud. Judging

Pram pals. Me and little Susan from next door, Remlap 1951.

from the album, little Peter was always buttoned up against the bracing Yorkshire wind inside a thick woollen coat with only his sandalled feet exposed. That is what little kids looked like in the Fifties: small, bright-eyed gremlins inside swaddlings of wool with their little, white naked legs sticking out.

Sometimes I was joined on my sand-castle construction site by a little girl of my own age or a bit older called Rosemary. She was the daughter of my parents' best friends. Most of their friends were fellow RAF officers and their wives. The Skagerraks, as I shall call them, were unusual in being civilians. They met over drinks in The Neptune. Rosemary's Dad, who I was encouraged to call Uncle Verner, was a Dane transplanted into the East Riding where he farmed a few hundred flat acres and went shooting for rabbits and wild duck in the woods and marshes that lay beyond the fields. That gave him and Dad something to do together, for Dad, too, was pretty handy with a shotgun at that time. The farmer's wife, 'Auntie Di', was a stern, dark, rather intimidating woman from the far side of the Humber. She seemed to give little Rosemary a hard time. For instance she once

Train ride, Withernsea Funfair, c.1953, though I question the 'fun'.

delivered her a terrific spanking after we had crashed our tricycles through the rose garden. I remember this dragon-lady towering over me and loudly regretting that she couldn't thrash me too (yeah, but you can't, can you, dog-face?).

I didn't much like the senior Skagerraks. Verner was a silent, brooding sort of man with blue Viking eyes and slicked back hair. I remember him serving dinner from an assortment of heavy, patterned crockery, and insisting that Rosemary ate every speck of horrible cabbage and mashed potato. As far as I was concerned, they could keep their farmhouse cooking. My idea of fine dining was baked beans, omelettes, chips, and that sort of thing. You're not half strict enough with him, they admonished. "Can I get down now please?" I had been taught that this was the correct form when you wanted to leave the table. "Yes dear". "Not you Rosemary, you'll stay until you've eaten that lovely bit of gristle".

Did I sense that there was something not quite right about this relationship? At any rate I was not surprised when Dad let out, in one of his senile rants half a century later, that it might have gone a bit further than friendship. Your mother, he shouted in his pain, had once

Little Rosemary and me on the shore at Easington.

had an affair *with a farmer in a field*. Mum retorted that the farmer's wife had been available for reciprocal favours which Dad had either been too innocent to notice or had rejected—and, if so, I can't say I blame him. Assuming there was anything behind Dad's outburst—for his fantasies were getting the better of him by then—that farmer was almost certainly Uncle Verner. The family album does indeed contain a shot of Verner and Mum in a field. He is holding a gun and grinning broadly, lord of all he surveys, and at his side stands mother, laughing at his Viking wit. So possibly my poor mad Dad had taken the idea from a photograph.

Still, it does bring in the interesting point of the dissimilarity between me and my younger brother Christopher. I was obviously Daddy's boy, with the same guarded expression, dark hair and big floppy ears. Chris, on the other hand, was blond, blue-eyed and a perfect pin-up for Nord Magazine. I examine the fuzzy snaps of Verner for signs of resemblance but find none. The dates might fit, for although we had moved on by the time Chris was born, we did continue to visit the Skagerraks. But, on balance, it seems unlikely. Genes are funny things. We would not be the first family of dissimilar siblings. Perhaps there is another flinty-

Laughter in a field. Mother and 'Uncle' Verner share a joke.

eyed, gun-toting Dane lost somewhere among the ancestors that makes his presence felt from time to time.

It was probably on one of those later visits that I noticed, with no great interest, that Rosemary didn't have a tinkle. Had we played doctors and nurses? Possibly, but I think I first spotted *la difference* when my playmate was fleeing knickerless across the landing with Auntie Di and her raised slipper in hot pursuit.

Father was very taken with the first more or less intelligible words I said, and repeated them, often. Let's get this embarrassing thing out of the way and done with. My statement was essentially an expression of confidence concerning the imminent return of a steam locomotive. Rendered phonetically, it reads as follows:

"*Da choofa-chain a-chum-back-a-minute*".

This was half-said, half-sung in a revoltingly smug way that made both parents go all smiley-eyed with happiness. Yes, I was very keen on trains. The parents used to take me to the railway museum in York or to the level crossing at Riccall to watch the great iron locomotives breathing smoke and fire, stinking of oil and steam, screaming past on the northern line. In those days every boy wanted to be a train driver. You saw yourself standing in the cab with the wind in your hair while your sturdy sidekick, called Bob, shoveled coal into the boiler. It was the best way of life we could imagine. This was why the first rock and roll programme on British television was introduced by, of all things, a train: *The Six-Five Special's steaming down the line / The Six-Five Special's right on time.* Even prototype rockers loved steam trains.

A couple more snapshots bear out this passion. In one, cut from the local paper, I'm at some toy show in my trademark woollen coat, my little face peeping over the table top, eyes level with the track. I'm staring at multiple trains whizzing over the points, probably controlled by a fat man with a moustache. Though I look as passionless as a goldfish, I was, I'm sure, dazzled by the tracks and signals and dinky little stations from yesteryear with their toy waiting rooms and ticket offices. All the wonders of train-land was there, spread out there for my delight: the signals and crossings worked as in real life, the locos ran at the right speeds and stopped properly at the stations to pick up the mail bags. There were little motionless passengers waiting ever so patiently on the platform with their hats and brollies, for days and days. And all around, life went on: sheep grazed the fields, plastic trees and bushes dotted the places where the night train passed on the way to the border, bringing the cheque and the postal order. There were even a few cars waiting at the level crossing (and, yes, let them wait for this is Train-land). You could lose yourself in this wonderful, alternate world ruled by trains. For a little boy from the Fifties, a layout like this was a dream made manifest by the miracles of tinplate and plastic.

The other snapshot shows me sitting rather nervously on the chintz sofa next to my baby brother, nursing a copy of *Timothy's Book of Trains*. I suspect the book was a prop. I spotted a copy once in a secondhand bookshop but it rang no bells; there was no steam whistle of recalled pleasure. I was only four and no doubt the book was read to me. While little Christy bounced and fidgeted, I seem to be eyeing the photographer distrustfully. I look as though I'm sucking an acid drop. Up until then the family album had shown me as quite a bonny little kid, with big-lashed eyes and the carefree face of a well-loved only son. Now, all of a sudden, I look awkward and suspicious. It marks the moment when the camera ceased to love me. It has never loved me again.

One random incident from toddlerhood became canonized as *the* first memory. I was waddling along the Easington garden when I slipped and fell down the rockery. I howled and wailed with pain and grief as Mummy dabbed the cut and unzipped the Elastoplast. Was there really as much blood as I 'remember'? Or is it not a memory but a memory of a memory, an incident recalled so many times that the original moment has been submerged under deep layers of exaggeration? Over the years that scrape, which has left no scar, was magnified into hideous wounds: a trail of blood from lawn to patio, a limb hanging by a thread, scraps of flesh left behind among the crocuses. Pain, then, is my first reliable memory, although it is caught up in a faint, almost indefinable sense of cotton wool and motherly reassurance.

I knew that certain things hurt. It was a bad idea, for example, to poke your finger into an electric socket. Wasp and nettle stings hurt. A smack hurt a bit, but not much (you only blubbed to make the parent feel bad). A splinter did not hurt until Daddy tried to get it out with a pin; ditto specks of grit caught in one's eye for which he sucked a corner of his hankie before fishing about in one's lids. I suppose a young child cries a dozen or more times during the course of its day. Some adults seem to think a crying child is a terrible thing, an indictment of a society in which such things are allowed to happen. But little children are always crying. They cry, and then they stop crying. It is their way of expressing themselves, and if you listen carefully you can tell whether the kid is simply drawing attention to itself or is really pissed-off about something, or perhaps just passing the time by making a noise. An unhappy child is something different. Perhaps you can spot a genuinely damaged child by the fact that it *doesn't* cry. At any rate, I seemed to cry and stop crying in the usual way, and I wasn't afraid of anything.

Mother kept this one in a silver frame calling it 'The Young Naturalist'.

Or rather I wasn't afraid of anything except one thing, and that thing was The Dentist. Why I was made to see the dentist so often I don't know, since there was obviously nothing much wrong with my teeth. *They* didn't hurt. I expect it was because dental care was now free, and mother, in her Palmer way, thought she should reap the greatest possible advantage of that fact. Fifties dentists were not the friendly, reassuring figures of today. Rather, they were gigantic figures of doom, waiting for you in their white coats and rubber aprons, rubbing their hands in anticipation. The chair had straps to hold you down if necessary. First they yonked open your little mouth and poked around for a bit with a nasty looking probe. Once the man found a shell of baked bean stuck in mine and everyone had a good laugh about that. When, inevitably, he spotted a bit of decay, the Dentist cranked up the old belt-fed drill. I can hear it now: "Wheee-*eeeeee*". While he blasted away, humming mindlessly, happy at his work, chips of molar and bicuspid would ricochet about the room and a faint trail of smoke exited from the back of your little mouth. Sooner or later the drill would burst through the enamel into the pulpy mass of tender nerve within, and then, as Bill Bryson puts it, your toes burst from your sandals. "Garghhh!" "Hold still. Nearly done". Whee-*EEEEEE*. "*GARGHHHHH!!*" Afterwards, as a treat for being such a brave boy, Mummy would take you to the shop to load up with dolly mixtures and jelly babies to begin the next round of tooth decay. I've found the more you go to the dentist, the more trouble you get from your teeth. These guys have *ways* of making you return.

CHAPTER SIX

Dad's Songs

Many years on, when we were growing up and Dad was getting old and testy, mother used to warn us not to disturb him when was singing. "It means he's happy". If so, he must have been happy indeed for when I was little for he sang all day long. As the sixteenth-century composer William Byrd noted, 'The exercise of singing is delightful to Nature and doth good to preserve the health of man'. Dad wasn't particularly musical—he never learned to read music or play an instrument or listen to anything that lasted longer than five minutes—but he was certainly quite a loud Dad. His repertoire varied from radio hits like 'Que sera sera' and 'Love and Marriage' to scraps of opera and forgotten songs from the music hall, the latter usually poignant or wistful rather than overtly comic. Perhaps because of my interests, the songs I remember best are about flowers and birds. There was the one about dainty mistress poppy on a warm and sunny day, who sheds her silken petticoat along the garden wall. And the cuckoo who singeth as she flies, and bringeth us glad tidings, and telleth us no lies. There was also a pretty, sad one that I used to think he had made up until I heard the Von Trapp family sing it in German. I suspect such tinsel tunes meant something to Dad; perhaps they were part of his dreams, like keeping bees and chickens, or shooting wild duck on the marshes; rural longings from his dreary coop in south London.

He seems to have been a Danny Kaye fan: 'Hoo-hoo-hoo-ha-hoo, that's the woody woodpecker's song'; 'wonderful, wonderful Copenhagen'. There were also snatches of opera in which the original Italian would be replaced by dum-de-dums and fa-la-las. The arrival of ITV brought a rich hoard of one-liners culled from the adverts, for in those innocent days every biscuit or tablet of soap came with its own jingle. 'Bridge-that-gap-with-Cadbury's-snack'—'You'll look a little lovelier each day…'—'Ambrosia, creamed rice!' So there is Dad, in his late thirties, lost forever in the past, as we all shall be one day, with his comforting warmth and big arms and loud, hooting, happy-Dad noises.

He also liked poetry, especially some of the classics from his own time: John Masefield, Walter de la Mare. W.H. Davies. They say that a person's sense of identity is found in the poetry they learned when they were young. I think that was true of Dad. He had a limited but obviously deeply-felt repertoire, probably from the poems he would have learned at school. One which he could still quote after his mind had gone was Wilfred Gibson's *The Ice Cart*—'Far from the grey and grimy heat/Of that intolerable street'—which conveys the sort of dreamy visions of far-off lands that Dad liked. From the war film *The Way to the Stars*, he had the tear-jerking *Johnny-head-in-air* off by heart:

> *Do not despair/For Johnny-head-in-air*
> *He sleeps as sound/As Johnny underground…*
> *Better by far/For Johnny-the-bright star*
> *To keep your head/And see his children fed.*

I might have been tempted to recite this one at his funeral except that I think I would have broken down. A bit of doggerel that falls flat to a generation like ours that has never known war meant something else to those that had lived through blitzes and bombings and bereavements.

Lines learned early enough never fade. Dad remembered lines like these after he had forgotten almost everything else. They seemed to animate him during his last, broken years in the EMI ward. When he came out with his stuttered line or two, his eyes would moisten and he'd sometimes even manage to crack a smile. Long after we were toddlers he'd stick with the nursery language we used in our Bill-and-Ben days. Christopher and I were his 'boys' to the end of his days, even when he got our names the wrong way round.

From my first comics, *Robin* or *Playhour*, Dad harvested a litany of Rupert Bear-like couplets. He mastered an entire alphabet including 'U for Uniform of Blue/Holding up the cars for you' and 'H for House with windows small/ With my brush I'll clean them all'. From Rupert himself came such cheery lines as: It's a bright and lovely day/Get up quickly, come and play'. Once, at the infant school, we were made to learn a kiddie's song about a fox and a hen that the teacher had made up: *Paul's little hen ran away from the farmyard/Ran down the hillside and into the dale...* Dad lapped it up. I would soon have forgotten the thing had not Dad sung it every day. I think his enthusiastic participation in my infant world went a bit beyond the purely motivational. He sang because he was loving the role of officer and husband and father, the ruler of his little roost: the airfield and bomb dump, his pretty wife and adoring son, the comfortable married quarter—the loving home life he had never had. Probably it also appealed to the child in the man. I think part of Dad, the emotional part, never quite grew up. He was like me in that childhood never quite lost its grip. The difference between us is that Dad was sentimental; he liked things sugar-coated. I seem to have lost my sweet tooth.

In one of our favourite games when I was about three, Dad used to dandle me on his knee while he recited some ancient lines from his own childhood:

Ladies go nim-nim.
Gentlemen go tree-trot, tree-trot.
The old man goes treeee-trot, treeee-trot.
And the huntsman goes gallop-gallop-gallop.

At each line his knees would mimic the respective horse of the lady, the gentleman and the old man until the final line when his furiously galloping knees would bounce me into the air, and I would shriek, "again, do it again!" ('again' is one of the first words a child learns). Once I got so carried away that I kicked him in the balls and was astonished by his reaction. What a fuss! I didn't know Dads felt pain; I thought mine was invincible. I used to brag about him in the playground. "My Dad's bigger than your Dad". "*My* Dad's the middleweight boxing champion". "That's nothing. *My* Dad's been to the moon". Some of the more stupid kids tended to believe me for, in his smart uniform and tall, slim figure, Dad did look as though he might just possibly spy for England, or fly a jet, or whatever.

Another oft-heard snippet was the gruesome parlour game they had played at 74, Marlowe Road. It was one of those Catholic games revolving around an absent-minded priest: '*The priest of the parish has lost his considering cap. Some say this, some say that, some say my man…*'—and at this point a name would be called out. 'Who me, Sir?' and you were supposed to respond. '*Yes, you, Sir!*' '*You're a liar ,Sir!*' '*Who then, Sir?*' "*My man…*"—and another name would be called and another idiot would join in the "game". Even when I was little this didn't sound much fun, and we never actually played it. I think the point of it was to show how different Catholics are to ordinary people.

Dad had more music for us whenever he gave me and my friends a lift to my first school in the village of Escrick. Depending on who was in the car, he would extemporise a rota-song along the following lines:

*Mark Oakland, Peter Jackson,
Andrew Dixon, Donald Benson
Roll on, roll on, roll on.*

I expect they took it in good part, being little kids. They certainly joined in with Dad's other catch-phrase as he motored along the Escrick road in his narrow black Austin 9 ('BBT 293'). "*Forty miles an hour!*", we yelled in unison as Dad clamped his foot on the throttle, and, going downhill with the wind behind him, eventually reached that fabulous speed. "He's all right your Dad", they would say. "Knows some nice songs. But that's a really crap car he drives." "It's our second car", I apologised. "Mum uses the Rolls to go to the film studios in York". "I didn't know there were film studios in York." "Yeah, there are, but they're, you know, secret. Don't tell anybody."

Finally there were Dad noises that were just noise. Instead of bursting forth with his latest air, he would simply chunter, or rumble, or make monkey-like sounds. They, too, probably meant he was happy. Dad, I suppose, wanted to shower a little well-being about. For a long time, I thought this was what all Dads were like. Admittedly, looking at other RAF Dads, with their moustaches and thinning hair, and long, serious faces, it was hard to imagine. But, then, you'd never suspect my own Dad's lighter side from all those photos of airfield inspections, the troops all lined up in rows, Dad accompanying the CO with his pale, solemn face, row of medals and highly polished shoes.

One of Dad's domestic chores was to answer my questions. I took it for granted that he knew everything, but what I really wanted to know was what he would do in a particular, usually dangerous situation. I suppose I hoped that some of his adult wisdom might be shared with little me. What he would *do*, for instance, if he was attacked by a tiger. He was pretty patient about it for the most part, although his answers, it seemed to me, often lacked imagination. What did he do about the tiger? He shot it, that's what he did. But, I would probe, what if you had forgotten the gun and left it at home? And what if you missed or just winged it? What would you do then? I mean, where was the back-up plan, where was Plan B? It seemed to me that he had not thought this tiger thing through. As for my supplementary about sharks, Dad's answer didn't convince me at all. Yes, Dad could swim, but he couldn't swim *that* fast. We both knew that.

He would, as I grew a bit older, tell me about stuff in the papers, such as the myxomatosis virus that was killing the poor bunny rabbits, or the frightful doings of the Mau Mau in Kenya, or about the latest RAF jet-plane (was it faster than a Spitfire? *Much* faster. Then was it faster than *two* Spitfires?). Sometimes he took me to see bits of his world—the office and the airfield and various concrete wartime bunkers and Nissen huts made of corrugated iron and smelling of damp. They weren't, to be honest, all *that* interesting. Back at base he was handy about the house with his ladders and brushes. Or he was outside gardening, or feeding the chickens with scraps—and that's another echo from early childhood, the rising, anticipatory mass clucking—clar-*clar* cluk-cluck—from the pen. I vaguely remember Mummy or Dad reading a story to me after putting me to bed and before kissing me good night. But they were not the sort to make a big thing about how they loved their little boy. That would have embarrassed both of us.

I think I felt reasonably comfortable with my parents. Children were more strictly brought up then, but, compared with what my father and mother had to put up with, my upbringing was pretty liberal. I did not, for example, have the Bible stuffed down my throat. I was taught good manners and the difference between right and wrong (the one being rewarded, the other punished). When not in the pushchair I spent a lot of time behind bars in the playpen, with or without a little chum. My toys were simple but colourful, and mostly made of wood. I had a set of bricks that you could pile on top of one another until they fell over. I had bats and balls, and a tinny spinning top, and an object with a long handle that made a pleasant clicking noise when you pulled it along. Living by the seaside, I of course had my bucket and spade, and a shrimping net. I had my own cupboard crammed with stuff like this, and a sudden recollection of one of those toys, bursting like a soap bubble in the mind, transports one back for an instant into those uncharted depths of childhood beyond the sunlight of conscious memory. Toys were not strewn all over the floor as they would be today. Life had zones and boundaries. You knew what you could get away with and what would result in a telling-off, or even a smack. You asked to leave the table and you didn't talk with your mouth full, or make a horrible noise as you ate. You were taught to say please and thank you at appropriate moments, and to hold a knife and fork properly. Those occasional light smacks left no emotional scar. Besides, I have generously forgotten them all except one, which I will describe in its place.

I suspect, and mother confirms, that I was a fairly quiet, self-absorbed child ("though you had your moments!" she smiled). At the age of three or four everything is intensely interesting: the products in the kitchen and the bathroom; any car or boat or train, the road signs (which you could buy for yourself in Dinky form), anyone's dog or cat or hamster, the contents of a shed or a cupboard or a shoebox. You could turn anything into a game. Wasn't life just one big game? One's comfort zone stretched to the stratosphere.

Father had a succession of postings in the early 50s, most of which left him in charge of another closed-down airfield or another pile of bombs or gas canisters. Counting temporary homes, such as the 'silly-light house', so-named because of the flickering beam of the nearby lighthouse, I must have toddled in and out of at least six different homes during my first five years. The parents had few possessions and the furniture in each quarter was rented. In most of his postings in the early Fifties, Dad was left more or less in charge of the base, which suited him. He could handle responsibility, could Dad. He could work happily on his own without much supervision. This meant that he was often without the company of fellow officers—and officers did not socialise with lower ranks—but while that might have been unfortunate for mother, he did not appear to mind.

Mummy was the home body, although when we were at RAF Riccall a lot of the dusting and hovering was done by our batman, Corporal Darrington, bizarre as that might sound now. Mum was always busy cooking and baking, producing an endless succession of jam tarts and gingerbread and little sponge cakes with angel wings stuck in the icing. When she wasn't baking she was knitting. We could barely keep up with her woolly avalanche of socks, jumpers and scarves. I was clad in home knitwear from top to toe. Since there was no possibility of us wearing these out fast enough, she started on cushion covers and tea cosies and cruet-swaddlers and bottle vests, and, once those possibilities were exhausted, began to stockpile knitted produce for the next RAF bazaar or jumble sale.

Mother was the dependable rock of my life. She was the hand you held. Once, I remember, I let go of that hand in a crowded place and slipped away. I remember the thrill of freedom, followed in no time at

Dad's life: another parade, another inspection.

all with sudden anguish and despair. Of course, the moment I started howling I was surrounded by a ring of adult faces. What's your name? Where's your Mummy? There was only benevolence in that mass of faces swaddled in Fifties wool: woollen coats, woollen hats, lovely warm wool all around. A policeman was summoned and my distraught mother located. "Wait till I get you home, you little monkey!" England seemed a kind and secure place then. There was a neighbourly spirit left over from the war and the shared austerity of the postwar years. No-one had ever heard of paedophiles, and murderers did not reoffend on account of their being hung. Some say that things are no worse today, and that we have simply become more cautious about risk-taking. Really? Get that! And then the pig flew past!

We were, as I say, a reasonably happy family. The parents had their moods, of course, and a child detects such things. When they were upset, I was upset, and that probably didn't help. Father required careful handling. He was generally well-intentioned, gentle and kind, and above all, gentlemanly. He was never violent nor unfaithful nor drunk. But the fine paternal weather could quickly turn stormy when something went wrong, or when he felt slighted in some way. He had

Mummy's boy, Easington c.1953.

a hyper-sensitive nature, a brittle sense of his own manhood, and, it was easy to suppose, a burning chip on his shoulder. He disliked being contradicted, and subsequent arguments tended to erupt first in angry shouts and counter-accusations, and then subside into a simmer which, in later years, could go on for days in which the singing most definitely stopped. The extent to which he governed his passion in those distant days is beyond my memory. My sense, and that is really all it is, is that this was his happy time. Years later he would look back fondly to the time when we were his 'little shavers' (one piece of Cockney he hadn't managed to shake off). Later on, when I was in my teens, we never really found enough to do together, Dad and me. His interests were essentially solitary, as mine were. And eventually his wisdoms and opinions seemed to me to be narrow and ignorant, his world, after all, a small one. A gulf opened up which never really closed. We stopped talking. I suppose that is why those faded memories of a warm home and loving parents still make me go slightly dreamy. They are the last faint echoes of a time when life was benign and uncomplicated, and when Dad's sense of manly pride embraced his family and home. He was looking forward to a close father-and-son relationship of the sort that he had never had. And, as things turned out, that I once had, and then, somehow, seemed to lose forever.

CHAPTER SEVEN

A Little Learning

Early in 1955 we were posted back to the East Riding, to RAF Riccall, close by the long straight road from Selby to York. Our quarter was a single-storey prefab that had served as the Sergeant's Mess at the now vanished wartime base. We were there because Dad had yet more bombs to dump in the sea. He was also in charge of supply at the nearby RAF Maintenance Unit No. 91 at Acaster Malbis. The old Mess was a funny place to live. Our new home stood bare and alone amid the ruins of hardstandings and pillboxes and mouldering huts. There was no street other than a concrete track, nor so much as an address that any of us can remember. Our quarter had been redecorated and furnished with chintzy armchairs, RAF utility furniture and—here's luxury!—an icebox. I now had a proper room of my own, where the Sergeants had perhaps kept their guns, with a potty underneath the metal-framed bed and a cupboard for my toys. I soon found kids to play with at a nearby farm, and in return I let them play in my personal concrete pill-box, just outside. In addition I had two grown-up chums: our batman Darrington, who was captive to little Peter's eager questions, and a local man called Jim who took me for short rides on the back of his motorbike. My strongest memory of those early, pre-school days at Riccall is of digging a hole which, I was confident, would one day reach the centre of the earth.

I first went to school in September 1955, a month short of my fifth birthday. It might have been a relief to get away from all the bawling and stinky goings-on at home, for I now had a little brother, Christopher Anthony. Born in York, six months previously, he had been another baby who seemed reluctant to enter the world. He was blond and blue-eyed and attention-seeking. I wasn't totally thrilled with the new situation. The family album has a shot of me rocking the tot and looking bored out of my mind. I managed to refrain from putting Harpic in his milk or sending his pram hurtling downhill (for unfortunately there weren't any hills). But I knew that from now on my exclusive claim to my parents' love would have to be shared, and no doubt, like any elder sibling, I resented it. Up until then photos show the cute boy with the dark fringe looking content and secure, the bright star in his little universe. Now all of a sudden I seem crestfallen. The prefab reeked of the damp, sweet stink of baby, shot through with the acidic tang of nappies and wee, not to mention the screeching at all hours, day and night. Big brother slunk about the stricken house and bided his time. His moment in the sun would come again. Wouldn't it?

The infant school lay at the far end of a long straight cul-de-sac in the nearest village, called Escrick. It was a tiny place, built of local stone and consisting of no more than a couple of rooms and a hard playground. It abutted a much larger school to which we traipsed for our horrible school dinner. I had no experience of pre-school and at first I think I found the new routine strange and disorienting. In the school photograph we have the frumpy, nameless teacher in her Paisley frock, the standing boys in their reach-me-down Fifties garb—shorts, sandals, Fair Isle pullies—and the sitting girls with their ribbons and plaits, like a row of Miss Piggies. I recognise only one or two faces: the broad smile of my sturdy pal, Mark Oakland, whose Dad owned a brickworks (another playground), a foxy-faced boy called Andrew Dixon who we sometimes gave a lift to school, and a girl named Molly who, after I failed to turn up to her birthday party—some complicated business with buses—had shouted, "You *should* have, you *should* have", over and over.

When the first shock of being banged up in this place had passed, I found the lessons, such as they were, pretty undemanding. First and last thing we chanted the Lord's Prayer and sang a hymn in our shrill infant voices, often 'All Things Bright and Beautiful', about all the lovely things made just for us by the good Lord in his celestial laboratory. Outside we threw bean bags and danced around a maypole. God knows why we had a maypole but we did. The girls were forever jumping up and down with a skipping rope and chanting their little rhymes. We boys played tag and pretended to be Red Indians by yelling *wha-wha-wha* and taking little kids hostage. In class we made nameless things out of matchsticks and pipe cleaners, and some smelly stuff called plasticine, which began in many colours but was almost immediately reduced by mixing to the colour of mud.

I suppose we must have learned something. That I came away from Escrick at least semi-literate must owe something to the school and its shelf of Janet-and-John books. Bill Bryson was right when he recalled how, in the strange world of Janet and John, 'the sun always shines. The dog never shits on the lawn. Everyone is at all times clean, healthy, strong, reliable, hard-working and white.' And pretty well-connected too. Janet and John seemed to have endless friends and relatives who did interesting things like keeping cows and horses, or running a grocer's shop, or sailing a boat. Yet this vapid pair never took advantage of such fantastic opportunities for fun. They were far too busy simply looking at stuff, and waving; a heck of a lot of waving. The episode with the train, for instance:

"Here is the train", says Father. "Look, John, here is the train". To rub home the message, there is a picture of John and his Dad, and probably Janet too, and the dog, all looking at the train and waving.

"Hello" cries Bob, the train driver, waving back. "See who is here! It is Janet and John. Look, look! It is Janet and John!"

Infants' school at Escrick. I am on the right, socks down, pully on the wrong way round.

Even at the age of five I must have wondered why the guy was so happy to see that pair of morons. But now it was John's turn to speak.

"Hello", says John. "Look, look, it is the train driver! Daddy, Janet, look, it is Bob! Bob the train driver! He is driving the train!"

And so they wave at Bob, and smile their milky smiles, and Bob waves back, and everyone is waving like mad, when suddenly a mist covers your eyes and you seem to see Bob reaching into his cab for the shovel, and then—Look! Look!—madly beating John about the head with it. "Look, it is Bob! Bob has a shovel! Bob is coming over! Ow, Bob has hit me with the shovel! He has a shovel and he hit me. Oh, he got you too. Shit."

The other thing I remember about Escrick is the school dinners. Up until now, I had been under the impression that food tasted nice. My diet at home was simple but nutritious: baked beans, chips, more baked beans, Mummy's Yorkshire puddings and that lovely lemon meringue that comes out of a little box (just add water and stand back). At school though, they produced terrible steaming tins of nameless stuff that didn't look like food and smelt like the liquid Mummy used to clean the sink. The worst, obviously created in an evil, atomic factory somewhere, was 'cheese-potato'. It was white, lumpy stuff that stank like a sweaty sock, and there was orange gunk on it that I knew was actually poisonous. Most of these Yorkshire kids knocked it all back with total lack of discrimination; it was just 'dinner' to them, like a cow eating grass. How I envied a little, pasty-faced kid called Donald who was on a special diet and so was left on his own to munch a carrot in the playground. I refused to touch their toxic cheese-potato and so these ordeals became a battle of wills between teacher, fearful that her young pupil would perish through lack of vitamins, and little Peter, convinced that it was all some plot to do away with him. I would roar and blub into my plate, sometimes with a great candle of snot dangling from a nostril and landing with a plop and a hiss into the fearful mess, until they gave up and sent me back to class in disgrace.

The school photo presents a simpering little Peter with his jumper on back to front, a sock fallen down and, probably, his pants sticking out of his shorts. I usually experienced trouble changing out of my clothes for games and, even more, struggling back into them again afterwards. It was hard enough even finding your stuff in the shifting pile of garments strewn all over the floor, as though washed up on the tide. And there was the permanent mystery of the missing sock. No matter how careful you were, no matter how hard you tried, a sock always went missing, and you never found it again. So another daily ritual was wandering around weepily, holding a lone sock in the air for all to see. When you are only five, a good cry always seems to clear the air.

Escrick infant school had no uniform, except possibly a cap, nor reports, nor tests. There seemed to be no clear way of distinguishing the swots from the thickos except in one or two outstanding cases, like the poor, tubby, special-needs boy who sat on his own table with a lump of plasticine. I have a random memory of colouring in a paper ruler in alternate stripes of red and green, my favourite colours, and being utterly disappointed by the effect, compared with those of more colour-co-ordinated boys and girls. And of making an ink stamp out of a potato. Potatoes were versatile things. You could make a potato head by sticking things into it, or gouging out bits as ammo for your spud gun. The bag they came in was kept for sack races, and for tag games we counted 'one potato, two potato, three potato, four'. Brilliant things potatoes. You can do almost anything with them, I thought, except eat them.

And that was school—a queer alternate life experience that made very little sense. You neither liked it nor hated it. It was just something you got through before going home and doing something else. You never asked yourself whether there was any underlying point to prancing round the maypole or making little giraffes out of pipe cleaners. It was just a great lump of cheese-potato called school. Eat it, and it was gone.

But I *was* learning stuff. I was a natural autodidact. I first started to discover the world beyond Janet and John in those books you saw only in the Fifties, the ones where you create your own pictures by tearing off perforated strips of images, like stamps, and gumming them in at the right place. There was one on Bible stories, another on the adventures of Davy Crockett, and a really good one with lots of fight scenes on King Arthur and his Knights of the Round Table. I went through them as to the manner born, and thus became an acknowledged expert on

Bible stories, King Arthur, Davy Crockett and, above all, flags. I had, it seemed, a retentive memory. Flags and their countries became my party piece. Daddy would wheel me out to describe the flag of Cambodia and name its capital city and main exports. My goodness, they said, and at his age too, while proud father beamed and puffed at his pipe, or at least he would have done if he had smoked a pipe. Box tops of the period always showed Dad puffing away, watching his clever son build a printing press, or whatever. That is what Fifties Dads did, along with wearing a hat and polished leather shoes, and a patched tweed jacket from Burtons.

The best of all these gummy picture-books was called Animals of the Past. For me it was a gateway into the wonderful world of vanished life; the progression of beasts over the immensity of time. These barely imaginable creatures, such as dinosaurs or pterodactyls, fed my young imagination. I was soon making endless drawings of animals with very

My brother Christopher in his pram outside our prefab at Escrick.

long necks, or gigantic horns, or with rows of hideous grinning teeth, all going about their business in a torrid, volcanic setting. Father, of course, showed them to our long-suffering friends and visitors ("oooh—and at *his* age!"). My passion for ancient life led to many a playground argument about whether the Thunder Dinosaur would really hold his own in a tussle with T-Rex, and whether they were really extinct, or might possibly live on somewhere, like that place in The Lost World. In these discussions my opinion inevitably prevailed. When it came to the prehistoric, it was acknowledged, throughout the junior circles of Escrick and Riccall Common, that little Peter was Dinosaur King.

Shortly after we left Escrick, the old Sergeant's Mess was pulled down. And among the debris, Dad liked to recall, they found a large drawing of a T-Rex, one of the last of my dinosaur portraits, with its triangular teeth and terrible red staring eyes, as though clambering out of the rubble to take one last stab at earthly domination.

"*Gae me a spark o' nature's fire*", wrote Rabbie Burns. "*That's a' the learning I require*". He didn't mean it literally of course; he was only striking a poetic attitude. But one way or another, nature was seeping into my life. As Konrad Lorenz, the animal behaviourist, noted in his heavy Austrian way, nature is 'ze best school at vich ze younk people learn that ze vorld hass significance und meaning'. Hence, 'ze chilt must haff ze closest poss-ible contact with ze liffing vorld at ze earliest poss-ible *opportunity*.' But although I agree with the old boy with some passion, I cannot in my own case isolate the moment when this truth came beaming down like a shaft of light in one of my Bible pictures. There was no eureka moment when, as Tim Dee describes it in the opening line of *The Running Sky*, a swallow 'flew into the garden of the house where I was born'. We probably had swallows too, but, if so, I didn't notice them. In fact, about the only wildlife yarn I can take away from that time is of Dad telling me about the squirrels in the wood, that dark line on the northern horizon. Proper *red* squirrels too. Of course I never saw one. Probably I only remember it because I didn't believe him. It seemed to me impossible that the wood, a very dull place, could possibly be the home of Squirrel Nutkin with his pointy ears and huge fluffy tail and unbelievably cute expression. Come *on*, Dad, you're kidding me.

Not that I would have noticed even if the squirrel had perched on the washing line. My world, like Squirrel Nutkins' tail, was fuzzy. No one seems to have noticed that little Peter was short-sighted. As for me, I probably assumed that permanent soft-focus was simply the way of things. I had got used to squinting at the world, trying to make out objects in the mist. And when I belatedly realised that my eyes were worse than those of other people, I hid the fact. It was only later, after we were posted to Harper Hill in the Peak District, that the teacher spotted my disability and snitched to the parents.

So I have no tales to tell of seminal encounters with swallows or squirrels or weasels. The wildlife I knew were the things I could see when they were under my nose. I could gaze at small life in a jam-jar, or pick flowers and press them in books. I could grow mustard-and-cress on wet blotting paper and plant a row of marigolds in the garden. I could potter along the beach, peering under stones and weed, and find dried-up starfish and empty shells, like castaway toys. I played with bladderwrack—nature's bubblewrap—and caught shrimps in my net. They were all part of the great playground which was the outdoors. I sploshed about in the sea and trickled the loose sand through my toes. At Riccall, I learned to climb trees: first saplings with branches near

On the chintz sofa with my new brother not co-operating.

the ground, like a ladder, but then, as I gained confidence, also taller ones with boughs to swing from. I learned how to annoy my friends with sticky buds and itching powder excavated from rose-hips. My nimble fingers could stitch together a daisy-chain necklace and shoot a plantain by looping the stalk around the bullet-shaped head. After a certain amount of practice I could make a sharp noise from doubling up a blade of grass and blowing it like a reed between two thumbs. The modern idea of 'look, don't touch' would have been, in the opinion of this free-range boy, unbelievably wet and weedy. Nature was *fun*. That was the whole point. It was there to be enjoyed.

No one yet knew that I had secret powers. My maladjusted eyes might be useless for spotting squirrels but they could focus really close. I had, in effect, a built-in magnifying lens. I could stare a beetle in the face and watch him twitch his antennae. I could make out the grains of coloured dust on a butterfly's wing, and see little, jerking specks in the pondwater and know that they were water-fleas. My jam jars were like Blake's grain of sand: infinity held in the palm of your hand. So I didn't start with the more obvious forms of life. I wasn't a birder or a bat-man. I was bug-boy, the explorer of the grassblade jungle, the microcosm of small ponds. Within the vast out-of-focus world, these were the points of sharpness, tiny living exhibits in the great museum of life.

Stealing the show at my brother's christening.

CHAPTER EIGHT

Childworld

That's the first thousand days of my life, and nearly all of it has gone beyond recall. Almost all I am left with is the soundtrack to those non-events. At Riccall, we rented a television, one of those early kinds with a screen about the size of a postcard surrounded by slats and grills and knobs. There was no channel changer because there was only one channel: the BBC. Programmes for the likes of me were confined to the magic hour between school and tea. On Mondays it was always *Picture Book*, a kind of little kid's Blue Peter, compered by a lovely Mumsy lady called Patricia Driscoll; in the Fifties, even young women looked and dressed like your Mum with their perms and frocks and row of beads. Patricia's catchphrase was: 'You could do this too. I'm sure you could if you tried'. On Tuesdays it was *Andy Pandy*, a wooden toddler on strings wearing a weird triangular hat who pranced about with his sinister sidekick, a rag doll named Looby Loo. The pair seemed to be just passing the time until the credits rolled and both of them would hop back into their wicker hamper, in a great hurry it seemed to me. I never really got Andy Pandy; he seemed a real dope. *Bill-and-Ben the Flowerpot Men* was the Wednesday watch, with their flobberdops and pobbleplops. Thursday was time for *Rag, Tag and Bobtail*, a wholesome trio of animal adventurers, a Wind in the Willows for nippers, a rather slow-paced number which, as one critic remembered, made *Waiting for Godot* look like the Keystone Cops. Even so it was a breeze compared with *The Woodentops*, which was Friday's offering: a bunch of thick wooden muppets on strings, including 'The Biggest Spotty Dog You Ever Did See', at which words the strings would jerk and the gormless canine flapped its wooden ears. You got out the old imaginary tommy-gun for the Woodentops—*da-da-da-da-da-da*—and a moment later it was all splinters and string and smoke coming out of the set. *Eat that you freakin' retards.*

First-generation television was a comforting load of old rubbish. Basically it was radio with moving pictures. Such drama as there was was based on sets no more elaborate than the stage. The mainstay was cheap family quiz-shows such as *What's My Line* and *Criss Cross Quiz*. Then as now they filled the gaps with imported sitcoms including one called *I Married Joan* about a supposedly comic broad married to a judge. Joan had a door bell that went 'bing-bong' which I thought was cool and very American, and can we have one, Mum? I stared uncomprehendingly at this adult comedy of manners for hours and hours. Well, I had nothing better to do. The adventure stuff, swashbucklers like Robin Hood and William Tell, came later, and all on ITV, which was obviously better because it had adverts.

From the radiogram, another large wooden box, came the popular songs of the era. They had pretty tinkle-tankle tunes, sung by gals in big flouncy dresses or crooners in dinner jackets. Practically all of them were family listening so you could join in with *You, Me and Us* (sung by Alma), or *Love and Marriage* (Frank), or *Papa Piccolino* (Petula), or *Que Sera Sera* (Doris), or, at the time of Suez, *Lay Down Your Arms* (Annie). From the studio of Walt Disney came 'Hi ho', 'April Showers' and 'Bella Nocha', the latter from *Lady and the Tramp*—the scene where the dogs share a bowl of spaghetti. It was all happy, era-defining stuff, proving that nothing much had changed in popular music since about 1870.

And then, all of a sudden, a discordant note crept in: music that your parents didn't necessarily like. Most of it came from America, and particularly from a restless boy with ants in his pants whose hair was all shook up with Brylcream. His name, we learned, was Elvis Presley. The Brits responded with some home-made stuff called skiffle in which the star was a grinning ferret-faced fellow called Lonnie Donegan. He sang *Puttin' on the Style*, a song I first heard at a pantomime. 'Whoa', you thought. 'What the hell is *this* crap?' They said it grew on you. No it didn't; it was just their brains going soft.

I much preferred the old-style music from my pile of gramophone 78s in their paper sleeves, made out of some incredibly brittle substance that broke and splintered if you dropped or even tried to bend them (and of course you tried to bend them; five-year-old kids are always testing the strength of stuff). These came as a job lot with our ancient wind-up gramophone; many were bitter songs about the Depression-men working on the chain gang, and folk with serious if hard-to-comprehend problems like the man who owed his soul to the company store (uh?). My favourite was a music-hall comedy song called *When Father Papered the Parlour* (the record label adding in brackets that 'He Had No Right To Do So!'). It was sung by an old bloke who sounded like my Uncle Rupert, and he had to pause between verses completely overcome by his own wit:

> *Wh-en—father papered the parlour*
> *You couldn't see Pa from paste.*
> *Dabbing it here, dabbing it there,*
> *Paste and paper everywhere.*
> *Mum was stuck to the ceiling,*
> *The kids were stuck to the floor.*
> *I never knew a blooming family*
> *So 'stuck up' before!*

Heh, heh, 'stuck up', get it? This was followed by gales of fake laughter: 'well, well, *ha ha ha ha*, well, *Ah-HA-HA-HA-HA*.' My father insisted that one about Tubby the Tuba, about a miserable brass instrument who wanted to be a trumpet or something, was even funnier than *When Father Papered the Parlour*. He was wrong about that, but he always appreciated a bit of pathos, did Dad.

The greatest hero of 1955—mine and everyone else's—was Davy Crockett. He was not someone whose lifestyle you could relate to—killing a 'bar' (a bear, that is) before breakfast was outside most of our experiences. But we watched the Disney film starring Fess Parker, with the long dull bit in the middle where our hero puts on a suit and goes up to Congress, whatever that was, to Serve a Spell, and we all knew the hit song with its chorus of *'Davee, Davee Crockett, King of the Wild Frontier'*. I felt obliged to Davy since he was on when Daddy took me to the cinema for the very first time, and we ate salted chips in the car afterwards, which was also good. Hard to explain his popularity; perhaps we liked him because he was brave and uncomplicated and had a sense of humour. It was this last quality that made him stand out. Most attempts to make a humorous western, such as Hopalong Cassidy, fell flat on their faces.

Television grew up with kids my age. As it happened I was able to watch TV only up the age of eight, for after that we lived overseas, and then they sent me off to a telly-less boarding school. Perhaps that is why those early TV memories are so intense. The theme tune to Dixon of Dock Green, for instance, still brings a slight tug to the innards, somewhere left-side of the stomach. In the mind's eye one sees the avuncular old London bobby dispensing his homely wisdoms under the blue lamp, an icon of that old forgotten sense of order. But once we graduated to ITV, it was thrilling adventure all the way with the square-jawed heroes of yore. First up was Robin Hood ('*Robin Hood, Robin Hood, Riding through the Glen*'; riding through the *what?*), played by Dan-Dare lookalike Richard Green with some great arrow action to open the credits. After Robin came William Tell ('*Come away, come away with William Tell…*'), a Swiss version of Robin who kicked off by shooting an apple off his boy's head with his crossbow; cut to a big grin of relief from the boy. Then there was Ivanhoe ('*Ivanho—oh, to adventure, bold adventure watch him go*') and The Buccaneers ('*Let's go a-roving. And join the Buccaneers!*'). They were all more or less the same, all heroic anti-establishment guys busy turning wrong into right. The ITV people knew what we liked. We were as keen on William Tell firing his crossbow in a remote mountain setting as we were on Robin with his longbow in the English greenwood. The heroes were so heroic and the villains so irredeemably villainous that even the most stupid kid could follow the story and know who to boo and who to cheer. Whenever Robin's arrow or Tell's bolt hit a bad guy there was never any blood, and he hit the dirt instantly and soundlessly with an obliging 'thunk'. The few women were all soppy and useless. We didn't really understand why they were there at all. Some of the heroes, notably Ivanhoe, had a boy or two in tow to help out with the adventuring. That seemed all right. Obviously any self-respecting hero needed a boy like us. Each programme was introduced with some manly singing, Gothic lettering swirling up the screen. And after an hour or so of olden-day ultra-violence we were ready for our tea, hopefully baked beans again with a poached egg and lots of chips swilled down with some sugary fizz.

The great thing about children's TV is that it bore no resemblance whatever to real life. Characters like Robin obviously lived a long time ago—exactly when hardly mattered—but they looked and talked like the stars of the 1940s in crisp mid-Atlantic accents. Westerns weren't real either. To begin with, TV played the Wild West for laughs, with the chunky, balding Hopalong Cassidy ('*Here he comes, here he comes!*') and the frankly foppish Cisco Kid ('*Here's adventure!*'). These guys never shot anybody. Big mistake. As even little kids knew, every western needs a baddie and it was the purpose of baddies to get shot and fall bloodlessly off their horse in the final frame uttering the word "ugh". This was where the Lone Ranger scored heavily, for he despatched the bad guys with *silver* bullets, which were obviously the best kind of bullet, and he also jumped on his horse from some hidden trampoline with a hearty "Hiyo Silver, away!" We were far too young to understand what a poser the Lone Ranger was, frankly camp in his mask and white hat, nor the sheer battiness of the '*fiery horse with the speed of light, a cloud of dust, and a hearty hiyo Silver!*' With the speed of what now? With a hearty hiyo *what*? "It's the way they talk in America", explained Mummy.

By the end of the decade, westerns were getting slightly more realistic, and they were on every night which was great: *Rawhide* ('*Rolling, rolling, rolling*' with the young Clint Eastwood), *Gunsmoke* (no singing here, just a close up of Matt Dillon's trusty six-gun being fired and then replaced, smoking, in the leather holster—the coolest opening ever). There were comic westerns (*Tenderfoot*) and girly westerns (*Bronco*) and epic westerns (*Wagon Train*) and even temperance westerns where the hero refused to drink anything but sarsaparilla—and so naturally got into lots of fights with whisky drinkers. There were westerns starring dogs (*Rin Tin Tin*) and horses (*Champion, the Wonder Horse!*) and probably sheep. We knew our way round the prairies of Wyoming and Arizona better than our own backyard. And then, quite suddenly, everyone got bored with big hats and six-guns and all the outlaws and sheriffs were put out to graze. Personally I blame the Beatles.

The home-grown stuff was equally escapist. The TV shows about school were not the places we knew but ancient places with clock towers and ivied turrets like the one in *Billy Bunter*, the Fat Owl of the Remove, played by 40-year-old Gerald Campion, or *Whacko!* where the genial Jimmy Edwards was never to be seen without his cane. It was what we had all got used to in comics, which, as George Orwell pointed out, were always at least thirty years behind the times. There, too, the choice was between public school and Bash Street, where mischievous working-class kids bait sadistic masters. Either way no one ever seems to learn anything.

The early consumer-culture shows were notable for the feebleness of their prizes. In *Take Your Pick* (catchphrase: '*Take the money or open the box!*') the top prize might be a fridge or a tinny 'treasure chest' containing a few tenners. What we were all waiting for, however, was for the moment when Betty from Blackpool won the show's booby prize, 'a comb without teeth for a bald man', or maybe a ticket for the next show. Betty was supposed to laugh good-heartedly, before clearing off back to Blackpool. On *Crackerjack*, the prize was a *pencil*, and to earn that you had to work pretty hard, holding an armful of cabbages or guessing blindfold the ingredients of some obnoxious substance fed to you by the bald man with a spoon.

In the Fifties, when even the crappiest shows were fresh and novel, we even watched the adverts. In fact we *especially* watched the adverts. This was the time of Halas-and-Batchelor style cartoons in which the hero gets all charged up by sucking mints or eating spinach. Some were, in today's terms, highly incorrect, such as the Ribena ad's line-up of singing blackcurrants, or the caricature Chinaman advising you to buy Esso for 'happy motolling'—or, for that matter, the lucky housewife who got a Hoover for Christmas.

They knew all about kids, did these advert guys. Cashing in on our natural greed, we were reminded that Fry's Turkish Delight was not only exotic and delicious but full of Eastern promise, which was obviously good, whatever it was. Sweets were healthy, too, or so we were led to judge from the sight of Big Fry marching into town bearing a vast choc bar on his massive shoulders. As for the Milky Bar Kid, he might look a wimp with his specs and geek-appeal but he wowed the girls with his mighty shout of "The Milky Bars are on me!" Every kind of sweet came with its own catchphrase. Polos were *the mint with the hole*, obviously the best kind of mint. Various chewy fruits were *made to make your mouth water*. Somebody's fruit pastilles had *the tingle-tongue taste*. Treats *melted in your mouth, not in your hand*, and your parent was implored never on any account *to forget the fruit gums, Mum*.

Adverts captured the tone of the Fifties perfectly. It was a time when all that girls cared about was keeping their man—the bloke with the hat and the packet of fags—and avoiding wrinkles from all the housework they were doing. It was a time when all foreigners were funny and everyone talked like the Queen, and so long as you ate enough Mars bars and drank enough pints of Guinness, perfect health would be yours.

Catch the decade in phrases like:

It looks good, it tastes good, and, by golly, it does you good!
(canned stout, that is).
You mean a woman can open it?
('yes, without an opener or even a husband!')
Look for the golly! The golly on the jar!
The harder she works the cuter she looks.
More doctors smoke Camels than any other kind of cigarette.
So amazing, such a treat/ Pour Ideal and watch them eat!
(this 'amazing treat' was tinned condensed milk.
Kids were used to worse then.)
Please. Don't be rude. On the road.
Blow in her face and she'll follow you anywhere.

And here's one I don't really like the sound of:

A finger of fudge is just enough to give your boys a treat.

I was still a toddler when sugar rationing ended so I was among the first children in a generation to receive their rightful share of chocolate, sherbet, liquorice and toffee. Some things haven't changed much in sixty years. Mars bars are still more or less the same although they seem suspiciously lightweight compared to the vast chocolate challenge of my boyhood. As for Cadburys Dairy Milk, it wasn't just a chocolate bar, it was an English icon, a substance which England bore, shaped, made aware, blest by the suns of home. How sad that it is now made in Poland. But other goodies have fallen off the counter never to be seen again; sweet cigarettes, for instance, which were marketed in packets just like proper ciggies. They were not only very sweet indeed—red icing indicated the hot end—but you could suck them to a sharp point and then jab the guy in front. Alternatively you could hang out with one drooping nonchalantly from your lips like James Dean in *Rebel without a Cause*. You even got a little card inside the packet, aeroplanes mostly. At Christmas your haul was never complete without a Junior Smokers Set in which, in addition to the packet of candy fags, you got a liquorice pipe, a chocolate cigar and some horrible stuff called sweet tobacco, all ensuring that you would know exactly what to do when your 40-a-day habit kicked in.

You could buy sweets for a penny (a unit of currency which is off the scale today: you got 240 pennies for a pound, and every penny was the size of a poker chip). The Penny Arrow, for instance, a strip of chewy toffee which came with a strawberry-favoured stripe running down the middle; guaranteed to extract the fillings lately installed by the NHS dentist. A penny could also buy you a gobstopper the size of a ping-pong ball which you forced into your gob for an hour of frantic sucking. It turned your tongue blue long before you worked all the way through to the little speck of aniseed in the middle. For a penny more you could snaffle a tube of Love Hearts with their mysterious messages of 'Blue Moon', 'I'm Shy' and 'Hey Daddio!' Or you could go for the sweet jars, standing in splendid multi-coloured ranks and annoy the woman behind the counter by asking for a pennyworth of this and tuppence of that, and in *different* packets please. Experienced kids always came away with the lighter sweets like pineapple chunks. But for sheer play value it was hard to beat the sherbet fountain which looked like a firework (with a liquorice fuse) and was impossible to eat without sneezing the stuff all over the place; usefully, it could double as a weapon, a sherbet-shooter. Totally forgotten now is that quintessential Fifties sweet, the Lucky Bag, containing all sorts of generally horrible sweets that couldn't be sold any other way, mixed up with little plastic toys and charms and the like. I suppose we kept on buying them in the hope of a lucky strike—uranium, maybe.

The top Fifties drink for the growing boy was Tizer, which came in heavy bottles with a rubber stop, and Dandelion-and-Burdock, the dark drink for tough kids. They bucked up the lively lad much faster than Coke. That's why you see grown men drinking expensive 'vintage' Dandelion-and-Burdock today: they are reliving their childhoods. Don't mock them. It's a sacred moment. Nothing this good ever happens again.

Iced lollies were always popular, even in winter, especially the posh ones that had ice cream inside. Eating the latter on a hot day was tricky, since the outside layer would slough off like snow from a roof, and if you weren't careful the last bit of melted ice cream would gloop onto your shirt leaving you holding the stick—one of the more apposite metaphors for life, I've often thought. There was also a lolly called a Zoom which was completely tasteless but we didn't care because it came in three (yes, three!) colours and was shaped like a space rocket. Space was a big, big deal in the early 60s. There was also a queer one covered in hundreds-and-thousands called a Big Chief ('*heap good inside, plenty colours outside*') that we bought not because it tasted good, because it didn't, but it was the coolest lolly to be seen with just then ("Hey, Wendy, fancy a lick of my Big Chief?").

The Fifties was, I maintain, the best decade ever for kid's toys. We were the first and last generation to play with electric train sets. We had all kinds of other 'sets': chemistry sets and Meccano and Bayko; we all had a shoebox-full of Dinky and Matchbox toys, as well as terrific battery-operated things made in South Korea that fired a volley of rockets while thundering along playing selections from the Royal Marines. We had guns that shot caps or bits of potato or ping pong balls—you could get shot with a wide variety of stuff in the Fifties. We had a small army of plastic toy soldiers, some of which could swap parts, so that, for instance, you could equip a gladiator with six-guns and a cowboy hat. And, since our attention span had not yet been rotted by computer games, or our vanity excited by Facebook, we even sort of enjoyed primitive things like yo-yos, marbles and Hula hoops. Every little kid owned a paint box and a tin globe and a kaleidoscope. Every boy had a stamp album with the foreign ones all glued in anyhow but those with the Queen's head on laid out patriotically in nice neat rows. And when not playing with all these excellent things we might be seen struggling with an Airfix model kit, slowly losing our cool inside a cobweb of glue with a wing stuck on backwards and the little plastic pilot rattling about, yelling perhaps, trapped forever inside his smeared cockpit.

Every kid had a bear. Mine was a battered old thing that had once belonged to my mother and had since lost its growl. He was called Tor, possibly from the growly noise he had once made, long ago, in his forgotten youth. Though balding now, he was still quite a good bear with long arms and a firm, resolute countenance, who managed to retain his dignity despite the terrible things I did to him (I have a slightly disturbing memory of roping him by the neck from the stairwell). Apart from Tor, I seem to have managed without fluffy animals, unlike my little brother Christy who shared his bed with a whole tribe of them, a veritable battalion of bears. His first and favourite, Nutney, was a yellow bear that went prematurely grey, probably from being slobbered over. After him came a curious homemade bear at which Christy took one horrified look before puking all over it. Understandably, it became known as Pongy Teddy, and, since it never lost its stink of baby chuck, did not become a fully integrated member of the family. Other bears included a giant called (imaginative name this) Big Teddy, and a cute one with a rubber nose called Koala because that is what it was. These were only the senior bears among a host of lesser lights that would be lined up under the counterpane at bed time, before which Christy might or might not crap on the floor. As for Tor, Nanna at length decided he had become too unhygienic to keep any longer and added his uncomplaining form to Grandad's garden bonfire: a Viking send-off, then, for Tor. Although grown up by then, I remember being shocked at this unexpected display of grandmotherly ruthlessness.

I suppose the Christmases you remember start at about five, for that is when the good stuff kicks in. The first present I can recall was a wooden castle for my toy soldiers, a fairly crude affair that looked as though it had been knocked up by one of Dad's airmen. You played with it carefully to avoid the splinters. Another was a junior bus conductor's outfit with a cap and a little gizmo that threw out a bit of paper when you wound it. It presumably records a time when my ambition to be Davy Crockett and shoot a bunch of 'bars' had given way to the more modest ambition of schlepping tickets on a double decker.

I still remember my first Dinky. It was a disc harrow, a farm implement painted in cheerful primary colours. I didn't have a tractor to tow it, and probably had no notion of what disc harrows did (they destroyed old meadows with their beautiful wild flowers, that's what they did). In fact it had no real play value at all, but I loved it simply as an object. It was the same when I spent a precious one-and-six on a Hornby water crane, a track accessory with no track to put it on. I just found it an intriguing object to stand on my locker and look at. Perhaps I was already of a contemplative frame of mind. I liked to look at things, pick them up and put them down again, and then think about them. It probably marked the start of my weird-kid syndrome.

Even so, every boy loves a Dinky. They were solid, surprisingly heavy, and with proper rubber tyres that you could send hurtling into the wall with cries of "vroom!" and "oooyah!". The bigger ones—'Dinky Supertoys'— were beautifully packaged in striped cardboard boxes, not that anyone kept the box for as long as five minutes. Today grown men with a nostalgia problem collect Dinkies, but they wouldn't have looked twice at ours because within hours the paint would be chipped and the little metal men driving the racing cars scarred terribly from dozens of high speed crashes. "I'm Sterling Moss", you'd yell, as your red Maserati smashes into your mate's blue Ferrari. "I'm Mike Hawthorne". "Vroooom!" "Ooyah!".

My best-ever Dinky was, strictly speaking, a Corgi, a top-of-the-range Bristol Bloodhound rocket which came with a special launch pad and a loading trolley. I asked for it for my eighth birthday. But long before then I had winkled it out of its hiding place at the top of the wardrobe while the parents were out, and played with it pretty thoroughly before shoving it back in the box and wrapping it up again. Come the big day, I feigned great surprise and joy, and then turned back to my comic. Eh, that Dan Dare—he was in pretty big trouble *this* week.

They say that the best everyday toys are junk plus imagination, and that certainly applies to a lot of stuff from the Fifties. There was a perpetual drizzle of what Americans call tick-tock toys, given away in comics and cereal packets: puzzles, plastic guardsmen, little gizmos that glow in the dark, tiny plastic bath-subs powered with baking powder, cardboard boomerangs, and junior detective's accessories such as a little plastic magnifying glass to search for clues ('Collect the full set!'). You never see them now because they are afraid kids might choke on them or something (yeah, or stick them up their noses; better not risk it). One freebie that came with, I think, *Beezer*, was a triangle of cardboard with a slip of folded paper inside that, when brought down smartly, made a loud crack, great for creeping up and making people jump. You had a good time with such things for about ten minutes and then moved on. We were consumers. We could turn any old crap into an instant toy; and then, like a spangle or a Penny Arrow, suck it and it was gone.

Come Christmas morning, you could expect something substantial inside the lumpy, well-stuffed pillowcase at the foot of your bed. We were expected to cry, "he's *been*", he being, of course, Santa. You pretended to be asleep when father tiptoed in with the bulging white bag. He didn't even bother dressing up. Inside you could expect to find at least one selection box of choc bars and sweets, and an annual of *Eagle* or *Topper* (middle-class comics had 'annuals', working-class ones 'books'). Digging deeper you might fish out a games compendium, enabling you to play ludo on one side and snakes-and-ladders on the other. Or a novelty item such as a torch with coloured filters or a puzzle with metal links that would come apart only when you made the right moves. There would be a book or two, probably some more plastic soldiers, and a weapon to add to your kid's armoury. There would be a pound from Nanna and ten bob from Uncle George. And after stuffing ourselves with chocolates all morning there was chicken for dinner, and crackers to pull, and a paper hat to put on for no other reason except that was what you did, because it was Christmas.

One day, inevitably, came the tearful Christmas morning when there was nothing to play with. For me the moment arrived amid the snows of 1962 when, having foolishly asked for a set of children's encyclopaedias, I found myself with nothing to do except sit there and read them, while my beastly brother enjoyed himself rather noisily with trucks and trailers and trains. But even that was one up on the Christmas of the Sand Machine. The parents had liked the look of it in the Gammages catalogue, a rollercoaster that, in theory, would excavate a load of special 'sand', deliver it by a cable-drawn hopper over various obstacles to its destination, and then return for more. We agreed it looked great. The trouble was you had to build it first, a task that defeated first Dad, and then Grampa, and then a succession of friends and relatives calling by for their glass of sherry and mince pie. "Eeeh, up it goes, oh, no, it doesn't". "Eh come on, *come on*, eeh, boogger!" "They diddled you, son". Each and every uncle and grand uncle and second cousin confessed themselves beat by the cat's cradle of ropes and pulleys and brackets that spilled sand all over Nanna's nice clean carpet but never in the receptacle labelled 'Sand'. And so, on Boxing Day, the Sand Machine went into the bathroom cupboard, a place where, curiously, toys were never seen again. It is still probably going the rounds, somewhere, spilling sand all over the place, sending brackets and pulleys spinning off in all directions amid curses and tears, before ponderously falling apart and collapsing in a rubble of red and yellow plastic.

Father and sons; the music box was mine, not his. Remlap, 1955.

CHAPTER NINE

Harpur Hill

Harpur Hill (or Harpurhill as it spells itself nowadays) was an insane place to live. At a thousand feet, Buxton is the highest market town in England, but Harpur Hill overlooks Buxton, and we overlooked Harpur Hill. We lived very nearly at the top of the hill, at the top of England so it seemed, with a terrific view whenever the mist and rain cleared for a moment. Yes, the local climate was pretty brisk. The trees had trouble growing anything like upright and eventually gave up the struggle and keeled over sideways as if trying to flee from the cutting wind. The *average* temperature of Harpur Hill was below freezing for all three winter months, and it was not unknown for cricket matches to be abandoned when a midsummer blizzard swept across the pitch. To match its location, the village was a bleak little place, a series of grim, terraced streets winding up the side of the hill eventually giving way to an equally unlovely military installation behind a security fence. Back in, say, the Bronze Age, the neighbourhood might have been quite attractive, with its limestone 'lows' (which is Derbyshire for 'hill', a local joke no doubt), its rocky defiles, its billows of hill and dale. But the surrounding lows had long since been chipped away for stone and cement. When they came to draw the boundaries of the Peak District National Park they drew a line, like the indentation of a jigsaw piece, round the environs of Harpur Hill. They didn't want the Harpur-hillians. You don't belong in our lovely new Park, it was implied. Your sort aren't what the tourists come to see.

Our house was on a cul-de-sac called Trenchard Drive, named after an Air Marshal with a big moustache. By local standards it was a roomy and well-appointed house set back from the road by a lawn with a windy, bush-free garden heading up the hillside at the back ending in a stone wall. The hill beyond became one of the great playgrounds of my boyhood: Fox Low, is its proper name, although we all knew it as 'Barker's Hill', maybe named after the farmer who lived a sensible distance below it on the far side. Parts of Barker's Hill were steep enough for tobogganing although you had to be careful as the ride terminated abruptly in a wall, into which I once walloped at full speed. The top of the hill is covered by flattish limestone blocks from which you can enjoy a stupendous view looking towards Buxton and the mock-tower known as Solomon's Temple, west over the moors to Axe Edge or east to a rather fetching viaduct on which you could admire the smoky trail of a steam locomotive. All this was country awaiting a brave explorer like me, a swell of green pasture and white rock, and full of nooks and crannies that kids like—little quarries with limestone blocks, copses with pits and pools, perfect settings for noisy games of war, chase and the Wild West.

The RAF was chiefly interested in Harpur Hill as a dump for bombs and explosives. Having cast an appreciative eye over the maze of tunnels left by the extraction industry, it acquired a big quarry off the Axe Edge road. The usual RAF mess of concrete standings, stores and bunkers sprang up, along with an underground railway. By the time we arrived the tunnels were full of all kinds of unpleasant things: incendiaries, canisters of mustard gas, even, it was rumoured, atom bombs. In one place was a withered heath where men in white protective suits burned

Father (middle) about to drop another bomb into the sea. Judging from the shorts and tropic gear, this must have been off Singapore somewhere, circa 1959.

gas canisters left over from the First World War. It looked like the Moon. After the RAF abandoned the place, in 1960, the tunnels were taken over for mushroom farming. Today, with a nice irony, it has become a Health and Safety laboratory.

We moved to the house on the hill at the onset of winter soon after my 6th birthday. The bitter cold and whistling wind eventually undermined all our constitutions. In my case it was bronchitis, which, when combined with a routine attack of measles, kept me bed-bound for several weeks. For Dad it was nephritis. The wind found a weak point in the small of his back for, in those days, RAF officers often wore battledress in which the upper tunic often parted company with the trousers, thus exposing one's middle to the elements. "Eeh", exclaimed Nanna, who happened to be staying with us one weekend, "he'll catch his death". He nearly did. The cold settled on his kidneys, which downed tools in protest, with the result that father's legs swelled up like prize marrows. Shortly afterwards he was taken away in a military ambulance and ended up in the home for fallen officers at Osborne in the Isle of Wight. He had been very ill. But at several points the entire family were coughing and sneezing and puking and knocking back the milk of magnesia and cod liver oil. Mother remembers it as a "rather trying" time, really.

After his brush with nephritis father decided to give up smoking and, by way of fortification, took a reeking spoon-full of baker's yeast each morning before setting off to work. As for me, there was, it seemed, a slight question mark over the state of my lungs; much later, a TB test indicated I had somehow acquired immunity, presumably after having come in contact with the bug, somewhere. If so, this was probably the time. My eyesight got worse too. Until now I had managed to keep my poor sight a secret, knowing that the National Health provided a peculiarly nasty pair of specs for boys like me. They had wire frames that stung your ears and humiliating round lenses that made you look like a cross between an owl and your granny. When, inevitably, teacher noticed that I couldn't see her big white letters on the blackboard, she snitched to the parents. I was dragged off to the opticians to be kitted out. There was, I knew, trouble ahead.

Until now nobody had bothered the bashful kid with the loopy haircut who knew the capital of Honduras. I might have been spanked a few times, but smacks were no big deal and soon over. The parents never nursed a grudge for they loved me, you see. But the young Harpur Hillbillies were the tough sons of quarry men with little tough kids' faces. It was important, in this primitive milieu, not to stand out. But, with my horrible new granny specs, I got noticed. I was a funny looking little kid anyway. My ears had grown faster than the rest of me and stuck out like Dumbo's. In between was a roundish face with squinty eyes and a nervous smirk that tough kids didn't like. Some of the Hillbillies spotted an opportunity. It could get boring in the windy playground. "Specky four-eyes", they screeched, "watch him cry, Speckeh, Speckeh-Four-eyes". One of my tormentors wore National Health glasses himself. Nothing made sense. "Peter Marry!" they shouted, "Who will you marry?" Dear me, the wit of an infant's playground in rural Derbyshire.

After a while they got bored and found someone else to pick on. Besides, I was not without friends and defenders. In the first category was my neighbour, a grinning, empty-headed kid called Michael who we once invited for Sunday dinner and who let down his family rather badly with his excited shout of "real chicken!" There was also little Martin, who was always going on about his pet hamster, a sagacious creature which could apparently perform all kinds of tricks—jumping through flaming hoops, riding a rodent bicycle etc.—though when I was introduced to the creature it seemed to have forgotten these amusing pranks and contented itself with scurrying up my arm and peeing on my shirt. But the boy I most liked to be seen with was Dennis, a robust lad, a sergeant's son who was able to look after himself *and* his mates. Once, for chatting during assembly, we were both dragged out to the front and told to sing. Dennis didn't care. "*Oh, see the sky/So blue so high/So very far away*", he bawled. But I was too shy to keep him company and just flapped my lips. "Well done, Dennis", cried the teacher, clapping her hands, as the hero finished his song, "And as for *you*..."

We ate our unspeakable school dinners under the beams of an outbuilding. I remember staring at my plate of stinking mush and thinking, what could be worse than this, a plate of sick, may be, which is certainly what it would turn into if I ate any. At the end of each gruesome meal we dumped the leavings into a bucket, bound for the local pigsty, which, in my opinion, should have got it *first*. I took to stocking up on breakfasts instead: bowl after bowl of hot, sweet Readybrek washed down with about a pint of chocolate Nesquik, which never managed to look quite so brown and bubbly as it did on the tin but it saw you through until the break. You could rely on good old Nesquik.

The plumbing at the little stone school was too primitive for a flush toilet and instead we had to make do with a terrible object in the yard known to everyone as the Thunderbox (so-named because, if you farted the sound would rumble and echo round and round like a distant storm). It was cold, dark and smelly in there. For me the Thunderbox was an object of dread. You opened the creaking door and stared up at the wooden ramparts on which you were supposed to clamber up before lowering your bare bottom over the terrible void. What if you fell in, I thought? Or what if, having pulled down one's shorts, some lout barged in (for there was no lock) and shouted out, "over here, quick, Specky Four-eyes is taking a dump!" It didn't seem to bother the quarry kids, but personally I would as lief crap over the wall as enter this evil place.

Then came the terrible day when I was taken short in the middle of the class. May be I had hit the old milky Nesquik pretty hard that morning. Of course I held out for as long as possible, but it was becoming distressingly clear that a visit to the Thunderbox was imminent. "*Please, Miss....*" "All right, Peter, you're excused". Out I went into the windy yard, and approached this hateful place. I peered round the door and, as usual the stink practically hurled me backwards. My innards turned to stone. Back I came, miserable and defeated. More agonised minutes passed by until, again:

"Ple-eese, Miss".

"But you've just been!"

"*Mi-iss*! I haven't finished, Miss."

"Oh, all right, off you go".

This time I forced myself, breathing as little as possible, to alight on the noisome throne to do what must be done, but there was evidently some impassable psychological barrier between need and performance.

I simply could not do this awful thing. And so it was a very sorry Peter that slunk back from the Vale of Affliction and slumped back on his stool with a look of martyrdom. After a minute or two I felt my guts heave and then roll on, remorselessly, irresistibly, unstoppably. There was a warm, slithery moment of relief as I kacked my pants.

Had anyone noticed? I sat there frozen, and after a minute or two little noses started to sniff and fingers to point. "What's that smell?" "Someone's done woppies!" "It's him!" "No, it's him!" It was me. The teacher, wondering what to do, hauled pungent little Peter out into the corridor. The head teacher was fetched and they conferred while I stood there whining with crap dribbling down my leg. The teachers decided to wash their hands of me, figuratively, and, if they had any sense, literally: "Send him home". So homeward plodded the dirty boy, bawling and howling, while dogs barked and Harpur-housewives peered and pointed from behind the net curtains. It was a foetid trail that I left all the way up the hill to Trenchard Drive.

Fortunately Mummy was home. She clucked a bit at the callousness of the school before taking charge of the situation, pulling me out of my polluted cloths and plonking me in a tin bath in front of the fire. Then, methodically, and without obvious repugnance, she sponged me down. It was a moment of true love.

One of the best things about the school was that they did a good Christmas. During the long count-down to the big event—it seemed to begin shortly after the summer holidays—we made chains of coloured paper and put tinsel, made of lead foil I believe, on everything. Above all, we sang carols in our reedy treble voices. *In the Bleak Mid-winter* had a particular resonance with Harpur Hill; whoever wrote the words, you thought, must have been here. The celebrations reached their climax in a party in which everyone got a nicely-wrapped present from a sack, generally a torch or a pen. There was also the Nativity Play in which a role was found for most of the class, with eager competition for the top parts, such as the donkey or the king with the golden gizmo. I should have been a king. I was booked for the part. Unfortunately Christmas that year coincided with another dose of Harpur Hill flu, and by the time I returned my part had gone—and to make things worse it had gone to a *girl*. In fact that year all the kings were girls. It was three simpering queens that delivered the goods to the doll in the straw. I plotted revenge.

My opportunity came when the school was putting on a little concert to which parents were invited, along with the head teacher of the big school down the road. Once again I had been denied my rightful share of the action. So while my classmates won glory performing 'There's a hole in my bucket, dear Liza' (I could have done that!) I was made to sit at the front with the duds and rejects who were considered too stupid to perform, even as the back end of a donkey. There we sat in our shame, the no-hopers, as the proud parents trooped into the hall telling each another all about their terrifically talented son or daughter and what a treat they were looking forward to.

It is hard, more than half a century later, to know what was running through my mind. My mother was there in her shawl, in the midst of a woolly scrum of other mums. That was confusing for a start: two separate worlds, home and school, had suddenly and unexpectedly collided. Was I now at home or at school? I began to fidget in my seat, and then to mess about. I tried to budge past rows of parents to sit with my Mum. "*You can't*", hissed the rejects. Oh yes I bloody could, for now I was in a state of uncontrollable excitement, hiding under chairs, pulling faces, waggling my fingers on my nose and doing my best to steal the show. Mother sat there frozen. Eventually the head of the big school came over, took me to the back, sat me down and told me to shut up. Even then I was too excited to stop jabbering. "Shut up", repeated the junior head.

"Who was the best behaved boy in school?" I remember asking mother on our way home. She did not seem to be very talkative so I repeated my question. "Not you", was her eventual, tight-lipped reply. "No, not me, but *who*?" I was sent to my room in disgrace, and I fancy mother wept with mortification. Eventually Dad came home and I heard words followed by an angry exclamation. Then he came clumping up the stairs and the door opened. Father put me across his knee and gave me the worst spanking I had ever had, which is to say, not all that bad. In fact I fancy it hurt him more than me, for I remember him roaring as he smacked away: "Arghhh!" and "ARGHHH!" we went in monstrous duet. Duty done, father descended to continue their sorrowful, uncomprehending discussion of little Peter's behaviour. After dutifully bawling for a few minutes, I picked up a comic, found some spangles, and settled down to read Dan Dare. He was having a tough time with the Mekon just now, but his trusty sidekick Digby would soon be there with the back-up guys.

Did I reflect that the reverse of the glowing pride my parents had in me was the depth of their shame when I disgraced myself and them in public? Years later, mother could never recall the incident without falling into inarticulacy: "You were… you did…oh, it was just *awful*". (Years further on, she finally discovered a phrase in which to encapsulate my perfidy. You made, she remembered, *"a rude gesture"*.) When exasperated by my behaviour, father would sometimes shout, "That's just typical *you*!" But this bit of street theatre was not typical me at all. I was normally shy and fairly quiet, if a bit of a show-off sometimes; no Dennis the Menace, me. What was the explanation? Was I rebelling against the injustice of my exclusion from both the Nativity Play and the school concert? Possibly, but I think I was much

Little Christy on the rockery in our bleak garden at Harper Hill.

too young to conceive of and then carry through a plan. I think it was more the novelty of the occasion, outside anything in my experience so far, perhaps allied to a feeling of resentment that overturned my usual caution and, as a medievalist would assert, released a little devil. Kids get these sudden surges of uncontrollability when something external seems to take charge of us—I have seen it in both my nephews. My mistake, if mistake it was, was to do it in front of all the young mums of Harpur Hill.

A note on the Jebel Akhbar rebellion, 1957

Sometime in 1957 father was called away to RAF Sharjah, a desert town in what were then known as the Trucial States, where Britain still had a military base and an airfield. It was close to modern Dubai, then just a creek with a small palm-fringed port served by picturesque sailing boats or dhows. There was some sort of flap on in which the Sultan, a good egg who had been to Sandhurst, was having issues with various commies and foaming fundamentalists backed by Saudi Arabia. We sent two squadrons of Shackletons to bomb the rotters in their caves and persuade them to run back to wherever they came from. To assist the bombers, we also had a squadron of Venom jets standing by, along with some chaps in armoured scout cars. Finally, when the rebels proved stubborn and difficult to dislodge with bombs and rockets, we sent in the SAS who scaled some cliffs and threw grenades at them. The upshot was that the bad guy, called the Imam, was sent packing, and our man, Sultan Qaboos, was installed as Sultan of Muscat and Oman. Those were the days in which you sometimes got a happy ending by dropping a few bombs and not agonising too much about the other chap's point of view.

Father had a bit-part in all this which lasted a couple of months. He had experience from his Berlin Airlift days of loading Shackletons, as well as of desert airfields during the war, and no doubt he made himself useful. He returned with a new clasp for his postwar General Services Medal and some more stamps for my collection. So all was well.

CHAPTER TEN

Games we Played

It was ironic that the bad boys should have teased me about marrying, because one of our games was about that very subject. It was the one where you stood in a ring with linked hands with someone in the middle. You played it only when there were girls to join in, for it was, undeniably, a very girly game. Once the chosen one was pushed inside the ring we waggled our arms up and down as we sang the following refrain:

> *The wind, the wind, the wind blows high*
> *The rain comes scattering from the sky.*
> *She is fair and she is pretty,*
> *She is the girl of London city,*
> *She comes a-courting, one, two, three.*
> *Tell us, tell us, who it may be.*

The answer, very often, was Christy, for he was now a blond, blue-eyed toddler, nearly as cute as I had been in my heyday. So into the ring went the baffled tot, peering up at the circle of leering faces. *Christy Marren says he loves her/All the boys say what they will...* 'Christy' was our pet name for him, one it took him years to shake off. I was, I regret to say, sometimes 'Pipsi', a name my parents used shamelessly in front of my friends. "Pipsi?" they would shout, incredulously. *Pipsi Cola*? Why do parents never understand that they are embarrassing us?

More often the girls played on their own, usually with a skipping rope and chanting things like "*sausage in a pan, sizzle, sizzle, sizzle, sausage in a pan...*" They were segregated for school games too, prancing about the hall in their blue knickers. Why did Fifties girls always wear blue knickers? I suppose no one asked because no one cared. As for boy's games, like tag or hide-and-seek, they usually began with a complicated counting system to decide who was 'it'. The standard one was *eeny-meeny-miny-moe*, which of course included the now notorious 'n' word as in 'catch a nigger by his toe'. Wikipedia insists that the usual word was 'tiger' and relegates our version to a footnote. It is nice to be old enough to know the truth. We were not being racist or consciously rude to those of Afro-Caribbean origin, and there were no black boys at our school to take offence. Yes, the Fifties are a far-off land.

Other versions were '*dip, dip, dip, my blue ship/Sailing on the water like a cup and saucer*'. Yet another, "*Eeny, meeny, hakka rakka/Rare rah, domi, nacker/Chikka pokka, lollipoppa/ Rum, pum, push*", and on that last word we shoved the 'it' guy out of the ring. Or there was "*One potato, two potato, three potato, four*" for which you stuck up your pair of bunched fists to be counted off. It could take longer to decide who was 'it' than to play the actual game. By the time we had sorted it all out the teacher was ringing the bell (a hand bell, made of brass with a wooden handle). Break's over. *Ding-a-ling-a-ling*. Line up in pairs to march back into school.

Possibly these little rituals came from nursery rhymes. Fifties kids still knew their Mother Goose; we were well-grounded in Little Boy Blue, Little Jack Horner, Little Miss Muffet and the rest of them. They were our shared culture: the kid's Golden Treasury. None of it made much sense—all those silver nutmegs and tuffets and sticking your thumbs into pies—but, as I say, life doesn't make much sense when you are only six. Does Father Christmas come down the chimney? Were there fairies in the bottom of the garden? We didn't see why not. We hadn't yet sorted out what is real and what is fantasy. Magic and reality were all mixed up. All told, it made the world a little bit more wonderful than it becomes later on, when all the magic falls away.

Some games were played mainly at birthday parties. Mother had hosted these since I was a toddler, serving out lashings of home-made cakes and jelly-and-ice-cream on paper plates and organising little games with the help of our wind-up gramophone. One standard was Pass the Parcel when each excited kid would strip off a layer of wrapping when the music stopped until the lucky one got the minuscule present in the middle. Usually it was sweets but sometimes it was just an Oxo cube, at which all except the unwrappee would skirl and hoot mockingly. Other birthday games included Statues, London Bridge and Musical Chairs, all with mother busy with the gramophone to ensure that every little kid, but most of all her beloved elder son, got their share of the glory. At intervals some child would start bawling, no doubt to attract attention to itself. Everyone brought a little present; tins of toffees from the officer's boys and fruit gums from the village kids. These agreeable little parties went on, with adjustments for increasing age (after, say, eight, we played out own games), until the sad day came when teen tastes began to intrude. Somehow Pass the Parcel doesn't do it when you are half-drunk on stolen sherry and lusting after the girl next door.

The roughest game was British Bulldog in which a couple of boys stood quavering in the middle of the playground as a great wall of schoolmates rushed towards them. The idea was for the former to impede as many boys as possible, grabbing them round the waist and twirling them round a few times, In practice it was a barely choreographed brawl. Sissies rushed off to hide, little kids went flying through the air, and boys like me broke their specs again; unfortunately there was always another free pair waiting at the opticians, just as there was always another round of free torture at the dentist's. Our deeply caring education authorities have since banned British Bulldog, along with conkers, marbles, yo-yos and most other things we used to enjoy. They were our own affirmation of the freedom of choice. The way we saw it, it was a free country. If you hurt yourself it was just tough cheese.

I was, I admit, in some ways a bit of a weed. I was suspicious of two-wheel bikes, not understanding how they could possibly stay upright, and so didn't learn to ride one until much later. I was afraid of the slides of polished ice along which bolder spirits went whizzing, until, splat, the wall halted their progress. I went to the swimming baths in Buxton with Dad but did not do any actual swimming. May be the reason was that the Buxton baths were hot—these were the last days of the Buxton spa—steamy, aromatic pools in which plump gentlemen with hairy tummies lounged about like sunning lizards. The last thing you want to do in hot water is swim in it. A proficiency in swimming actually might have been a good idea since I often visited the quarry ponds alone with my net and jam-jar, and they were clear, deep and treacherous. But no one seemed to care.

What I *was* quite good at was climbing. There were few climbable trees at Harpur Hill where they struggled to get much taller than a bush, but there were plenty of crags and quarries, rocky scoops in the hillside out of the wind with blocks of stone to practice on. Climbing is easy enough when you are little as you weigh almost nothing and, once you get your leg over a branch or boulder, you can just haul yourself up. The quarries were natural playgrounds, out of sight of peering adults. They resembled the sets of TV westerns—actually they were far more realistic—and so ideal for gun fights, or building outlaw's dens out of loose rocks. At least once we talked about a filthy game we had heard of called Postman's Knock but I don't think ever we got very far with it. As I say, normal boys didn't really care what girls looked like with their clothes off.

One of the Harpur Hill crazes was for 'transfers', coloured film you could float off the paper and attach to your skin like tattoos. You could get a whole page of them for twopence—curly dragons vying with views of Dovedale—and plaster them all over your arms and legs like a sailor. Another was for collecting Brooke Bond tea cards, which were so popular that the village shop, Sharples, had a little corner bin where you could swop yours for those that never turned up no matter how much tea you drank. Most of the swops were in appalling condition having been used as flickers—that is, repeatedly zapped with a bent finger across a table or at a wall. To collect the full album we must have drunk an awful lot of tea. The cards themselves smelt of tea, and also, once stuck in the threepenny album, of Bostick. Even now one sniff of a fifty-year-old Brooke Bond tea-card takes me straight back to the Sharples swop-bin and the little stone-built school on the corner of the road.

Another of these mid-Fifties epiphanies was stamps. Stamp collecting was one of the stock boy's hobbies back then, and even village stores sold packets of stamps from around the world. Multicolour printing was still primitive; most stamps were in only one colour and the designs retained a flavour of where they came from. They bore names like *Deutsches Flugpost*, *Correos Espana* and *Magyar Posta*, from places where people paid for their stamps in kopecs, zloties, forints, pennias, and (I loved this one) *pies*. They revealed the great strangeness of the world, the otherness of distant nations and their different preoccupations: kings, presidents, dictators, and the things they took pride in: railways, airports, landscapes with castles, ships, coal mines. We liked the fact that, having invented them, British stamps didn't have the name of the country, only a portrait of our young and glamorous Queen half-turned towards us. But we were sorry that our stamps were so few and boring. All the same, there was something rather noble about these little scraps of gummed paper with their solemn-faced rulers and funny designs. They were gateways to new places, faraway lands, unfathomable people. So stamps too joined my childhood wonderland.

I liked knowledge. You didn't get much of it at school. Your parents had very little (work, not knowledge, was what they knew), our relations even less, and most of my friends had little use for it. Instead you found knowledge in books, and sometimes in unexpected places like tea-cards and stamps. There were many other such gateways: children's encyclopaedias, educational comics, the great natural world itself—gates that it seemed only I knew how to open, or was even interested in opening. Knowledge was everywhere but no one at Harpur Hill seemed to bother with it much unless it helped them to dig the garden or mend the bike or make some money. It seemed I had been given the blessing of the inward eye. The inner world, I was starting to discover, was my solo tramping ground. That was fine, but I do wonder now whether I had any close friends just then. For I remember books far better than boys.

Harpur Hill marked the time when, so to speak, Columbus discovered America. I was reading. All of a sudden, words shivered into meaning and gave up their secrets. The paths of literacy lay ahead. I became a fierce little reader. I had grown out of my first love, for steam trains, and what I craved now was nature books. Unfortunately there weren't many, not affordable ones anyway, and few of them made any concessions to six-year-old boys. To assist my interest in ponds, Daddy bought me the *Observer's Book of Pond Life* which had some smashing plates of water fleas, flatworms and other small fry of ponds and streams, but a deadly dull text. I soon knew the names of the thrillingly magnified mini-beasts, even when I couldn't pronounce them. *Chlamydomonas*, for instance, came out as 'Chillyman Donas', and so became another fun word for Dad. I stopped drawing dinosaurs and turned instead to the invisible jungles of slipper animalcules stalking diatoms and monads, of boss-eyed flatworms gliding over reefs of algal filaments and sponges. I couldn't understand why no one else was interested in this stuff. It was great. Pleased by my wide-eyed reaction, Dad bought me another Observer's book, this time on geology. If it failed to get me excited about rocks, except as stuff to climb on, at least the book contained, as I was careful to point out, a page or two about dinosaurs, whereat Dad picked me up and whirled me round the kitchen hooting with delight: "Dinosaurs! Wooh-wooh! Dinosaurs!" I loved Dad when he was happy.

I loved the idea of wildlife and nature, too, but poor sight and an absence of family holidays had hitherto limited my explorations. It was at Harpur Hill, wearing my horrible National Health glasses, that I was able to discover pond life for myself. Despite its drawbacks in other ways, Harpur Hill was a great place to wander. Beyond the rocks and crags there were little woods in the cusp of the hills, and further out, deep quarries and their secluded ponds. Further out still were the bare moors of Axe Edge where you could find purple orchids with spotted leaves

The view from Barker's Hill (Fox Low) with our house in the middle distance, and beyond the hills I wandered as a boy, currently being turned into cement by quarrymen.

and gather bilberries that Mummy made into delicious pies tasting of the Dales. I felt relaxed and unworried out of doors. I liked swooshing through fallen leaves, and stamping in puddles, and running or rolling about in the long grass. I loved the smell of hay in the meadows, and the medicinal reek of certain weeds, and the queer textures and smells of wild mushrooms. My squinty eyes spotted bugs and hoverflies on Dad's marigolds, tortoiseshell butterflies fluttering and weaving over the nettle patch, and the various wayside flowers which at some point mother and I started ticking off in the book as we found them. I found that when you picked a flower, or caught a water bug in your net, and took a really good look at them, you remembered their names, just like that—because they interested you. But if you simply glanced and walked on, then you didn't.

As I say, I could come and go more or less as I pleased so long as I returned in time for tea. I suppose Mummy sometimes asked me where I was going, and what I got up to, but she rarely tried to stop me. For a week or two during the summer holiday I even managed to get some of the quarry kids to join me in netting for newts, water boatmen and tadpoles. They liked watching the small scale violence taking place

Self with pond life. I think the jar contained two large leeches.

inside the jam-jar, for instance when a diving beetle sank its jaws into a taddy (the kids said they had sharp teeth and when I said, no, it was a modified mouthpart called a mandible, they told me to belt up, Four-eyes). Soon they got bored in that sudden way boys have, and found something else to do. But I was quite happy on my own, paddling in the cool, dangerous water, feeling the weed cling to my legs and listening to the hum of insects in the mint-scented air. And inside my head was this ever-eager but ignorant apprentice naturalist asking questions of his master. The master, of course, was me, me and my massive, indeed omniscient, knowledge.

That was how I learned about nature: partly from books, partly from wandering about in countryside that still seemed rich in wildlife despite the complete lack of country parks and nature reserves. I lived in a child's paradise of limestone hillsides and buttercup meads, clear ponds and rippling streams. But my passion was essentially solitary. It was years before I discovered that I wasn't alone in my feelings for the wild world. The nub was that the natural world is revealed more readily to those who are patient and prepared to keep quiet. In company, little boys are almost never quiet. Perhaps that is why lifelong naturalists have often had an unusually solitary boyhood. It was at Harpur Hill, that tough, cold place, that I learned to become a young freemason of pond and hedge.

CHAPTER ELEVEN

Wet Holidays and Cold Playgrounds

Teaching infants wasn't about programmed learning. There was no syllabus at our little stone school, or set periods of work, or homework, or end-of-term tests, or even a school report. Apart from chanting the time-tables more or less daily we casually soaked up such information as came our way. We assembled in the little hall and sang a kid's hymn, repeated a kid's prayer and were then spryly tinkle-tankled out by the ancient part-timer who played the piano. Much of our class time was spent larking about. We bashed tambourines and tingled triangles and sang kid's songs. That was 'music'. We scribbled cranky pictures with wax crayons and poster paint: art. One term we set up a little shop in the corner of the classroom where we learned how to add up the purchases and give change from a ten bob note: Economic Theory and Practice. We played with brass weights and a balance and thereby learned that there were sixteen ounces in a pound but only fourteen pounds in a stone. A set of copper jugs of gradually increasing size taught us that two pints made a quart and that the biggest, bucket-sized jug held a whole gallon. I would have been amazed to know that in twelve years' time I could drink that much beer in a single evening. We learned the temperature in Fahrenheit, and our height in feet and inches. All completely useless knowledge, you will note, rendered irrelevant in an instant when Grocer Heath sold Britain to Europe. My generation still mourns the passing of our bobs and tanners, our furkins and hogsheads, our yards and furlongs, our rods, poles and perches. They were part of our sense of Englishness, our endemic mixture of quaintness and practicality, our once strong sense of tradition. No wonder everybody hated the Grocer with his hectares and his litres and horrible new money called pees.

When it came to practical skills, such as our weekly round of handicrafts, I was mostly rubbish. My raffia mats were about average, but I could never manage to make a decent ashtray. Mine inevitably cracked or crumbled during the baking. This only mattered because we were always making clay ashtrays and were allowed to present the garishly painted final product to the parents who, as everybody knew, smoked like chimneys. While neglecting the sciences and most of the arts, the school did take a little trouble to teach the Harpur Hill-billies to be good with their hands, against the day when they would be chipping rocks or mending motors, just like their Dads.

My writing and spelling were still dreadful, but at least I could read. My most useful book was a kid's encyclopaedia which started with our insides and ended with a comprehensive overview of how to build a radio or understand how an internal combustion engine worked. When I was little, some of the pictures used to terrify me, especially the double-page spread of May Day customs: Mummers, hobby-horses and the Jack-in-the-Green. Perhaps it was their strangeness that made them fearful, just as little Christy used to cower behind the sofa whenever Michael Bentine and the Bumblies came on the telly. Even now he quivers slightly whenever I remind him of the Bumblies. These things leave a scar.

In the clutches of Santa.

We read animal stories that hinted at the merciless of the natural world. Chicken-licken, for instance, might be a funny story but it ends with the whole lot of them being eaten by a fox. At Remlap I had devoured Mum's schoolgirl library including my favourite *Insect Ways on Summer Days*, stories told by insects about themselves which were at once instructive and savage. Behind the childish banter you understood that survival for the very small is a ceaseless struggle, that life in among the grass-stalks is not only cruel but utterly uncaring. How awful it must be, I thought, to have nowhere to hide, no place to be safe. Aesop's fables, too, hinted at life's pratfalls for the unwary (did I sense even then that his animal stories are really about *us*?).

On the other hand Enid Blyton's Famous Fives and Secret Sevens seemed to me the purest fantasy. Real kids were nothing like that. Ditto Billy Bunter, the lying fatso, whose escapades invariably ended either with a feast or a whacking. Reading such stuff was as easy as eating Ready-brek; everything was more-or-less pre-digested for you. You could swallow the whole tale without chewing. As far as I remember no one taught us to read; or at least not at any level beyond Janet and John. It was another self-discovery: the magic and the music and the light and the sheer pleasure of words. No one was shouting at you or mocking you or ordering you about. It was just you and the inward world, and it was good. Better in many ways than the real world, the one you were stuck with.

At playtime, while the tough kids played their tough kids' games, I would tend to hang about on the periphery, exchanging jokes and stories with little Martin Bennett. Martin's repertoire of smutty jokes was much more extensive than mine. When you are seven, toilets are hilariously funny (*Oh dear, what can the matter be/ Three old ladies locked in the lavatory*). So are bodily functions. Martin talked about a very funny book called *Flushing Waters* by I.P. Green, and a hilarious Chinaman called Hoo-flung-dung. Knowing few jokes, dirty or otherwise, I responded with would-be lewd tales about a lanky girl in our class called Eileen, for instance of how Eileen got locked in the lavatory and attracted rescuers by waving her blue knickers. Occasionally we would escape over the playground wall to the sweet shop as much for the thrill of breaking out as the penny chews and aero-bars we stuffed ourselves with. Once, I remember, there was a tremendous snowball battle in the more spacious grounds of the junior school down the road. Worldly-wise Martin warned me that the big boys often hid stones inside their snowballs. So it was fortunate, perhaps, that it took me most of the lunch hour to wrestle my dysfunctional way into boots, jumper, scarf and mac. It was all over by the time I shuffled out, padded and muffled from head to foot, a little lad in armour.

In September 1958 our class moved up the road to the junior school, a much larger, relatively modern one situated in a close off the Buxton Road. But before that we had our first proper family holiday. Father booked us in at a farmhouse near Porthmadog on the far side of Wales which we were to share with our neighbours, the Butlers. It was a tough journey for our creaking, wind-up Austin and it took us most of the day to get there via such amusing places as Mold, Betws-y-coed, Dolwyddelan and Penrhyndendraeth (the further into Wales you went, the longer grew the names, or so it seemed to me). The Butlers had been on the beach for hours by the time we coughed and chugged into view (there was no car park; we just used the beach), having taken the wrong turning at Ysbytyfan and ending up in Cefnddwysarn. It was hot, as hot as I ever remembered, and the Welsh sun glowed down on real golden sand, quite unlike the mud-like substance I was used to in Yorkshire. I made straight for the rock pools, wonderful weedy worlds of limpid light in which you could see anemones and watch translucent prawns scuttling past shaking their feelers. There was even the odd fish, some blenny or rockling, darting into a cranny with a flick of their finny tails. Dad, who had been badly flustered by the Welsh roads, had wandered off. He returned eventually, all smiles, to inform me that he had seen the biggest butterfly ever, almost as big as a bat. Was it a Purple Emperor? A Camberwell Beauty? No, said Dad, it was only a Peacock. But the biggest Peacock he had ever seen. Probably he had tried to catch it for me. Wow! What a great place! "Daddy, can we come here every day?" "Whenever the sun shines", promised the happy parent. When Dad was smiling all seemed well with the world.

It poured with rain for the rest of our stay.

Our first proper holiday turned into a series of damp excursions into the interior. We took the mountain railway to Ffestiniog, past misty glimpses of waterfalls and dripping greenery. We made the obligatory visit to Snowdon, or rather the car park at the bottom for the mountain was hidden in cloud. We dodged from shop to shop in a wringing-wet Llandudno. You learn a certain amount about your parents during a wet week in Wales. For example, that they cannot last more than ten minutes without a cup of tea (the old Blu-its gas stove coming in handy for occasions when no tea shop was in sight). Consequently Mother spent the other half of the holiday looking for places to pee. During the enforced dead-time at the farmhouse waiting for the rain to stop, I learned how to milk a cow. I can still remember the rough feel of those long red teats and the swish and tang as each thin stream of milk hit the bottom of the pail. I proudly presented the Marrens and the Butlers with my jug of still-warm new milk with its soft bubbles gathered round the brim. All the same I much preferred the bottled, pasteurised stuff that manages to be cold, white and completely tasteless which is what every growing boy expects of milk. At other times on those cool, grey mornings we were so bored we sat on the stone wall counting cars. An old rattletrap of a tractor passed about once a minute, and we got to about nine before jacking it in and kicking an old can round the yard.

One day, as we were on our daily drive through the sodden valleys father took me into his confidence. He told me quietly that I might be getting a little sister one of these days. She would, he thought, be called Patricia—PM, like me, and almost certainly, I reflected bitterly, she would be 'Patsy' to my 'Pipsy'. I might not have caught all the details for Howard, the Butler lad, a beefy boy of twelve, was entertaining us from the back seat with his extensive repertoire of Scout songs.

"Pipsy?"

"Yes, Daddy".

"Would you like a little sister?"

"*Patsy-atsy-ori-ay*", sang Howard, appropriately, if unconsciously.

"Will I be getting a little sister?" It sounded all right to me.

"*A ram-sam ram-sam, gooly-gooly gam-gam*", selected Howard.

"Mummy and I are thinking about it. We think she'll be called Patricia".

"I said—*boom, chukka chukka chukka, boom boom*!"

"It's a nice name, Daddy…urm, where will my sister come from, Daddy?"

"Well Mummy and Daddy will decide and then…"

"*YAKKA YAKKA BANG BANG, BING-BANG-BOOM*!"

In fact I had no interest in whichever shop or ward or salon little Patsy came from, but I wasn't against the idea in principal, despite the inevitable repeat of prams, pushchairs, playpens and stinky goings-on. But I heard no more about her, and whenever I asked whether little Patsy was due yet, my parents seemed to want to talk about something else. Mother indeed feigned complete ignorance. Perhaps then my phantom sister was only a passing whim of Dad's, brought on by Welsh home cooking and misty views of Tremadog Bay. I often used to think of my lost little sister; poor little Patsy who was no more than a wish and a dream.

On the last day the sun finally broke through the leaden skies of the Lleyn to mock us as we crammed our leather suitcases into the Austin for the return haul to Buxton. This experience did not seem to dampen my parents' enthusiasm for summer holidays on the west coast, though it dampened everything else. They did it again in the Sixties, choosing Cornwall as a potentially sunnier alternative. And needless to say it poured with rain most of the time.

The junior school was a short bus ride from Harpur Hill although we often walked it, for the walk home from school was quality time. It was the happy hour when you bought and ate sweets, played flickers or marbles, and told dirty jokes. With kid's TV, followed by tea, followed by bedtime in short order there weren't many other social opportunities until the weekend. Why were Fifties' parents so keen on you getting you into bed so early? What could a boy do with all that sleep?—about eleven hours of it in my case. Half of the precious few peak years of Kidworld, it seems to me now, were wasted in the cot.

I did not much like the new school. The big kids looked enormous, like giants or trolls, and one or two of them cast ominous glances at gawky little Peter, shivering in his specs. At some point their stares turned into threats, and, scared, I told mother. She announced her intention of accompanying me to school and having a word with the head teacher ("Oh, *Mum*"). But Mummy, though an epic worrier, often experienced trouble turning intention into practice, and decided that if she ignored it for long enough the problem would go away. "Just don't provoke them", she advised. Oh yeah, I was raring to do that, wasn't I, to these hulking great brutes. As it turned out she was right. They soon got bored with baiting me and found some other geek or fatso or nitwit to beat up. I was spared. For now.

It didn't matter anyway. We were about to move on, to another, far greater adventure. This time, unlike his other postings, father could choose whether or not to go; it was to be some kind of reward for his part in the emergency at Sharjah, and also perhaps as compensation for a rotten posting among the cold hills of Derbyshire that had at one point nearly killed him. It would, they said, be so hot we would be able to run around half naked all day long. Better still, we need only go to school in the morning. I vaguely imagined a distant palm-green shore, similar to the one in Masefield's *Cargoes*, with galleons dipping past the tropical strand with their euphonious loads of sandalwood, cedarwood and gold moidors. We were going almost as far away as you could go without starting on your way back. We were off to the island of Singapore.

CHAPTER TWELVE

Singapore

There were a few obstacles in the way before we could get the hell out of Harpur Hill. A lengthy sojourn in the tropics required injections from great glittering syringes that to my eyes looked about the size of trombones. Dad decided that we could do without the most notorious one, the dreaded TAB 'Booster', which made your arm swell up and darken like an aubergine. But we had to suffer the rest, and to receive them I was taken, with a heart of lead, all the way to Manchester. I had never seen such a huge city before. In fact I'm not sure I had ever set foot in any kind of city before, unless you count York. I have a distinct memory of Manchester's dark, coal-fire filthy streets, the lamps gleaming dimly in the fog and damp. Despite the Christmas lights, everyone looked harassed and miserable. In one of the stores a tired Santa, his cotton-wool beard askew, was dispensing dibs of fake cheer from a pasteboard cave. I had seen through the leery old fraud some time since, but I agreed that I'd been good, took his proffered colouring box, stared blankly into the Polaroid, and went on my way. "Happy Christmas, ho ho ho", he called after me, but it wasn't. It was the most rubbish Christmas ever, homeless at Remlap with an unplayable sand machine and all our toys smashed together in a hamper for sending on; those, that is, which had not been simply junked, or 'sent to the poor boys in Africa', as Dad liked to joke.

Come the day of the great journey, two days later, we set off by train and coach to the dark aerodrome at Blackbushe where our plane, a Hermes, awaited. Today the commercial flight to Singapore takes about ten hours, but in the Hermes it would take at least three highly charged days, assuming nothing went wrong, such as an engine falling off. And things often did go wrong, and the engine did fall off. Two years previously a Hermes had crash-landed at Blackbushe killing eight passengers. At the Singapore end another Hermes had bellyflopped onto the concrete in the midst of a storm and finished tail-up in the monsoon drain. Cruising at a majestic 270 miles per hour with a fuel tank not much bigger than a bath tub, our flight plan envisaged a series of hops from one airport to the next: from Blackbushe to Brindisi, from Brindisi to Ankara, and so on via the desert strip of Aberdan, through Karachi and Delhi and Calcutta and Bangkok, before finally heading south on a favouring wind to descend on Singapore around the New Year, give or take a few days; we might make it in what was left of '58; or it might be the next year, 1959. The seats faced backwards since in that position, they believed, you had a slightly better chance of surviving a crash. It was the first time any of us, apart from father, had been in an aeroplane. Nervousness aside, there must have been a feeling of shifting continental plates. I had just turned eight. In all likelihood, by the time I saw England again I would be nearly eleven, an age which seemed far off and unimaginably grown up. I was leaving cold dales, grey skies and icy playgrounds for a new world I found hard to imagine except that it would be steaming hot and teeming with Chinamen.

 I wiled away the tedium of the journey by reading my new book, *Prehistoric Animals*, which had cool pictures of dinosaurs and primitive mammals bearing a wild assortment of horns and tusks. "Oh no, he's far too young for that", the shop lady had protested, holding the book behind her back, but the parents only chuckled knowingly. So there I was, immersed at the bottom of the Cambrian seas (500 million years ago!), as we took off into the rainy December night. I had reached the coal swamps by the time we were eating our revolting breakfast in Ankara, and by the time the view below had turned into endless plains of rock and sand, we had at last reached the Mesozoic, which, as every schoolboy knew, is the very best bit of life on earth. "Look", exclaimed Mummy, "here we are at Aberdan in the Persian Gulf! Daddy was here a year ago. Look at all that sand!"—"Uh? Oh, right". And, after a glance at the uninteresting view of Aberdan, it was back to the ceratopsians battling it out amid a remote and bosky backdrop of mesas and cycads. We were late for our supper at Delhi, and I handed the congealed mess to the hungry airman sitting next to me. I lived on tinned mandarin oranges and boiled sweets, which were handed round before each flight in a little wicker basket; we sucked them with all our might to counter the effects of cabin pressure. Once, after an even longer-than-usual delay, we were served a double helping of cake as a gesture of contrition. At Karachi, we stopped over while mechanics stared up at the engine, scratching their heads and arguing that something didn't sound right. By the time we reached our destination that small plane and its misadventures had almost become an alternative way of life.

We landed at Paya Lebar airport in Singapore on a warm still night that smelt of roses and sewers. We were an hour into New Year's Day, 1959. Waiting in the deserted airport lounge to take us to our temporary quarters in a guest house near the Singapore River was Squadron Leader Des Butters DFC. A burly, taciturn man with a military moustache, we didn't much like him to begin with, nor his pretty wife Alvis, nor their hefty son Tony who did his best to divert me with his pet terrapins paddling about in their tank. After three nights of little sleep, I was in a daze. And, Christ, wasn't it hot? The air was damp, thick and curiously effortful to breath. Contrary to what I had heard, it rained like stair-rods every day in Singapore; within a second you would be drenched and steaming from head to toe. Not that it mattered because your shirt and pants were stuck to your skin in any case. Sleep wasn't made any easier by mosquitoes whining in your ear, oblivious of the incense smoking from the 'snake coils' by your pillow.

The mozzies loved our pink, tender skin and fresh European blood. Fresh meat! When driven half-mad by their itchy bites you nearly raked your skin off, or, with a finger nail kept long for the purpose, carved a cross in the pale lump. In either case, infection often followed and in my case erupted in boils, one after the other. I was also made to suffer by ferocious Singapore ants. They were bright red, like little devils, and made their neat, oval nests in the trees, especially the small, white-barked frangipanis that I liked to climb. I spent much of our first few months with bandaged knees, or sitting on a rubber ring to take the weight off the festering lump on my bottom. Every now and then I would be taken to the clinic at Fort Canning for another jab of penicillin in my nethers. I never got used to those painful jabs. Nor did little Christy help matters by peering eagerly down the long corridor to spot the white-coated man approaching with his cloth-covered dish, and announcing with glee, "the prick's coming, Peter!"—at which I would howl with grief and apprehension.

Yes, the climate took some getting used to. But, bites and boils apart, we children adapted to it quickly enough. I was soon exploring the hinterland of the guest house: the kampong by the river with its ditches full of iridescent guppies, the brightly coloured butterflies, the strips of jungle bush bearing huge strap-shaped ferns with dark sergeant's stripes running up the back. The grown-ups suffered more. They sat in the shade under swirling fans, and grew fractious as their blood sugars plummeted. Mother held whispered rows with Dad, now clad in tropical whites, with shorts and big socks, after which she would retire to their room, close the blinds and take a well-earned rest. She took to threatening Christy and me with a wooden spoon. She managed to catch him a crisp swipe across his little bum a couple of times, but I was far too nimble. The wooden spoon became another family joke, a sort of mock threat. There was also a little local difficulty with an elderly guest who watched us narrowly as we played on the swings, lacing his

Morningside Guest House, Singapore where we were stuck for a few months in early 1959.

tea from his flask. Once, in the shrouded dining room he tottered over to complain about the noise we were making. "It's not *your* fault", he leered at us. "It's your mother's". All tears, Mum complained to Dad, who stalked off in pursuit of the bothersome old perve. "Len, Len! Leave it, Len", cried Mum, "he's not worth it!" But I enjoyed violence as much as the next kid and hope he smacked him a good one.

Some of the other guests were more amenable. One was Frank Makin, who used to call my little brother 'grumpy-chops'. Poor Frank: he didn't have long to live. Three years later he accidentally walked into a whirling propeller that "killed him instantly", i.e. cut his head off. Another was Ellen Bryce, a young schoolteacher who gave me my first chemistry set, and who later married our dashing neighbour, 'Jock' Cassels, a World War Two flying hero. Each of these new friends took kindly notice of Christy and me, fed us with biscuits and treats, and examined with interest each bug or dinosaur bone or guppy I showed them. I had never known such sympathetic adults before. Almost like big kids, I thought.

As I quickly discovered, life in Singapore could be very different from Harpur Hill or the East Riding. I teamed up, as one does, with a group of guest-house kids, lying about my age to gain ready admittance. One of the first photos Mum took with her new Instamatic was of us playing with snakes, lent to us by the gully-gully-man or snake-charmer. We were not allowed to touch the cobras, which lay coiled and dignified in their rattan baskets, ready to sway their flattened necks at the call of his pipe. But the man had plenty of spares that didn't bite: small pythons he kept in a canvas bag which we were allowed to drape about each other's necks or wrap them around our middles. You could, I found, tie a loose knot in a snake and watch it travel all the way down its body—a smooth tube of muscle—until at last it unravelled with a single contemptuous twitch. It never occurred to me that the snake might not enjoy this treatment; to an eight-year-old it was no more than an animated plaything. I could never understand why some people, grown-ups especially, were frightened of snakes. They were lovely, especially the cobras with their hoods, their cold eyes and their black, flickering tongues. Spiders were good too, especially big, hairy ones.

Not long after our arrival Singapore went mad for Chinese New Year. In England we were used to bangers on bonfire night, but Singapore bangers came in bunches of thirty or more, all tied up with string, and they fired them off like ammo belts, with a mighty crackle. That said, these grown-ups had no idea how to put a banger to good use. At Harpur Hill we stuck them on the end of a bicycle pump, or chucked them under the feet of the school fatty or dimmo and laughed as he bounced. In Singapore they simply hung a few hundred of them from a branch, then cackled and waved their arms as the things popped and spluttered to their conclusion. They loved a good bang and a clatter did the Singaporeans, believing it woke up their gods or something.

Another Singapore festival at around that time was Thaipusan in which some of the locals thought it great fun to trog along carrying a sort of bower over their heads, which rested on their shoulders by means of sharp spikes. The bleeding procession happened to go past the guest house, and, although Mummy did not wish us to see it, we peeked through the gates anyway. It was noisy and colourful and rather eerie. The bleeding ones seemed to be in a trance—opium no doubt—

Playing with snakes, Morningside, 1959.

and took no notice of their camp followers dancing about, clapping and clashing gongs. There were other daily reminders of violence and pain. The chickens for our evening meal were despatched in the yard. They seemed to know what was coming, and ran away as fast as their little legs could carry them. Unfortunately there was nowhere to hide; the chicken man hoisted each one by the legs and, with a deft stroke of the knife, severed their throats. Sometimes the stricken chicken would survive for a minute or two and run about spraying blood in all directions, head hanging to one side. Somehow it was unsurprising to find that Tiger Balm Gardens, one of Singapore's big attractions, and just round the corner, was a colourful torture-fest of painted dragons and lurid gods and fiendishly imaginative punishments for the damned. This, one thought, is the sort of thing that happens when you let yourself go in a hot climate.

Life had changed in more mundane ways. The overhead sun at mid-day was considered dangerous to Europeans and we were supposed to stay indoors and take a siesta, a rule we grew to ignore as our pink northern skins turned hard and brown. School began early but ended at mid-day; they tried to make up for the time differential by giving us homework, which we carried home in rattan hampers. Clipped to the hamper, we also carried a wood-and-paper Singapore brolly, which, since the rain nearly always fell vertically, was flat-topped so that the heavy drops bounced off with a merry clatter. After the routine afternoon storm, the air would clear and cool, and everyone moved out on to the veranda for tea. Come half-past-six the night came on like thief, quite suddenly, as though someone had pressed a dimmer switch. Often, the dark was heralded with a glorious light-show streaked with copper and crimson and gold when even the grown-ups stopped talking for a moment to take in the spectacle.

Many staples of the British way of life were missing. We became reconciled to life without the telly, and the local radio was mostly caterwauling. We hardly bothered with newspapers either (though we had comics sent from the UK). Instead of television, we went to the cinema, either the big one downtown or one of many makeshift ones in army huts, or under a rattan roof in the open air. We bought a Black

Box gramophone, an elegant wooden construction that could play up to ten records, one after the other, and played it all the time. As a family we were suddenly better off; pay was higher, taxes lower, and for the first time in their lives my parents became conspicuous spenders. So far we had accumulated relatively few possessions. We arrived in Singapore with hardly more than our suitcases; but by the time we left, two dozen large wooden crates were needed to hold it all. My parents acquired a taste for Chinese vases, bought mainly from itinerant vendors who patiently unwrapped their wares and set them out for inspection on the veranda floor; and, if none took our fancy, he patiently and sadly wrapped them all up again. From Tangs, the grand pagoda-style store on Orchard Road, the parents acquired a couple of camphorwood chests and a nest of little carved tables that fitted together, one inside another. I remember a marbled green vase-lamp that lit up from inside, ash-trays in the shape of Siamese fish, octagonal waste-paper baskets decorated with little paper Chinamen, a pair of handsome Singapore-lion bookends among other knick-knacks of the Orient. My own prize possession was a proper Chinese Mah Jong set made from bamboo

By the old pagoda, looking eastwards to the sea. The Marrens, Singapore 1959.

and, it was said, the bones of dead Chinamen, enemies of the regime perhaps. Dad, characteristically, bought almost nothing for himself. Singapore clutter filled the family home for the rest of their lives. Like generations of Anglo-Indians before us, Eastern vases and the like became permanent fixtures. Quite naturally, without trying, we were ceasing to be English. We had turned into Colonials. And life in the sunset of Empire, I thought, was just fine and dandy. Faraway England had ceased to call me home.

CHAPTER THIRTEEN

Manners Makyth Man

The emblem of Alexandra Junior School was a palm tree with a crouching tiger. It bore a strong resemblance to the label on a bottle of Tiger beer, the beverage of choice for the armed forces. In place of a uniform we wore a couple of pinned badges on our white T-shirts. One was green and bore the school's borrowed motto of 'manners makyth man'. Man, you notice, not woman, even though girls were in the majority in my class. The other was a little metal shield coloured red, blue, green or yellow. They represented the four school houses, each named after a famous army general: Slim, Wavell, Alexander and Montgomery. Their purpose, I suppose, was to encourage healthy competition, though, since we had no sports teams or any other kind of after-school activities, it availed them little. The exploits of the four generals, still of recent memory, were commemorated in crude tapestries hung in the school hall. To begin with I was in Montgomery, whose OK colour was a military green. Later on, for some reason, I was transferred to Alexander whose shield was a cowardy-custard yellow. Was he, you wondered, the general who ran away?

Apart from our badges, we boys wore well-pressed T-shirts tucked into khaki shorts and white socks stuck into open-toed sandals. The girls wore simple green dresses with white collars. The school photograph, taken in mid-1959, has us lined up around a horse-faced teacher in a big skirt called Miss Toy. We were all white; there were no Malays or Chinese at our school, and no one seemed to think there was anything wrong with that. We were mostly forces kids, and forces kids stare straight ahead without smiling; I seem to have been an exception though my ingratiating simper is fortunately half-hidden by a big grinning girl. Most of our teachers were women, led by the headmistress, the redoubtable Miss Boswell MBE. Miss Boswell was so proud of her MBE that she flaunted it on all possible occasions, even signing herself Boswell MBE, which Dad thought was a bit off; she should take a leaf out of her own school motto, he said.

We caught the bus to school. Ours, I think, was called 'K2'. They were noisy, single-decker transports at their last gasp, with spluttering engines and bad suspension. Whenever we overtook some other chugging rattletrap a great jeer rose up and gestures would be exchanged. School started at 8.00, which meant we had to catch the bus at about 7.30, which meant we got up at about the same time as an English milkman. But since, in the tropics, you tend to rise and retire with the sun anyway (and, as I say, there was no telly to keep you up), it didn't really matter. The school was a former army barrack on top of a hill; in Singapore most British institutions tended to be on hills to catch the breeze. Built of some mud-like substance, its classrooms opened directly on to balconies; and from its high vantage point Singapore stretched far away in a green-fringed maze of streets and buildings, right out to the docks and the massed sampans and junks on Singapore River. In those days there was hardly a high-rise building in sight. You could see the grand old Raffles Hotel in downtown Singapore from miles away. Surrounding the school was the old parade ground which became our hard playground. There was nary a bush or blade of grass, and any idea of escape was discouraged by a chain-link fence. Our

Miss Toy and her class, self half-hidden at the back, Alexandra School 1959.

games of hide-and-seek must have been feeble for there was effectively nowhere to hide.

The highlight of the morning was the handing out of milk at half-time. There were three kinds of milk for growing forces kids. First up was 'white milk', which came inside cardboard pyramids that were tricky to open without squirting the stuff all over yourself and your neighbour. Straight milk appealed only to a few whey-faced vegans and sickies. Next, those who had opted for strawberry-flavoured milk, another pretty dopey option, got their turn to dip into the crate for their little bottles. Finally with a roar and a great scraping of chairs came the surge of boys for their rightful half-pint of chocolate-flavoured milk. No self-respecting forces boy would be seen with anything else. It's a man's drink.

That was one highlight of the school day. The other was going home. In between were several lowlights. Whenever I hear certain hymns—'New Ev'ry Morning is the Sun'—'Ride on, ride on in Majesty'—I am transported back to morning assembly at Alexandra School, among the little kids at the front, with phalanxes of progressively bigger kids stretching behind us all the way to the languid fourth formers lounging at the back. One hymn contained the line 'at intercourse at hearth or board/ with my beloved one', which we all found screamingly funny and would study the teacher's faces closely as they sang it. 'Onward Christian Soldiers' was another popular choice, with its image of an army of singing nutters and Satan's host taking to their heels, like Zulus, say, or fuzzy-wuzzies. I gather it isn't anything like so popular now.

Morning assembly was never other than a bore, but far worse was lining up after break before returning in an orderly crocodile to class. It could get pretty warm out there on the asphalt, and every now again someone, probably one of the white-milk drinkers, would sag and flop out of line, and occasionally hit the dirt in a faint. I remember thinking that this would be unimaginable to the folks back home. Heat, in Britain, is a pleasant summery thing in which you can chase a ball, or sail a boat, or simply loll on a sun lounger. But real heat on a bad day on the equator is something else, and you don't want to have anything to do with it when you can escape to the nearest shower or bar. That is why, in the old days, they used to wear a solar topee or pith helmet. The idea was that the harmful rays bounced off the hat keeping your head safely nice n' cool. If, for one unthinking moment, you removed it, your head would instantly sizzle and burst like an orange in a microwave.

I suppose discipline at Alexandra School might have been stricter than at Harpur Hill or Escrick, although I don't recall anyone being hauled out and shot. There was certainly a cane on show in Miss Boswell's study and stories went round the playground of terrible whackings and other tortures. One day our art teacher, who I thought at first to be a fairly decent old stick, over-reacted rather badly when, for a dare, we pressed our chalk drawings against one another's clean white shirts. Perhaps having groaned over our lack of talent once, he did not care to see it again, paraded about the school on our backs. At any event he roared his displeasure and hauled us out to face the headmistress MBE. They discussed various modes of punishment like medieval gaolers arguing over the respective merits of racks and thumbscrews, but eventually consoled themselves with the thought that, whatever they did to us, our parents would do it worse when they found us covered in chalk. So home I went and presented myself to mother. "Tch", she said, handing the shirt to our amah, Ah Lan, for washing. And that was that. What sort of parents did these people think we had?

At the end of each term we had the odd test or exam which enabled the teacher to assign us a position in class. Did I come top? I probably should have come top. In the first year I received a book-prize as 'top boy', but there were only eleven boys in the class and at least two girls were ahead of me. Horsey Miss Toy praised my "lively imagination" but not my spelling or handwriting. Perhaps influenced by the T-shirt episode, the art teacher found my daubs 'unimpressive', while the music teacher, having witnessed my less than half-hearted attempts to sing and dance, put me down as 'unenthusiastic'. In my second year I rose to second overall (and another book, *Five Go To Kirrin Island Again*). Shrewish Miss Tetlow believed I showed promise but noted that I was easily discouraged or bored, and inclined to ramble, as well as being "rather a chatterbox!" Back with Miss Toy for the third form, my performance suddenly plummeted to seventeeth, which she tolerantly put down to spells of sickness. We were back in England before I had the chance to soar back to form in the end-of-the-year test.

My school reports—they are the first substantial documents to survive from my interrupted childhood—include a section called 'N-study', nature study that is, in which I might have been expected to excel. Back at the guest house, I had created a little museum with my friend Debbie. We decorated a shelf with shells collected from Changi beach, and claimed that our prize specimen, a spiny Murex shell, of the sort that provided purple dye for the emperors of old, was rare and valuable, and well worth paying good money to see. There was a jam jar of guppies, some ferns and flowers in borrowed jugs and glasses, and some white butterflies with coloured undersides that I housed in more jam jars with punched holes in the lid. There was also a bone that I was convinced must have belonged to an Allosaurus. We left a cracked saucer by the door for tips. Unfortunately our Museum of Singapore was soon wound up after a misunderstanding over another live display. I had caught some hermit crabs and Debbie put them in the bath. She liked them there and refused to let me take them to their rightful place, next to the guppies. Our subsequent dispute ended with me threatening to give her a good bashing, at which point her mother stormed in

On the swings at Morningside, little Debbie looking on.

shouting, "And I'll bash you!" We made it up but by then Debbie had lost all interest in the museum and so instead we used the room to read comics. This early burst of enthusiasm for 'N-study' failed to develop into anything more ambitious. Downtown Singapore was no place for a nature ramble. Our nature table could not have been very impressive, and no doubt the teaching was uninspired. At any rate, Miss Tetlow thought I seemed to 'often display disinterest' (sic) in the subject that has animated my whole life. Please Miss, not 'disinterest'. 'Boredom' is what it was. I knew all that already.

Since we only attended school in the morning it did not dominate our lives as it did back home. One did not even know one's classmates very well apart from those that lived down our way. One of the few co-operative events I remember was an end-of-term concert in which each form had to participate, although it was no more than taking the stage to roar a rustic song in unison. Ours was 'John Barleycorn', and, failing to understanding that John was only a head of cereal, I took the whole thing to be some kind of torture-fest on the scale of Thaipusan or the Tiger Balm Gardens. Poor old John Barleycorn, I thought, what had *he* done to get ground, crushed, hung-up, and clods piled on his head. They certainly had it in for poor old John. It seemed to me a strange choice of song for a parcel of 8-year-old kids at their first public performance. Still, we must have learned something at Alexandra School. I went in as a keen reader, but otherwise practically illiterate, and emerged able to do joined-up hand-writing in the then fashionable Marion Richardson style, and also to combine consecutive sentences into some kind of sequence or argument. I was inclined to give most of the credit to comics—especially the Classics Picture Library, where you could read boiled-down versions of *Moby Dick* or *Don Quixote*, with lively pictures and great balloons of speech escaping from the character's mouth. Learning, in my opinion, wasn't about the hours you wasted in the ex-army barracks doing long division, or gilding pine cones for Miss Tetlow's rotten nature table. It was about what you did when you weren't at school. It was what you found out on your own, or among chosen friends, things that flashed an intense image in your infant mind and made you want to find out more. Life, I felt, is so much more involving than school.

CHAPTER FOURTEEN

14, Adam Drive

We were lucky in our allocated quarter. It was probably the best slice of luck that came our way in Dad's entire service career. But we waited a long time for it. We stewed at the guest house for three months before learning that we would not, after all, be heading for some RAF dump, like Tengah or Seletar, but to a pleasant cul-de-sac in the rural heart of the island, close by Sime golf course and the MacRitchie reservoir. Our good fortune was related to Dad's off-base job in the Singapore docks. The house on Adam Drive—our Singapore Eden—had been intended for a more senior officer (it had a Wing Commander's fridge, observed mother, with wonder). It stood on a terrace set into the hillside and open to pleasant breezes with a hibiscus hedge running along the front and a lawn kept neat and well-watered by our caboon, or gardener. In one corner stood a banana tree whose tight bunches changed from green and

Front of our house at Adam Drive, now preserved as a 'fine example of colonial architecture'.

tart to black and slimy in a twinkling. The house was separated from the road by a flight of concrete steps with a rail running alongside on which columns of red ants would parade, sometimes bearing aloft bits of leaf like green banners. We overlooked a bowl of grass crossed by pipelines and pock-marked with the ruins of concrete military installations, and beyond that to a Malay kampong sheltering among the palms. At the far end of the house, connected to it by a covered way, was the detached single-room flat of our Chinese housemaid or amah, Ah Lan. She called Dad 'tuan' and Mum 'mem'. I expect she just called me 'Peter'. Round the back under a rattan shelter rested, and rusted, our black, beetle-like car, a Standard Vanguard, which, in exchange for a fuel consumption of about twenty miles to the gallon gave us a theoretical top speed of about fifty.

We may not have known it but our house stood on land that had been a battlefield and later a prisoner-of-war camp. We were on a line defended by the First Battalion of the Cambridgeshire Regiment, the so-called Fen Tigers, during the fall of Singapore in February 1942. They held off the Japanese for three days in one of the few creditable engagements of that time. And after the invasion had swept on towards Singapore City, and the prisoners despatched to Changi jail, the place was a scene of utter devastation, houses razed to the ground, lawns scarred with shell holes and slit trenches, and bodies lying where they had fallen. A year later the area became part of vast, treeless camp of attap huts, built by British and Australian prisoners. Our garden would have been part of the women's camp which held around 1,000 prisoners. Although conditions here were less harsh than in many camps run by the Japanese army, many died of disease and malnutrition. By the end of the war at least 4,500 soldiers and civilian internees had passed through, 300 of them children. And yet, only fifteen years later, you would hardly have known there had been a war, still less a notorious camp. Only mysterious concrete standings and the odd pill-box stood as silent reminders of those terrible years.

We had a fine set of neighbours at Adam Drive. Nearly all of them had exciting war records. Jock Cassels, for example, should by rights have been dead, for he had served nearly four full tours of thirty ops each when just one was enough to snuff out the lives of so many pilots. At the top house behind a tall hedge lived Harry White who flaunted two bars on his Distinguished Flying Cross for various feats of gallant pilotage. Just down the road was Des Butters, who had flown in the elite Pathfinder Squadron and so had led the way to the bombing of Dresden. We were quite keen to hear about their Battler Britton-like dicing with death, but they were modest men and seemed to regard it as all done-and-dusted. It occurred to me that Jock and Harry, and especially Des, would between them have killed quite a lot of Germans. All of them now had off-base jobs in security or intelligence. We all got on like a house on fire and before long life for mother seemed to consist of one long round of coffee mornings and tea-party afternoons eked out by shopping trips. In the evening they often attended dinner parties held by incoming ships, or in the army mess, or by one of Dad's wealthy Chinese contractors. Singapore was, I should think, the highlight of their social lives. It might have been the sunset of Empire but we Brits of the post-war officer class still knew how to live the good life.

Each day Dad set off in the black beetle to his whitewashed office in the docks where he supervised 'movements' of freight cargo from the ships of the Ben Line (Ben Lomond, Ben Loyal, Ben Lawers, Ben Cruachan, we knew them all). He also made sure that bombs arrived at the right depot, or were stowed on board the right ship for dumping at the bottom of the South China Sea. Des Butters and another neighbour worked nearby on the dockside. Mr Chua, the man who supplied anything up to 2,000 coolies for dock work, enjoyed hosting parties and dinners for his white officer friends. So Dad was in his element. Dad was all right.

As for me, eight year-old boys don't have to wait long before the neighbouring kids start poking their heads over the hedge. "I'm ten too", I lied to ten-year-old Roger White, who led the delegation. Roger was soon teaching me Mah-jong and another game called Buccaneer where you sailed around a board picking up pirate treasure and then losing it again. In keeping with every board game ever invented, with the possible exceptions of Monopoly and Cluedo, it had strictly limited play value.

My closest friend in those early days was Edward Smalley, who was a year or two older but deferred to me handsomely when it came to dinosaurs and other scientific topics. Edward set himself the task of copying out my best dinosaur book by hand. "Skip the bit about evolution", I advised. "It's dead boring". With Edward I began to explore the hinterland of Adam Drive. The pipelines were fun to walk on especially when the consequences of falling off grew ever more thrillingly serious as the ground fell away. As we became more pipe-experienced we took to running along them and then jumping off into the long grass below, which resulted in many a tot whining home with a twisted ankle or bloodied pug. Even more promising was an area of rough ground beyond the pipes which we called the Battleground. On the very first day Edward and I spotted a big snake sunning itself on one of the concrete hard-standings left over from the war. "It's probably a cat snake", I hissed, with what Keats called a wild surmise. "Is it dangerous?" asked Edward, hopefully. "Very. And it can spit poison at you from quite a long way off, and it aims at your eyes". "Wow, can we make it do that?" "Worth a try." So we lobbed stones at the unfortunate snake which eventually gave an annoyed hiss and slithered into cover. As indeed did we. "Did you hear it spit?" "I think I saw a great gob of it go past. It just missed me." "Good job we took cover then". "Yes, or we might have been blinded for life, and die in horrible agony and stuff". "Probably." "Wow. Can we make it do it again?" We looked for more snakes but didn't find any. It was probably harmless but we might very easily have trodden on some unexploded shell or mine. No one seemed to mind.

Poor Edward. By the time I met him again, twelve years later, he was a young RAF officer, and had lost all interest in snakes and dinosaurs, and everything else that once united us. He seemed to have time only for RAF technicalities. He died young, of cancer of the kidneys. So did his handicapped sister, Makita. So, in due course, did their glamorous German mother Magda, leaving their father, one-eyed Wing Commander Ted (another stout chap), all alone. And Harry White's wife was killed in a car crash in 1960. We were with young Roger White and his sister Rosemary when it happened, larking about in the garden without a care in the world. And then Jock Cassel's wife, Ruth, ran away to Australia taking with her their daughter Vicky (Christopher's great friend); Jock eventually got Vicky back through the services of a private sleuth. And, as I say, he went on to marry our mutual friend Ellen, who promptly died of leukaemia. What a lot of tragedies.

One of the things we did a lot of was swim. I arrived as a non-swimmer and left as a fairly nifty adept of all the styles, as well as a seasoned snorkeler. There was no good swimming beach in Singapore, its coastline being mostly mud, concrete or filth, so we did most of our swimming at the Island Club, a golf club on a breezy hillside with an open air pool and a high diving board. I was taught to swim by the club coach 'Johnny' Johnson, who had been some sort of swim-champ in his youth—an Olympiad, Dad said—but was now reduced to lining up officer's kids along the shallow end and ordering us to kick our legs. The proper stroke for officer's boys, he told us, is the crawl. Breaststroke is for sissies; and the butterfly is for show-offs, and we want no showing off here. After a while he encouraged us to demonstrate our manhood by taking a dive off the high board. When it came to my turn I remember holding my arms out in the approved manner and looking down at the upturned faces in the pool about fifty feet below. "Go on", shouted Johnny. "Come on, Peter", added the parents. "Dive, dive, dive" chorused the little kids in the shallows. But it was the Harpur Hill thunderbox all over again. Terrified and embarrassed in equal measure, and feeling more than a tad exposed up there in the stratosphere on my trembling board, I eventually took a run-up—and jumped. I was eight, and knew the meaning of shame. I swam underwater to the steps, and, in the gathering silence, took my sorry ass off to the shower.

Little Christy proved even less courageous. As a resolute non-swimmer, he was confined to the detached toddlers' pool where stray turds prowled the waves like evil brown submarines. One day the parents handed him over to Johnny, beseeching the swim-champ to teach the toddler a few strokes. But Chris was stubborn, as well as cowardly, and clung to the side-rail like a limpet. Eventually Johnny simply took hold of his little white head and ducked it underwater. Up he came, spluttering, "Wahhhhh!", as Mummy led him off to the towel.

Swimming was the one sport I became fairly good at, though I was never fast enough to win races (what's the point of being fast, I reasoned. You get there in the end). Chris, on the other hand, has never been very keen on water activities.

The best Singapore swimming was on some offshore islands to the south with hot white beaches sloping down to reefs of coral. The islands were deserted for they had only recently been cleared of wartime missiles. Fortunately Dad was able to pull a few strings and get us on a jaunt there on an RAF barge called a Z-craft. Our destination was the thrillingly-named Alligator Island or Pulai Pawai (though, as I could have told them, there are no alligators in Singapore. Ours were *crocodiles*). It turned into a fairly adventurous day. To begin with I was one happy boy sporting with my new flippers above the colourful reef where thorny urchins and long black sea cucumbers slumbered in the depths. I felt I had all of a sudden become part of nature, a curiously intense experience I much enjoyed. But I wasn't used to diving, and when a sudden wave jammed the ping-pong ball in my kid's snorkel and I received a mouthful of warm, salty water, I thought I must be drowning. I looked around for a helping hand. Not far off sat the ferry man in his sampan; we had towed him behind us over the bouncing waves in his little boat and he wore that inscrutable look that all Malays put on in public. "Help, help, hurry, you blurry sampan man", I yelled between splutters. But the other thing sampan men do, apart from looking perpetually bland and unruffled, is to take their time. It took him a while to notice me, splashing there, shouting my head off, and even longer to take hold of his paddle and make his way, ever so slowly, towards me. Perhaps he stopped for a smoke on the way. I felt I had drowned several times over before he eased alongside and extended a brown, leathery hand. "You took your time", I gasped. I was, I intimated, not waving but drowning. "Ah *tuan*, all things come to he who waits". Dad, who was sitting, lean, brown and preoccupied, on the beach, seemed more disgusted than anxious about my adventure. Perhaps he thought I was showing off.

The adventure was only just beginning. The commander of our craft had misjudged the tide, and, as the waters receded, the boat became impaled on the sharp coral. Waiting for high tide would have meant spending the night on the beach, and rather than risk an encounter with the fabled alligators of Pulai Pawai, he radioed for relief. Unfortunately, to reach the rescue vessel, which had wisely anchored well off-shore, we had to cross the reef on foot, in our flip-flops. Two men who had gone out to the boat slipped on the coral and returned bleeding profusely. A rumour went round, probably started by me, that they had been savaged by a shark. The boat was tiny and so we had to leave some of the grown-ups behind on the desolate beach. They were last seen building sad little fires of coconut husks and driftwood. Father and I took a berth at the back of the boat under a rippling RAF flag. It was getting dark; a storm blew up and suddenly out there, far off, we saw a waterspout, a menacing line between the heavy clouds and the ocean swell, heading straight towards those marooned on Pulai Pawai. What a great day! "Can we come back soon, Daddy?" We did, but no one will ever again swim over those once pristine reefs. No sooner had the islands been cleared of bombs and guerrillas and booby traps than they were commandeered by the Singapore government for target practice. For the past forty years they have been bombed and shelled and strafed, and their beautiful coral blown to bits. And our beloved Battleground is now crossed by the pan-Singapore expressway. Well, it was only waste ground, and the Singapore government has never been one to let things go to waste.

The best swimming of all was at a place across the Causeway in Johore, called Kota Tinggi, where a bright jungle river passes over rocks in a series of falls and pools. It was the most beautiful place I had ever seen. It required a hot journey in the beetle to get there, past stalls selling delicious looking ices, which Dad refused to let us sample because, he said, they would probably give us typhoid. We brought along a yellow inflatable dinghy of the sort used by shipwrecked aircrew. On our first trip, the area, which had been swarming with communist guerrillas a few years before, had just been re-opened and the romantic jungle setting was unsullied by commerce. The waters were pure and clear and deliciously cool, and only a few hardy folk ever went there. Alas it was not long before the place became a major attraction, strewn with rubbish and sordid half-eaten meals of rice, and then brutally commercialised by car-parks and kiosks and lavatories and water slides. We stopped going.

Another, less successful trip into Malaya was to the beach at Mersing, reputedly one of the best shores on the peninsula, but in reality not much more than an expanse of mud by a smelly river. The swimming was not tempting. The most exciting thing at Mersing was a moth. It was an atlas moth, and it goes without saying that it was the biggest moth I had ever seen because the atlas moth is the biggest moth in the world. It had great velvet wings with little triangular windows inside, and wing-tips like the heads of snakes. Over the years, that already-oversize moth kept on growing in my mind's eye. Before long it had grown to the size of a dinner plate, a moth the size of a rook. It must have been, I reasoned, a particularly *big* atlas moth. "That moth could eat my shorts for breakfast", I japed. Of course I knew that atlas moths did not eat clothes, or indeed anything at all, but the parents didn't, and they chuckled obligingly at my infant wit.

One day me and my pal, Philip Wood, a bony kid with bulging eyes and buck teeth, and a funny way of pronouncing his 'r's, decided

Little Christy in the dinghy, self swimming underwater, about to upset said dinghy, Kota Tinggi, Johore.

to walk over the golf course to the MacCritchie reservoir for an illegal dip. For some reason we took little Christy with us. Having paddled and swum to our heart's content in the island's cool, clear water supply, we decided to take what seemed to be a short cut back and were soon lost in the maze of houses by the Dunearn Road. Christy's contribution was to lose a flipflop and so we had to take it in turns to piggyback the hot and blubbering tot. We arrived home hours late. Mother was in a state of, if not panic, at least querulous concern: "Where have you *been*? Do you know how worried we've been? You *naughty* boys." After we had failed to return by tea-time, she had gone over to the Wood house to look for us and had then discussed the situation with Philip's mother at some length without coming to any definite course of action except, probably, to order the amah to make them another pot of tea. In general there was little incentive to wander far in Singapore even when, like us, you lived in what passed for countryside. There were no rights of way; it was hot, and your path was constantly blocked by spiky bushes bursting with ants and (we imagined) cobras. But the parents were lucky we didn't have bikes.

Peter takes over dinghy; little brother pissed off. The camera has mercifully pixillated the smug expression on my 10-year-old face.

By definition one's best pals come singly. They were the ones who occasionally came to stay over or I would also spend the day at their place (if they came over, you had to go over to their place, that was the rule). Dad huffed and puffed when one of my friends came from the ranks rather than the officer class. He gave me the impression that the dads of corporals and sergeants were all tattooed and sweaty, and mostly drunk, while their wives sold their favours on the Bukit Timah Road. But in fact they were great. They took us to the Singapore Swimming Club which was loud and smelled of fried food, while the pool was stuffed full of yelling kids. Then, afterwards, their Mum, back from the Bukit Timah Road, would dish us out a terrific mess of eggs, burgers, tomatoes, chips and beans with lashings of HP sauce. They were friendly and nice and great fun, and I always wanted to go again, at which Dad huffed and puffed some more. Perhaps the parents were relieved when I took up with a quieter boy, an albino called Simon who was not up to much horseplay. Instead we fed his hamsters, played board games or simply slopped around his shady garden reading comics. Comics are best read in company so that you can read out all the best bits. Somehow, when you read comics on your own, as I did during a spell of Singapore sickness, you find yourself feeling lonely.

If I had kept a diary during the long high noon of my boyhood, it would have been packed with small and inconsequential doings: messing about, falling out and making up, eating sweets and playing games. When I first came to Singapore, the 'in-game' was played with plastic Hindu charms you could buy at a shop in Tanglin; you bagged the other guy's (or, just as likely, girl's, since they loved charms) by flipping yours over it. Quite apart from the game there was an entrancing oddness about all the eight-armed gods and little transparent animals that were supposed to win you good luck, or enhance your looks, or something. This was also the year of the hula hoop. Being lithe and supple we were soon whirling one hoop around our waists and another round an arm while attempting with mixed success to get a third one going round a leg or even, with medically ill-advised wags and wobbles of one's head, round our necks. When I think of hula hoops it is always little Debbie, whirling her coloured hoop with a look of the utmost concentration: a vision of loveliness that makes this now stout old man turn mistily nostalgic. My last glimpse of lovely Debbie was in the Singapore barbers (great because you could read Tom & Jerry while the Chinaman cut your hair). Debbie was getting a crop, doubtless at the whim of her angry, Peter-hating mother. I often wonder what happened to her.

It was not all bright noonday sun of course. There were clouds in that imperious tropic sky. One of them was a Bunterish lout called Cook. The smaller houses and bungalows along the lower half of Adam Drive were occupied by what mother called 'the Bricks and Works people' whose job was to keep the military supplied with construction materials. Their kids, being of lower status, were filled with envy and spite at the sons of the war heroes further up the hill, and so would try and pick a fight as we waited for the school bus. Cook was a year or two older, and twice my weight, so he usually won our brief tussles, though not always. His bullying stopped abruptly when I began bringing our big dog, Punch, with me. Punch was equally prejudiced but in the opposite direction. Had young Cook laid one finger on his master he would have found the seat ripped out of his pants and yellow, germ-ridden teeth sunk into his bloated, wobbling bottom. And so he found some other kid to bother.

Even so, a few of the works kids were worth knowing. One boy called Alan had that rare wonder, *an interesting Dad*. Alan senior owned the best train-set in town, a proper model railway with superior track accessories and first-class rolling stock. Unfortunately he refused to let us play with it except under supervision, which meant in effect that he controlled all the switchboxes and told us when to change a coach or flip the signal. He also had a stamp collection, which was large but very dull, consisting mostly of heavily postmarked Penny Reds without a single football team or royal wedding in sight. I sighed at all those pages of dreary old Queen Victoria. Didn't he realise they were all the same? Even when they shared a few of our crazes, adults were so strange about it.

The Works n' Bricks crowd could be your friend one day, simpering with their eagerness to oblige, and the next spitting with hate and fury. Such was my on-off friendship with a large but simple, curly-haired boy called Joe. Joe's parents took us to the Botanic Gardens to throw peanuts at the monkeys (which, being rude and contemptuous of tourists, would otherwise amble up and snatch the whole packet). Joe had a mercurial temperament. Once, while we were larking about in the savannah-like Gardens, I lost patience with him and thumped him on the side of his knobbly head, whereat Joe made a loud animal cry and ran off into the bushes. I had to tell his parents that I was frightfully sorry but their son had just run away and was probably at this moment being mugged by macaques or worse. "Did you hit him?" asked Joe's Dad. "Yes, but not very hard, and he was being annoying, as you know". "Yes, I know", sighed Joe's Mum, "but he gets upset when you do that". We eventually found him, crouched low and gibbering among the banana fronds. Joe plotted revenge but he was too feeble-minded to present any serious threat. I remember once throwing an apple at him, and, to my great surprise, hitting him squarely in the eye, at which he threw out another wretched howl.

I was growing up from a small pinkish boy into a medium-sized brown one. I wore a cheap Japanese watch and slightly better specs with tortoiseshell frames. I had a cat called Whiskers. I read books like the Famous Five, or Doctor Doolittle, or Moomintroll, straight through, though I preferred comics. I had a train set and my own collection of stamps, which I bought from a man called Mr Fish at the big store in Raffles Square during Mummy's weekly shopping trips. I had a microscope with three different magnifications, and a hoard of interesting objects: coral, shells, matchbox labels, Models of Yesteryear. Apart from boils and the odd spell of fever, I was healthy. I was skinny but well-nourished, sufficiently loved, free to wander, and, usually, with a sufficiency of playmates. Of England I retained only a fading memory of frost and wind, bleak northern hills and cold, muddy shores. I felt no great longing to return. I was eight, coming on nine, approaching ten, and life under the blistering noonday sun was sweet.

Footnote on some of our Singapore neighbours

Group Captain Ted Smalley 1920–2008. Father of my pal Edward. One-eyed RAF Support Command chief, later CO at Hartlebury and head of something-or-other at RAF Andover. "He would have been an Air Marshal but for his swearing and fondness for a tipple" (Dad).

Squadron Leader Jock Cassels DFC 1922–2009. Father of Chris's little chums, Vicky and Andrew. Bomber pilot completing a humongous 119 operations over Germany. His damaged Mosquito crash-landed in Sweden where Jock was eventually repatriated in exchange for a German POW. Retired from RAF in 1965 but continued to fly for air defence and train cadets.

Air Commodore Harry White DFC, AFC 1923–1990. Father of my pal Roger. Flew in wartime Beaufighters, then Mosquitoes. Shot down lots of Germans. Retired from RAF in 1977 to become Chief Executive of Swale Borough Council.

Squadron Leader Des Butters DFC. 1923–2012. A great if gruff pal of Dad's. RAF bomber pilot who gained a wartime commission after heavy losses over Nuremburg, and later flew in the elite Pathfinder squadron. Bombed lots of Germans. We saw him again in Germany in the mid-60s, often asleep in one of our armchairs after a heavy lunch. He and his wife Alvis lived to a great age and both died at almost exactly the same time. Their funeral was held jointly.

View from Ah Lan's flat across our neighbour's roof to the grounds I wandered as a 9 year-old boy.

CHAPTER FIFTEEN

Songs of the Island

More than any of my other childhood homes, Singapore had a soundtrack. So many memories of the place are bound up with songs, and the reason was the Black Box gramophone that we played all day long. For ever afterwards the sound of Henry Hall playing Whistling Rufus took us back to languid Singapore afternoons, tea and cakes served by Ah Lan on the rattan table, and shrill children's voices from beyond the frangipani trees. Thanks to the Black Box I can still sing all the airs from *South Pacific* and *High Society* and *Oklahoma*, although the nuances of The Girl Who Can't Say No were way above my little head (say 'no' to what? Anyway why couldn't she say 'no'? If you offered her a plate of sick, would she say yes? I mean, would she?). Perhaps my later passion for classical music had its origins in our EPs of Percy Faith's string-band playing popular film classics, or the Hollywood Bowl performing moonlit numbers by Greig or Massenet. Thanks to Singapore evenings, I can never hear certain tunes without smelling the canna lilies. As time went on, more contemporary tunes joined this traditional fare. Mother developed a liking for the quavering voice of young Johnny Mathis ('*A certain smile, a certain face / Can lead the unsuspecting heart on a merry chase*'). Dad, for his part, fell for the husky charms of Helen Shapiro, though mainly, I think, because he seemed to quite fancy her.

We saw in the Sixties at the Repulse Bay Hotel in Hong Kong, overlooking the bay of that name, a place of old-style colonial charm, with swarms of tiny Chinese waiters, each with a carefully folded napkin over his arm to mop up our spills and messes. Our holiday combined a short cruise across the South China Sea in a troop ship called SS Nevassa with a shop-fest in the stores of Kowloon. If we had sailed the Seven Seas for a year in the Nevassa we would never have found anywhere more like the place we had just left. Hong King was a chillier, hillier version of Singapore, still low-rise, apart from a few apartment blocks, still full of oriental charm with its open-air markets and dusty wooden shops smelling of camphor and incense. The Repulse Bay was noted for its cuisine, and I ate my considerable way through such new delights as Baked Alaska and melba toast and chunks of fried chicken surrounded by all kinds of baked fruit which you ate with your fingers. The downside was that the sea was too cold to swim in and there was nowhere to roam. We simply shopped till we dropped. The parents went nuts. They bought jade ear-rings and Mikimoto pearls and a handbag made from the skin of crocodiles for Mum; a Noritake dinner service in fine bone china, a carved teak chest lined with camphorwood, and a tailor-made suit or two, stitched up by a Chinaman in an afternoon, for Dad. For my part I lobbied hard for a Schaeffer Schnorkel fountain pen, which, I argued, would buck up my writing no end, but somehow their largesse fell short of that. Just as well probably: it was too fat for my kid's fingers; it would have been like trying to write with a bicycle pump. In the evening we might go to the cinema to watch some incomprehensible yarn set in olden-day China or India with a cast of thousands, and the kind of acting you last saw at Harpur Hill on Parent's Day. I imagine Hong Kong bored us pretty quickly, little Christy and I trailing behind

In the breakers, Victoria island, Hong Kong, Christmas 1959.

the dazzle-eyed parents, snivelling and whining, demanding to know *when* were we going home.

Our second Singapore holiday, a year later, was to the island of Penang off the north-west coast of Malaya. Unlike Hong Kong, Penang has big sandy beaches fringed with palms, and is everything a boy could wish except that the sea was infested with jellyfish and sea-snakes so toxic you had no hope of regaining the shore alive. So one tended to paddle cautiously among the rolling breakers or watch the gully-gully man on the beach with his box of tricks; a very good gully-gully man, this, for, to my vast surprise, he pulled a ping-pong ball from my mouth (now what was *that* doing there?), a card from my ear and possibly a live chicken from my pants. We stayed at the Runnymede Hotel, another colonial timewarp, and one that had seen better days. You could tell the good times were over from its empty, echoing ballroom with its silent ceiling fans and the special hotel railway ticket office, now locked and deserted, as was the swimming pool. We hired a Morris Minor which little Christy promptly decorated with sick. If the parents had come to the island expecting another shop-fest they were disappointed. There was a temple full of snakes which sounded good but it was dark and smelly, and the snakes were so heavily drugged as to appear dead. I seem to remember reading a lot of comics, including a storyboard version of Hamlet in which huge speech bubbles went all the way down the page—'whether tis nobler in the mind to suffer... what dreams may come...will *fardles bear?*'...oh, for Chrissakes, you thought, quit yakking and top the guy! As far as I could see, all the characters just stood about talking nonstop until the last two pages when they all fell down dead. Come on, you wanted to yell, *stop messing about and get biffing.* Shakespeare, I thought, could learn a thing or two from ITV's Robin Hood. *He'd* have dropped the bad guy on page one. End of story.

Our lasting memory of that trip was not the island so much as an incident on the way out. To save money, Dad had booked us on an RAF Valetta, a titchy troop plane lacking civilised amenities. As it lumbered towards Kuala Lumpur, little Christy couldn't help noticing that something interesting was going on with the starboard wing. He watched in fascination as first an engine cowling came loose, flapped a bit and then, with an ominous rattle, detached itself and slid off into the air. "Um, *Daddy*?" Father looked up from his book, glanced out of the little porthole, and Chris swears it was the first time he heard an adult say "fuck". Dad went forward for an urgent word with the pilot, with curious little Christy trailing after him. The plane made an unscheduled emergency landing and we passengers took shelter in a Nissen hut while the crew stalked off in search of a replacement. Flights were still a bit of an adventure in those days, which is why a lot of people preferred to stay at home, or go the slow way by boat.

Both the Runnymede and, alas, the Repulse Bay are now among the world's missing hotels. The old Repulse Bay burned down at the end of the Sixties and was demolished. As for the Runnymede, it became an army barracks and now stands desolate and forlorn, its timbers rotting, its roof fallen in, its pool gone, the walls covered in creeper. No one knows what to do with it but, as almost the last remnant of colonial architecture in downtown Penang, they don't want to knock it down either. One day, perhaps, it will burn down in the same mysterious way as the Repulse Bay. No boy from 1960 would recognise Hong Kong today nor Georgetown, Penang, either, nor even the Singapore that we once knew and loved. All gone, the way of Nineveh and Babylon, alas, alas. In those bustling places the Fifties is already archaeology.

Another of the sounds of Singapore was the merry bark of our big dog, Punch. A racialist mongrel, an upmarket version of the pi-dogs that lurked around the village kampongs, we acquired Punch after a brush with burglars. One night a little burgling man had shimmied up the drainpipe and into the parents' bedroom. Mother woke up to see a tiny figure creeping about and peering into cupboards and drawers. She nudged father who sat up with a frightened roar and the man scampered off towards the far end of the house where Christy and I slept, before jumping out of the window. Punch would have had him for supper. Unfortunately, being, as I say, a racialist cur with an unexplained grudge extending to all Orientals, he had a go at the caboon (our gardener) and the man who came up each evening to turn on the lights. He even snarled out of jealousy at Christy and me during afternoon tea, when we would smack him on the nose to make him snarl again. Once he had graciously accepted a biscuit or a slice of cake, he would forgive us and bound about the garden barking in sudden high spirits. He was an escape artiste, usually able to find some way out of the house after we locked him in, and so to come lolloping after our chugging beetle as we set off to the shops. Come the day when it was time to return to England, we passed him on to another family living a mile away—but we hadn't left him for five minutes before Punch was back, bounding up the drive, wagging his tail and grinning his stupid grin. Had we forgotten him, he seemed to say. I think of Punch when I see our old toy soldiers that my nephews now play with, many with missing heads or chew marks where Punch had joined in the fun, all those years ago. And I can still hear him slurping water from the lavatory. It was a habit he had.

When I listen to the faint echo of distant Singapore afternoons, another sound is the tinny whirr and whiff of my Tri-ang Princess as she did her rounds over and over on the trestle table in the play room. Round past the plastic yellow-and-red ticket office on the platform, under the footbridge, past the water tower to the little stand where a

Father, sons and racist dog in the garden at 14, Adam Drive.

special mechanism in the rear coach would pick up the mail and dump it at the far end of the track. Then, picking up speed, the maroon Princess with her train of coaches would pass out into the English countryside, summarised by some plastic fir trees and a badly-painted papier-mâché tunnel, and so on back over the level-crossing, where a queue of Matchbox toys waited patiently forever, and so to the station again. Round and round it went, and I maintained interest by adding the odd piece of rolling stock or track accessory from time to time. The Princess on her eternal round is forever Singapore, just as the sound of sleet hitting the windows is Harpur Hill and the distant swoosh of the grey North Sea a wired-in, genetic memory of Easington. They are the murmurs of my lost worlds, sounding faintly like dreams until the day I die and they finally cease to be.

I would like to say more about Singapore wildlife but in truth we hardly noticed any. Instead of blackbirds and robins to welcome the dawn there was the *chick-chack* of a little wall gecko as it snapped at a fly. The most exciting things to be found in our mown-and clipped acre were big, green, evil-eyed mantids, and equally green lizards that lived in the bushes, their long thin tails trailing behind. One of the few birds we could recognise was the Mynah which, in addition to a fine, full-throated screech, could imitate the sounds of ice cream vans and police sirens. There was another one that sometimes called in the evening, a descending melancholy whistle that ended with three or four repeat notes, deepening the sense that the bird had just had a very bad day. I have since listened to Singapore tit-babblers and orioles and tailor-birds on the internet but am unable to identify our dismal songster. Perhaps, then, it wasn't a real bird so much as a phantasm, a trick of memory, only loosely based on what perhaps I really did hear from the garden, one warm, scented dusk. They say house geckoes and green lizards are rarely seen in Singapore today. What have they done to the place?

Among the many and varied smells of Singapore I would rank Ah Lan's mouth-watering pot roasts near the top. Ah Lan had long been used to cooking the English way for her tuans, though with subtle twists of her own. She would soak our vegetables in purple potassium permanganate to discourage the bugs and it left a faint chemical taint.

The house smelt of polish: one kind for the linoleum and some lavender-scented stuff for the RAF-issue furniture. The streets downtown had a warm, tropical pong compounded of fish drying in the sun, food stalls with their little garlicky cakes and roasted shrimps, the sweet stink of monsoon drains, and the fug of human sweat. Singapore smells were hot, muzzy and damp. The cool scents of an English spring, the miasma of wild roses and honeysuckle, the smell of cold rain on fresh grass, were only fading memories, and, at least to we acclimatised kids, not much missed.

As for Oriental cuisine, most of us regarded it largely as a joke. I could never nerve myself to sample the big, stinky durians which were lying around for the asking. By some mystery of the biological process they smelled like an open sewer. But others liked them, as they liked even less tempting foods. A man emerged most mornings to collect the crickets in the dewy long grass, no doubt for a jolly fry-up back at the kampong. They ate soup made out of bird spit. And, we heard, they buried eggs in some kind of compost for about thirty years until

Guy Fawkes at Adam Drive with Christy and his little chum Vicky.

they had turned into a rotting, greenish jelly, and then swallowed them, smacking their lips and slapping one another on the back. You could shorten the process, we gathered, by soaking the eggs in horse piss. People paid good money to dine out on bugs and spit and pissy eggs. But we were getting used to the strange otherness of grown-ups. And unfortunately the parents never ate anything as interesting as that.

It didn't make a sound, but one of the indelible memories of Singapore are those vast, flaming sunsets, best seen from the top of our hill when the sky grew incandescent behind the silhouetted palms, burning gold and orange fire, then cooling to pink and dark blue, bleeding with dark wounds of crimson. The dying embers were followed by the yellow tropical moon rising in the velvet night, the crenelated band of the Milky Way arching overhead. You could lie on the coarse, dry grass of the lawn and gaze upwards into eternity. I didn't know the stars then, and was blind to the procession of heroes and beasts across the night sky, but I was certain that the stars were much brighter than they were in England, shiny diamond points in a Guinness-black

Happy family, Adam Drive 1960.

sky. The stars might be strangers but Singapore was home now. It was hot and pungent and other-worldly, but we had grown used to it, and on the whole we liked it. By comparison, the mother country was an increasingly far-off memory, a cold, cloudy place we had lived in when we were little; Christy could hardly remember it at all. By the time of my father's new posting—in what would be summertime in distant England, but in Singapore just a shade less humid—it was as if we were returning to a foreign place. In fact we were not so much returning as leaving home again.

CHAPTER SIXTEEN

Back to Blighty

It is now 1961, the year that reads the same when upside down, the year we returned to England, to the old life of RAF stations and redbrick married quarters in windy places. I was now ten, Christy an increasingly useful five, mother a still fairly youthful 38, while father had reached forty and was losing his hair. I was brown and lithe, and although I might have looked a bit of a wimp, I was strong and more self-confident, and had learned to think for myself. Outside school hours I could do more or less what I pleased; I wandered my world under the tropical sun, defying gravity on the pipes, clambering about in my friend's tree-houses like a monkey, playing about on the plentiful ruins of the Second World War. The parents contributed to my entertainment by taking me to the beach or the aquarium or to matinees at the army cinema. I saw them not so much as guides (for I knew *far* more about fish and coral and stuff than them) as chauffeurs. And on tedious shopping trips along Orchard Road, it was understood that they would take us to the Cold Storage milk bar afterwards and allow us fill our faces with some frozen wonder, a 'Victorian' banana split, say, or a multi-coloured thing in a very tall glass called a Knickerbocker Banana Skyscraper into which you would dip the long spoon into those creamy depths. My weekly pocket money of a Singapore dollar (about 10p) might not seem generous by today's standards, but it was augmented with Dinkies—army tanks and howitzers were all the rage now—and Tri-ang rolling stock and floods of comics. In exchange we were expected to be well-mannered and a credit to them, to go to bed promptly without whining, and ask to leave the table after a meal. And if the parents had had a row, as they occasionally did, for heat bred fractiousness, we were expected not to tell anyone. But we told everyone, adding imaginary detail where one felt it necessary to enliven an otherwise dull and unconvincing narrative.

Father liked to put on a stern patriarchal face at dinner time, as 'master of the house', a phrase that obviously gave him great satisfaction.

When in the right mood he could still be quite amusing. He would tell us about the motorcycle adventures he had had with his great friend Willy (the one who was killed at Anzio). He found amusing names for farm animals. He invented an elaborate fantasy about road signs and cat's eyes, which he called 'parkers', and said they were a secret army that marched at night and morphed into new signs by day. There was a new bullying kind of road sign that (as it were) bellowed at you: *'Get in lane!'* In those relatively polite and genteel days this seemed a bit rude. How about a please and thank you? Whatever next? A no-entry sign telling you to *'Fuck Off!'*?

Perhaps the parents could not be blamed for failing to prepare their eldest for what lay ahead. For instance, they never bothered telling either of us about The Facts of Life. Evidently they had thought about it for on the top shelf of a bookcase was a slim volume titled *Sex Instruction for the Under-nines*. I had read it eagerly, but the subject matter seemed to be conveyed in nudges and hints, and from an adult's perspective, such as how to react if your child accidentally caught you At It. Little Christy claimed he once had, standing there haloed in the doorway like a rabbit in the lights (he also claimed to have seen mummy naked in the shower but had noticed nothing remarkable). Probably it was just as well the parents decided not to broach this difficult topic. I knew enough from playground gossip to be getting on with, and I also knew that, whatever they said, it would be horribly embarrassing.

Perhaps this *laissez-faire* attitude to child-rearing was connected with their own easy lives in post-colonial Singapore. The island had gained its independence the previous year, but it still felt like part of the Empire. It felt safe. Nothing much ever seemed to happen in Singapore. We had our amah and were members of the Island Club, and enjoyed a standard of living better than all but the wealthiest Chinese or Malays. We lived in the middle of the island in a well-guarded cul-de-sac with a big dog to frighten away the burglars. And if we were lucky to have parents who were inclined to let us run free, I might add the modest suggestion that they were lucky to have us as their children. We were not emotionally needy, and demanded little from them except that they keep us fed and chauffeured about and provided with treats. For our part, perhaps we might have liked Dad to wear a DFC medal ribbon, like everyone else, but at least he looked smart and officerly, while mother looked positively chic in her Singapore frocks. They were there when we needed them, which, you might argue, is the perfect parent-child relationship really. Chris still rates Singapore as our best time ever as a family, even though he was barely more than a toddler at the time. I rate it as second-best. The best was yet to come, shortly before everything fell apart.

We arrived at Singapore with hardly more than we stood up in. We left with more than two dozen large wooden crates that filled the porch and spilled over into the lounge and made, for Christy and me, a pretty nifty wooden castle to play in. Mother, I think, was glad to see the back of Singapore. She had never accustomed herself to the climate and missed her mam and pop, and the homely things of England, the bottle of milk on the doorstep, the papershop just down the road. I was more apprehensive. Three years is a long time when you are young, and my chief memories of England were of the cold and, at school, the horrible food. But at that age you live for the day, like an animal. For our new quarter, which, we learned, was to be in a place called Longstanton, on the edge of the Fens, I imagined a house in some nook of the hills by a cornfield with some tall, billowing trees that amazingly went brown in autumn when all their leaves fell off. Like a medieval Book of Hours, I thought of the English spring arriving sweet and bright, with cuckoos singing their glad tidings and Morris men prancing about the square waving their hankies; in summer swains in smocks would harvest the sheaves with their scythes and sprawl in the haystack afterwards with a milkmaid apiece, drinking zider from big, stone bottles; and come winter—roaring log fires and roasting joints—we would be out there building snowmen and duelling with icicles. I had forgotten what snow was like and even little brown kids get tired of living in an oven. From that safe distance the cold of an English winter seemed no more threatening than a cool, refreshing Knickerbocker Glory.

For the journey home father had wangled a berth on another troopship, SS Oxfordshire, sister ship to the Nevassa that had taken us to Hong Kong. The voyage would take at least three weeks and we would stop off at Columbo in what was then Ceylon, as well as

Aden and Gibraltar, before heading north towards the misty shores of old England. Father would work his passage, in a separate cabin, by helping with the ship's accounts. I would have to attend the ship's school, which was a rotten swiz because it was very nearly time for the summer holidays. The cruise of the Oxfordshire represented an entr'acte between one thing and the next. But, at the time, it felt like just another adventure.

As it turned out, schooling on the sea was perfunctory; we spent most of the time designing posters for the various entertainments onboard. The real education lay all around us, in the marbled sea from which occasional shoals of flying fishes would burst forth, and in the deserts of Aden and Suez, where the traders descended on us in little boats laden with leather *pouffes* and stitched sawdust camels and inlaid trinket boxes. The ship tried to keep we kids entertained. There was a nightly cinema, and a fancy-dress parade in which I felt very silly dressed up as King Neptune, in a paper crown and draped in a net, from which mother's little cut-out fishes dropped out one by one. I also remember curling up in the cosy kid's library in the bowels of the ship reading *Treasure Island* and feeling like Jim Hawkins inside the apple barrel. I was learning that you could lose yourself in a book far more than when watching a film or TV. Years later, when I reread *Treasure Island*, I was transported back to that little cabin library with the sea streaking past through the porthole and the steady thrum of mighty engines taking us home, or, as I saw it, away from home.

England, when it appeared on the horizon one chilly morning, looked less than wholly welcoming. It was July, but we disembarked wearing jerseys, and with a nippy wind blowing up my shorts. While we waited for our temporary quarter and Dad's papers were sorted out, we spent a week or two at Remlap. The gramps were pleased to see us, of course, and, oh my, hadn't we grown? From my perspective it was more like Remlap had shrunk. The house was no longer a palace of small delights, nor the narrow garden an adventure playground. I sullenly announced that I wanted to go swimming, and set off down the March to the river with three generations of Marrens and Palmers trailing in my wake. The Soar might have been flecked with chemical froth from the shoe factories; there might have been roach floating belly up, but it was water, and in it I dived. Christ, the cold! I dived straight out again and sat there shivering on the bank while Grandad exclaimed over and over that he had never seen such a thing in all his born days. A lad swimming in the Soar! Nanna agreed: "Well, I never did! You little monkey, you'll catch your death!"

We did our best to turn Mountsorrel into a kind of poor kid's Singapore. There was the Pit, which was fractionally warmer, but the green weed pulled at your feet, and when I fell off the railings and tumbled down the bank into a nettlebed, mother said this sort of nonsense had to stop. We tried sliding down the banks of the Tips, the Mountsorrel granite quarry, on flattened-out cardboard boxes, as we did in Singapore, but this time it was little Christy that brought things to a close by bloodying his nose and running to mother. Then he buried his savings in the garden and couldn't remember where. We were in limbo. There were no kids to play with and we were bored. Moving from 'Singers' was a crock, we said. Why hadn't they requested a double posting? Mum, we're *Singapore kids*. We hate England. England sucks. *Mu-um*.

Eventually and not a day too soon, we were moving on in a new car, a white Morris Oxford ('WRY 40', a number which was also a description of Dad). We were back to basics again: just a change of clothes and other necessities in a couple of cases. The rest of the crated hoard was consigned to a warehouse until we had somewhere permanent to live. Our new station was a disappointment. Instead of the hoped-for fine, square officer's house there was a single-storey cabin in a field. It was called an OTMQ, which stood for 'Officer's Temporary Married Quarters'. I think it was OTMQ number 11. Our new home looked as though it was made of cardboard with a flat asbestos roof and a coal bunker stuck on at one end, like the tender of my Tri-ang locomotive. Chris and I shared a small room at the back. In only one respect did the new place match my imaginings. There was indeed a cornfield, recently shorn, between the RAF houses and the airfield hangars beyond. But the skyline was flat, and there was no garden to play in. In a few days' time it would be time for school again, another village school, probably full of angry yokels who hated snotty RAF kids. And beyond that lay a greater threat to my happiness. In a year's time I would face the Eleven-plus, after which this talk of boarding school, about which I was hearing more and more, would become a pressing reality. But, for now at least, that particular storm could bluster and roar off-stage. I still had a year left.

CHAPTER SEVENTEEN

High Noon

I was contemplating our new home by the cornfield and thinking of Singapore when the kids started to drop by. They came in small groups, older ones, younger ones, and a few shifty looking ones from the village. The most promising was a boy of about my age called Paul Petra. He was the son of an exiled Polish pilot who had joined one of the Polish Air Force squadrons in Britain. After Poland was betrayed to the Soviets, the man stayed on, took a British passport, joined the RAF and married an English girl. In due course, Paul, too, became an officer in the RAF. You would not have known he was half-Polish were it not for his (probably anglicised) surname and an upright and serious quality not typical of English boys. As was my custom, I began to explore the place with Paul as my guide. And to my surprise, it wasn't at all bad. Longstanton—the long, stony *tun* or homestead—lived up to its name as a straggle of houses along a mile or so of street. Open country was never more than a few yards away. The parish was divided at the crossroads with the larger portion known as Longstanton All Saints and the smaller, slightly posher remainder, Longstanton St Michaels. Like most villages at the edge of the Fens it was made of any old stuff they could find—brick, flint, mud, corrugated iron. All Saints had a steepled church, St Michaels, a tiny, reed-thatched, and now redundant one, with a wishing well in the yard. There were a few outlying farms, called Follies, a couple of pubs, the school, and the village shop called Pennix. That was it. What made Longstanton stand out from its neighbours was the RAF. At the outbreak of World War Two the grass airfield between Longstanton and Oakington had been converted into a bomber base—RAF Oakington, later home to the famous 627 Pathfinder Squadron. Barracks and red-brick family quarters sprang up almost overnight: an officers' quarter among trees in St Michaels known as Thatcher's Wood; a humbler one without trees for lower ranks in All Saints called Thornhill Place. At one time there were more RAF personnel than villagers. And a lot of them were killed: 600 crew in 258 doomed bombing planes. At one point the deaths averaged three a week.

After the war, RAF Oakington became a base for 'mixed engine training'. The lumbering drone of Lancasters, Stirlings and Liberators was replaced by the thin whistle of Vampire jets and the rumble and hiss of piston-engined Varsities. Many of the student pilots lived in caravans by the airfield. There were further reminders of the war in the form of mushroom-shaped concrete pillboxes known as Oakington Boxes, which, I noted with a practised eye, had potential play value, for example as redoubts to defend against salvoes of crab-apples or volleys of snowballs. There was a training ground with ropes and walkways dangling from trees which we could play on, or at least nobody seemed inclined to stop us. There were lots of ponds—a pond in every paddock—as well as an elm wood full of small, crater-sized pools carpeted with duckweed. There were tracks leading towards outlying farms, ideal for off-road, rally biking, especially when they passed through slow streams with broad and generous allocations of mud. And finally there was the airfield itself, closed to traffic most of the time but not to kids on bikes. In one corner was a wrecked plane into which you could clamber and whose basic controls—wing flaps and tail-planes—*still worked*. This place, I thought, was all right. This place had potential. It wasn't Singapore (it was September and already felt cold), and we badly needed a decent house and a big garden, but it would do.

In the meantime it was time for school again. The village school, called Hatton Park, was a modern single-floor construction made mostly of wood with big glass windows and a flat roof. There was the usual hard school yard, with a sand pit for the little kids and some fallen logs for the hearties. There was also a big, deep pond, but most of it was fenced off for safety's sake. It was with mixed feelings that I noticed the grounds included a paddock large enough for a game of football. This time there was a school uniform. In place of T-shirts and sandals we wore a dark blue cap, a matching blazer with a badge (a shield bearing the Golden Hind and a gleaming sword, for reasons nobody cared about) and instead of a Singapore hamper I carried a satchel. It was a combined infant and junior school so that, for the first time, Christy and I would attend the same school. But he was at the bottom (the sand-pit kids) and I was at the top, Form 6, among the big lads, the log-walkers, the ball kickers, the ones that had reached the awesome age of ten.

Mummy insisted on accompanying me to school that first day. Her parting words were, as usual, an admonition *not to get into fights.* Unfortunately she said it out loud, too loud, and in front of a group of village kids who were already casting a critical eye over the geeky new posh boy in specs. "Heh, heh", snickered one of them, a toughie with a crew-cut. "His Mum said he mustn't get into a fight, huh, huh". "Yeah", agreed his mate, a black-haired Goth. "His mummy won't let him". "Won't she? We'll see about that," said another, a dirty little kid with smouldering eyes. Will we? Oh great, I thought. Here we go again.

Sure enough, on the stroke of four they were waiting for me just outside the school grounds. This was obviously a ritual, a rite of passage

Geeky kid. Smiling for the school album at Longstanton, 1961.

for RAF kids (though, I reflected bitterly, Paul Petra seemed to have escaped it). I was given the choice of fighting either the crew-cut or the Goth. I chose the Goth: a bad call since he was as strong as an ox, while crew-cut was a mouthy, backward boy who acted tough but was easy to knock down, once you got over his thick-kid aggression and glowering look. As I say, I chose the wrong one. Someone held my specs while I squared up to my new enemy inside a ring of gleeful, expectant faces. For a short while we grappled and I heard someone mutter, as if in disappointment, "he's stronger than he looks". But nowhere near strong enough, unfortunately. Before long he had me down, flat on my tummy, and pulled my head back. "I surrender", I sobbed—the wisest words I had spoken all day. The Goth very decently got off and stood back, and that was that. With a kind of boy's formality I was assisted to my feet and my glasses handed back. "Officer's pet", snarled the little, furious kid. I staggered home feeling weak, unmanly and pathetic. Drying my

Christy at Longstanton, 1961. Doesn't look much like me, does he?

eyes, I entered the cardboard temp where Mummy was busy preparing tea. "Did you have a lovely day, dear?"—"Oh, *wonderful*."—"Didn't get into fights?"—"As if!" I felt a little apprehensive the next day, but, would you believe it, I found I was now an accepted member of the gang; practically everyone was in the gang, if only for safety reasons. The intention, it seemed, was not to hurt me, or at least not *much*, but to show the new guy who was boss. Of course, being in the gang meant having to endure endless games of football. But they were tolerant of my evident braininess and contrasting lack of sporting talent, and were often considerate enough to put me in goal.

The parents were feeling the pinch again. Train-sets and knickerbocker glories were out of reach for the moment and instead, for my eleventh birthday, they got me a box of cigarette cards from a small ad in *Exchange & Mart*. But I was learning that expensive stuff isn't always the best. I liked things that tickled my imagination, and I loved my little cards even though they were all from broken sets. Many were about wildlife, especially, for some reason, fish—a quiet day by the river was obviously ideal for getting in some quality smoking time. Other cards were about subjects of more than passing interest such as ancient Wonders of the World, or the street cries of Old London town, or the strange uniforms of royal officials, none of which had the slightest relevance to everyday life but were, for that very reason, part of the great national pageant of weirdness and wonder. I had acquired a taste for educational cards from Brooke Bond tea, which had by now reached a terrific series on African Wildlife, with an even better one to come on Tropical Birds. We also used to buy big square cards sold with pink wafers of bubble gum that showed flags on the front and some interesting facts on the back, including "Hi, how are you?" in every known language. Even the tough kids collected them. In a school composition entitled "What I did today", little Christy decided to focus on my birthday. Still unsure of his orthography, he managed to raise his class teacher's eyebrows by informing her that brother Peter had celebrated his big day with 'a thousand cigarettes'.

Longstanton was the start of other longterm passions. That autumn father took me to London. In exchange for hanging about while his tailor measured him up for 'civvies', he took me to the London Planetarium and Madame Tussauds. It was through the severed heads of Robespierre *et al.* in the Chamber of Horrors that I became interested in the history of the French Revolution, and revolutions generally. Knowledge of the past is rarely much use in a strictly material sense, but it seems to me that a sense of history makes one's mind a more interesting place, and one's conversation perhaps a mite less boring. Life, it seemed to me, makes more sense when you know where things come from, and why they happened like that.

The Planetarium, too, though disappointing in its special effects, fed a craze for astronomy which has never quite left me. Many were the cold nights I stood outside with Dad's heavy binoculars scanning the heavens for nebulosities and double stars. Lacking a star atlas I tried to make my own on the blank side of a sheet of wallpaper but could not make the constellations fit together right; I was too stupid to understand that it was impossible since the heavens are curved. In due course, having learned a bit more about ascension and declination, I took and passed an 'O'-level in astronomy as my one bit of purely voluntary schooling. It still amazes me how few people know the constellations and are therefore denied the sight of starry heroes, flying horses, and all kinds of celestial pots and pans circling above our heads. Admittedly, the night skies have grown less inky black than they were at Rampton Drift, Longstanton in the fall of 1961.

Another moment that set my young imagination on fire was a little book about moths. We had gone to Willingham to buy some fireworks—little squibs for the November doorstep—and, having five bob to spare, I decided to add another Observer's Book, on the Larger Moths, to my collection. I knew the butterflies already but their mothy cousins were a complete surprise, equally beautiful and enticing but in a different way. While butterflies had colours, moths had textures and patterns, and, in some cases, hairy bodies, like winged mice. They were more obviously of animal nature; butterflies are more like spirits or flying flowers. There were noble hawk-moths shaped like torpedoes with the elegant, narrow wings of fighter planes; eggars and prominents like winged teddy bears; gorgeous damask tiger-moths and silver-lines with bright green wings. The book crammed in tips on where and how to find them all. A light came on behind my greedy little eyes but this was autumn and for the time being there was nothing to be done about it. But I knew there and then that this was going to be something big; possibly the next Big Thing in fact.

My first moth collection was nothing to boast about. I had been studying the techniques for mounting and displaying dead insects and was aching to give it a try. I found some dead moths in the lavatory. Having given up the ghost some time ago, they were too stiff to set, so I simply spread their wings on a bit of rag and stuck them in place with pins. Then I threw them away. Not long afterwards, and joined by some of the village lads, I started looking for live moths; they must, we reasoned, be out there *somewhere*. And so they were. One day we were larking about in someone's front garden and suddenly there it was, sitting on the trunk of a laburnum tree: a big, white moth with black spots all over its wings. I knew what it was: a female Wood Leopard, probably newly emerged from the trunk where it had lived as a caterpillar, stealthily munching the sapwood. We were not sure what to do next. Clearly we had to kill it, but it suddenly seemed a shame. Prodding it with a pin didn't seem to do the job and in the end an impatient boy called Lefty got his sheath knife out. By the time he had finished carving up the poor Wood Leopard no one seemed to want it. But, we all agreed, it really had been a fine looking moth.

Then came a breakthrough. It turned out that the author of my Observer's Book, Richard Ford, ran a natural history supply service called Watkins & Doncaster from some house or bungalow on the far side of London. I managed to get hold of his catalogue and when I opened it my eyes nearly popped out of my head. There were pages and pages of the most amazing things to help the young naturalist catch moths, and to do many other excellent things too, like netting plankton or turning roadkill back into three-dimensional animals with the help of wadding and glass eyes. There were nets and boxes for catching butterflies, but also weird stuff such as a special lamp for drying freshly-mounted caterpillars (you blew out the guts with a glass pipette, as if you were blowing a bird's egg). Best of all you could actually buy mounted specimens of moths which Mr Ford had thoughtfully preserved from old collections. And a special cork-lined storage box to put them in. And some labels with their names on. From then on, nary a day went by without our pestering Dad to take us there. Eventually he gave in and even gave me an allowance in advance of my birthday. To find the Moth Shop, all we had to go on was the very rough street plan on the back of the catalogue. But we got there in the end, and located the shop as an unprepossessing house midway along a long tree-lined avenue. I got out and knocked on Richard Ford's door.

All things considered he and his son Robin were very patient with his unexpected visitors that Sunday afternoon. My pal Jonathan and I went through one naptha-scented cabinet of dead moths after another, murmuring things like, "um, maybe I'll have that one, no, no, on second thoughts—you can put that one back, Mr Ford—I'll have that one, no, not that one, *that* one"—and so on, until our cardboard boxes were filled wing to wing with pinned and labelled specimens variously banded, tufted or spotted, and costing anything between tuppence and (for a beautiful Spurge Hawk-moth caught in Germany in 1899) four bob. But Richard Ford was a naturalist, not a mere tradesman. "Any fool can *buy* a moth", he pointed out, rather sniffily. What you should be doing, fine boys like you, he said, is *looking* for moths, by searching for larvae, and digging for pupae, and smearing tree trunks with a mixture of treacle and beer. Yes, I thought, but how much digging, how much treacle and beer, would it take to get my lovely Spurge Hawk-moth? A lot more than four bob's worth, you bet.

A day or two later I was showing off my moths to our neighbour, young Stephen, a simple, curly-haired boy whose parents would sometimes lock him out of the house, fearing, I suppose, that he might break something. Letting him anywhere near fragile objects, such as dead moths, was a bad idea. When I showed him my prize hawk-moth he responded with an incredulous poke of a dirty, snot-stained forefinger. "What, *that*?" The long-dead moth lurched on its pin. I roared with anguish and the next moment young Stephen was wisely fleeing down the stairs and down the garden path with the outraged young scientist in hot pursuit. But Stephen was used to violent reactions to blunders of his and had learned to run. He dodged between the caravans and was away before I could get at him.

Despite Ford's words of encouragement we found moths hard to find. The ones that came to the porch light, or we found floating in the loo in the morning, were much duller than the lovely specimens in the Observer's book. Caterpillars were slightly easier to find, but the ones that spun a web in the hedge, and which I managed to rear through, produced pathetic little mothlets no bigger than a fingernail. Our best find was the caterpillar of a Puss Moth, the one that, in Alice in Wonderland, sits trippily on a mushroom smoking a hookah. It was plump and green, with a saddle the colour of Morocco leather, and two little kittenish tails frisking at the back. As did Thomas Moffet, 400 years ago, we 'found it on a willow feeding greedily'. A day or two later it made a silk cocoon on a piece of bark with which it blended into near invisibility. I was away at school by the time it emerged. Taking a leaf from Ford's book, I told the parents to feed the baby moth on sugar solution soaked into cotton wool. But the poor thing got stuck in the cotton and, struggling, lost all its legs but one. Mum called it Peg-leg. I realised then that raising moths was another thing I was going to have to take charge of myself.

CHAPTER EIGHTEEN

Golden Afternoons at the House on the Hill

Shortly after Christmas 1961 we had a wonderful stroke of luck. A quarter had become available not in the expected clutch of identikit RAF houses at Rampton Drift or Thatcher's Wood, but in the top half of a Victorian mansion called The Mount (it stood on a slight rise that counts as a hill in those parts). It was a rather ugly house, slab-sided and four-square with gaunt three-sided bay windows at the front. Standing on its lonely eminence the house looked bigger than it actually was. Being close to the airfield, it had been taken over by the RAF and divided into an upstairs and a downstairs flat. Upstairs included the former servant's quarters in the attic; downstairs got the extensive cellar. But the best thing about The Mount was that it came with several acres of park, a private playground that was guaranteed to boost my popularity. On the lawn soared three giant redwoods, the nearest of which held out an arm for a swing. Further down the slope stood a walnut tree which a Tawny

My gang at The Mount, Jonathan doing his monkey impression in the foreground.

Owl had made its own, and some climbable yew trees, in one of which we built a den. Right at the bottom was a sunken garden with some fruit trees. My great friends Jonathan and Martin lived just down the lane, while beyond lay the empty, barely used airfield with its ruined outbuildings and plane wrecks. In a day or two an army lorry came chugging up the drive bearing the two dozen crates we had last seen on the tropical porch in Singapore. At last we were home again.

From the start I adored The Mount extravagantly, more than any of our temporary homes before or since. Who needed formal playgrounds when a few yards away hung the ropes for the airman's PT strung from tree to tree? Who needed them when there were concrete pill boxes left over from the war, and pig pens, and isolated farmhouses with barns full of hay? Even the corn, being taller and looser than it is today, was playable for you could make tunnels and mazes in them simply by trundling along on all fours. Better yet was my pal Peter's place, a working farm near the Huntingdon road called Noon Folly. Once, Peter's farming Dad let us sit in the trailer while he cut the silage and blew a hail of juicy chopped-up grass at us through the hopper. Mother was resigned to us returning home after a day's exploration spattered with mud and smelling of the farmyard but even she was surprised when I returned painted grass-green from head to foot like a goblin. Equally hazardous was a prize Berkshire boar of uncertain temper which we enjoyed teasing. Looking back, it was a wonder any of us survived, really.

This extended adventure playground demanded a form of transport. Heaven knows why, but until then I had never learned how to ride a bike; every village boy had a bike; even little Christy rode one. I think the reason must have been logic: not having grasped how motion relates to gravity, I could not make out how they stayed upright. Fortunately the nearby airfield made an ideal practice track. I can still hear my mother shouting, "*pedal, pedal, pedal*", the idea being that once you got up enough speed it was impossible to fall off. Experience suggested otherwise, but after scraping both elbows and knees on the concrete, I eventually mastered it. It was a glorious, life-affirming moment. The parents bought me a squeaking old black push-bike from the local bike-shed; every village, in those days, had a bike bloke, rugged of visage with week-old stubble, silently knocking old busted bikes back into shape, and mending your puncture for sixpence. And so, all of a sudden, I was Bike Boy, more at home on two wheels than two legs. Among the first fruits of this newfound freedom was being able to escape school at lunchtime—for Hatton Park was no closer to a fine dining experience than any of my previous schools—and cycle jauntily home for soup and sandwiches.

With a bike you could explore further and build up your map. Perhaps I should explain. At school, the headmaster, a decent chap called Furnell, had read us *The Hobbit*, and as part of the fun we had copied out the map of Middle Earth, complete with goblins and dragons. Straightway Longstanton was transformed for me into a kid's Middle Earth full of toyland Mirkwoods and homely Rivendells, where my friends lived, or the orc-haunted wastelands near the railway where the tough kids hung out. There was even an Enchanted Stream at a place called Abb's Folly where, no matter what you did, you *always* got wet. Soon we were designing Middle Earths of our own on the back of sheets of wallpaper, crammed with unbelievably hazardous places and crawling with monsters. On little Martin's map there were no Shires or Homely Houses. You couldn't go a step in any direction without getting captured by uber-orcs, or turned into some hideous wraith, or sacrificed to some sci-fi gobbler in a cave. When I pointed out that the good guys had to live *somewhere* he thought for a moment and then pencilled in some offshore island free of predators, but even then he couldn't resist adding 'Bewair of Hobbits!' Martin's imaginings were much more savage than you might have expected from a quiet lad whose happiest moments were spent spotting trains on the Huntingdon line. Old Tolkien had awakened the slumbering beast.

Dear Martin. It was just a lark for him, those imagined lands. Was it just a lark for me? I could feel the tug of Tolkein's world drawing me in. As something to dream about it was better than toy soldiers and model railways because this place was a land; it had geography, woods and mountains, and dragons to fight (though absolutely no girls to love, not that that was a problem then). I think I may have been one of those boys that lived half in the real world and half in my own fantasy, re-invented from books and stories. I told stories on the way back from school, extemporising as I went along. I liked my inner world. Perhaps I needed it. I would need it more, very soon now, when the orcs and goblins began to creep out into the open, and shadows fell across those Elysian fields.

Our time at Longstanton was too precious to waste on holidays. Instead, whenever Dad felt the call of culture, as he occasionally did, we would head off to some museum or centre. One day, he announced that we were all going to visit the fields and cottages painted by his favourite artist: John Constable; Constable Country. In his youth Dad had been a great reader of library books and the elegiac paintings of Constable were to him a vision of the English countryside at its most bountiful and poetic, far beyond the mean streets of South London. So, here we were, on a pilgrimage into the soul of bygone rural England. Eventually the white Morris pulled up at a half-timbered cottage by a small, rather dirty river. "*There*", announced Dad. "*Constable Country!*" It looked like anybody's country to me. We had trees at home, for Heaven's sake. After five minutes even Dad decided he had seen enough of what was left of *The Haywain*. He didn't seem sure what to do next. Perhaps another long-cherished dream was unwinding into bitterness and disappointment.

I stuck my head out of the car window to accost a passing peasant. "Hey, my good man, what else is there to do in these here artistic parts?" "Why young maister", he returned, "you'm be wantin' Grimes Graves. That's where young maisters allus end up after seeing Constable Country. But you mind um bonks young Sir, or ya'll get bladdered in slutch." To Grimes Graves!", roared me and my mate, Stuart Greenleaf, who had come along for the ride.

Grimes Graves was in every way an advance on Constable Country. Nowadays, I imagine, these ancient tunnels in the East Anglian chalk can be viewed only from a respectful distance through safety glass, but in those days no one seemed to care if you descended the ladder with a merry cry and crawled off down one of the numerous tunnels and shafts where prehistoric Anglians once wielded their picks and shovels.

You went in pink, so to speak, and came out as white as a polar bear. It was jolly educational too, I thought, for you learned exactly what it must have been like to be an ancient flint miner (*great*, that's what it was like). On the way back, Stuart and I, now high with excitement, devised a game in which we would shout a random letter of the alphabet at every car or pedestrian we passed. "BEE", yelled Stuart, as father nipped past a kerb-crawling granny in Newmarket. "EFF", I screamed at the startled driver of a bus on its way to Barton Mills. And then we pulled horrible faces through the rear window, sticking out our tongues and waggling our ears. Even Dad joined in the fun by tooting his horn derisively. Ah, what it would be like to be ten again. You can have fun *anywhere*.

Another of Dad's trips, this time to the airfield at Waterbeach, was a Damascene moment for my brother Christopher. It was our introduction to flying in a glider. Each of us was taken aloft in an open, two-seat construction, sitting proudly, if a little nervously, side-by-side with the pilot. I remember the sudden silence after the roar of the winch, and then soundlessly soaring over the chessboard fields and the winding River Ouse, a thousand feet below. Chris had to be contented with a shorter ride after something went wrong with the winch, but it is he that still remembers the name of the pilot, the make of the glider, and every small detail of that distant Anglian afternoon. For me it was just a ride, as good as, but no better, than the day Uncle Rupert and I sat at the front of the old wooden rollercoaster at Great Yarmouth and roared as we rattled down and into the tunnel at the bottom. For Christopher, though, a passion had been ignited, and then left to simmer for a few years. From that moment he knew what he wanted to do when he grew up, and that was to spend as much time as possible flying gliders. Just once or twice in life something clicks into place, quite unexpectedly, and you realise that your life has been changed forever—and nobody knows except you. For him it was a short ride in a glider. For me, as I say, it was a big spotted moth in a laburnum tree by the pigsty. You don't say anything. You just *know*.

That year even school was quite fun. No great effort was required. The lessons were not challenging. I was in a class of about thirty, aged between nine and eleven, and ranging from jolly clever (me) to what they now call 'differently intelligent' or frankly unteachable (that was Stephen, the leader of the pack). A Miss Southgate took us through a forgettable rota of reading, writing and 'rithmetic, while I yawned and watched the world go by through the big window, or doodled secret codes on the desktop. The best bits were when headmaster Furnell, took over. Most of his contributions were extra-curricular. A man of hobbies, he generously shared them with us, or at least those of us able to concentrate for long enough. He read us his favourite books (*The Hobbit, Brendon Chase, The Lion, the Witch and the Wardrobe*), and let a few of us borrow his precious volumes of *Lord of the Rings*. He encouraged us to collect pond life, and press wild flowers, and arranged astronomy evenings in which we took it in turns to peer through his small reflector at the moon and the planets. We got through a lot of exercise books with George Furnell for, despite his enthusiasm, he had little staying power. We would start a promising topic on, say, the Aztecs, say, only to halt after a week or so because he had thought of something better, the Tudors, maybe, or a digression on contemporary politics.

From this distance it seems like one long lark, but there were occasional attempts to keep classroom discipline. Everyone was frightened of the teacher that took us through our paces in Country Dancing, the dreaded Miss Robinson. As headmaster, Furnell had summary powers of corporal punishment and occasionally used them. I remember him once tucking the school's black boy, Claude, under his arm and spanking him on the bottom. With his head upside down and peering out through the back of Furnell's coat, little Claude's face registered no expression at all, as though this indignity was happening to someone else. Furnell could also taunt you through mockery. He was a good mimic. My catchphrase, according to him, was "eh, what, pardon?" since it seemed to him that I always had trouble hearing the first time round (very likely one's mind was elsewhere). He was a trooper, and I was sorry to see his name on a bench in front of the school on a later visit. He had died young, evidently of heart failure, not many years later. RIP.

When not adding, dividing or writing a composition, we seniors dabbled in the creative arts. A select few of us warbled and peeped on home-made bamboo pipes in the tiny school library. We played about with poster paint, and clattered about the hall to the rhythms of Miss Robinson and whatever beat combo she had assembled. At the end of it all Furnell decided I had come top in everything. 'An excellent year's work', he wrote on my report, although I question the 'work'. The only exception to all this excellence was Country Dancing, in which Miss Robinson noted my unwillingness to excel. Furnell probably thought I was only goofing about, but the sad truth was that I had no sense of rhythm. I danced like a drunken duck. My toes did not twinkle; my flat feet shuffled aimlessly, and no little Angela or Wendy would go anywhere near me.

On and on went the golden year. Eye-spy books; cockle-picking at Hunstanton; Famous Five-style cycling adventures. Because we chased after them that summer, I chiefly remember the butterflies. They were my first true love: the tortoiseshells and admirals, the holly blue jinking along the garden wall in a twinkle of white and powder blue; the orange-tips fluttering from the waysides lined with foaming 'keck'. Each sweet childish day lasted as long as twenty in the slow lane of middle age.

Best I could do. A blurry shot of The Mount, Longstanton, in 1962.

It was summer and the village was a lush leafy oasis amid the level Anglian corn. If there was a rumble of thunder beyond the harvest sun, I disregarded it. Children dwell in the present, and, as the days grew shorter again, and shadows moved across the grass by tea-time, Peter was still playing with his friends in the big friendly garden, out in the farmyards and the airfield, under the wide open skies of Middle Earth.

CHAPTER NINETEEN

At the Crossroads

Towards the end of the summer term the school hosted a grand sports day. Athletic kids converged from Histon and Girton, Willingham and Waterbeach, Swavesey and Over, for the chance of winning a little coloured ribbon in the sprint or the sack race or the egg-and-spoon. I was taking part in most of these on account of having cheated in the heats. With split-second timing I had jumped the gun enough to give me a head start without earning a disqualification. Alas, this cheat did not prosper. At the end of the day Paul Petra was festooned in ribbons like a general, and even the unathletic Martin wore a yellow one for his prowess in the egg-and-spoon. But poor Peter's sports shirt remained spotlessly and ribbon-lessly white. I cycled home dishonoured. Sport, I said to myself, you can stuff sport. What does winning prove? That you're a loser, that's what. "Oi, Petra, can I borrow your brain? I'm building an idiot". And so forth.

Around that time we sat the Eleven Plus, the exam that determined once and for all whether we ascended the sunlit peak of a grammar school in Cambridge or sank without trace into the secondary modern at Swavesey. I vaguely remember three or four tests, mostly involving sums or 'composition'. After one of them, Furnell came up to me with concern all over his warty face. "You didn't do as well as you should have done. Are you sure you are feeling all right?" I thought for a moment before replying. "Sir", I said, "now that you come to mention it, I find I'm a little breathless. Oh dear me, do you think I might have a cold coming on? Or worse, it could be flu. I think its flu. Do you think they will take my illness into account?" It was a total lie that was actually true for the very next day I went down with chickenpox. Hoping for sympathy, I put it about that I had caught 'brain fever', but the village kids saw that as a great joke—"*you* with a sick brain, haw, haw, haw", they mocked.

I passed all right but Furnell was right. I had not done myself justice—a year of larking about at a village school had seen to that.

Most of my classmates would shortly be heading off on the school bus to Swavesey to be taught journeyman skills and leave at 16, no better educated than their parents. All except my crew-cut friend Stephen, the gang leader, who was destined for a special-needs institution to try and mould this unpromising clay into something useful to society. As for me, my future was still unclear. My parents had begun to study the prospectuses of schools close to home and then, ominously, others further away. Now and again I would overhear them in earnest discussion though without evidently coming to any particular conclusion for a day or two later I would hear the same thing all over again. Well, I thought, that's their problem. They are bound to get it sorted out in the end. Heck, they are grown-ups. Grown-ups know what to do.

Recovering from the pox, I took a short break in London with my grown-up friend Ralph Hale and his wife, who lived childless in their semi in Wembley. I had performed a small service for them by occasionally visiting Ralph's aged, senile grandmother during our weekends in Mountsorrel. After half an hour's gruesome conversation she would send me on my way with a couple of bob or a packet of fruit gums. Evidently my visits cheered her up a bit. This was to be my reward. Ralph knew his man. It was to be a long weekend of high-pressure cramming as if preparing for the general knowledge section of Mastermind. We took in the zoo and most of the museums, while in my scant moments of repose a little girl next door taught me to play Scrabble. Travelling with Ralph on the tube, I remember the crush of the morning rush hour, every man dressed alike in a mac and a bowler hat and carrying a brolly. In just a few years' time all those bowlers would disappear forever. I grew curiously attached to my little wallpapered room in the Wembley semi, and especially to Ralph's large library and albums of bird stamps. When Dad came to pick me up, I started to blub. Clearly I was under a lot of stress.

Mother and father, meanwhile, resumed their hopeless discussions. They felt no need to involve me in them, and, to do them credit, I do not remember wanting to be involved. My education, as far as I was concerned, was a matter for them. I trusted their judgement. I knew nothing about schools and GCEs but had long since taken it for granted that I would be sent away, for that was the accepted fate of any RAF officer's boy who passed the Eleven-plus. Boarding school held few terrors for me. I remember even quite looking forward to my new life. School, mother assured me, was nothing like that film of *Tom Brown's Schooldays*. No one nowadays got tossed in a blanket or roasted in front of a fire (and that was true enough if only because my particular school had no fires). That kind of thing had been stamped out, insisted Mum.

There was just a chance that I would not be sent away at all. Their first and eminently sensible choice was Perse School in Cambridge, which was only a short bus ride away. Jonathan warned me that if I joined that nest of snobs, no village lad would ever speak to me again. That might have been a risk I was prepared to take, but in the event Perse School didn't want me. Possibly my exam results were insufficiently impressive; possibly my parents baulked at the required interview; I don't know. At any rate, when Perse demurred, the parents were not disposed to argue but moved on to the next choice, some boarding school in Norfolk. It might have been Gresham's School at Holt, another sensible choice, which combined ancient stones, decent countryside and excellent exam results, and which they, or rather the RAF, could just about afford.

Wherever it was, we were offered an interview, but in the meantime mother had had a brainwave. The solution was obvious! It had been under their noses all the time. Why not send me to school near my *alternative* home in Mountsorrel? That, at least in her eyes, would take the sting out of my absence with the reassuring thought that Nanna would be close at hand. There were, she discovered, *two* grammar schools for boys in Loughborough, and both of them took boarders. One was Loughborough Grammar School, an independent, fee-paying school of good repute, top sports facilities, an impressive academic record and lots of successful ex-pupils. For some reason, Mum chose the other one. This was Loughborough College School, something of an unknown quantity. It was, it seemed, an ordinary grant-maintained day school but with a house for boarders a twenty-minute walk away. The board was a good bit cheaper—at that time about £150 a term—and the school was distinctly un-posh. Mother knew little or nothing about its level of academic attainment. The great thing for her was that it was only a bus ride away from my grandmother's and that it took boys from forces backgrounds like me: the sons of middling majors and captains and flight lieutenants who could not afford public school fees but could run to a boarding house in Loughborough.

As my parents saw it, this was the best way of providing me with the stable schooling they were convinced I needed. Neither of them had any apprehension of what boarding school was like. They probably thought of it in some vague way as a hearty Greyfriars sort of place, of tuck shops and pillow fights and toasted muffins. I say 'probably' because that is how I myself imagined myself it from comics and TV series like Billy Bunter and Whacko! You will be among boys of your own age and background, they assured me. You'll be with other new boys, and you'll find you have lots in common. And, besides, Nanna would be hovering in the background, would she not, like a fairy godmother, in case young Peter needed an occasional reminder of home comforts.

And so it was that, towards the end of a cloudless summer of free-range fun, we took off to Loughborough in the white Morris to take a look at my new school and meet the headmaster, a Lt Col. Gordon H. F. Broad OBE, BA (Oxon). The place where I was to board for the foreseeable future, may be until the end of my schooldays, was an orange-brick Victorian villa on the junction of Ashby Road called Field House. The head lived there with his wife, a housemaster and 50 boys aged from 11 to 18. The head's wife acted as matron. Colonel Broad turned out to be a huge man, about six-foot-four in his socks, with a bald egg-shaped head, a grey moustache, and a rather intimidating expression from behind his horn-rimmed glasses. On this occasion he was fairly genial and called me Peter—though, in the absence of the parents it would always be 'Marren' or 'young Marren'. As we left he patted my head.

After tea with the owner, we were shown around the house. We mounted the hall staircase to the boys' dorms on the first floor. I would be in the 'baby dorm', an unheated end room with seven beds dispersed on the bare, shiny lino, and otherwise unadorned apart from some lockers and hard chairs. I would come to hate the wallpaper, which featured rock-and-roll bands and dancers, with a boiling intensity. Mother was taken aback by the state of the beds—primitive iron constructions whose springs had gone so that the thin mattresses slumped down towards the floor. The place was evidently run on a shoestring. It was in fact owned by the local authority and the Labour Council then in power was not inclined to lavish resources on 'elite' establishments like this.

With that brief glimpse of my future we went into town to purchase a maroon blazer with its school badge, a matching cap with a yellow band, a long scarf, and a grey suit to wear to church on Sundays. I was, I think, still feeling fairly upbeat about the new adventure. Although, God knows, I had been called Daddy's or Mummy's boy often enough, I was not in fact emotionally close to either of my parents. Children of the armed forces were not like the American kids on TV, forever cooing "I love you, Dad" ("and I love you too, son"). I was an officer's boy and I had never said anything like that in my whole life. I suppose, if you thought about it, one did love them, in a way, but in middle-class, postwar England, you kept your cool about emotions of that kind. Rather, you looked to your parents to provide pocket money, and keep you warm and well-fed and reasonably happy. In general I felt I could manage pretty well on my own. I was looking forward, not without a certain, ill-focussed unease, to making new friends ("boys from the same background"), living a boy's life and learning interesting and possibly even quite useful stuff at school. I'd be all right, I reckoned.

I would, I realised, need a new bike. I dropped a pretty strong hint that anyone who brought me that lean, green machine in the shop window at Bennett's—one of those great, long-lost village shops that sold everything—would find in me a grateful suppliant for the rest of my breathing days. That took care of the bike. Nanna bought it for my birthday, as I knew she would, and it was duly delivered to the school a few weeks later. Mum made me promise to keep it padlocked at all times. Her own parting gift and advance birthday present was less exciting. It was a pigskin writing case containing a pad of Basildon Bond and an admonition to write regularly and often. What a rotten swiz. This stinky so-called gift was school kit, not a proper present, which, by definition, was a thing you could have *fun* with. Thanks a lot, *Mum*.

In the last days of freedom that remained to me, life at The Mount never seemed sweeter. The roof was being re-tiled and a high and rickety bridge of planks circled the house. The moment no one was looking we were up the ladders in a flash and racing each other round and round the roof while the scaffolding creaked and wobbled. We weren't scared of heights. On the airmen's PT course just over the hedge we limbered up the ropes and swung from tree to tree like monkeys. We had daredevil biking fun tearing down the bank of the sunken garden at full speed, bouncing over the bumps. Life felt sweet as the shadows of late summer lengthened from the garden wall; rows of swallows twittered from the wires and the attic was filled with the scent of stored apples. I was eleven, healthy, happy and clever, with plenty of friends, indulgent parents and the whole village, and its farms and airfield, as my playground. And behind it all was my growing love of natural history, that immense canvas of wonders coloured by intense, unfathomable curiosity. Childhood just went on getting better and better. You thought, just then, that it would never end.

The End

(Of Part One)

PART TWO

I have a theory that boarding schools are good training for writers because it is so desperately lacking in privacy: you make space for yourself by having an interior life.

Simon Mawer, English writer and contemporary

CHAPTER ONE

Loughborough College School

The school my parents had chosen for me was a forgettable, red-brick, flat-roofed barrack of a place on a hill. No one outside the area would have heard of it. May be not many inside it either, for my new school was out at the edge of town between the old railway line and the top of Thorpe Hill. Loughborough College School had originated as a feeder for Loughborough College (now Loughborough University), which specialised in engineering and sports. The school's official history manages to delve much further into the past to find an ultimate origin in the whim of a seventeenth-century Loughborough mayor called Bartholomew Hickling. This worthy was concerned that virtually no one in the town could read and write. Most of them had no particular need to, but what mattered to Hickling was that they should be able to read the Bible for themselves and so prepare themselves for Heaven after their unbelievably awful lives on earth. Consequently he set up and endowed some chapel or outhouse with a blackboard and plenty of birches. But that is really neither here nor there. To all intents and purposes, my school originated in 1917 as a 'junior college' set up to supply motivated local lads for Loughborough's burgeoning engineering and pharmaceutical industries. It became a fee-paying grammar school four years later in 1921.

The school's ambiguous status caused difficulties from the start. The local education authority viewed its upkeep as the responsibility of the College, but the latter preferred to wash their hands of it. As a result, some dilapidated wooden huts on William Street, intended as a temporary expedient, became the school's permanent quarters for the next thirty years. By the 1950s, the huts had begun to rot and fall to bits; in the despairing words of the headmaster, 'floors, roofs, corridors and walls are mouldering away'. The parents of one prospective boarder brought their son all the way from Bolivia to see this fine school (they had heard) in the English Midlands. They took one look at the rotting huts and took him straight home again, all the way back to Bolivia.

Until his retirement in 1952, the school's head was a local man called Alfred Eggington, known to all and sundry as 'Eggs'. He was a good egg was Eggington. With the face of an unusually self-satisfied vole, he did his best to imbue the place with a public school ethos that belied its reduced circumstances. Exceptionally for headteachers at that time, Eggs' academic background was not in the classics but in chemistry. He had taught maths and general science before taking over the junior college shortly after its establishment. Since no parents of a bright boy with any means of avoiding doing so was going to send their son to the disgusting huts on William Street, academic achievement was unlikely to be the school's proudest boast—and indeed not a single boy between 1930 and 1940 made it through to university. Eggs might have responded that it was not *that* kind of school. What mattered to him was character. He set about trying to win the school a reputation in handicrafts and sports. He wanted big, strong Loughborough boys that were good at games. He longed for the College School to lead the field in woodwork. To get the most out of his boys he introduced a house system, naming each group after ancient tribes, so that you became a Dane or a Celt or an Ancient Briton, or whatever. The school magazine was called *Limit* (later changed to *Summit*); and that gave you the general idea: Eggs' Danes and Vikings were expected to push themselves to the limit, kicking balls and creating nifty wooden nicknacks under the eye of a terrifying old brute called Burford. Eggs seems to have been a sentimental old booby. After retirement they had him back regularly to present prizes when he would invariably start blubbing and telling the yawning masses that those had been the happiest days of his life. He became something of a Loughborough institution, a perpetual busybody, serving as a Liberal on the county council and chairing the local education committee, culminating in a stint as mayor. He lived to a full century, and is remembered in a block of flats on the campus known as the Falkner-Eggington Courts, or Falk-Egg for short. Don't ask me who Falkner was.

Eventually the education authority scraped together enough money to build a new school on top of Thorpe Hill. It was a purpose-built utility designed by the county architect, a certain T.A. Collins, who described it as a "three-storey building built on the principal of vertical circulation". He did his best to cheer up its austere brick-and-glass Lego shape with a set of terracotta moulds displaying the signs of the zodiac, and, in honour of some forgotten local legend, he plonked a bronze boar in the middle of the paved quad. A long corridor ran the full length of the school via several short flights of steps, with the hall and a small library at one end and a detached block for geography and biology seniors at the other. There was a relatively generous provision of laboratories for budding engineers and chemists, as well as shops for the wood and metal-work artisans. There was also an extensive sports field on the cold, windy hilltop between the school and the railway. My school was beset by other schools. Next door lay the local Secondary Modern, called Garendon, while across the road was the De Lisle School for Roman Catholics, where our own few Catholics went for their religious instruction. All in all Thorpe Hill provided an economical means of segregating a lot of local kids well out of town where they were least likely to bother anyone.

Around 1950 the school admitted girls for the first time after a merger with the local college of art. 'Eggs' had been less than wholehearted about this. For one thing girls were a potential distraction, and sure enough boys were soon punching holes in the rotting walls to get at them. "Like salt in meat, too much might be too much", he protested (spoken like a chemistry teacher, Eggs!). By the time the school moved to Thorpe Hill it had also acquired a Sixth Form, who were dressed in smart black blazers to distinguish them from their maroon-blazered juniors. The new school opened in 1956, but right away it was apparent that the local authority had miscalculated. Even without the juniors the place was bursting at the seams. Built to hold about 800 pupils, there were in fact more than a thousand baby-boomers to accommodate. Classes spilled out into the hall, the balcony, stockrooms, even the new Mormon church halfway down the hill. The juniors were forced to take their school dinners at horrible Garendon. And the first years were unable to leave their huts down town and join the school until my first term in autumn 1962.

This was the institution my parents had chosen for their clever boy that fatal summer. Had they investigated further, they might have discovered that the school's record in sending its brightest pupils to university had improved slightly, but was still unimpressive. Apart from a freak quartet accepted into Cambridge in 1963, the last year of state scholarships, few boys or girls managed to win a place at a senior university. The usual goal for College kids who managed to pass their 'A' levels was not university but technical college—above all Loughborough College—or one of the nearby teacher-training establishments. What strikes me most, when learning about my old school acquaintances on Friends Reunited, is how few of them seem to have left the Loughborough area. This was basically a local school for local kids qualifying for local jobs. And so, as I occasionally found myself wondering, what the hell was *I* doing here? The usual kick-backs for suffering at public school—influential friends, useful contacts, a red carpet into Sandhurst, Oxbridge or a City Bank—obviously didn't apply. Even the school's future as a grammar was in doubt. Under the Leicester Plan, sooner or later we were destined to become part of a bog-standard comprehensive, and after that a Sixth Form College with the younger boys kicked across the road to Garendon.

What drove any parent outside the area to send their boys to Loughborough College School? It seems that the common thread was some connection with the town. My friend Simon Khosla, for instance, was born there. His father had been a pupil at the school and had gone on to study engineering at the College. It was a place he knew and thought well of, and he could think of no better future for young Simon than to send him there in his turn. Some boys were dumped there as the result of a messy divorce and an evident wish to place their teenage son some distance away. As for me, it was, of course, the Mountsorrel connection—although for most of the time my granny's home might have been on the moon for all the benefit it brought me. Time and again I must have asked myself what I was doing at a far-away school that was no better than the one back home, and quite possibly worse. And always the same answer crept back like the echo of a bell. It was to be near my grandmother.

A note about The Boss

Gordon Broad, the headmaster, was universally known, and for sufficient reason, as Boss. This boss was most definitely in charge. He was physically, as well as figuratively, head and shoulders above his staff. His massive presence was made all the more scary by his slightly magnifying specs, and when he was angry his parade-ground bellow would fill the assembly hall or, back at the boarding house, shake the pots in the conservatory. When you got to know him you understood that his bark was worse than his bite and that Boss was a shrewd, intelligent and basically kindly man. But his bite was nonetheless pretty bad, as anyone who had been caned by him knew very well, and at Field House in those days that was everybody. His attitude, generally, was of a regimental colonel with a rather backward battalion to train.

Boss took over from Eggs in 1953 when the school was still festering in the huts on William Street. Although he was in every way a more imposing figure than the grinning, blubbing Eggs, Boss was not a local man and did not talk with the soft, flat accents of Leicestershire; he was an upper-middle class Mancunian, and so an outsider. He had been educated at Tonbridge School, one of the most expensive, and by all accounts, one of the most brutal, public schools in the land, notorious for beatings, bullying and buggery. I do not know what lessons young Gordon Broad drew from his time there but buggery, at least, was seldom practised under his headship. He won a scholarship to Balliol College, Oxford—noted for clever boys from the right background—where he graduated in modern history. Boss was still of military age when the war broke out, and lost no time in joining the Royal Artillery, though he was soon seconded to the Army Education Corps. He spent his time reminding soldiers what they were fighting for, with special reference to liberal values and postwar reconstruction. Boss rose to Lt. Colonel, earning an OBE and a mention in despatches: a good man. Could go far. With that record he had no trouble finding a headship of a small rural grammar school in Lutterworth. By then he had married the snobbish, unhappy woman we knew as Fanny by whom he had two children, an older girl and a boy we knew only as Brat: Brat Broad.

When he took over the running of Loughborough College School, Boss was only 42 but he looked more like 60. His headship extended to the boarding school, known to us as Field Hole, or, as I shall generally refer to it here, The Hole. Hence he was rarely off duty; boys to the left of him, boys to the right of him, boys all over the place: there was no escape. He shared his meal times with us, took us unwillingly to church, flicked us our letters after breakfast, inspected our dormitories on Sundays and occasionally played ping-pong with selected senior boys. Once or twice he even challenged me to a round of Mah-jong, and of course I beat him despite his poor sportsmanship (for he claimed lots of non-scoring chows to get out quickly, which even his boy Brat thought was a bit off). To cap it all he marked 'O' and 'A' level exam papers that kept him partially confined to barracks in summer. He was a dedicated and determined man was Boss: a Liberal with a mission.

True to his principles, Boss was a reformer, going through the motions of organising staff committees to spread a little democracy about. Not surprisingly, he was keen on rugger and the Combined Cadet Force, and in the early days sometimes took the parades himself. In his view you went to school not only to learn but to acquire character through extra-curricular school activities. For dedicated backsliders like me who intended to get through to the Sixth Form with the minimum of effort, this emphasis on hearty participation required a certain amount of dodging and ducking. The school history, written in 1972 by some toady, faithfully records some of the Boss's favourite phrases: 'a healthy mind in a healthy body'; 'stretching their talents to their full extent' and so on. Perhaps he took his exhortations seriously, but I suspect it was basically make-believe, part of the Liberal tradition of always trying to say the right thing. Boss set about turning Egg's ramshackle edifice into a modern school by introducing streaming, with an accelerated 'A' form 'for the more able', who would, among other things, have to study Latin on the outside chance of winning a place at Oxbridge. He also decided that everyone would learn French, doubtless to the great joy of old 'Jock' Chalmers, a grizzled veteran who had taught the language longer than anyone could remember, probably since Napoleon.

Off duty, Boss's great passion was playing bridge. Boss was very good at bridge. He and his partner carried off the trophies of the Leicestershire Contract Bridge Association on at least 13 occasions between 1949 and 1972, and I believe he also played bridge for England once or twice. Once, probably when the Boss was captain of the county team in 1964–65, Omar Sharif was among the top players that gathered at the Hole for a heavy session round the card table. We boarders craned our necks round the swing door to catch a glimpse of the star of Dr Zhivago and Lawrence of Arabia. At last someone spotted him. "He's small", he hissed to the scrum of film fans behind. "He's a tiny little guy. I can't believe that's him". He was about the size of a hooker in the under-14s. But I guess most of us would look big on a camel.

All things considered, Boss was an underachiever. He presided over our third-rate school for year after year, right up to his retirement in 1970. There was obviously a weakness somewhere. Possibly he had a rather limited sense of humour. He didn't seem to smile or relax very often, and for the reason you only had to look at the sour-puss standing next to him: his wife, Fanny. In those days he was more respected than liked. But many of us can remember little acts of kindness—a great many in my case—to counterbalance the occasions when he lost his temper when things got a little slack. Many have remarked on how his comments on our leaver's reports have proved uncannily prescient. He was a shrewd judge of boys and how they would turn out (I say boys; there were girls at our school, of course, but he left them to the benevolent care of a Mrs Park). Boss and I usually rubbed along fairly well. Perhaps he felt rather sorry for me at first, the only boy of scholarly potential in a house full of sweaty rugger types. Boss didn't have many scholars. I was his token scholar. And I didn't at all mind him feeling a bit uneasy over the plight of poor little Marren, as I was henceforth known. For, as I will now relate, I was feeling very hard done by.

CHAPTER TWO

A Hole and its Rules

After our interview with Boss, we came away with a copy of the prospectus and the House Rules. There seemed to be a great many of these rules and, one evening by the fireside at The Mount, mother and I went through them together. There would come a time when I knew them word-for-word, for copying out the rules was a favourite punishment of the nastier kind of prefect. You could, I thought, sum them up by the ant-heap formula that says anything not forbidden is compulsory. Church, for instance, was compulsory, and so were grey shirts and socks, wearing caps when outdoors, going to bed and getting up on-the-bloody-dot, and not talking after lights-out, or during prep. On the other hand you could forget about going out when you liked,

The Hole today. Partly rebuilt and extended since my time, this is the front which was out of bounds. On the roof is the pergola where one hero once hoisted the matron's knickers.

wearing informal clothes, watching television, or having a bath when you wanted (and with hot instead of lukewarm water), or keeping food except in the nominated tuck tin, available for a precisely allocated ten minutes each evening. These, along with most other kinds of normal life, were all forbidden. The rules were enforced by prefects who were given a fairly free hand in their interpretation. Their effect was to regulate our lives from the moment we rose from our broken beds at 7.15 to lights out for juniors fourteen hours later. Even weekends had a set routine of walks, inspections and religious observance. The keener boys spent their moments of leisure polishing their army boots or putting their rugger shorts through the mangle. I was one of the lucky ones. By tacit agreement with the Boss, I was allowed to see my grandmother on Sunday afternoons, where I would watch television, enjoy a hot bath in private and fill my face with fried food before returning, with a sorrowful heart, on the four o'clock bus to Loughborough.

Most of these rules were, I imagine, standard fare for boarding schools across the land. It was largely because of the attitude of prefects that their effect was perhaps harsher than intended. Full-grown forces boys liked to impose and punish, partly through a heady sense of empowerment, partly to boost their own sense of *amour-propre*, but mostly because they had been through it themselves. It was a tradition; it was the way things were done here. In prep, for example, which occupied every weekday evening from 5.30 to 7.15, we were supposed to ask permission to leave our seats, or before whispering something to a neighbour, or to go for a pee—permission which might or might not be granted, depending on the boy's mood. Moreover, since prep was allocated for homework, and nothing but homework, the presiding boy was often disinclined to let us to do anything else, such as read a book. Naturally we did our best to cheat the system. I generally finished my prep well before the bell rang for cocoa and I remember spending one vacant half-hour drawing a map. A map of Wales. The prefect in charge spotted it and whisked it up.

"What's this, Marren?" All eyes left their algebra and French verbs and fastened on me.

"It's a map" (what does it look like, you twat). "It's a map of Wales."

"Hmmm, I didn't know Wales was on your syllabus. I'll have a word with Mr Sharpe [the geography teacher] tomorrow". He handed back my drawing. *"And woe betide you if you're lying"*.

I spent a sleepless night.

Punishments for minor infringements varied. If the prefect was in a good mood, you might get off with polishing his shoes for a week, which was far preferable to the alternative of 'a page of logs'—an exact written-out copy of the mathematical tables of logarithms which would then be tested for accuracy, and, if it failed to satisfy, had to be repeated. Writing out the rules took longer still, and both took care of your free time. Corporal punishment was the prerogative of the Head Boy who was permitted to whack junior bottoms with a slipper at a public *auto-da-fé* in which other prefects would pile into the room to cheer on the whacker and further humiliate the whackee.

All told, there were rich opportunities here for persecution. Prefect power was upheld by Boss who no doubt saw the system as conducive to character-building. Perhaps he also saw it as a kind of officer-training. Discipline, after all, was what had won the war. Boss himself, and his Housemaster, could punish misbehaviour by up to six strokes of the cane, a duty carried out fairly regularly, for example on the victims of a dorm raid. It was scarcely possible to survive long at the Hole without being logged or slippered or caned. I don't think it bothered anybody unduly, and the great thing about a beating is that it is soon over and done with. What was worse was psychological persecution. It was applied most enthusiastically by the little rat-like prefects who had been bullied mercilessly in their time. Power gave them an outlet for all that pent-up hatred. To us juniors, the system was an object lesson in the arbitrariness of justice, in the waywardness of punishment. That, at least, has left its scar on me. I have done my best ever since to snipe at abused authority, at what we used to call the little Hitlers. If it is possible to follow an instinct back to some point of origin, it was probably in those early days at the Hole that I first became sceptical of those in power, and especially anyone who seemed to wish to exert it over me. I'd had enough of it. No, I wasn't going *there* again. (At least one boy I knew there feels the same way).

Partly in emulation of public schools, but also because the education authority refused to pay for cleaners, the Hole had a system of fag duty in which groups of juniors took it in turns to clean up with brushes and brooms, and to clear the tables after breakfast and supper. There was more scraping and scrubbing to do before Sunday morning inspections when the Boss and his duty prefect liked to find a sparkling bathroom and a dust-free dorm. One way or another we became pretty nifty with a brush and pan. We brushed the boards of the cloakroom where our lockers lined the walls; we brushed and cleaned the old boiler room next door where our boots and shoes were stored, and then the cold, tiled floor next to the chilly lavatory where, if you had a mind to, you could reach over the partition and surprise the boy next door by pulling his chain; and then on, past the bike sheds to brush the dusty outhouse that served as our common room. Upstairs lay more dusting: the wooden loft with its naked light bulb, reached by a flight of wooden steps, where the ping-pong table was housed. All needed a good regular brushing, and all were inspected afterwards. We must have been a fairly clean Hole, most of the time.

This place had been purchased by the county education authority back in 1933; at just over £4,000, it cost more than the school. Before a dual carriageway removed half the grounds in 1964, the Hole had a pleasant front garden, an orchard, some greenhouses and vegetable gardens at the back, and, beyond the garden wall, a paddock lined on one side with trees. It would have interested none of us, I'm sure, to know that the house was of some slight architectural merit and is now listed at Grade 2. From the front, before it was hidden from sight behind a fence, you would have seen a handsome brick villa in the Queen Anne style with sash windows and a tile roof topped with a cupola and weather vane (reachable by a risky crawl up the roof from one of the dormers). But the front and all the grander parts of the house and the front garden were out of bounds to boarders. We spent our leisure hours in the paddock or the meaner quarters at the back where servants once boiled the master's linen, and hay was stored where the ping-pong table now stood. We did not live comfortable lives. My feet rarely touched a carpet nor did my bottom find anything softer than wooden chairs and benches. For most of the year it was dark by the time we were released from prep.

Neither one's feet nor one's bottom would have grieved unduly about these mild austerities. The main drawbacks to life at the Hole were not hard chairs but cold, hunger, fear and loneliness. In winter we froze; the only warm place was in your narrow bed. The food was inadequate and we were nearly always hungry. You would return from holiday or a free weekend feeling comparatively well fed for a couple of days, until it wore off and that familiar nag of hunger returned. We spent our pocket money on food but you had to be careful. You would not want to let them catch you eating it. Once Fanny spotted some boarders guzzling chips in the street, a sight she found disgusting and worthy of punishment. In a spirit of let-the-punishment-fit-the-crime Boss purchased a large quantity of chips, laid them on the table and ordered the offenders to eat the lot. That'll teach 'em, he thought. They won't eat chips again in a hurry, oh no. Needless to say the chips were despatched lickety-split and one of the boys even had the nerve to ask for more. So that didn't work.

I might have suffered from hunger more than most since I was rather fastidious and could not bring myself to make up the deficit by gorging on school dinners, the traditional boarder's standby. Suppers at the Hole were of slightly better quality than the ghastly mid-day dinner at school but they were never sufficient. We filled up on bread and jam; each of us had a personal jam jar in a window locker; Hartley's New Jam or tinned IXL, we thought, were the best. Fanny used to insist we be given no fresh bread until the old loaf was used up, a system which would have ensured that, by the time we ate it, the bread was stale. We got around that by slipping the old bread out of the window where the rats could take care of it. We could bulk out our rations with our personal tuck tin, but this was available only at 7.15 when a greyish fluid they called cocoa was served through the hatch. My parents had arranged a five-bob-a-week account for me at the nearest grocers. I tended to spend it on fig rolls, not because I liked them particularly but because they were cheap, and you got a big bag full for your bob. Good for keeping you regular, too, taken in sufficient quantity, for constipation was another occupational hazard—something to do with the porridge, I shouldn't wonder. Our morning porridge was kept warm for us in a metal urn; it usually had a thick crust, like ice on a pond, by the time it was served, and tasted metallic, but at least it was warm and filling. Even so, I wasn't surprised to learn that porridge was a word for the rigours of imprisonment. It was only at home that porridge, mashed potato, swede, and even semolina, actually tasted quite nice.

As for the unheated dorms, after the first term I begged my parents to buy me some long trousers (shorts were the prescribed leg uniform for first formers). It was partly because I did not want to be the only kid in the house in shorts, but I was also glad of my new trousers during the Siberian winter of 1962/63. Our head boy, a Pat Smith, cited the Hole's subzero temperatures as his reason for emigrating to New Zealand as soon as possible. The cold—cold beds, cold linoleum and bare boards, cold sinks, cold toilets, cold, soggy football pitches—was his abiding memory of the Hole, fifty years on. Trudging back from school, one passed humble homes where a comfortable yellow glow from behind the curtains suggested Dickensian scenes of Loughborough boys warming their toes by the fireside and watching Dr Who from a comfy armchair. I had the same feeling of envy when I was occasionally invited into the Hole's inner sanctum to play with Brat. The touch of the carpet and the comforting glow of the fire, the softness of the furnishings! In what luxury did these people live!

For young Marren, aged eleven and very much alone, the worst aspect of life in the Hole was the more or less complete absence of kindness. Twenty years on, our school was renamed a Community College in which, so the online prospectus claims, 'all members should feel a sense of belonging and inclusion'. You didn't get much sense of that back then when the Hole felt more like a Borstal than a 'community'. You could say our lives lacked the feminine touch. There was no matron, no maternal shoulder to cry on, only Fanny. Nor did we receive much sympathy from the College doctor who visited us once a week. Convinced that our sickies were simply lesson-dodgers, which, to do him justice, was often the case, he would diagnose an all-round epidemic of 'Mondayitis' and warn you not to darken his surgery again for a long time. The doses of penicillin he stabbed into my bottom were extraordinarily painful, and he got around the problem of a sty in my eye by pulling out the lashes and then lancing the boil with his scalpel. Others told me he had an excruciating way with verrucas. He was not a man to be trifled with.

George Orwell's abiding memory of his prep school was one of disgust: the overcrowded, underfed, under-washed life of boys crammed together. Things had not changed all that much in my day, half a century later. Disgusting memories pile up: the collapsing beds, farts, smelly feet, the cat shit under the bench at prep ("don't disturb it!"), of being constipated for days together. On top of that, there was, in my case, a more or less permanent state of anguish over a missing toilet bag or pullover, of forgetting to wash one's PE kit, of being unable to finish one's homework. And simmering gently in the background were the heartache summits of loneliness and boredom. At the start of each term it was Betjeman's 'Doom! Shivering doom!'—though I'd trade his Marlborough for my Hole any day. You endured, because you thought you had to, in fee-paying institutions that had much in common with prison but which nearly everybody accepted as the decreed fate for boys of our sort. All this, they said, was building our personalities, toughening us up, doing us good. On that, parents, teachers, prefects, all those with authority over us, were in full agreement. It takes a rare eleven-year-old to argue with such unanimity.

CHAPTER THREE

Arrival

The fateful day came soon enough. It was on 11th September 1962 that I pulled on my new maroon blazer and knotted my maroon-and-yellow striped tie and was taken away in the white Morris, away from the warm nest of The Mount to whatever tank of pike awaited me in Loughborough. Mother insisted on coming too, and kept up a reassuring banter all the way. I was bound to make *lots* of new friends. I must remember to write *every* week and padlock my bike and, of course, *keep out of fights*. At length, the deceptively mellow, orange-brick front of the Hole swayed into view. While my parents had a word with Boss, doubtless to remind him that little Peter needed to see his granny every Sunday, I was shown around the place by a second-year boy called Steve. He seemed friendly enough, though his slightly over-eager Boy Scout manner indicated he was on his best behaviour. "I *think* you'll like it here", he kept saying. I had an open mind on that point, especially when he pointed out my locker (which lacked a lock) in the humblest position, right down at floor level with a label that said, simply, 'MARREN'. Up till that point I had always been 'Peter'.

I would share the Baby Dorm with six others. Steve introduced me to a large, plump, black boy from Nigeria called Charlie. They invited me to take the vacant bed between theirs, all chums together. It was at that moment that I spotted the white Morris slipping down the gravel path. We had already said our goodbyes, hastily in my case for fear the parents would say or do something that made me blub. All the same, it came as a slight shock to realise that I was now alone among strangers for the first time in my life. Steve broke into whatever reflections I might have been having with a breezy invitation to inspect some other outhouse or locker room or boot rack. "Come on, you're in Field House now. I *think* you'll like it here".

As the afternoon wore on, more dorm babes arrived. There was Steve's great chum Dim, a pretty boy from Rothley where his parents ran a pub. Dim could easily have lived at home and caught the bus to school; perhaps, then, he was here for character-building purposes. Arriving next was the dorm captain, a small, sneering sort of boy called McCretton, who, Steve warned, could be hard on newcomers. Last to turn up was a handsome, sulky, carrot-haired boy called Nigel King, the son of an army captain, who seemed cautious and watchful. I could not help noticing that all these boys were a year older than me. They were in the *second* form, I, the first. Moreover, Steve aside (and he soon changed his spots), they did not go out of their way to make the new first-year feel welcome. It began to dawn on me that mother had been less than thorough in her investigations, and that her confident assertion that there would be *plenty* of boys my own age was not well grounded. My remaining hopes rested in the vacant bed by the door. It would be occupied in about a week by a boy from Rhodesia named Musson. Musson was the boy for me. What castles in the air I built for Musson and me; Musson and Marren: the similarity of our names was surely a good sign. Nothing is so bad that it cannot be improved by sharing. What larks we would have, once young Musson had, with my help, settled in.

Those hopes were dashed when the missing Musson finally appeared. A large boy still wearing his old school blazer, he turned out to be a second-year too, and no more inclined than the others to treat little bespectacled Marren as an equal. Mine, I realised now, had been the only parents in the whole wide world to decide to send their eleven-year-old boy to this particular boarding school.

It had never occurred to them, or me, that I might find myself without a friend. Unfortunately for me, the social structure of the Hole was based on quasi-military lines in which I found myself at the very bottom. Those on the next level up needed someone to despise in order to boost their own self-esteem and I was the only candidate. Perhaps if I had been a hearty boy, impatient to muck in on the rugger pitch and the parade ground, I might have been accepted more readily. The Hole liked tough, thick-skinned boys. The quintessential boarder was a soccer captain or cricket champ or a loud, pint-sized NCO smelling of dubbin and blanco. Unfortunately I wasn't made that way. My looks and build were against me. I was a gawky, weedy little kid with mother's boy written all over his twitchy little face. They soon found an appropriate nickname for me. I was Clarence, because I looked like the sort of kid who is called Clarence on TV and in the comics. As I free-wheeled down Thorpe Hill on my flash green bike, someone called out: "Hey, Clarence, your back wheel's going round", and, unthinkingly, I turned and looked. So that became my catchphrase: "Hey, Clarence, your back wheel's going round!"

Standing in the bleak backyard by the bike shed I asked Steve, who, for want of a better, I still regarded as a friend, who *his* best chum was (for such things are important to boys). "Well, Dim, obviously", he began, and that was fair enough, for he and Dim were indeed inseparable. "Then—let me see—probably McCretton", he went on, for the two of them had been given a hard time by bullies the previous year and the experience had bound them together as fellow sufferers (Steve, so he told me, had more than once been basketed, that is, stuffed inside the laundry basket and pushed down the outhouse stairs, "and *then* they poured ink on me. Think yourself lucky"*). I decided I might as well drink this bitter potion to the dregs. Well, who next, I asked, wearily. Who is your *fourth*-best friend? "Musson. And then King". Steve paused, and then added, offhandedly, "and then you, I suppose, and right at the bottom, way out of sight, Charlie", and he made some gestures suggestive of the bottom of a well. Charlie had started bullying his dorm mates, as well as developing serious hygiene problems, and people had begun to avoid him. "If only you were a second year", concluded Steve with a pitying look.

That might have been a good moment to mount the green bike and clear off to granny's, leaving a note on the broken bed with that old Irish farewell, "Think of me no way but this—may the wind rise up to greet you and may the cold rain piss on your backs". There were several such moments during that first term. Another came on letter-writing day. My first letter home had been a masterpiece of evasion, admitting

---

* Hence the expression: 'Some people are like Slinkies—not really good for anything but they bring a smile to your face when they're pushed down the stairs.'

that, while Burf, the woodwork teacher, had threatened me with a good hiding, I had, on the other hand, persuaded somebody to give me some salad cream to go with my slice of Hole corned beef. I liked salad cream. Salad cream reminded me of home. That, I thought, was the sort of thing that would make Dad chortle and Mummy smile. For my second letter home, though, I nearly came clean. Had it been sent, it would have caused some serious soul-searching back at The Mount. I lied, I wrote miserably, when I said I liked it here. It's a rotten dump. It's the most despicable hole. But please don't worry, I went on (some hope). I was also worried about how to spell 'worry'. Was that one 'r' or two? I decided on one, but it didn't look right to me. I was frowning over this when McCretton sitting opposite said or did something that tripped my emotional wire. I burst into tears. The duty prefect leapt up, sent McCretton flying off his chair and skidding over the bare boards, then picked me up and pushed me outside. Words must have been said, for that night the baby dormers were relatively quiet and considerate. My unfinished letter was returned to me. I tore it up. It felt like a watershed moment.

There was, it seems, sympathy for my plight among some of the older boys, and also from the housemaster 'Tes' Egan, who was youngish and a decent stick, for a PE teacher. Once a fourth former from the dorm next door, happening to overhear the mockery of my dorm mates, came in and made a fine, old-fashioned speech straight out of *Tom Brown's Schooldays* about decency and fair play. I could barely restrain the tears. "Don't take any notice", remarked Steve, after he had gone. "He's a loner. He won't last long. He doesn't have any friends. A bit like you, really", he added, thoughtfully.

Another good moment to call it a day was The Affair of Fanny's Bedroom. Boss and Fanny slept in separate rooms off the main landing. One morning I awoke feeling bad. All I wanted to do was stay in bed and die. "What do I do now?" Either they did not know or they saw another opportunity for a rag. I was advised to tiptoe along the dark corridor, through the fire door on the landing and knock on Fanny's door. Really? It sounded a bit rum, but if that was what you were supposed to do… so I did. I tugged on my dressing gown, and, after hesitating a few moments, knocked lightly on the forbidden door. "What? Who's that?" came a muffled voice from within. Innocently I opened the door and stuck my head round. "Er, Ma'am, it's me, Marren, I'm feeling sick". Go back to your room, she commanded, and we'll see about that later. She didn't sound angry. But she was. *Bloody angry. Furious.* I fancy Boss had been given an ear-wigging, for after breakfast he had some hard words for all of us. He had decided, he announced, to punish everyone from the fourth form down. We were each going to write out forty times the precise procedure for reporting sick, and it was clear that this did not include disturbing his wife, nor peering round her bedroom door. Threats and curses rained down on my head as we worked on our lines that night, but they had a bantering edge to them as though it was tacitly accepted that there were others to blame apart from idiot me. It occurs to me now that this would have been another perfect moment to shimmy down the drainpipe, leaving a box of cheap chocolates and an insulting note on Fanny's pillow, before cycling off to freedom. Somehow these things never occur to you at the time.

"I never thought you'd actually do it, you bloody fool". Orwell was right about the strange honour of adolescent boys. A boy has no sense of proportion. He may be a mass of egotism and rebelliousness, but he lacks the necessary accumulated experience to give him confidence in his own judgements. Hence, by and large, he will accept what he is told. I was in the Hole against my will. I could easily have talked my parents into taking me away, with sufficient justification since I had been sent there on what could be construed as a false premise, namely that I would be among friends, *boys of your own age*. But to do so would have entailed an admission that I was unhappy and unpopular; that I was an abject failure. Boys, perhaps especially middle-class boys from military backgrounds, used to believe that misfortune is disgraceful and so something to conceal at all costs. Besides, not exposing your true feelings to an adult, even one's parents, seems to be instinctive from the age of eight upwards. Christopher Hitchens went so far as to suggest that it is the business of the boarding-school boy to protect parental innocence. If so, I think I managed it pretty well. My parents remained perfect innocents. I never told them the full story of my suffering in the Isolator that was the Hole. It was permissible to mention details—woodwork masters, maths homework, lumpy porridge—but I held back on the rest knowing what an agony of distress and indecision it would cause them. They wouldn't, I was starting to realise, know what to do. And so, for them, the Hole experience was all about jolly pranks, the apple-pie beds, the nicknames, the eccentric teacher with a permanent drip on his nose.

Perhaps one incident will illustrate this determination to keep home life and school well apart. Shortly before we parted that first term, father had tried to press some money into my hand. I remember the place where we were standing and that the hand-out was substantial, a handfull of bright half-crowns. I had never been offered so much money in my life. It would have been a very handy supplement to the Hole's miserly two bob a week. But I refused to take it with some nonsense about how it wouldn't be fair on the others. I must have known that this was a guilt offering and that acceptance would have made father feel better. But just at that moment I didn't want his money. What I wanted was for him to go away. He was confusing me in my mind about whether I was at home or at school. A boarding boy wants parents that are above all inconspicuous ("Oh, *Mum*, please, *don't* kiss me, not *here*"). He should have given me the bloody money earlier. Parents, I thought, with a sudden realisation that came as a shock, can be really stupid sometimes. You can't necessarily rely on them. You can't necessarily tell them stuff. That came as a shock too. I had, perhaps for the first time in my life, produced a sequence of thought.

CHAPTER FOUR

Veritate, scientia, labore

'By truth, wisdom and hard labour' ran the school motto, emblazoned in Latin on every school report and library book and prefect's blazer. Or, alternatively, it might read: '*With* truth, knowledge and industry'. The ablative case is hopelessly vague. What with sticking their verbs at the end of their sentences, like an afterthought, there must have been tremendous scope for being misunderstood in Roman times. Anyway, it wasn't really *our* school motto. It is that of Loughborough College and my school had simply purloined it, along with the College coat-of-arms, which was a wavy cross with little gizmos in the corners: a peacock for pride, an open book for the learning of, and so forth. It is exactly the sort of badge you might expect in a place like Loughborough: all about working hard with no hint of irony or of enjoying yourself along the way. Or, as Alan Clarke might have put it, it's an appropriate motto for a solemn little place with a corncob up its arse.

"Allen, Blanchard, Bone, Brookes, Carrington, Clements, Creber,..." The morning register of Form 1D rang through about thirty names—surnames, that is. Christian names were reserved for girls, and we were all boys. Our form inhabited a wooden hut, one of three acquired to house the first years until there was room for them inside the main school building. The huts smelt of varnished wood and the blackboards, being new, squeaked horribly. We were arranged in separate rows in alphabetical order with Allen, Blanchard and company at the back while anyone unlucky enough to be called Zygote or Yarbles was right up at the front within gown-swishing distance of the teacher. But there was one boy who was in front of everybody, even Zygote. He was a kid called Evan, a little monkey of a boy with short black fuzz on his curiously flat-topped head. Evan was so thick he was made to stay behind in 1D after all his classmates moved onwards and upwards, and do his lessons all over again, properly this time. He is probably still there now. Evan had a way of clambering underneath his desktop when attacked by the teacher, clinging to the lid with his rubbery arms and legs. Sitting right behind him I watched his antics entranced. I thought this desk manoeuvre of his quite brilliant and once tried it myself, but got stuck and then brought the desk over with a crash. Evan might not have learned much, or indeed anything at all, but he knew all the hiding places on his desk.

I was in the second row, behind Evan and between my friend Bill Leivers and some other, long-forgotten boy beginning with M, Mattock or Muffin or something. Our day was divided into periods of half an hour, five in the morning, four in the afternoon, with an hour for lunch and two fifteen-minute breaks inbetween. Our subjects included English, which might have been all right, but for now the severities of grammar outweighed the dalliance of literature. There was also history, geography, French, maths and 'general science', with an hour or so each week devoted to art, music and woodwork, plus half-an-hour for C-of-E-approved RE (Religious Education, that is). Twice a week we would troop off to the reeking changing rooms for PE and Games; never exactly a highlight for me. Before all that, at nine o'clock sharp, we assembled in the school hall to sing a hymn, recite a prayer and hear the sports results, plus a list of awards, detentions and canings.

Every class had a form teacher who took the roll call. We were lucky. Ours was a benign young history teacher with flowery handwriting called Brian W. T. Williams and, since he was Welsh, he was known as Taffy, or Taff, as he might have been, Taff Williams. We came to an understanding, Taff and I, or so I thought. The rest of the class could write about the ancient Sumerians or whatever but I could do pretty much what I liked. For my first essay I thought history needed a bit of context so I wrote about evolution. "Very interesting", commented Taff, "but now, about these ancient Sumerians…" But the funny thing was, whenever I mentioned some arcane beast, such as *Gyroptygius*, he *corrected my spelling*!

Until that September day in the piquant hut, my schooling had been larky and ad hoc, a bit of 'composition' here, some adding or dividing there, a smattering of music and drawing and so on. This sudden onset of academic rigour struck me with the same horror as it did millions of others. Some of it was all right. Geography, for instance, began with maps and conventional signs, which was quite good fun, and a reminder of those sub-Tolkien maps I had drawn of my village and its hinterland ('Here be Feylds. Ther are cowS'). In General Science a moon-faced man named Cooper showed us how to make oxygen in a bell jar by the reaction of heat on two powdered substances. Life-giving air from powder! Fabulous! I wanted to do that. I could tell chemistry was going to be a big thing in my life shortly, and it certainly sorted out Christmas this year (and I reckoned they owed me, big time).

But other subjects were harder to fathom. Maths, for instance, had hitherto been about numbers, which you could figure out, more or less, but now for some reason there were letters as well. Let the quantity be 'a'. But why should it be bloody 'a' when it was obviously a number of some sort, 19 or whatever. I just didn't get it. And if maths was puzzling, French was an insult. The teacher, a diminutive old sweetie called Mrs Park, gave us all a little French book that starred a boring little brat called Toto, who lived in Paris and so spoke French. Sort of. It seemed that Toto spent his whole time staring at stuff as though struck dumb in wonder. *'Voici Toto'*, we read (yeah, hi Toto, you little fuck). *Regarde Toto*. Look at Toto. *Toto regarde la table*. We look at Toto while Toto looks at the table (and why, incidentally, do the Frogs think a table is feminine?). "*Oui*, Toto", replies his *père*, wearily, "*elle est une table*". After thoroughly banging this table business into the ground, *petit* Toto moves on thoughtfully on to the next thing, which is a chair. And after looking at the *chaise* for what seemed like several hours, he then decides to check out the *window*, and you got this delirious vision of beating the creepy little shit around *le tête* with the leg of his broken *chaise* and then chucking him out of the *fenêtre*. But Mrs Park was happy. What a great way to learn a foreign language.

Each subject came with its own teacher. The days when we had a Miss Krebopple to teach us a bit of everything were over. These teachers wore long black gowns, often chalk-stained and tattered so that they looked like crows as they strode down the corridor, their black rags billowing behind them. We had to call them all Sir, or, in a few cases, Miss or Ma'am. From the perspective of a small boy in shorts they were a curious mix, a bit like a box of cheap chocolates, some soft-centred, some hard and gritty, and a few who were just plain nuts. Among the former was poor old 'H-T', the maths master. He had been in action with the Merchant Navy during the war and the experience left its scars. He dithered and mumbled and shook. He retired shortly afterwards, and I was not altogether surprised when, a year or two after that, we were told he had died. The Boss made us sing 'For Those in Peril on the Sea' in H-T's honour. It was what he would have wanted, said Boss, although I had my doubts about that.

Our English master, Mr Cobberley, suffered from a severe form of Parkinson's disease which had withered his arm. He tucked the useless limb behind his gown where it shivered and flapped and, as it were, waved at you as he scribbled on the blackboard—a waste of time incidentally for no one could read his spidery writing. God knows how he managed to coax his old sit-up bike up Thorpe Hill. We devised cruel nicknames for him: Creep, Big Chief Broken Wing and so on. Everyone could, and did, do a 'Creep' impersonation. He was rather sweet, actually, and often told us that these were the best days of our lives and how proud we should be of everything.

In overall charge of the first years was a cadaverous old devil we called Pussy—probably because he had a habit of creeping up on you before clouting you one. A perpetual dewdrop quivered from the end of Pussy's long beak. When, eventually, it dropped with a splash, a sister droplet instantly formed in its place and hung there in its turn until gravity did the rest. When he served school dinner you waited with baited breath: when and where would it fall? Bets might be taken. Plates were snatched away. Then, with a terrible splosh, another bit of Pussy hit some luckless bastard's mash. Unusually Pussy taught all sorts of things from English to general science (his sprinkler nose fizzing little piles of chemicals as he stalked the lab). His catchphrase when teaching English was: "*no we-wes, no it-its, no then-thens*'. To repeat any of these words twice in one sentence was the mark of an illiterate, warned Pussy. Later on, with the gathered informality of age, we began to call him 'Puss'. "Puss the Magic Dragon", we sang, "lives in Hut Three", or at least he taught there. We, fortunately, lived in Hut Two.

The most fearsome of all the masters was old 'Dickie' Burford, better known as Burf the woodwork teacher. He had a partner in the metal workshop called Ben. "Burf-and-Ben", we sang, to the tune of the Flowerpot Men, *"Burf-and-Ben, Work-shop-men!"* Burf had been part of the school for as long as anyone could remember. Now he was nearing retirement, angry and hairless apart from a terrible little black toothbrush moustache. He seems to have been one of those people, not rare among school teachers, who pass their lives in a permanent state of irritation. Almost on my first day Burf had a go at me. Evidently he found my dovetail joint lacking in finesse. There were errors in this joint. His way of remonstrating was to crouch down to your level and thrust his face forward to look you in the eye. From about three inches away you could make out every bristle of his horrible Hitler moustache and catch the sour whiff of his breath. "Do you want a good hidin?" he would ask with apparent curiosity. "Eh?" *"Do-you-want-a-good-hidin?"* "Yes Sir, I mean, no Sir". *"Then do it properly,* boy". Someone remembered cutting himself quite badly with a chisel: blood all over the place. Burf's reaction was to threaten to clip his ear. "I never cut myself again", laughed the boy. Lesson learned.

Another Burf story concerned an illicit book that some enterprising boy once kept on the Grand National. Burf's horse came nowhere, whereat the angry woodwork teacher informed on the lad, who received his due of a whacking. But to do him justice, Burf would probably have done the same even if his horse had won, at least after he had collected his winnings. Like H-T, Burf retired only to drop dead almost immediately. I imagined him quite literally exploding with rage at having no boys left to frighten. I had read of such cases in the history books. Attila the Hun, for instance, one moment top guy of the ancient world, next minute, boom!, all exploded. Terribly sad.

The boys in my class were all local lads, either from the town or one of the little brick villages about, with names like Kegworth (pronounced *Kegg-eh*), Barrow (*Barra*) or Queniborough (*Quen-eh*). Those from Shepshed prowled about in a glowering pack led by an enormous lout called Harvey. "Giz us yore brake mun-eh", they would snarl. "I ain't gorrote", you'd reply, politely. Most of them spoke like my grandad:

"gerrout me rowd" (excuse me); "gizzit ere" (may I have it, please?); "yavin owt teet?" (care for a nibble, my man?), "are ain't yorn" (it doesn't belong to you), "gun gerraz a cob" (would you mind fetching me a bread roll?), "av no truck wi'im" (I have doubts about his trustworthiness), "bit parky up me coggie" (oh dear me, there's a hole in my bathing costume). The class fat boy, Yarbles, was seen as a bit of posh, being the son of a publican.

For a week or two I was regarded with a mixture of curiosity and suspicion. "What's it *lark* bein' a Boarder?" they would ask, one after the other. I said it was all right, but when they kept up this cretinous barrage, I began to invent stories. We were kept in chains most of the time, and don't tell anyone but I'm here on a secret mission. We're building a space rocket, actually. "*Gerron*!" I assumed the leadership of a troop of fellow geeks, mostly gangly, bespectacled beanpoles of high IQ but low social status. We were the Marren Gang. As an identifiable clique we received threats from rival gangs, the Killerz from Kegg-eh, say, or the Bashers from Barra, though we were far too timid to respond. There was one particularly annoying kid, a half-wit called Jake, who was always challenging us to a fight. The odd thing was that he was absolutely no good at fighting. One grew weary of knocking him to the ground and kicking his arse for him. Like the black knight in Monty Python, he just didn't know when to stop. He was no problem, but all the same I needed to watch out. Speaking with what they saw as a posh-boy's voice marked me out as a class enemy.

One way of endearing yourself to the masses was to do well at games. This was not an option I relished, but for the first term I did make a small effort. After all, I could swim pretty well ("got yer coggeh?"), and, thanks to hours of fun on the airmen's training course and not weighing very much, I could shin up a rope as though born to the gym. Being without my specs for rugby, I could never see the ball coming and usually ran off in the wrong direction, but I could at least tackle. Since I was a Boarder, the games teacher, Tes Egan, who was also housemaster at the Hole, showered undeserved praise on my footling attempts to grab the ball. "Oh well done, Gianessi", he would cry as the big Italian boy brought down a racing forward. Then I would jump on top, quite pointlessly. "*....And* Marren", he felt obliged to add. Gamesmanship paid dividends. Once, in the gym, a snarling killer from Kegg-eh was contesting the ownership of a rope with me when the top lout, Harvey himself, strolled over. Uh-oh. With a sharp word of command he ordered the fawning minion to take himself off, adding over his shoulder to me that "eeza tosser". They liked a show of physicality, did these hard lads. I only wish now that I'd smacked the little tosser's head as he slunk away.

My form, as I say, was 1D. If you thought we were thick you should have seen form 1E or 1F (there were, for reasons lost in history, no forms 1B or C). Form 1A represented our academic elite. 'A' stood for 'accelerated'. So brilliant were these geniuses that they took their GCE 'O'-levels a year early and so, by skipping the Fifth, ended up in the Sixth Form at the age of fifteen. In pursuance of this futile goal they were given more homework. On the other hand the boys of 1A did not have to carve wood under Burf's threatening eye, nor endure being lined up in stiff battledress to be shouted at on wet Wednesday afternoons. 1A was a caste apart and no one seemed to have much to do with them. They even had a classroom in the main school instead of in the huts outside. Why was I not among these privileged swots? Because someone had blundered. That mistake was rectified after the first term exams.

At that time boys still outnumbered girls by about four to one. This was in no way disadvantageous to the Marren gang, for girls were beneath our notice unless they were particularly pretty, in which case we were terrified of them. Dark faces were also rare. We had a few white Europeans: Poles, Ukrainians, Italians, the sons of wartime exiles. The Hole boys included a Szota (Showt-a), a big strapping Pole, as well as Charlie from Lagos, and, later on, three boys from India and another from Hong Kong. But the Hole-dwellers were seen as a separate caste, being middle class. The day boys and girls were mainly, I would say, provincial small-town working class, as well as homogeneous and white.

In no time at all I was feeling ashamed of my school, of the town, of the whole bloody county. This was no way to carry on, but frankly I felt uncomfortable here, marooned among people who did not talk like me, or act like me, or, as far as I could see, even think like me. At village schools this never mattered much because village schools were only a lark, and nine-year-olds are the same the world over. But by the time you reach eleven or twelve, self-consciousness starts to take charge. Something wrong here, I thought. What would Biggles have done? Or James Bond? Make good friends with Harvey, probably. And then bump him off and screw his girlfriend. What to do, what to do? So I did what I always did when in difficulties. I lay low and bided my time. And then I did nothing.

Kite flying with little brother on Mountsorrel Hill on a day off from the Hole.

CHAPTER FIVE

Alarums and Excursions

Almost as soon as I arrived at the Hole, faithful Nanna sent me a short letter to remind me that she came to town on Saturday for her shopping and that we could meet, if I liked. Well, yes, being desperate for a loved and familiar face, I did very much like. That day Fanny was doling out the juniors' pocket money and I cunningly took the opportunity to ask if I could spend the day with my granny. "Is there a letter?" I produced Nanna's note that, strictly speaking, should have been addressed to Fanny, not me, but, much to my surprise, it was good enough to get me a day pass. We met in what would become our usual trysting place in Loughborough's newly opened Wimpy Bar, where, with a happy smile, I told my startled grandma that I would be coming home with her on the bus. Never in my life did I appreciate Remlap as I did then, for its modest comforts, its greasy home cooking, and its small but friendly telly. It was to be my air-raid shelter in what looked like a long war. From then on I took the bus to Remlap about once a week, usually on Sunday afternoon, sometimes with a friendly boarder in tow. Once I even took Nigerian Charlie to meet the gramps, though he seemed ill at ease, and left a trail of mud over the living room carpet. "Is he your friend, that blackie?" asked Nanna, nervously.

All went well until the day she poisoned me. She had rounded off my usual kid's lunch of tinned oxtail soup (with white bread to dunk in it) followed by fried fish-and-chips and a cream pastry I had chosen that very morning from the market. As bad luck would have it, it was infected with salmonella, and so it was a very sad and puking little boy who returned to the Hole that evening. There was the most tremendous fuss. "What did you eat?" demanded the Boss. I told him, leaving out the infected pastry. "Oxtail-soup-and-fish-and-chips!" he repeated incredulously, as though I'd been supping with the three witches in Macbeth. He repeated it for Fanny's benefit: "this boy has been eating *oxtail-soup-and-fish-and-chips*!" What was wrong with that? Christ it was better than the crap they served us with at the Hole. But for a while they saw Nanna as the toxic nanny in a house of germs. Future escapes to Mountsorrel were accompanied by health warnings especially about lunch—no dead dog's tails, mind, and watch out for those eyes of newt.

That first term at the Hole lasted about 100 days according to the calendar but more like three years in Kidworld. The day before father came to pick me up for the first of two 'free weekends' at home crawled by like an arthritic snail: a day that was like a year, a year whose days are long (thank you, Oscar). When the school bell finally buzzed, I biked furiously Hole-wards and there was my Dad waiting in the hall in his uniform. It was one of only two moments in my life when I found myself unable to speak a single word (the other was when I had to put down my poor ailing doggie). "Hello Peter, how's tricks?" asked a smiling Dad. After a few gulps and heavy breathing, I managed to say: "Daddy!" As we set off in the Morris I very properly apologised for this loss of self-control. "Don't mention it", said understanding Dad. "I expect your Ma will be just the same." In fact she was fussed and bothered because we were late, and she had had to keep our dinner warm in the oven. It was pheasant with roasted potatoes and sprouts followed by apple crumble and custard, and I gobbled it all down in front of the television. Yes, I could do anything I liked that night.

Father had bought me the birthday present I had carefully chosen for him: another little box of set moths from Watkins and Doncaster. I had made a long list of specimens I wanted, in the hope, of course, that he would get the whole lot. But, being Dad, he didn't think I could possibly want all those dull little things and so selected only the biggest and most colourful ones on the list—sleek hawkmoths, tiger moths as bright as Airfix paint, and fawn-coloured eggars like winged teddy bears. So it was a happy, and, for once, well-fed, eleven-year-old that sprawled in the big armchair watching Bronco and batting away the boring questions about dorms and baths and whether I had packed a clean vest. They were in no hurry to send me to bed either. I had grown in their eyes; I had aged more than a few weeks since I left The Mount.

I had grown up at Hatton Park School too, where I sauntered down at half-term to visit my old chums and teach them some rugby.

My tackling class went down a storm, and when I strolled into the classroom afterwards, being unwilling to clear off just yet, the teacher, Miss Southgate, gave me what I considered to be an adult-to-adult look as if to say, what can I do for you now, oh attractive stranger? I liked this new turn of events. "Respect!" I thought. I'm getting a bit of that at last. This must be what it's like to be grown-up, I thought.

On that first Saturday, one of the last warm days of the year, I held my twelfth birthday party. Kids big and small trailed into the park bearing little gifts of toffee and fruit gums, one of them with a little silver William IV sixpence sellotaped to the packet. There is still a residual glow from that distant afternoon at The Mount, like Wordsworth's 'emotion recollected in tranquillity' only the other way round. It was as though I had never been away, that the past weeks at the Hole had been nothing but a dream, and that life could go on now as it always had, carefree and full of friends, warm and comfortable, safe from spiteful second-years and prefects. We village boys laughed and played together on the lawn, dashing in and out of the trees as the autumn sun cast long shadows on the grass and my mother called us in for birthday tea. Could life get any sweeter? And then I opened my eyes and it was Monday morning with the bell ringing and a damp patch on the pillow, waking up, in Cyril Connolly's words, 'with all the accumulated misery of the mornings before'.

Still, you can't be miserable all the time. Boys quickly get used to a routine, and even at the Hole, with every half-hour mapped out for you, so to speak, there was time to please yourself. You could, for instance, glue together and paint a plastic model. My Kawasaki Hien monoplane fighter was much admired in its snazzy jungle camouflage and dinky red propeller. And you could read; I had discovered James Bond and enjoyed the clipped conversations and lashings of ultra-violence, though the hero's addiction to women was a mystery to this young fan. We were sometimes allowed out to the Odeon cinema on Saturday night to sneak into A-rated films like Dr Strangelove (in this case by getting ourselves 'adopted' by two louts, and, once inside, getting the hell away from them). There was also a film club at school that ran schoolboy classics on Friday evening (Guns of Navarone! Cockleshell Heroes!

HMS Defiant!). And the occasional big event at school, such as the school play or Speech Day when the masters paraded in their best gowns and hoods, and some senile old buffer would dish out the prizes and tell us how lucky we were.

Among the best fun was Guy Fawkes's Night, when we built a huge bonfire in the paddock and roasted foil-wrapped potatoes in the embers. Dressing the Guy was a useful way of getting rid of worn-out school uniforms and so the scarecrow we hoisted onto the bonfire looked very much like one of us in his tattered school cap and tie, with a satchel across his shoulders and a pair of last season's winklepickers sticking out from under his trousers. This was one of the occasions when the Boss allowed our youthful spirits to let rip. Each of us had a tin of black Cherry Blossom polish in our pocket for administering a debagging, by rugby tackling a boy to the ground, pulling down his trousers and plastering his bottom with blacking. Some boys were so terrified of the scrum of yelling kids heading their way that they took off like hares over the paddock wall and down Ashby Road, and were quite possibly never seen again. That November pretty well every junior kid's face and bum was black with a mixture of banger burns and boot polish. I loved it. It took about a week for the excitement to die down.

At about the same time, the fair came to Loughborough: one of those ancient travelling fairs that date from the Middle Ages and which are used to test-drive the latest wild rides. It filled the market square and ran down the side streets for what seemed miles, all coloured lights and dodgems and waltzers and ghost trains amid an overarching fug of fried onions. The best rides... were the scariest. As a veteran of the funfair at Withernsea in those far-off Yorkshire days, nothing fazed me (the ghost train, for instance, was a joke). I remember seeing big kids, even grown-ups, practically melting with funk as they waited for their turn on The Looper, a terrifying rotating cage for two in which your stomach ended up somewhere between your ears. Another good one was The Rotor, a giant spinning drum that rotated at exactly the same speed as an LP, leaving you stuck to the sides as the floor slipped from under your feet. The more daring gravity riders turned themselves upside down as they whizzed round and round with a kind of frozen joy on their faces. The

Rotor was so exciting there was even a deck for spectators. It has long since been replaced by a doubtless safer and more sensible engine called The Gravitron. Some of the senior boys might be seen ambling along with a girl in tow, possibly having won her at the shooting gallery or coconut shy. All I ever managed to win was a goldfish, but it was jolly good fun nonetheless.

There were also alarums and excursions in the dorms. There's no denying it, it could get a bit noisy in there sometimes. Dorm raids were risky since the raiders were rarely caught and it was usually the victims that were punished (see Chapter Seven, *Figures of Authority* for an account of one ill-fated raid). Another merry prank was to 'apple pie' someone's bed by pulling up the lower sheet and folding it back over the counterpane so that everything looked hunky-dory until the victim tried to slip into bed. It was a kind of bed wedgie. The fun lay in watching the sucker's face when, slipping into bed with a sigh after his hard day. he fetched up short, knocking his knee against his chin with a shout of "bastards!" With a bit more time to spare, you could also undo the bolts that secured the bedframe so that the whole caboodle would collapse in a heap. This was always extremely amusing, especially if the suspicious fellow had first inspected the sheets for signs of an apple pie. One could also loosen the top of someone's hot water bottle so that the scalding hot water would splash all over the victim the instant he clutched it to his bosom, though this was possibly too vicious to be all that funny. Once, probably during the term when I seemed to be ill a lot, they isolated my bed with towels on a string. It was quite funny the first time. The point of it all, I suppose, was to rub in the fact that jolly japes are apt to erupt at any time, even in bed, even in your sleep: there was never a time when you could be off your guard. It is amazing the fun an imaginative boy can find in an initially unpromising situation.

After lights out we often told stories which were intended to be either scary or 'dirty'. I quickly picked up the ribald songs about dicky di-does and something called a thrashing-machine. One of the boys offered to introduce me to a strange habit he called 'tossing'. In my innocence I couldn't see the point of it, but this boy seemed to enjoy it, whatever it was, and could be heard rattling about in his bed after dark until someone, probably Charlie, threatened to kick his arse. Naturally all this banter revived one's speculations about the mystery of sex. For years I had known and not known. I knew that boys and girls were shaped differently in certain ways and that babies were made by the act of sexual intercourse—though at first I misheard and thought it was 'sexual intercalls', like ordering flowers over the phone. I had a vague idea that married folk only did it once in a while, like, say, once per baby. Nonsense, scoffed my interlocutor. They were at it the whole time, like rabbits. Surely not? Not my parents at any rate, or my grandparents, or any of their friends (the very idea!). I knew these people and they just weren't like that. At all events, I resolved to get to the bottom of all this and, at the first opportunity, told Mummy what I had learned. *Is it true*, I demanded, looking her sternly in the eye? "Yes", she said, simply (well, *you might have bloody told me*). Grown-ups certainly know how to keep a secret. That was the beginning and the end of my sex education; the end, I suppose, of my innocence. Good grief, I thought. Like bloody rabbits! *Like James Bond*!

CHAPTER SIX

End of Term Report

Towards the end of term we, the pupils of 1D, in the Hallam Hut smelling of leather and varnish, undertook tests in all the major subjects. Having overcome my aversion to Toto and algebra I felt I had done all right, in fact possibly a bit too all right. Had I done badly the case for removing me from the Hole might be made. The Boss showed surprising interest in my progress. Then one day, about a week before the school broke up for Christmas, he called me to his office. I was to pack my things at once, he said. Uh? My father, he explained patiently, had been called away. He was going to a place called Labuan, in Borneo he understood, to assist in the putting down of some insurrection. Father was on his way to pick me up right now. Boss had agreed to release me before the term was up since it might well be some time before young Marren saw his Daddy again. So he won't be back for Christmas, I stammered (Christmas without Dad would be…it would be like turkey without the sprouts, I thought). No, said Boss, almost certainly he won't be back for Christmas. Get along with you now, and pack those bags. Have a word with Mr Williams [the form master] first.

On balance this should have been brilliant news—a whole extra week away from the Hole! Shame about Dad, of course, but he had been away before and he would probably want to buy me an extra good present by way of restitution. Yet this unexpected windfall was the straw that broke the dam of my pent-up anguish. I found Taff Williams and tried to tell him I was off home right now, and so toodle-oo and all that. But instead I found myself blubbing helplessly into the crook of his chalky gown. I was an over-wrought little first-year. Taffy decided we should go and have a word with Pussy, the fatherly overseer of the newbies. Pussy, with a fresh dewdrop trembling on the end of his beak, stooped to take a good look at this tearful kid and observed that "he's had a good cry already, and, look! Look! He's about to have another one!" "Arghhh, boo-HOO-HOOO". "Off you go", said Pussy.

END OF TERM REPORT

The Mount was looking wintry, the grounds dark and brooding with a premonition of frigid blasts from the Urals. But the fire was blazing, and, as before, there was something tasty in the oven and something good on the telly. The Hole seemed a safe way off by the time my first school report arrived by post a few days later. The school did a good report, all written out in ink on thick paper, tinted pale blue for extra gravitas, with the school crest on the back. This one was further embellished by the beautiful, foliated handwriting of Taff Williams, like a medieval manuscript. But, instead of contenting himself with 'good' or 'satisfactory', and so saving himself ink and energy, Taff had something to tell the parents of *this* boy.

My school report: 'Sensitive and a disposition to panic are proving drawbacks...'

After a while, school reports become routine and no one takes any notice of them. This one, being the first from the Hole, and by far the most in-depth report ever devoted to poor little me, made a great impression. For a start I had come second, and a *good* second too, only pipped at the post by some beast called Thorpe. That meant that I would be heading straight for Form 1A next term. Most of the teachers had given me the old thumbs-up. Taff professed to finding my knowledge of history 'quite startling', and even H-T, the crumbling algebra guy, believed that I had finally settled down to 'good, steady industry' (good, steady *what*?). Mum thought the handwriting of Burf the woodwork tyrant (he, predictably, was less enthusiastic) had great character; and so it had—the letters looked like little mallets and saws, digging into the paper . One saw now why the report was written on thick paper. Poor creepy Mr Cobberley had scrawled a word or two that looked like 'eserrt qrrgsss', but he, presumably, was happy too.

It was the form-master's comments that brought me up a bit. Taff must have inscribed them with the splash marks of my tears drying on his gown. '*Sensitivity and a disposition to panic are proving drawbacks to him*', were his words. But I was 'of academic bent already', he continued, and, since I was obviously OK in the old brain department, he thought 'a measure of justifiable self-confidence' would ensure me a good 'career' in the school. What the hell does that mean, I asked Mum. Doesn't he realise that I am leader of the Marren Gang? "Don't swear, Peter. It means you are shy, just like I used to be at your age". That was Mum, of course, always relating things to her own, very limited experience. That didn't seem to me to offer a full explanation of Taff's extraordinary choice of words for a boy that had come so very nearly top of the form in, I would like to emphasise, rather trying circumstances. What it actually meant was that, in Taffy's opinion, I was a pathetic cry baby who should make a real effort to pull himself together double quick before some lout smacked him one. Or to put it more succinctly, little Marren should 'man up', pronto. Fuck him, I thought. Now, what does 'Tes' Egan have to say?

Egan was housemaster at the Hole, and, as I say, he felt sorry for me. He had pretended to be impressed by my rugby tackling and so gave me my best ever games report: '*Shows commendable courage and tenacity*'. Not 'skill' you notice. But with his housemaster's hat on, Tes found me 'still a little diffident'. Why did they all feel the need to use hard words? I had no idea what 'diffident' meant, although I knew Giant Despair had a wife of that name in *Pilgrim's Progress*, and she was a bad lot, as well as a woman. Not good then. Once again, Mum was on to it. "It means shy", she said. "He's saying you're shy, like I was". So, that's two 'shys' already. Again, I thought this fell some way short of a proper explanation. 'Tes' had in fact noticed that little Marren had retreated so far into his shell that it was practically impossible to communicate with him. One day, after separating me from my opponent in some scrap, he insisted on walking with me to school (I was performing in a gymnastics display for a parents evening, and was full of justifiable dread).

"Well, what was that all about, Marren?" asked Tes.

"Oh, nothing, Sir."

"Were they picking on you?"

"Me? Oh, no. No,"

"Because if they are, I'll discourage them. Are you having trouble with Charlie?" he asked suddenly.

"Sir?"

"Because if he's bothering you, I'll enjoy belting him from wall to wall".

He said this with some vehemence. Clearly the thought of knocking the daylights out of plump Charlie was very pleasant to him.

"No, no", I said, truly. "It's not that". Questions, questions. Why doesn't he leave me alone?

I never did tell him what was bothering me. He was a grown-up, and a PE teacher besides, and he could not possibly understand my predicament, even if I was able to put it into words. Besides, expressions of sympathy from figures of authority had a tendency to make me blub. What I might have said was: "it's like this, 'Tes', I'm feeling a bit lonely, harassed and unhappy, and I'm not feeling so great about this fucking gym display either, so, thanks, but if you don't mind I'll deal with it in my own way". For, knowing Tes, his solution would have been to give me extra PE. He was incapable of realising that some boys dread games on account of our being no good at them. They expose us to mockery and humiliation. The only sensible strategy for the likes of us is to keep a low profile, and, if possible, organise a duffer's league of lankies, fatsos and all-round ball-dodgers. But PE and organised games was Tes's life. Being mostly brawn himself, he could not imagine what it was like to be mostly brain—to be a little brainy geek surrounded by big brawny blokes. And besides, he had decided against all evidence to the contrary that I was capable of performing creditably, if I really tried. "We'll have you in the Junior Fifteen next term", he promised.

As for Boss, whose section followed in a kind of summing up, he considered all of the above to be 'a good report on a boy who has courage and a growing personality'. By 'growing' he meant that I did not yet have a discernible personality. I was just a small, frightened boy. So, altogether, I totted up two references to 'shy' and two to 'courage'. Here, perhaps, was the key, but neither of my parents were capable of grasping it. It occurs to me now that shyness and courage are related; they indicate, surely, a tendency to suffer in silence. By banging on about the courage he claimed he saw in me, might the Boss be telling the parents, albeit obliquely, that I *needed* courage?

"A very good report", said mother with finality. "Form 1A!" You could tell she was pleased. "How hard you must have worked!" (I had done as little as possible). What did I want for Christmas? Here I had my answer ready. "Get me", I said, "a *Chemistry Set*".

Although school science had been one of my weaker subjects—it was mostly physics and so incomprehensible—it revived my love of chemistry, or, to be more precise, the wonderful phizzes, pops, stinks and bangs that can take place when one substance is heated with another. In those days chemistry sets were far more impressively stocked than the pallid apologies you get today—all baking powder and starch, with warnings on anything that isn't actually edible. The bare list of a Merit chemistry set circa 1960 sounds magical: litmus blue, methyl orange, flowers of sulphur, tartaric acid (which sounds thrillingly dangerous, though it isn't). The American ones even had radioactive stuff. On the box, which was of impressive size, there was always a picture of a boy about my age with neatly parted hair, wearing a collar and tie, and happily pouring coloured liquid into a tube while proud Dad tugged at his pipe. He didn't know that the boy was making explosives, or possibly drugs.

I set up my lab on the trestle table in the spare bedroom after packing up the old model railway for the last time. For the experiments I had in mind, I needed more dangerous ingredients, and so mother's shopping list now looked something like this: one doz. eggs, two botts milk, lettuce, one oz (approx.) potassium nitrate, small loaf (sliced), small bottle dilute hydrochloric acid, one pkt. tincture of iodine, soap, one oz manganese dioxide, one box standard pins. The pins were for my insect collection.

The chemist shrewdly spotted that my list was a combination of substances that, properly mixed, would make a neat small bomb and refused to hand them all over. But that was OK; you just picked up the missing stuff at a different chemist. I also collected useful stuff from the kitchen: starch powder, Epsom salts, aluminium foil, tungsten wire from spent light bulbs. There was, of course, a much wider range of substances to steal at school, but, as one quickly learned, certain compounds, sodium hydroxide being one, were apt to burn a hole in your pocket. My career as a midget chem-head did not last long. One day, suddenly bored with mixing chemicals, I tipped the whole lot into my largest beaker and ran it up with the old bunsen. There is, I am sure, still a stain on the ceiling of that corner room at The Mount where the Christmas present met its final conflagration.

A few years later, when I thought all that was behind me, I beheld a collection of all the elements in the Science Museum: bottle on bottle, displayed in proper periodic order with indium, dysprosium, boron, mendelevium and the rest of them; all the fundamental matter of the universe in a single box (and what did it matter that most of the elements looked more or less the same?). A flame lit up behind my eyes. One day I was going to *do* this lot. And, as it happens, I did, more or less. Apart from mendelevium. Don't have a spot of it in the garage, do you, by any chance?

By the time I was blowing up the spare room, father had gone off for his adventure in Labuan, which, as I had discovered in my kid's atlas, is a little island off the coast of Brunei with an air strip and some oil tanks. In doing so, Dad managed to miss the coldest, longest winter of our time, the season when England turned into Greenland for a month or two. It began to snow on Boxing Day, and it snowed and snowed, all day, and all the next, and all the week after. Great stalactites of ice hung from window sills and broken pipes. Dunes of snow covered the grounds until you practically needed a team of huskies to reach the shop. We dug trenches to the car and down the path, lugged hod after hod of coal up the stairs from the cellar, and installed a paraffin stove in the bathroom (at some risk of death by carbon monoxide poisoning, as I suppose I should have realised). It was great fun for us village lads, larking about building igloos and fighting running battles up and down the frozen garden. It was less fun for mother, left alone in a large and indifferently heated house with two snow-covered boys. It must have occurred to me that if it was getting a bit chilly at The Mount, with all its attendant comforts, it was going to be very much grimmer at the Hole while this arctic weather lasted.

Funnily enough, I don't think I cared. I was getting used to saying goodbye. I was buoyed up by the prospect of joining the accelerated swots in 1A, and, having evidently acquired courage and a growing personality, I was not as forlorn as I might have been, indeed probably should have been. Besides, as mother kept reminding me, "it will get lighter in the evenings now". This was obviously a great comfort to her, but perhaps she meant it metaphorically as well as literally. Life was lightening up. It would never be quite so dark again. And so it was with a stiff-lipped cheerio that I stuck on my horrible cap, shouldered my satchel, and trudged down resolutely through the drifts to the waiting car.

A note on the Malaya–Indonesia confrontation of 1961–66

The reason for my father's sudden posting to Labuan was his recent experience of RAF freight movements to and from Singapore. In 1961, Malaya, independent since 1957, was about to hook up with the former British colonies of North Borneo and Sarawak, as well as

Singapore, to form the confederation of Malaysia. The plan had British support but the leader of Indonesia, a stinker called Sukarno, had other ideas. He regarded himself as top dog in the region, and, besides, he wanted a slice of oil-rich Borneo for himself. So he backed the North Kalimantan National Army (Kalimantan was their name for Borneo), a proxy guerrilla band whose job it was to grab as much land and oil as possible while Sukarno spouted all the usual rubbish about freedom and Socialism. By the time father joined the British forces at Labuan, the guerrillas had tried and failed to seize the oilfields and capture the Sultan of Brunei. The British lion roared as loudly as it still could and sent in the Ghurkhas. The British forces under the splendidly named General Walter Walker were based on Labuan island in the placid waters of Brunei Bay. Father busied himself with loading Valettas, a troop-carrying aircraft. In those sticky early days the SAS ringed the airfield in case of attack. After a while, the tension lessened, and Dad, with a hole in his trousers, came home. Trouble with Sukarno continued for several years until he was unseated in a coup in 1966, after which relations were normalised and the confrontation fizzled out, the way they always do. Until next time.

CHAPTER SEVEN

Figures of Authority

Before I went to boarding school there were very few people in my life who had both power over me and the determination to use it. My parents rarely interfered in our day-to-day escapades. Nor did school hold any terrors, with the possible exception of Mrs Robinson, the Country Dancing fiend. But all of a sudden, the world seemed to be full of power freaks intent on keeping me in order. Quite what they all expected from me I was never sure. Perhaps it depended on their mood but a state of abject and terrified submission seemed to be the broad intention. My life had taken a sudden downturn; it seemed to me to be unnecessarily harsh. The design of those in power, insofar as I could understand it, was to make a man of me by expelling what was left of the boy.

The most senior of these figures of doom was God, or, as I prefer to call him, for purposes of insult, 'god'. Until then I had more or less taken god for granted. Even though he didn't make much sense (where exactly was heaven, and what was there to do when you got there?), I sort of half-believed in him in much the same way as one wanted to believe in Santa Claus. God seemed to be a well-intentioned kind of guy. Like Santa, he had a kindly bearded face. At least when in disguise as Jesus (as seen on TV that is—for Jesus was a big star in the Fifties) he seemed to be a caring sort of chap, going about in a long white robe dispensing wisdom and solace to the downtrodden and oppressed— and being nice to little children. God, you thought, is on my side, except when I'm naughty. But once I entered the Hole ('abandon hope, all ye who enter here'), god seemed to have changed his mind. At morning assembly, under the glare of the black-robed masters, he required, in the words of the hymn, 'praise and praise without ceasing'. He obviously liked praise; plus a regime of constant self-abasement. If he had seemed fairly benign and Santa-like when we were infants, it was as if he was waving his celestial cane now that we were teenagers.

The worst thing about god was the hour he took from our lives every Sunday morning. For us, god's place was the small, undistinguished Victorian church in the housing estate of Thorpe Acre, built to house the workers of Loughborough's Brush factory. Its single bell would toll funereally as we trudged along in our macs and grey Sunday suits. We crammed the back pews, juniors at the front with our chewing gum and noughts-and-crosses, seniors at the back with their Parades and the racing results. Boss planted himself a few rows to the front, well within glaring distance. He had this habit of turning round during a hymn and, if we were misbehaving, cranking up the volume to an appalling roar. In front of him sat row upon row of elderly ladies in hats, horrible great woolly things shaped like bells or cushions or beehives. The service, conducted by a youngish vicar with a strong resemblance to Bamber Gascoigne, with added pimples, was standard fare: unvarying, wall-to-wall Christian grovelling from start to finish, apart from the sermon, and that never seemed to have anything to say to us.

My parents had never tried to impose god on me. I considered myself fortunate to have as a father a lapsed Catholic who hated the church and a mother who, though nominally C of E, never went there (and grandparents who did but were believers of the most humble and diffident kind). I was therefore unprepared for this angry, pissed-off god who, in exchange for our attendance in church, morning assemblies and prayers before and after every meal, offered us only a fraudulent and entirely pointless everlasting life by way of bait. God obviously thought we were idiots ("This party's going on forever. And you *can't* leave. You've got to stay. The boss said so, and he also insists you have a great time"— Christopher Hitchens). Halfway through every church service we chanted the Nicene Creed, a summary of what we supposedly believed in. It went on and on and I still know it by heart, both versions. I was enough of a historian to realise that the Creed was nothing but a knock-down compromise imposed on the church by Emperor Constantine, criminal, mass murderer, and stupendous shit. You didn't have to believe in the old brute 'god' in order to hate him. Perhaps I might have come to a different view had not church attendance been compulsory and RE rammed down our throats in class every week. My inevitable disbelief might then have been tinged with regret. But my teenage self was not inclined to forgive him for those lost Sunday mornings.

In my third year I did attend confirmation classes, and was eventually confirmed in the Christian faith by our pimpled vicar. Confirmation was a rite of passage expected by teachers and parents, like winning a school prize or the colours. Like those at the Feeding of the Five Thousand, I was happy to take the lord's fish—quite literally, for the Sunday School's proximity to the chip shop was the main reason for our sudden interest in Christianity. And a good slurp of saliva-laced 'British' sherry at 'holy' communion always made the time go by just that little bit faster. All the same, my reception into the Church of England had this much going for it: I did not have to hand over any money; I did not have to sign anything. I was not asked to make any pledges of any kind. A mere whispered 'yes' would do nicely when asked by the bishop if I was ready.

As a newly fledged atheist, I felt it my duty to try to undermine god's weekly half-hour in the RE class by getting them to discuss topics like evolution or the origin of the universe. "What was in The Beginning?" asked the teacher. The Big Bang, I asserted confidently. "Well then, who made the Big Bang?" was her triumphant follow-up. "Particle physics", I answered, without hesitation. I had no knowledge whatever of particle physics, but was willing to seize hold of anything to beat up that old fraud, god. RE, as far as I was concerned, was a waste of good science time. No one seemed interested in making the slightest effort to make religion interesting or palatable or relevant. Nor, in the spirit of the times, were they afraid to use it as a moral bludgeon. Once, in one of our would-be moral debates, I found myself having to defend the then white-minority regime in Rhodesia. We were all playing a part. It was not a subject I knew much about, or on which I felt strongly one way or the other, but the object of the exercise was to present an argument, and so I did my best. Yet just when things started swinging my way, the teacher suddenly burst forth with hair-raising tales of injustice, of brave Zimbabwean dads beaten up by cops, of their orphans begged for bread in the street. She wouldn't let it go until every member of the class had been shamed into voting her way, leaving poor lone Marren as the token Nazi.

Unlike god, Boss did not demand ceaseless praise, only instant and total obedience. He was, for most juniors, a rather remote figure, and one to approach with trepidation. You seemed to want to cram in the word "Sir" as many times as possible in a single sentence: "Good morning, Marren". "Ah, Sir, *good morning*, Sir, er, er, Sir". "Get along with you then". Boss seemed to go along with god on most practical points. An onward Christian (Liberal) soldier was Boss. But while the vicar could only preach about the everlasting punishments that god had in mind for sinners, Boss had a more proximate instrument of correction in the form of the cane. Most boarders got whacked on the bottom sooner or later and a few must have felt pretty sore throughout their stay. One of the commonest causes of a caning was the dorm raid, a small pitched battle in which some larger boys tore in, messed up the beds, threw blankets and pillows about, and then got the hell out before the housemaster turned up. It was rarely the wreckers that were punished, unless they were caught in the act, but those I shall call the wreckees. The theory, I suppose, was that we had wrecked our own beds. Early in my second year, our dorm had just been shaken up in a fairly good-natured way by the fourth formers next door when Fanny turned up, and in no pleasant mood. She screeched blue murder at the state of the room with pillows in the corners and sheets hanging from the windows. While she ranted on, my friend Mich unwisely continued to salvage his bedding instead of standing to attention like a sensible boy, and so drew her wrath on to himself. As the Boss led them down the hall stairs for a whacking, Fanny kept pointing to the hapless Mich. "*He's* the worst of them. *He's* the ring leader". Poor Mich was so obviously innocent that the Boss gave him only the same punishment as the rest: two strokes each, probably the minimum possible with his furious wife urging him on.

Everyday authority was delegated to Boss's earthly archangels, the prefects. To us little kids, these huge guys from the Upper Sixth were almost grown-ups, at least twice our size and weight, and with deep, loud voices. Their role was to enforce every petty rule in the house, of which there were, of course, plenty. It was a moot point—one I was too inexperienced to judge—at what point their legitimate duties turned into licensed bullying. Most of them had been through the mill themselves. Some, I'm sure, pretended to think that discipline was good for us, and that we would be glad of the toughening experience when we joined the army, or the prison service, or whatever. Like the chastened rebels in Lindsay Anderson's film, *If*, we would want to thank them. The harshest prefects tended to be those keenest on games and the CCF. Almost by definition they were also the loudest and dimmest. The brighter ones, like 'Big Gum' Wardrop, pride of the Hole, bound for Downing College, Cambridge in the autumn, were gentler, and may be had more on their minds than tormenting the helpless. Prefects were capricious. You had to watch their moods. One day they might indulge your carefully phrased banter, while on another the same exchange might land you with a page of logs. They themselves broke the rules at every opportunity. They met at forbidden coffee bars in town such as the notorious El Chico, haunt of chain-smoking, chick-chasing bandits. Years later, when Boss was nearing retirement, he confessed that he knew that some of them had abused his confidence and exceeded their authority. But he never interfered and always supported them in public.

Yet Boss could be surprisingly subtle. Once, when the Sixth Form was in disgrace for making a hullaballoo in the corridors and waking the whole house, one of them attempted a little *divertissement* by seeking to get me caned for visiting my grandmother. Boss elected not to tell the sneak that I had his full permission to do so, and, for his benefit, said loudly that I would be joining a punishment battalion the next day. But while the others picked apples, Boss invited me for a friendly stroll round the garden. I think we talked about flowers and trees. After an hour or so, Boss addressed the boys in the trees, sympathetically enough. "When prefects are in trouble", he advised, "it's as well to keep your head down." "And thank you, Marren," he added, "for your help. Very much appreciated. The rest of you can go. And mind yourselves".

Below the level of house prefect a kind of corporal's authority cascaded down the years if only because, in the last resort, the older boy was bigger and stronger than you, and could, if he chose, push you around. Even the Baby Dorm had an official in the diminutive form of McCretton who, by virtue of his dorm captaincy, occupied the central bed. His authority was limited, and, in the case of aggressive boys like

Charlie, purely nominal. But there was one person who could be pushed around by everybody, the one at the nadir of the inverted pyramid, and for a couple of years that sad sap was me.

The accumulated weight of all this authority felt crushing. I was, I think, made mildly paranoid by it. Once, over porridge, I looked up to the hulking rank of third years opposite and suddenly burst out, "You're all against me, the whole rotten, stinking lot of you!" Perhaps the porridge was particularly disagreeable that morning. One of the third years seemed surprised. He hardly knew who I was. "I've never said a word against you!" he pointed out, truly enough. Ah well, you probably will, I thought bitterly. It was easy to suppose that anyone not your friend was your enemy, and, since you didn't have any friends, that was pretty well everybody. There was little point in trying to fight back; the only way was to retreat into your mind-world where scalding repartee and violent revenge could be doled out, just as in the comics when the geeky kid takes off his specs, dons a masked cape and becomes Tiger Boy. For example, I could make Pussy drown inside his self-created dewdrop, and little McCretton could be made littler and littler until, with a merry stamp of his slippered foot, Tiger Boy crushed him like a bug. Sometimes I would base their comeuppance on one of the American horror comics Charlie lent me, such as the X-beams flashing from my magic specs or the agonising blasts of electricity from the ray-gun hidden in my satchel. At other times it might amuse me to spare the cringing creature and let him off with an annihilating word of warning. And then, just as the cowed villain was slinking out the door, I'd change my mind, and blast him into space. 'KPOW!', as they said in the Batman comics. 'A far, far better thing, toss-pot'. 'PTANGG!' '*Hasta la vista* scumbag'.

This very trying year had an upbeat ending. I was finding schoolwork quite interesting now, since joining the A-stream. At some point towards the end of the summer term, a large boy not noted for his academic attainment remarked: "you realise you're going to be top boy, don't you?" No, I hadn't realised that. It hadn't occurred to me at all. I hadn't done much revision, unlike my fellow baby-dormers who sat up in bed each morning trying vainly to cram thirty weeks of neglect into one panic-stricken swotothon. My thoughts were not on exam results but on the approaching weeks of glorious summer at The Mount when I would shed my year at the Hole and, like a butterfly, soar off into the benign Elysian sky.

It was with that prospect in mind that Boss found me lounging by the heap of coke outside, whistling with my hands in my pockets. He had a prefect in tow. "There's your rival, Salter", he said. "Top of IA. *Top of IA!*", he repeated. The odd thing was that he didn't seem to be talking to me, for whom this was definitely news, but to this Salter, who shot me a look. "Gosh", I said, to their retreating backs. "Does that mean I'm clever, then?"

It probably meant I was in the wrong school. Still, I had pleased the Boss. 'He has the makings of a scholar', he wrote happily on my pale-blue summer-term report. 'It unfolds striking prospects for the future'. Except that, with Boss's terrible writing, it looked more like 'stinking prospects', which seemed a bit ungenerous. But even that was not the best moment of the year. The best moment arrived shortly afterwards with a hymn called Dismissal, traditionally sung on the day before the school broke up for the summer:

> *Lord dismiss us, with thy blessing,*
> *Thanks for mercies past received.*

Small mercies, I thought, and the lord's blessing was, as usual, balanced by his threat to make those returning 'more faithful than before'. Well, that wouldn't be difficult. The great thing was that I was going home. Home where Dad was waiting by the white Morris, home with mother welcoming me into the bay-fronted lounge with hugs and home cooking, home with my friends and another round of carefree fun and adventure ahead; six spacious weeks in which life could resume as it had before, happy, free and full of possibilities.

CHAPTER EIGHT

Last Summer at The Mount

The Mount was still there, half hidden behind the big redwoods on its little hill, with the Varsities warming their engines on the airstrip beyond. By summer 1963 I had moved from the room I had always shared with Christy to the vacant one at the back, where my chemicals and specimens were stored, along with cages of caterpillars, my microscope and my row of reference books. There was probably some half-built Meccano crane in there too. My parents had given me a Set 6 as an advance birthday present and for being such a clever, 'courageous' and hard-working boy (ho ho). I loved the more advanced Meccano components, the brass and enamelled gears, the eccentrics, the arcane sprockets and couplings and crankshafts, but the models were a bore to build and the fiddly little nuts and screws were forever working loose. The cranes looked all right in their green and red livery, especially when you managed to sneak in a few more gears, but shortly after the fleeting moment of pride came the realisation that it had taken you all day to construct this half-assed object and, whoa, hang on, this thing's a bloody *toy*—and I'm a young biologist. I felt I had done with toys now.

For the times were a-changing, that summer of 1963. Even twelve-year-old kids could sense it. TV, for instance, was no longer the safe, sound but rather dreary thing we had grown up with. The new programmes on prime-time telly were gritty, modern and realistic. There was, for example, Steptoe and Son, a variant of Hancock in which the comedy-crook Sid James character was replaced by a wheedling old git of a dad forever dragging down his son's 60s aspiration for a better life. The new cop show, Z-Cars was much more brutal than Dixon of Dock Green. You wouldn't want this lot anywhere near your home. The Z-cops snarled at one another in incomprehensible northern accents and tore round the neighbourhood in fast cars, sirens blaring. Dr Who, the new sci-fi series, retained the familiar grandpa figure but got us all drawing pictures of monsters, especially the daleks with their hysterical speak-your-weight commands. All these shows had memorable theme tunes; they—and what was to become known as the Liverpool sound—defined the summer of '63. The new era was chrome-plated and had tail fins. We were over reassurance and into excitement. It was as if the baby boomers were at last taking over from their fussy, respectable parents.

The Brits were getting good at pop. Not long ago we were all whistling Moon River and other tunes that could equally have been sung by your Dad or even your grandad. But now, on the new pop show Ready, Steady, Go!, the only grown-up in sight was the elderly DJ in his shiny suit and dentures, telling us in conspiratorial tones that four lads from Liverpool were about to play their hit single 'She Loves You'. The words were mere pap—'she loves me, yeah, yeah, yeah!'—but the stuff these mopheads packed into it was amazing: the guitar chimes and arpeggios, the harmonies, that dissonant last chord and those headshaking 'whoos' that ought to have been faggy but somehow weren't. Mother clucked her tongue over their long hair (*hardly*, Mum), tight trousers and Cuban heels, but we knew at once that something wonderful was happening, and that, even in Longstanton, we could share it. We started to check out what else was going on in the hit parade. The top of the pops that week was a song called 'Bad to Me' by Billy J. Kramer and The Dakotas, and that too was written by Lennon and McCartney. These guys were so brilliant they were writing everybody else's songs! My love affair with the Beatles lasted about three years. I collected gum cards with their pictures on, and noted all their banter, and bought as many of their EPs and singles and LPs as I could afford. We knew all their hits in our house. Even Dad (actually, *especially* Dad) could sing them.

Meanwhile the boys' lives resumed after a fashion. We continued to head off on cycle expeditions, raced pine cones or now-battered Dinkies down improvised race tracks of sand, played about in the farmer's pig pens, swung on RAF ropes. We chased butterflies with our baggy nets and ammonia jars, and set them slightly more professionally than before. We generally managed to come home plastered in mud with bits of hay sticking out. But it wasn't quite the same as before. For one thing it was cool and cloudy most of the time. For another a distance had grown between the village lads and me. My best mate Jonathan had been poached by my rival Lefty, a troublesome, loutish fellow from the wrong end of the village. We no longer had so much to share and talk about. We were friends but no longer intimates. You did the same things as before but, I don't know, somehow the gloss had been removed, the light dimmed, the sun obscured by cloud. Or maybe I was just getting older.

Moreover, I discovered that even the sweet apples of Longstanton could contain maggots. There were wolves in those Elysian Fields. One day Jonathan and I were cycling past one of the mushroom-shaped, wartime pillboxes, unique to our corner of the world, when we were ambushed by a gang of older youths and 'kidnapped'. They forced us inside the concrete bunker at knifepoint. What was in their minds I do not know, but after doing their best to frighten us, they eventually got bored and cleared off. Jonathan was robust enough to fraternise with the louts and treat the whole thing as a bit of a joke. I, on the other hand, had been genuinely frightened, and shocked that even home turf

Mother and her two growing boys, Remlap, 1964.

had become a place of danger. Let's tell Dad, I suggested. "Nah", said Jonathan, who had already shrugged it off, "c'mon, race you to the gate".

Another small maggot was the day of the car crash. Father was taking me back to the Hole one foggy night when he bashed into the back of a lorry. There were no seat belts in those days and we both banged our heads, in father's case somewhat bloodily. "You all right?" he managed to say. Not one to waste words in an emergency was Dad. "Yeah, but *you're* not". I had never seen Dad covered in blood before. It sort of dragged him down to my level. We returned in a hire car to The Mount, father fretting the whole way about what 'your Ma' was going to say. But I was feeling quietly triumphant. If I played my cards right I might get at least a whole week's extra holiday out of this. But no, after a day recuperating at home, they sent me back. They were worried to the point of obsession that I might miss some irregular verb or equation or Saxon king. What a waste of a good car crash! My parents, I thought, were getting pathetic.

I found I had time on my hands, that summer. Sometimes I accompanied Dad to the big RAF tool-shed where he was trying, ever so slowly, and with many rethinks, to build a flat-bottomed rowing boat called a pram dinghy; in the end he got two squaddies to finish the job for him. He took us to the RAF gun club to fire revolvers and automatics at little targets, just like they did on American cop shows. This was quite good fun, and it made you feel very grown-up, standing there in a combat stance with a powerful handgun ready to blow away the cardboard villain. But somehow these sessions failed to cement a bond. Dad, I was beginning to grasp, was essentially a loner, impatient by nature and not very good at sharing a task. He could give orders, or he could do it himself, being fairly handy about the house and garden, but partnership, even with a willing son, was not his forte. His self-control was also getting questionable. Once he and Mum had had some row and they seemed inclined to take it out on us. I wasn't having that, so, collecting Christy, I got the bikes out and informed my kid brother that we were running away. But after we had cycled over the airfield and round Oakington a few times, we got bored with the adventure and came home for tea, by which time normal relations had been restored.

And yet... Dad was basically kind and well-intentioned, and almost embarrassingly proud of his boys, but there was no doubt about it, we were growing apart. Did I blame him for the miseries of the past year? Did I resent the fact that he had played what seems in retrospect to have been a rather passive role in my education? Did he find it difficult to come to decisions? I was only twelve and I didn't have the faintest idea. They might be your parents but they were also grown-ups. You couldn't discuss things with them as you did with your mates. It was impossible. I'm not sure why, half a century later, but it was.

You could, I discovered, love your father without necessarily liking him much. Dad was diminished in my cold twelve-year-old eyes. It was Mum who wrote nearly all the letters, short, practical missives, full of sensible advice. Dad wrote only when he had something to announce: that he had bought that globe I wanted with Green Shield stamps; or he had got hold of some book I needed. His role was to drive me back to school and pick me up for free weekends and holidays. We didn't talk much about school except as a joke. Only once did I nearly let the cat out of the bag. Before dropping me off at the Hole, we usually stopped off at Remlap first for a cup of tea. On one such stop I remember slipping on some steps and landing painfully. Instead of getting up and brushing myself down, I decided to stay where I was and cry. Oh dear God, don't take me back to that place. Dad seemed surprised, then baffled. What on earth was the matter? "Is it that *Charlie* fella?" he suddenly burst out. He had absolutely no idea. And so, after a second cup of tea, I pulled myself together and he drove me back to the Hole.

Chris once remarked that I was never quite the same person again after that first year at the Hole. I sense, viscerally, but with no real evidence, that he was probably right. I felt at odds with my world. I had grown distrustful and made friends less readily. My fixed memory was of the white Morris turning down the drive; as Sir Bedivere had cried to the departing, fatally wounded, King Arthur, "what shall become of me, now ye go from me and leave me here alone among mine enemies?" My year in solitary taught me about survival and the mechanisms you subconsciously put there to achieve it. At that age I lacked humour, that is to say, any sense of irony or perspective. The consequence was a growing inwardness, an unwillingness to confide, a sense of hopelessness at being trapped in a situation from which I could see no escape. It is known in the trade, not that I would have known, as a 'survival personality'. Once ingrained, they say it is hard to lose. One of its symptoms is a difficulty in forming close or intimate relations. I have noticed this in me, but I have also seen it in my brother, and certainly in father, and so it may be simplistic to ascribe it entirely to my sufferings at the Hole. Perhaps it's a defective gene. A certain passivity must, I think, have been there already, for otherwise I would have surely have gathered my wits, hoarded my pocket money, and got out of there, after first setting light to the curtains.

School had obviously not harmed me intellectually; by the not-very-demanding standards of a flat-topped school in Loughborough, I was top of the class. I had, insisted Boss, the makings of a scholar. At school I merely felt out of place. But nothing could reconcile me to life at the Hole. I used to make a point of saying, towards the end of the holidays, that this would be my *last* meal at home, the last pee, the last glance in the hall mirror. We called this litany 'The Lasts'. It was a family joke. Or rather, I pretended it was a joke. And the parents pretended to be amused.

Come the day I remember leaning against the long window of the dining room in my hated maroon blazer counting the swallows on the line. About twenty, I think there were; all off to sunshine and South Africa, the lucky little buggers. This time, I'd been told, at least I would not be alone. The Boss had said that I'd have at least one friend of my own age, possibly more than one. Show the new boy the ropes, he said. Make him feel at home. Yes, I thought, I'll look forward to that. And I'll have the lines ready: "I *think* you'll like it here. I think so."

CHAPTER NINE

Clarence Knows the Ropes

At some point during that autumn term I fell ill. The Hole had a sick bay next to the baby dorm which doubled as Brat Broad's bedroom when he was in residence. Hence it was warm and cosy, and well-furnished with books, many of them lurid paperbacks about murder and crime, and so well worth checking out. I moved in, with some sort of fever, and spent a blissful week on my own with Brat's books and a borrowed radio. It was spoiled only by the painful shots of penicillin injected into my bottom each evening by the cadaverous college doctor, who agreed reluctantly that this, for once, was not a case of Mondayitis. Exactly what it was I never discovered. Possibly a nervous breakdown. After my first night in the isolator, dorm-captain Nigel King stuck his carroty head round the door. "Did you have a good cry last night?" he wanted to know. Uh? "*I said did you have a good cry*". From behind him came a Glaswegian growl: "Fuckin' crybaby wanker". It seems that I had kept them awake by raving in my sleep. Evidently I had been complaining about something nasty in the sickroom, may be the ghost of a previous sickie. It was very rum. I had, I thought, slept like a top for once, uninterrupted this time by snores or farts or the grinding of teeth. So, even when parted from them, I had managed to annoy my dorm mates, and some of them were not of a forgiving nature.

The day I began my second year was one of my happiest at the Hole. There was not one new chum but four and they put us in a room all together. We exchanged dirty jokes long into the night. The social structures of the Hole were based on who you shared a room with, and it could mean the difference between happiness and misery. It was in the fellowship of the dorm that you spent your leisure hours, chatting, reading, pillow-fighting, and, for those so inclined, some quiet wanking in the small hours. Our comfortable fivesome seemed a rare stroke of luck. Even the beds were comparatively comfortable.

It couldn't last. As House juniors our proper place was in the baby dorm, from which there came mutinous rumblings. After a few days we were obliged to move back into the old, hated room with the rock 'n' roll wallpaper and the broken beds. Here we were joined by Nigel King, who seemed none too pleased to be placed in charge of a bunch of little kids, and a new guy, a tough, mop-headed Glaswegian we naturally called Jock. Jock was a primitive boy. We all sprang from apes, but in Jock's case he had obviously not managed to spring very far. I should have spotted at a glance that he would need careful handling. Watchfulness was the word. But I was all too evidently full of myself as a Hole veteran, one that had survived a whole year and, as the Boss had put it, 'had learned the ropes'. Jock was not inclined to take advice from any younger kid, least of all a soft-looking A-streamer in specs. He was delighted to learn they had called me Clarence. "Clarence knows the ropes", he kept repeating. "He knows all the fuckin' ropes, does Clarence". I think he was being sarcastic.

Trouble was brewing. You might be surprised to learn that I was quite good at fighting. By generally choosing my opponent with care—the inoffensive Dim made a useful stooge (and I'm really sorry about that, Dim)—I usually won my fights. My tactic was simple. Punch the sucker in the face hard, and then, whilst he's still in shock, grab him in a neck-lock and squeeze until he goes limp. Works every time. Even quite aggressive boys can be shocked by an unexpected show of ultra-violence. The downside of this essentially pre-emptive strategy was that I had earned the reputation of being hot-tempered and goadable. There was fun to be had in teasing me into a state just short of mayhem. They pretended that rage filled me with ungovernable strength, like the Incredible Hulk, when the normally shy and mild-mannered Marren would transform before their eyes into something thrillingly dangerous. None of this was true, or even likely, but Jock was intrigued, and so he started to push me around. One day, while I was cleaning my teeth, he pushed me once too often. The floor was slippery. I pushed back and Jock went head over heels and banged his flattish head against the rim of the bath. Perhaps he banged it quite hard, because, instead of laying out retribution there and then, he withdrew into a state of threat-full muttering. He vowed to sort me out well and truly the following night. And instead of conceding that his fall was just a lucky fluke, for which I was of course extremely sorry, and then arranging a late evening at school, I stupidly baited him. I was egged on by Nigel King who seemed to appreciate a bit of reckless, nay suicidal, verbal fireworks.

The next evening, all bravado gone, I lay low. The thought of being beaten up by this psychotic Rob Roy now terrified me. Had I been capable of examining the situation dispassionately, I might have realised that I still held some useful cards. For a start he would not dare to thrash me too badly and if he tried someone would almost certainly stop him. Contrariwise, being much smaller and weaker, I was free to do my best to damage him in any way I liked: an eye jab, say, followed by a smart knee in the kisser and a trenchant boot in the balls. One way out of the situation, then, might have been to astonish the bugger with a display of homicidal fury. But this was risky. A more prudent course might have been to hide in the paddock until lights out, or simply to run away and keep on running. By tradition, the only fights allowed in the dormitory were pillow fights.

Alas, a long day at school thinking about Jock and his knotty fists had driven any such calculations out of my mind. And so it was in a panicky state of irresolution that he eventually found me, cowering in the little white-washed room where the cadets polished their boots. His leery chimp's face lit up. "C'mon", he challenged, pushing out his prickly, Desperate Dan chin. "Hit me". With amazing speed a crowd gathered eager to witness the massacre. "C'mon, Clarence, hit me!" "Go on, Clarence, *hit* him!" No one seemed inclined to break it up. I looked around desperately. "Hit me! *Hit me*!" Oh Christ, what now?

Then a way out dawned. Of course! The boarder's stand by! The last resort of the true coward! I knew exactly what I had to do. With all the force my trembling arm could summon I swung my fist through its full arc and smashed him in the face. Not Jock, but the guy standing next to him.

Possibly it was Dim again, who knows? It is helplessness that produces the worst extremes of rage. As I saw it there was justice here since in a situation like this anyone who was not for you (in which case they would have tried to stop it) was against you. At any rate, it was a catharsis, a sudden release from fear. I sprang at the crowd who had gathered for their sadistic pleasure, laying into them right and left, a bashed nose here, and a thick ear there, joyously yelling my head off. The mob parted, then contracted, carrying me off bodily into the cloakroom where as many of them as would fit tried to scramble on top of my kicking form. I remember catching one older boy, with whom I normally got on with quite well, a lovely boot in the face with my free leg. Over he went, groaning. I was still struggling and shouting and lashing out when a huge Fifth Former came in, brushed them off like insects, and carried me outside. The crowd followed, but as with the police, so with my saviour: "Go away, there's nothing for you here, nothing to see. It's all over. Go home". I heard young Steve telling anyone who would listen that, "We should report this, he's not safe". "*You* won't be safe tonight", I yelled back.

That night the inmates of the baby dorm, friend and foe alike, were surprisingly subdued. Someone might have had a word with Jock and told him to go easy. The Scotsman sneered a bit but there were no more physical threats, or at least not for a while. His challenge was, of course, another rite of passage. In his brute way, the older boy was asserting his dominance, his senior place in the peck order over one who, it seemed to him, had pretensions. Gonna nip *that* in the bud, thought Jock. He seemed to enjoy hurting and humiliating weaker kids. The only way to deal with predators like him is to hit back or use your superior wits. They never teach you these things. You either pick it up, and live, or you don't and suffer the consequences. I had trouble with Jock, year in, year out; not all the time—there were days when he could be fairly amiable—and not just me, but I was on his list. When he was in a bad mood, there were always boys like me to cuff and kick. It might, in retrospect, have been better to take a beating after all.

It should never be said that all this violence, physical and psychological, did us no harm. 'I think we were all damaged by it', commented Auberon Waugh, 'which is why Britain is such a screwed-up hopeless country now.' Fights are ephemeral; you have your scrap and it's over. What is worse is social exclusion. At school it was enough that I sounded posh for the lower orders to regard me as an alien and a snob (and for me to see them in turn as oafs and oiks). It is normal for state schools to persecute the middle classes, and lately some of the teachers have joined in, which no doubt accounts for the decline of spoken English and civilised standards generally. The joke today is that we all, toffs and berks alike, regard ourselves as middle class yet insist on acting and sounding like plebs. You only have to listen to some public-school-educated young man straining every vowel to sound like a docker's lad from Deptford to realise that the class system has been turned on its head. It was otherwise, back in 1963. We have turned around on a course my school would have thoroughly approved of. *Vicisti* Loughborough!

CHAPTER TEN

Third Form

When I returned to school in the autumn of 1964, most of the boys sounded rather odd. Their voices had broken during the summer holidays and suddenly they sounded like little men, albeit with squeaks and rasps, like badly tuned cellos. The syllabus had grown up too. For we A-streamers it was the start of two years cramming for GCE 'O' levels. Among the teachers chosen for the task was the dreaded 'Jock' Chalmers, head of French, whose stiff, white hair was cut *en brosse* like a scrubbing brush. His distinctly uncheery slogan was: 'you have two choices. You can work hard willingly or you can work hard unwillingly.' His catchphrase was an exclamation: "eh!", spoken not as a query but as a statement. Jock had taught foreign languages in exactly the same way since the reign of Queen Anne, that is, with a heck of a lot of homework and full-scale tests every week. It was said, too, that he had a whippy way with the cane that stung the bum most horribly. Luckily, for every problem the diligent schoolboy has a solution. I shared homework with another boy who, for a consideration paid in glacier mints, ensured that I could continue in complete idleness even under Jock's gimlet eye.

For geography we had 'Slosher' Brown who couldn't tell you the capital of Iceland without covering you in spit. He was also noted for the deadliness of his aim with the blackboard duster. One moment you were casually chatting to your neighbour and then, suddenly, crack, you were at the centre of your personal universe of stars and chalk dust. Our new form master was Timmons, the history teacher, who, being newish and nondescript, lacked a nickname, although 'Doggy' might have done since he had a tendency to bark. Although I was good at history, Timmons did not seem to appreciate me. "You're lazy, Marren, lazy", he growled. That was two 'lazys', a kind of double idleness. Since I had come top of the form again in the second-year exams, and, moreover, always came top in his subject, this seemed a trifle unfair. What more could I do? But in the Timmons scheme of things I had come top in the wrong way. "He seems to coast along relying on his natural ability", he sourly noted at the end of my gleaming report, "not by hard work". Timmons resented success without apparent effort. My way was not the Loughborough way.

Nor did our new housemaster at the Hole, a man we called Keyhole Kate, have any kinder words for poor little Marren. "He must join in more," was always the gist of his comments. But join in what? "He needs more often to offer his services". What services were those, Kate? Given that everything not forbidden was compulsory, there didn't seem much room for freelance keenness at the Hole. What Kate was really getting at was my attitude. He had caught me with a porn mag (see next chapter for all the lurid details) and then he had had caught me sneaking out to the chip shop with a first-year in tow, and so, in his eyes, corrupting him. I was failing to conform. My lack of enthusiasm for boarding school life was obvious to him. He thought I needed shaking up. Not that it mattered what Kate thought; my parents had lost interest in my school reports and Boss wasn't all that bothered either, so long as I stayed near the top.

One autumn day at the Loughborough fair I managed to win a goldfish inside a plastic bag. With a flash of imagination I called it Goldie. Spotting Goldie on my locker with a pebble or two and a bit of weed for company, Kate confiscated it for his own room but generously allowed me in once a week to greet my little fish and clean out his bowl. On the first Goldie clean-up day, a friend accompanied me to Kate's room for a good snoop round. "Look at Kate's toothbrush", he chuckled. It was indeed a sorry specimen. It looked as though Kate brushed his shoes with it. But it gave me an idea. Once a week Kate's scuffy toothbrush became just the thing for scrubbing out the goldfish bowl—ooh, that's a really stinky mess you made just there, Goldie, need some hard scrubbing to get that out. After a while even Kate got bored with Goldie's pointless meanderings and handed him back. Goldie ended up in Nanna's bird bath, a rather callous choice of home, perhaps, but I doubt whether the fish cared one way or another. A goldfish in a bowl is not so much a pet as an object-lesson, a warning of the futility of existence without purpose.

Ever since then I have tried consciously to do something worthwhile or creative every day. Without it, I find, you go to bed feeling sick with ennui and self-loathing, and that's no good is it?

This might be the appropriate moment to relive my caning: a tragi-comic episode involving nothing worse than a broken bed, lost dignity and a sore bum. Our hospital-style bed-frames had bars through which, if you were supple and skinny enough, you could wriggle in and out of. It was a nice trick if you could work it, and, having watched others do it, I naturally thought I could too. Unfortunately I had not allowed for the critical moment when, bent double with your head nudging your feet, it suddenly becomes impossible to move, forward or back. Completely stuck in this compromising position, I hollered for assistance, instead of which the whole dorm chortled and whooped with glee. Hearing the commotion, Fanny, who never seemed to be far away from the keyhole, burst in, took one incredulous look and called for her husband. "Look! Look at this!" She was all for having me whacked there and then, and certainly my posture would have been most convenient for the purpose, but Boss decided to show me a little compassion. "Come on now, get him out". In a trice I was out of the frame and standing there in my pyjamas, red-faced and feeling, dare I say, rather foolish. Fortunately for me, Boss seemed quite amused. "Now then, Marren", he said, while the rest of the dorm stifled their giggles. "What were you up to? *Experimenting* were you?" That was it (thanks Boss!) "Yes, Sir", I answered, "it was a foolish experiment that went sadly wrong and one for which I offer regret and an apology". "Well, don't do it again, you'll damage the beds". With a glance around the room, he left with Fanny in tow, shaking her head. The others felt no need to disguise their disappointment. *"Fuckin' teacher's pet"*, growled a familiar Scottish voice near the window.

A few days later a group of us were fooling around in the cloakroom and taking it in turns to be spun around inside the wicker laundry basket. My spinning was, I felt, getting a bit rough, and I was considering whether to shout at them to stop when suddenly the whole room fell silent. With no more wit than a hamster I yelled, "Get me out of here, you wankers".

"Is that Marren again?" came a terrible voice. Yes, Sir, it's me. "Come on, get him out".

I rose from the basket like the morning sun.

"Well, Marren?", said the Boss, "did they put you in there or *were you experimenting again*?"

There was only one possible answer (yes, that was it!). "Yes, Sir, I'm afraid it was another experiment, one for which I …"

"Come with me".

I was one of the few who had not yet been caned, and it was probably just as well to get it over and done with. You're not a proper boarder, they said, until you had a full and proper whacking. It was another rite of passage (those endless rites of passage). A no-cane boarder ranked as an utter weed and wet; a nonce, brown-noser and creep; definitively not one of us. I followed Boss into the hall in a trance-like state, wondering what it would be like. He disappeared into his study and came out with a thin stick with a curved handle. Where, I wondered, did they get these things? Did the school suppliers maintain a stash of sticks of different sizes? Was the teacher measured for arm length and swing before being sold a customised cane of his choice? Were they able to choose from a variety of types from deadly thin whippers to stout, sturdy whackers? Did they really sell canes fitted with telescopic sights like that one in Molesworth? Did the man really think I had been rolled in the basket for an *experiment*?

"Bend over." Could this really be happening to me?

Whack, whack and—oh really, Sir!—another whack. The Boss obviously felt the need to be seriously discouraging.

"Don't do it again!"

We had solemnly shaken hands, and I was out of the hall and half way down the corridor before the pain kicked in. *Yow*, that really *hurt*. The boys in the cloakroom were concussing with laughter. I knew my lines and played up in a suitably modest way, later exposing my impressively striped bum to public gaze as custom required. "Wow, there's blood on that one, he really got you there!" Yeah, that's the last 'experiment' I'll be doing for a while, I thought, as I prepared for sleep, lying on my tummy. "Join the club, mate". My sergeant's stripes were seen as an honourable wound, especially as I had virtually volunteered for them.

The Third Form was, I think, my nadir, the crappiest of all the crappy years at the Hole. But it started well. I was at first the appointed captain of a small dorm with five others of my age, most of them newbies, all amiable and refreshingly normal. But before long the pack was shuffled again, and I ended up in the 'Eight Dorm', the biggest dorm in the Hole, among all the rogues and psychos I had earnestly hoped to avoid for the rest of my stay. It was so unfair. "Why is it always me", I wailed. "It's someone else's turn to suffer. What's wrong", I continued, indicating my new friends, "with *those* guys?" But answer came there none. I was judged the most senior on account of having been there the longest, and so they chucked me into that long, cold room like a floppy-eared rabbit into a pack of wolves.

As it happened, this year had spawned a particularly vicious set of prefects. One of them, a surly, sallow-looking yob, had, for some reason, taken a dislike to me. "I don't like you, Marren", he would hiss. He wanted me to care that he didn't like me. His way was to trip me up for some misdemeanour and make me write out all the rules of the Hole, pretend to find a mistake and then make me do it all over again. I had, I suppose, excellent grounds for an appeal on grounds of victimisation, but that was a line that was somehow never crossed. A couple of mates—and let's inscribe their heroic names here—*Balsdon* and *Michelson*—showed their solidarity by helping me write my lines. That brought them into the firing line too, but, as we knew he would, our tormentor eventually lost interest. Here again, the Boss eventually came clean. "I had trouble with him", he admitted. "I had little to choose from that year. There had to be prefects, but I made only one of them a *school* prefect, and that was only because he was Head Boy. They were probably the worst we ever had", he went on, "with one possible exception". What exception was that? (great mates now, Boss and me). "Your lot", he replied, smiling broadly.

Probably I was feeling well sorry for myself. First I had been fished out of my sunlit boy's world and dumped into this disgusting pit. Then the RAF took away my country playground and moved us to a mean street in North London. And now I was being denied civilised company for the *second* time and thrown among angry gorillas. Over and above all that, I was nearing 14, an age which one knew instinctively was going to be particularly gruesome, neither one thing nor the other; a man struggling to escape from a child's skin, in my case most reluctantly. And a bit further on, the parents would be moving to Germany again, leaving their hapless son to sojourn at Remlap for weekends and half-term. My boyhood, it seemed to me, was over; my friends were flown, my garden was full of weeds and in general life sucked. Who was doing this to me? Who was writing the script? To modify a passage from Evelyn Waugh's *A Handful of Dust*, 'a whole imaginative world had come to grief…there were no more brilliant butterflies glittering through the forest glades, no bare feet on the tidal strand, no cycle rides on golden afternoons…' It was the hell of a way to end up, I reflected bitterly, as I trudged up Thorpe Hill in the rain before remembering I'd forgotten my PE kit.

My anger took passive forms. I decided I didn't care about their pissing, third-rate school and its squalid boarding house. I couldn't have cared less if 'Doggy' Timmons thought me lazy or 'Keyhole' Kate unwilling. I slacked off games. I cheated my way through French homework. I stole bars of chocolate and spent Fanny's pocket money on Woodbines. I retreated into my shell some more and, like Goldie, lived from day to day. Five days ended the school week, two more the weekend. Four more weeks and one earned a weekend at home, alone in North London. Another five and it was half-term, then Christmas and the New Year, and then there was only another year to get through. One day all this would be over. It was only a matter of time.

CHAPTER ELEVEN

The Visible Man

At last we reach the dirty bits. Or, rather, no, not exactly. I took no interest in the opposite sex until I was nearly 15, and they took no interest in me for at least three years after that. Nor do I intend to make the same mistake as Cyril Connolly who famously claimed, in *Enemies of Promise*, that he had never masturbated until he was 18, or possibly 25, or was it 40? My discovery of the pleasant art of wanking will be for ever shrouded in the mists of discretion. All I will say is that I was initially disgusted by the 'tossing' I witnessed all around me at the Hole, but later on found it quite amusing. A pal of mine used to perform a dumb-show of two boys masturbating, one with a tiny, indeed invisible, imagined penis and the other with a whopper the size of a rolling pin. He made the more fortunately endowed one look pop-eyed with effort, tongue hanging out in imbecile concentration, the other an angry little fellow, searching desperately with finger and thumb for what should have been there. I thought it was the funniest thing I had seen in my life. And then there was that other time when I was caught massaging someone, and it was exactly that, a massage—I had been promised two bob!—and not what the Hole's dirtier minds suspected.

The best part of our biology lessons was on the workings of the human body. According to the syllabus the man was supposed to be telling us all about the rabbit, but he had obviously taken a broader view of his responsibilities. In particular, he wanted to warn us about the perils and temptations of Sex. And so, when we reached the eagerly anticipated Reproductive System, he was ready with his charts and diagrams, including a most instructive one of a willy and a vagina and little running dots to show where sperm came from and where it went. One day soon, he told us, with a wink of experience, our voices would break, our groins would sprout a thick bush of hair, and we would suddenly become interested in girls and try and remove their clothes. But we should desist, he went on sternly, because although we might soon begin to *look* physically mature, our sense of responsibility would lag years behind. We were not ready for fatherhood *yet*, he concluded, oh no, not by a long chalk. We might desire, but fulfilment must be delayed. Something to look forward to, suggested this nice middle-aged biology teacher with a twinkle in his eye, because sex is so *very* nice, even *after* you are married.

None of this was exactly news. As I say, I knew what Bond had done with each and every one of his lady friends. Moreover, since the Chatterley trial more explicit paperbacks were now on sale, such as *The Perfumed Garden* and *The Tropic of Cancer*, although, since they were not illustrated, you didn't half have to use your imagination. We had also seen pictures of naked ladies, for example in the bedraggled and sometimes stained copies of *Parade* one found stuffed down a cistern or behind a radiator in one of the Hole lavatories. But in those days the pictures were always discretely shot or airbrushed, so that you never caught sight of a bush and only rarely a bare bum. The only place where you could leer at ladies without a stitch on, bush and all, was a special magazine for nudists called *Health and Efficiency*, and there the ladies were usually playing volleyball or playing the piano, having absent-mindedly left all their togs behind. By no means all of them were young and pretty either; some looked more like men with a pair of joke tits about their middle. But, as I say, one's curiosity at this stage was largely scientific. The reproductive system was certainly interesting (the things they get up to!) but only marginally more so than the workings of the digestive tract or the miracle of the inner ear.

It was therefore largely in a spirit of anatomical inquiry that I told my parents what I wanted for Christmas 1963 (the year sexual intercourse began, according to Philip Larkin). I wanted a Visible Man matched by a Visible Woman. These were special twelve-inch high model human beings who displayed the secrets of their insides to the admiring world. Transparent plastic shells represented the skin with the blood vessels beneath, and tucked inside lay all the bones, muscles and organs, including the naughty bits, all snuggly fitted together. Visible Man stood four-square with a solemn yet vacant expression, his palms open and outstretched as if to say: 'here I am, come hither and check me out'. His partner was on a smaller, heart-shaped stand, half-turned in submission to her partner, with a coquettish half-smile on her plastic face. I am not sure what kind of tableau I was planning here, and perhaps wisely, they bought me the Man only. Out came the paints and brushes, and by Boxing Day my Visible Man stood proud but alone with his grey lungs, yellow stomach, shiny brown giblets and mad blue staring eyes. You could take him apart and then put him back together again, like an autopsy. For at least three days I thought he was terrific.

In furthering my extra-curricular studies of human anatomy I had acquired a Teach Yourself book, one of those educational self-help manuals in modish yellow-and-black jackets that were such a big hit in the Sixties. With one of these, the autodidact could introduce himself to Modern Greek or Motor Cycle Maintenance, or may be even build a modest nuclear power plant in the back garden. With my *Teach Yourself Anatomy* you could probably perform some basic abdominal surgery. But the picture that most disturbed me was a drawing of the female pudenda displayed in graphic detail. What the hell? *Did James Bond know about this?* If so he kept damn quiet about it. There was not the slightest hint of all this anatomy, tucked away between a woman's legs, in the centrefolds of *Parade*, or even among the hearty tennis players of *Health and Efficiency*. Potential there for a bit of a shock on your wedding night, what! (And how much, you wondered uneasily, did they know about *our* bits? Were they even interested?)

Real girls were hard to come by at the Hole. There was no particular cachet in dating a Boarder. You had the opportunity to meet girls at school, of course, and may be to hang around with them afterwards, but there was little space or freedom in our lives for courtship at least until the Sixth Form. Nevertheless some boys seemed to manage it. Pretty-boy Dim went steady with the same girl for years, but since he came from Rothley, only a few miles away, he scarcely counted. Carrot-haired Nigel King found himself an Amazon, a giantess at least two years older than him, and more than a head higher, with whom he would trail hand-in-hand along Ashby Road on Sunday afternoons like a boy with his mum. Me, I hardly even spoke to a girl before the Third Form. Most of them went around in giggling packs in their no-favours uniform of blazers, knee-length grey skirts and white bobby socks. You would overhear them chatting soppily about domestic science or horses or hockey, or one of those tedious "I-said-to-him-and-he-said-and-then-I-said…" monologues, none of it the least bit interesting to a normal, healthy 13-year-old boy.

But towards the end of that year I remember doing a double take down at the college baths. Until then one would hardly have bothered giving the girls in our class—a particularly dowdy lot—the time of day. Now, suddenly, here they were, much more interesting in their bathing suits and, I noticed, inclined to be quite friendly in their turn, at least to those of us who had managed to put on a bit of muscle around the shoulders. By then the more street-wise girls were ditching their white socks and putting on stockings or tights, raising their skirts a little and finding other ways of making their uniforms marginally sexier. By the Third Form we were suddenly talking about and thinking about girls quite a lot, in some cases all the time. After lights out at the Hole, we competed as to who could tell the dirtiest story. I had little knowledge and absolutely no experience, but I did have a certain amount of imagination. Fanny, listening at the door in horror, rounded on me one morning. "Your language is getting filthy, Marren. *Filthy*. Your parents would be *shocked* to hear you". That was true enough. They would be and they were. There had been stern words the day they overheard little Christy singing one of his elder brother's rugby songs. In vain did I protest he had got it all *wrong*: it *wasn't* four-and-fifty virgins, and they *didn't* come from Easterness. And it's a *dicky-di-do*, I added, and not what he said.

As John Lennon sang on *Rubber Soul* around this time, "girl, girl, *aaarghh*." When would I get my hands on one or see one naked? Everyone seemed out to thwart you. One dreadful old perve of a teacher used to scan the periphery of the sports field with binoculars for signs of what he called heavy petting. Prefects yelled at us to keep our caps on and pulled down over our eyes. Older girls rebuffed one's clumsy overtures or half-baked witticisms. Even Nanna inadvertently joined my tormentors by getting it into her head that a girl who lived on her street was somehow my 'girlfriend'. In fact she had hardly deigned to notice me. "Hello", I wheedled, passing her on the way to the bus stop. She looked at me, and then the other way.

What worried me more about Nanna was a piece of would-be pornography I had written during an idle moment at Remlap and then mislaid. Nanna enjoyed reading my little stories—"I think you've really got something there", she would say. She would not have enjoyed this one, although it was pretty mild—mainly about a girl undressing and being ogled by a bloke in a cupboard. For weeks afterwards I studied her face for any signs of having read such a piece of filth, but she looked as guileless and innocent as ever. Perhaps, then, Granddad had rolled it up and used my shame to light his pipe.

Another time girls got me into trouble was after I had paid someone a bob for his dog-eared copy of *Health & Efficiency* in which a comely nude lady was baking a pie in the kitchen. We were just admiring the way her tits juddered over the pastry when there was a whispered warning from our look-out. I barely had enough time to stuff the magazine down my trousers before Keyhole Kate poked his head round the door. "You're looking guilty about something, Marren", he spotted. "Oh, am I Sir?" (fuck off, Kate). "Very guilty". I didn't think this warranted a reply, and after a glance around the common room, Kate stalked off and we continued our minute examination of the kitchen goddess. Suddenly there was another hiss: *"He's coming back"*. This time I wasn't quite quick enough. I slipped the magazine behind my back. "Show it to me, now". "Show you what, Sir?" I asked, trying desperately to jam it into my belt. "You know very well. Come with me". And so I dragged after Kate, the pie lady peeping out from the back of my pants, the Jezebel. We stopped in front of the boiler.

"I don't want to see your filth, Marren", he conceded. "But you will burn it now".

Several denials later, he supervised the destruction of a perfectly serviceable copy of *Health & Efficiency* with all the righteousness of a Gauleiter burning books in the Marktplatz. A twirl of flame briefly licked over a notably healthy and efficient female form and she was gone from my life. Life was such a bitch. "I'm keeping an eye on you, Marren", warned Kate.

At some point this sense of longing turned from the generalised to the specific. They became attached in the first place to a rather louche girl called, I think, Maureen. She had a dark fringe that half hid her face and below her school dress, worn as short as she could get away with, were chubby thighs and long shanks clad in dark stockings. She was the kind of girl that went out with members of the First Fifteen. I doubt I even spoke to her, although I may have been lurking by as she hung up her coat or went to her locker. I remember one day during the summer holidays, treading the wet sands of North Cornwall and thinking wistfully about all the fun we could have had and, with a vicious kick at a passing crab, realising we never would. She fuelled my fantasies for a few weeks before I ditched her and moved onwards and upwards to that blond in 4D.

All things considered it is surprising that the boys of the Hole were not inclined to experiment with one another a little more. No one, as far as I know, nourished a curt kind of love for their little fag, nor did I witness any moony glances over porridge, or tiptoed wanderings down the passage after dark. No one was expelled for offences that could not be named publicly. Perhaps our daily contact with girls at school overcame any same-sex inclinations and steadied our thoughts in the correct biological alignment. Hole friends were mates, not *mates*. But in any case I fear that any incipient gayness would have been dealt with severely by the Jocks of this world—as I knew only too well after that little misunderstanding over the massage ("do that again, Marren, and I'm going to cut your balls off, see?").

As for self-abuse, some of the habitual tossers did make an occasional show of their tossing. I heard about, but thankfully did not witness, a mass wank in the baby dorm which ended with one fellow soaking himself and his neighbour with a jet of pee. No, we were all, or nearly all, normal confined teenage males dreaming of some distant shagathon when years of accumulated frustration would finally explode in a glorious sexual conflagration beyond the mind to grasp. In the meantime, a snatched moment of gratification with a dog-eared copy of *Parade* would have to suffice.

WHERE THE WILD THYME BLEW • PART TWO

CHAPTER TWELVE

Charlie and Other Hole-dwellers

Only one group photograph was taken during my incarceration at the Hole, and that was in summer 1964, towards the end of my second year (and still the second youngest boy in the house). The front garden was about to be taken away for a by-pass which would also remove half of our paddock, and Boss thought it a suitable time for a picture. We lined up on the forbidden lawn in rows, shoulder to shoulder, big guys at the back, prefects sitting importantly on chairs on either side of Boss, and we baby dormers crouched cross-legged at their feet. I remember Tes Egan, the PE teacher, murmuring some pleasantry as I made room for him, calling me by my nickname, which I suppose he meant as a matey greeting. The boarders variously grinned or glowered at the camera, and the moment was frozen for all time with a click. Looking at them now I see 40-odd ordinary adolescent youths, some with vacant expressions, others pensive or smirking, a few staring steadily ahead, not deigning to smile: army boys no doubt. One or two bozos, caught unawares, were facing in the wrong direction. Some of those faces I hardly recognise now. But one can still sense which were benign and which invoke a faint recrudescence of ancient fear and loathing. My own smirk and shank of floppy hair I acknowledge with shame.

Standing at the back and among those not bothering to smile is a lone black face. Could anyone, least of all those who had the misfortune to share a dorm with him, ever forget Charlie? A big plump lad from Lagos, Charlie was tall, Charlie was strong, he was loud and he was mean, but what you noticed most was that Charlie had a serious hygiene problem. It wasn't that he just whiffed a bit after exercise or after beating up some kid. Every boarder was well used to the reek of post-match rugger jerseys and cheesy adolescent feet. No, the thing about Charlie was that his body odour actually *hurt*. It assailed your nose and stung your throat; it made you gag and your eyes smart. Charlie was borderline toxic. Perhaps, since he seemed to be morbidly afraid to expose his genitals, it might have been a simple matter of not bathing very often. He was less shy about his farts, which were fully African in their volume and intensity, like the bellow of a wounded elephant. After a while there was a certain rush back to school to secure a bed as far away from Charlie as possible.

The thing I liked most about Charlie is that he didn't bully me more than anyone else. In fact, in my first year we were, as fellow outcasts, almost mates, at least to the extent of sharing comics. Charlie had some remarkable comics; not Eagle or Rover, as in my case, but doubtfully legal American *noir* thrillers of sweating hoods in dark alleys and nasty goings on in the crypt. Not that Charlie would have gone anywhere near a crypt. Once, knowing he had nowhere to go, I invited him home for a weekend, but when he found out we lived in an isolated house in the country he made his excuses. Country houses to him were haunted houses. Perhaps it was something to do with his Ibo culture—his father was apparently a minor tribal chief—but Charlie had no trouble believing in the supernatural as a real, threatening presence. He was

The Hole-dwellers. Self on the ground to the right of 'Tes' Egan, the housemaster. Charlie is the dark face on the back row.

frightened of being alone in the dark, and so the housemaster was being crueller than he knew when, as a punishment, he sent Charlie into the cellar to shovel coal. In no time at all he ran out jabbering with terror, and claiming to have been accosted by some malevolent spirit.

Charlie had his own style of humour. He once made imaginative use of a set of darts, first throwing them at our bare feet as we made ready for bed, and later, after lights out, chucking them at the wall just above the beds. I still remember that 'thunk' of a dart a few inches above my face, which was under the pillow. It wasn't that Charlie actually wanted to have someone's eye out. It was just that he wasn't very responsible.

Seeing things from his point of view, it cannot have been easy for him. He was a long way from home. His was the only black face in the whole school. All the same, we had boys from India, who integrated pretty well. My friend Ali eventually became head boy and so did Simon Khosla, whose father was from Bombay. Charlie seems to have had an unhappy childhood and claimed he had been beaten by his father, often and severely. Why his parents sent him into exile at the Hole I cannot remember, but they evidently weren't keen to have him back during the holidays. Did we subject him to racial abuse? Only, I think, behind his back. For a short time I kept a diary which I hid in my locker under a pile of clothes. One day, during one of the flu epidemics that left half the Hole-dwellers bedridden, Charlie wiled away the boredom by rifling through the effects of absent boys, and it was then that he discovered my secret diary. He read it out loud, guffawing with mirth whenever he came across some critical or insulting reference to my fellow boarders. He was less amused to find himself referred to as 'Kaffir', his Hole nickname, although, as I say, only behind his back. Oddly enough, he did not follow through his intention to make me suffer for mentioning him in this disrespectful way. Perhaps he felt some small twinge of conscience for breaking into what had, after all, been a private journal. At any rate he told me, not without a certain dignity, that my name-calling had wounded his feelings.

If there was any racist at the Hole it was probably Charlie himself. More than any of us he seemed obsessed with skin colour, not so much his own as other people's. How far was he joking when he asserted that Simon Khosla, who was half-Indian, was "blacker than I am" and joshingly called him 'wog', 'coon' and 'black bastard'? Another 'coon', according to him, was Rick, a big Polish boy who would magically acquire a deep tan from only an hour or two in the sunshine. For my part, when he heard of my ambition to be a zoologist, Charlie knew me as that "dirty, dirty zoo-keeper". Was it all rooted in an inferiority complex? Charlie was in many respects a bad boy but so many of the stories about him make you smile. And (which I'm coming to in a moment) they can also make you wonder about the workings of fate. There were, as Martin Amis once said about a character, 'chinks in his coal-black armour, God bless every one of them'.

What might have lain at the heart of things was Charlie's near complete lack of empathy. He was a loner: it was Charlie *contra mundum*, a struggle in which he would be prepared to cheat, lie and bully without a qualm. He seems to have a soft spot for my friend Kosh, but mainly (says Kosh) because Charlie fancied his German mother. Charlie liked blondes. In return for a percentage of his pocket money, Charlie ensured that Kosh did not suffer unduly from predators like the egregious Jock. Jock's eyrie was the ping-pong room and one day, when Kosh had managed to offend him in some way, he was ordered up there for a slapping. He obeyed but had first bribed Charlie to come up the stairs a moment later. Jock only had time for a couple of routine cuffs before Kosh's minder got to work on the angry wee bully, ending up by smashing him over the head with a cricket bat. Not *quite* hard enough, in my view, for the Scotsman lived, but Kosh experienced no more trouble from that quarter.

During my third year at the Hole there was a short-lived craze for shop-lifting. Most of us slipped a few chocolate bars and trinkets into our blazer pockets and called it a day. It was Charlie who raised these teen rites into a whole new level of professionalism. Charlie lifted so much that he would auction the loot in the outhouse on Sunday nights. By this and other means he usually had plenty of money which he used to bet on horses. By the time he left in summer 1967 Charlie was a fairly hardened piece of goods. He might have fluffed his exams, but life at the Hole had at least taught him what he was good at.

It was Charlie's bad luck that he left school just as the civil war in Nigeria was getting under way. As a Catholic Ibo from a prominent local tribe he was barred from returning home. Instead he headed for London, where he had apparently made useful contacts. Charlie became a 'wheeler-dealer'. In the words of someone who knew him well, 'he found himself with no funds coming in and ended up delving into the worst, seediest side of it...he made choices that had ramifications'. He met and married a Scottish girl, described then as a 'total nomadic hippie spirit', by whom he had a daughter and a son, also named Charles, in quick succession. Then he left her; 'it was a disaster from the start'. The hippie looked after the children and took cleaning work to make ends meet. Charlie dropped by from time to time. Then, around 1986, he was killed in a car crash.

And how do I know all this? Because his daughter is the actress Carmen Ejogo, star of a dozen films and numerous TV shows, including her own video show on BSkyB. She told a reporter on *The Evening Standard* about her lost dad. Charlie's boy, Charles junior, too, became briefly famous when he won the jackpot on the first Dragon's Den TV show with a clever idea for a vending machine for disposable brollies. He took out a patent, went into business with the help of the Dragons, and presumably made a pile of money. I see a little of Charlie in the images of both of them, but his dark spirit has somehow been transformed into light by the good-looking, optimistic faces of his children: the children he never saw grow up. Look on it as a kind of generational redemption. His short, sordid life turned into a parable. In the end, and beyond the grave, Charlie did all right.

I hold out little such hope for another of the Hole's oddballs, Chong from Hong Kong (I have of course changed his name). He was only there a year but I remember him well for I occupied the bed next to his. One night the boys amused themselves by unscrewing the bolts that held my bed together while I was in the bathroom so that, when I got into bed, the whole thing collapsed. Chong thought this the funniest thing he had seen in his whole life. Long after the laughter had died down he was still convulsed with merriment with this high Chinese giggle: *hee-hee-hee*. You went to sleep, then woke up and there was Chong still sitting up, still giggling, *heeee-heee-heeee*! He was probably still laughing at breakfast and all the way to school. The next night he tried undoing the bolts of my bed again, but this time I caught him and told him to fuck off.

Poor old Chong, I don't think he enjoyed his short time at the Hole. He wanted so desperately to make an impression. For example, he would have us know that he was an expert in the martial arts. He used to practice, stripped down to the waist and surrounded by a circle of little kids as he practiced his kicks and chops with many a "*Ha*!" and a "*Heee-ahh*!" He informed them that mastery of these skills took years and years of training, probably in some monastery high in the mountains. It was a matter of disciplining the mind as well as the body, explained Chong, combining the traditional *yong* of courage with the *yang* of humility. Wow, said the little kids.

It was only a matter of time before someone challenged Chong to a fight, oriental martial arts versus western-style boxing. But the great match was postponed time after time, because, as Chong explained, his blows were so deadly that he could not be held responsible for what might happen to his challenger. If he was hoping to make the guy think twice, it didn't work. The dare-devil challenger was determined to have his bout with the high-kicker from Hong Kong. The day came, bets were taken, and Chong limbered up for hours, preparing himself with heavy breathing exercises and mystic chants of "Haahhh!" and "*Wooo-gahh*!"

At last the protagonists squared up. But before Chong had time to utter his first "*Ha*!" the challenger casually straightened his arm and knocked him flat. Yes, the Kung Fu champ had bit the dust. The fight had lasted about ten seconds. Needless to say everyone was bitterly disappointed and some of us began to wonder whether what Hong Kong Chong had told us was strictly true, in the western sense of the word. Did he, for instance, know the slightest thing about Kung Fu? With his reputation as the new Bruce Lee in tatters, Chong became known as 'Pineapple Chonk', after the suck-'em-till-you-drop cubic sweets.

He also fancied himself with the ladies. A regular chick magnet was Chong, or so he claimed. By way of evidence he demonstrated his dancing prowess, a sort of civilian version of his Kung Fu moves. I for one was pretty impressed. All eyes would be on Chong as he knocked them out with his macho strutting and Nureyev-like pirouettes. Just as he had practiced for weeks before the great fight, so Chong could be seen hopping and skipping about, dancing up and down the stairs, in and out of the bathroom, as the day of the school dance approached. But, come the day, the Chinaman found himself gated for some misdemeanour and confined to barracks. He danced alone that day, and may be every other day too.

Chong only lasted a year. His reputation sank even lower when he became the prime suspect for a number of petty thefts. Whether he was innocent or guilty, whether he left of his own accord or was pushed, I do not remember, but he was said to have left in some style. He got someone to give him a lift to Birmingham, and, knowing our man, the driver demanded the fare in advance. At Birmingham New Street Chong thanked the guy and went on his way, whistling probably. He had reason to be happy for he had just nicked back the fare.

My great friend at the Hole, at least in my third year (for it tended to be a different best chum each year) was Kosh, Simon Khosla, the sturdy son of an Indian father and a German mother. We all had our reasons for being at the Hole. In Kosh's case, Loughborough was where his father had studied engineering. He was actually born in Loughborough. But now his parents were about to divorce, with his father remaining in Bombay and his mother returning to Germany. This left the 13-year-old Kosh, who up until then had barely needed to tie a shoe lace himself without a servant rushing up to do it, high and dry. The poor bastard saw his parents only once in the six years he was at the Hole. Fortunately he took to Hole life pretty well. He was droll, friendly, tenacious and adaptable. He could pull a range of funny faces which was a useful asset. I remember crying with laughter as Kosh simply recited the names of all the dopiest kids he could think of, with a face for each one. It was Rowan Atkinson and the schoolmaster sketch ("*Bab*cock...*Bland*... Carthorse...*Dint*...") fifteen years *avant la lettre*. Even now it makes me smile. Yes, Kosh, those certainly were a cheesy bunch of kids.

Kosh, as I say, was a good laugh. He was also sturdy and loyal, and in his little vulnerabilities rather endearing. Years later, I was unsurprised to learn, he had become a good businessman too. An early example of his ability to make something from almost nothing was his patronage of Charlie to ward off bullies. The Boss obviously spotted potential in him too for, despite his conspicuous lack of academic achievement, Kosh ended his time as head boy, not only of the Hole but the whole school. From my point of view the problem was that he was a bit *too* popular. A boy called Johnny (the one that had biffed the King Fu champ) stole him from me. Johnny was a boy of reckless courage, of dark imagination, mad, bad and dangerous to know; a much more charismatic character, I dare say, than me. Friendships at boarding schools are made up of interlocking circles, circles within circles, and once formed they are hard to break. I found myself physically removed from the warming rays of Kosh by the geography of the Hole, and socially by the jealous spirit of young Johnny. It was all a long while ago but I can still feel a distant echo, a faint bat-squeak of jealousy, from that sudden and, to me, baffling process of estrangement. One moment you were soul-mates, and the next, all of a sudden, while you were still sort-of friends, you were in different teams. You walked to school with someone else. You sat at a different table at prep. And rarely, now, shared that great bonding experience, the magic dust of schoolboy stories: those gales of laughter at someone else's expense.

Johnny seemed like another lad who could go far. He was a fiery character, with curly red hair to match; as Shakespeare might have put it, he was quick in quarrel, slow to forgive (unless he felt like it), burning with lore and stratagems. He was bright—possibly the brightest boy in the house, including me—but everyone generously overlooked that on account of the fact that Johnny never seemed to try very hard. He was brought up in Dar-es-Salaam, where perhaps he had some experience of the dark arts, for he had an abiding interest in the supernatural. For example, the day Charlie emerged from the coal hole, jabbering with funk, Johnny offered to sort things out using hypnosis. To our surprise, Charlie agreed and went under pretty promptly, although all that could be got out of him was an incoherent babble about his sufferings at the hands of his Dad, back in Lagos. When he came to, he chased Johnny round the paddock.

Later on, Johnny claimed to have found traces of a malign spirit—dubbed the Field Hole Fly—in the dark recesses of the attic behind a walled-in fireplace. Kosh, who followed him in, remembers the tunnel as bitterly cold, even on a warm summer's day. They found an apparently forgotten stash of objects in there, including Boss's long-lost degree certificates. Johnny had read up on the occult with the intention of cornering and, if possible, communicating with the Fly, though before he could do that he was expelled.

Johnny had already got into a fist fight with the housemaster. I played an unwitting part in the ultimate cause of his expulsion when, having left the Hole earlier in the year, I returned with the intention of taking the boys out for a night on the town. Johnny was duty prefect that day but he wasn't going to let a little thing like that prevent him from joining us. He returned loud and drunk on whisky and beer. He might have got away with it even then, but within a few days he compounded his offence by some equally outrageous stunt whereupon the Boss told him to pack his bags.

What happened next I learned later on. Johnny had a place at university to study medicine but in the meantime he took himself off to Morocco. After some upset with a girl, Johnny wandered out on to the beach and slashed one of his wrists. He survived but the apparent suicide attempt meant the end of his medical career; instead he studied biology, passing out in due course, and with his customary minimal effort, with a first. In the meantime he took up boxing in which his natural agility and aggression took him to the top of the university championship for his weight. Then he learned to dive, and earned a lot of money on Aberdeen's offshore rigs. But by then his inner demon was getting the better of him. He burned his money on booze and by the time of Kosh's wedding in 1980, at which Johnny was best man, he was a physical wreck. There were no wedding photographs because, after insisting on taking them all himself, Johnny found he had forgotten to put any film in the camera. Half-starved Johnny ate and ate all day long. Sometime after that he was diagnosed as a manic depressive. He ended up in an asylum—ironically in Loughborough—where his day job was picking up balls from a golf course. 'A brilliant guy', concludes Kosh, 'on the verge of madness, and then turned into the negative part, sad to say'. Did the shadow of the Hole haunt his young life? Who can say?

The other faces on the fading picture must have their stories. Some ex-boarders have pegged pictures and terse resumes of their lives on Friends Reunited, and what they have in common is their ordinariness. Many of them seem more eager to tell you what car they drive (Fiats, Toyotas), or how many kids or grandchildren they have, than what they actually did. They post images of unrecognisable old buffers sitting in the park, or at the wheel of their fucking Toyota, or grinning under the Christmas tree with the grand-kids. If the purpose of our school was to prepare us for respectable lives of quiet mediocrity, it seems to have succeeded well enough.

CHAPTER THIRTEEN

Escaping from Kenmore Avenue

If the crappiest thing that ever happened to me was the Hole, the next, in strict order of crapitude, was school holidays in North London. Up till then we had been lucky: the frozen peaks of Harpur Hill had been followed by a spell in the torrid Orient and then a half-share in a Victorian mansion with its own park. So we were overdue for a stinker and, towards the end of 1963, it came: Dad's stint at the Ministry of Defence. In career terms this was potentially a buck-up. But it meant that we would no longer be living in the country but in deepest suburbia. Even so we should have found a more congenial home than 236 Kenmore Avenue, a lego-house on a long street of 235 identical lego-houses. Presumably the parents had concluded that it was no worse than anywhere else in Kenton or Finchley or Edgware, a bow-windowed Thirties-semi built for the kind of Pooterish clerk who worked in the city. Each identi-home nestled behind a coy strip of privet. You parked your car on the street outside, under a lime tree that wept sugary juice onto the bonnet. If the parents didn't feel the come-down, the humiliation, I certainly did. If The Mount had been an oasis, this was the desert.

But Dad was happy: it was nice being at the centre of things for once, with Air Marshals and Defence Ministers padding the corridors; far more stimulating than his supplier's job at RAF Oakington. And Chris was happy if only because a good day-school had been found for him nearby. But Mum wasn't happy. She could not be proud of the dark house with its lumpy rented furniture, and with no friends of her own age and background. Both our new neighbours were elderly, and, some said, mad. One was a former assistant in a physics lab. He had known Chadwick and Soddy, which was jolly interesting to me, but Mum did not really care about neutrons and atoms. In fact I'm surprised she didn't have a nervous breakdown.

And of course I wasn't happy either. The neighbourhood had little to offer a country adventurer like me. It did not take long to explore the glum back garden. Even after Chris and I found some ants to roast on a tin lid, we agreed that this had the makings of the crappiest posting ever. You could walk and walk in any direction and all you found was more Kenmore Avenues, apart from the odd park or playground steaming with dog shit. How could any boy live in a dump like this?

There were a few compensations. There was a decent local library and I got to know all the London museums, and the zoo, and Westminster Abbey. One could visit the Odeon on Belmont Circle at some slight risk of getting stuck in one of the thick London fogs that could descend without warning, and a much greater risk of treading in the monstrous piles of dog shit everywhere. What I really missed, even more than the open horizon, was friends that you could call on, at any time, without warning, and instantly find fun stuff to do. It was dawning on me that yet another consequence of boarding school was this social dislocation. I could, I suppose, have joined some youth group but I never got round to it. Instead I loafed about the house getting on everyone's nerves, reading, drawing, playing my records and building Airfix model aeroplanes.

I had the feeling that my boyhood was ending. I remember joining in some game in the paddock with some younger kids when it suddenly struck me that I was too old to be playing at cowboys and Indians. With a dawning sense of self-consciousness, you felt a fool running around and shouting, "bang!" Almost without noticing, you were no longer living in Kidworld but in a new place called Teenland, in an untried era of pop music and sport and girls and, God help us, dancing. Even cycling had become questionable once I realised, belatedly, that my mean, green machine was really an old man's bike. Teen cycling required derailleur gears and cable brakes for speeding along with one's bum in the air and that set expression the sporting biker is expected to wear. My once-adored bicycle ended up in Granddad's cobbling shed covered by old sacks as if in shame. I couldn't be seen riding that old thing. It was too embarrassing.

This was all rather academic because, when I came home, I had nowhere to cycle to and no kids to cycle with, apart from Chris and even he was starting to develop interests of his own. We all agreed that there was only one thing for it: we would have to go on holiday. Up till now we had had remarkably few family holidays. But the parents had distant, happy memories of Cornwall where they had honeymooned about on the beach at Perranporth. By coincidence, Grampa's younger and more dynamic brother Fred had just bought Jamaica Inn, the lonely pub in the middle of Bodmin Moor made famous by Daphne du Maurier. God knows what visions had stirred in the mind of the stolid Fred when he decided to turn publican. Perhaps he envied great-uncle Mort who managed a string of pubs in Loughborough. At any rate, Fred and his wife and son (called, with crisp Midlands logic, 'Sonny') moved bag and baggage to Jamaica Inn and invited us to join them as their guests over Easter.

In those pre-motorway times it took all day to get there. I still recall the moment when the gaunt grey building at last rose into view as we crested the hill. The menacing pirate on the inn sign swayed and creaked in the wind, but inside there was a roaring log fire in a vast hearth and a pleasant fug of pasties, beer and cigarettes. My room was called Patience and there was a pitcher and ewer on the dresser. Chris was next door in 'Joss' while the parents shared a grander room called Francis Davy.

Jamaican Inn at about the time Uncle Fred owned it.

The place was haunted, warned Fred. He'd seen a ghost disappear into a wall. As he said this, the pirate sign gave a loud creak and briefly his hideous face appeared at the window. Fred's wife didn't like the place at all, and even mother, I remember, seemed rather nervous.

That was the old Jamaica Inn, barely changed from the time of the novel apart from a small gift shop in one of the stables. It was not then, as it is now, a motorway service station with beams. It ought to have been a great adventure, but sadly it proved rather a bore. You must see Dozmary Pool, they said. It was where King Arthur sailed away after the 'last weird battle in the west', which was all very well but what we saw when we got there was a small pond on a windswept moor. The parents were not great walkers. We looked at the pool for a few minutes and then went back to the pub. I was too young to join the merry throng in Mary Yellen's bar so I wiled away the time shoving logs on to the fire and reading Agatha Christie or (for the third or fourth time) *Lord of the Rings*, or feeding coins into the juke box in the buttery bar. The hit parade was particularly stellar just then: 'Bits and Pieces' by the Dave Clarke Five, noted for knocking the Beatles off their perch, 'Needles and Pins' by the Searchers, Dusty singing 'I Don't Know What to do With Myself', Cilla with 'Anyone Who Has A Heart', and a whacky new beat group called Manfred Mann with their song about picking up girls called 'Do Wah Diddy'. We were quite a vocal family quartet as we motored along the coast from Boscastle to Bossiney to Tintagel singing along to Light on the car radio.

Fred tired of Jamaica Inn very quickly. His wife Madge missed her friends and neighbours and the barman was helping himself from the till. He sold the inn at a profit to the thriller writer Alistair MacLean and bought a villa in Torquay. Ten years later, new owners cashed in by building a sort of Wimpy bar alongside the old stones and ravaging the surrounding moor with the biggest car park this side of Plymouth. Ten years after that the poor old inn became marooned on a traffic island between the old road and the new dual carriageway. The last time I was there I queued with a bus party of old folks for a rotten warmed-up lunch. I suppose we can blame Daphne du Maurier for that. Jamaica Inn is a horrible place now; as the French say, *tout passé, tout lasse, tout cassé*; everything passes, everything breaks, all things wear away. I would not go so far as to assume Fred must be turning in his grave, for he was a canny Midlands businessman and I'm sure he would have done much the same thing. Old Fred had his head screwed on right.

In due course, the parents decided on Cornwall for the summer too. But rather than choose a conventional resort, mother consulted the small ads in her magazine, *The Lady*, and found a small terraced cottage down a cul-de-sac in a place called Delabole. It was remarkably cheap and when we got there we realised why. Delabole, though handy for a rugged bit of coast, is not the kind of place you see on post cards. It is the other Cornwall, a bleak, bare mining village perched above the biggest slate quarry in Europe. It was where Jamaica Inn's roof had come from. Dad took to pronouncing the name dolefully, as De-la-BOLE, as if to emphasise its windy, rain-swept despondency. Still, we could all agree on one thing: it was better than 236, Kenmore Avenue.

Mid-Sixties summers were cool and wet. Like our holiday in Wales, six years before, it rained most of the time. Cornwall couldn't get enough rain that year. But one magical evening the clouds parted briefly and the parents took off on their own, perhaps to try and recapture their carefree days of love on the sands. They returned, eyes sparkling, to tell us of this marvellous place they had found: a perfect beach not all that far away with hardly a soul on it. It was called Tregardock, described by John Betjeman as a cove sheltered by 'gigantic, slithering shelves of slate'. We set off there the very next day. Sadly, by the time we had trudged down the muddy track to the beach lugging deck chairs and surf boards and beach towels, the parents' romantic mood had faded. Mother settled herself speechlessly on the slatey beach while father wandered grumpily off. Eventually he returned holding a jam-jar which he had stuffed with grass. He was still upset by their tiff, but in a strangled voice he managed to croak the word 'fritillary'. "Dad, you're kidding?" But sure enough, if you looked closely you could see a bedraggled, half-crushed butterfly at the bottom of the jar. It was a male Dark Green Fritillary. I had never seen one before, nor any other kind of fritillary either, and, despite its ill-treatment, it still looked lovely with its speckles and spots on warm golden-brown wings and silver-spangled green underneath.

We were thrilled: this place not only had sand and surf but it had great butterflies too! From then on we brought nets and collecting gear on top of everything else. Tregardock became my little English heaven, a place where you could lose oneself amid the waves and the weedy world of rock pools, and when the tide was in, beating against the slate cliffs, you could roam over the cliff-path to 'Tregardock Mountain' where the late-summer butterflies darted and dipped among the heath.

On wet days the parents looked around desperately for something to amuse us. Quite likely, left to themselves they would have been content to have a lazy day in, walk to the paper shop, make another pot of tea, and see what was on the rented telly. As it was, they felt the call of parental duty without having any clear idea of what to do. One miserable day we went to Looe which was holding some sort of festival. We were dragged along from one catchpenny attraction to the next, bored and increasingly fractious, spending money but not enjoying ourselves. "We are mugs", summed up mother at the end. *"Just mugs"*. Neither she nor Dad had serious interests in which they could try and involve us. If anything it was the other way round. Butterflies, I suppose, filled that vacuum. At least father and son could share the modest thrill of bagging a bright fritillary on a thistle.

As for me, I was the monarch of miles of gritty sand, standing barefoot on the wet, veined shore feeling the ebb tide between my toes. I imagined Atlantis-like dramas as I built walls of sand with crafty breakwaters and piers to divert the tide on to young Chris's feeble effort next door. 'Cold wind, warm slate, so mercilessly smooth', wrote Betjeman. Chris would have agreed with that when he went arse over tip on the slippery rock and bloodied his pug, possibly on the same day that mother's arm swelled up so remarkably after being bitten by a sand-fly. But when the sun came out, I was happy enough roaming the tideline, hitting the waves with my wooden surfboard, and just enjoying the moment. I was, I thought, getting quite good at being on my own.

Soon enough it was time to return to Kenmore Avenue. Time enough to swelter in the holiday traffic queues. Time to play our car-journey-tedium games such as guessing the brand of the next petrol station or (my own favourite), Fifty British Fish, in which you took it in turns to name a different fish, or song-bird, or whatever, until the rest of the family gave up in boredom. And then, towards dusk, the long streets of lime trees and suburban villas until the Morris chugged to a halt outside our own unloved semi. And a week or two after that I could start on another round of 'Lasts': it's my Last Breakfast today, you know, and, look, here's my Last Cup of Tea; and now, please note, I'm heading for my Last Visit to the Loo. "Yes dear, and don't forget to pack your vests and pants". The one thing you could say about 236, Kenmore was that leaving it was so much less heart-wrenching, less altogether soul-shattering than the Via Dolorosa past the green lawns, the park trees and the homes of friends that used to tear me away from The Mount.

CHAPTER FOURTEEN

The Black Blazer

We finally saw the back of 236, Kenmore late in 1965, after two years in which mother thought in all sincerity that I was better off at the Hole. That was the good news. The less good news was that the family was off to Germany now: back to the land of my birth. That offered the prospect of more interesting holidays but it also meant I would have to spend my free weekends and half terms at Remlap. Fortunately the Christmas break was not far away, but to reach the homely nest I needed to pick my way across London to Gatwick airport where the BAC 111 was waiting to take me to Wildenrath and our new temporary home, near Cologne. That may not sound a big deal but I had never travelled on my own before, and I felt distinctly apprehensive. Dad hadn't helped matters by forgetting to send the air ticket. As for mother, she hoped I would be all right but she told Nanna that "knowing Peter, the thought makes me sick". 'Knowing Peter'? What exactly did that mean? It was the same when Dad lost his temper and yelled, "that's just typical you!" What was? What was typical? They never tell you.

After a heavy session with Boss to sort out the missing ticket—it turned out that Dad had wangled some deal with the airline but had forgotten to mention it—I made the transition from bus to train to taxi to plane without mishap. Piece of cake, in fact, or so I thought until the underlying tension seeped out of my brain that night and morphed into nightmares. Waking in a sweat, it took me some time to work out where I was. And then I realised: I had no idea. Perusal of a map of Europe revealed that we were in some small town or base or suburb called Volkspark. Father was working at the big RAF base at Rheindahlen near the Dutch border, supplying munitions to smaller airbases in Germany from maintenance units in Britain. For the time being we were in this nice big German house with a cellar and tame jays in the garden, and a long lounge with wooden panels, and empty rooms and cubby-holes all over the place.

That was the merriest Christmas for a long time. The parents were visibly happier; in one of the few spontaneous gestures of affection that I remember, Dad clapped his hand on my mother's knee, which she banteringly pushed away. This modesty is another thing that vanished in the Sixties. By the Seventies you could hardly walk across the park on a warm day without treading on entwined couples. Where was I? Ah yes, Christmas 1965. What was it about those few weeks somewhere in Germany that left such a warm glow behind, like the bright embers of a log fire moments before it turns to charcoal. That Christmas was nothing and everything. My presents were pretty average: a small telescope which we instantly put to good use spying on the neighbours, and an electric shaver for removing the incipient bum-fluff from my cheeks (in parenthesis this was practically the last time I remember what I got for Christmas, for I was growing up, you see). We did nothing out of the ordinary; a few visits to the RAF cinema, sitting on loose chairs in some Nissen hut; a shopping trip to Cologne (much more flash than any British town I had seen); a winter drive in the hills known as the Eiffel. Perhaps it was because there was no telly. Instead we ran all our records through the Black Box and played cards or roulette, or I would find a comfy place to curl up with Christopher's stash of *Look and Learn* or *Sergeant Fury and his Howlin' Commandoes*. However this year my Christmas pillowcase included Keble Martin's *Concise British Flora* and I knew that, after butterflies and moths, wild flowers were going to be the next big thing. But the root cause of that distant midwinter glow might have been psychological. Very soon now I would turn into a stroppy, chippy adolescent at odds with everything. Christmas at Immendorfer Weg was, in retrospect, a brief moment when everything seemed all right again; when the parents were happy and we were happy, and the world was full of small delights. For once I found I was quite looking forward to growing up.

By the time of the next holiday, at Easter, the family had moved to Rheindahlen and to a nondescript quarter at the edge of the sprawling NATO base. At the back the long garden led to a strip of woodland on sandy soil with cornfields beyond. The wood was good for making dens, which would then be raided by youths from across the field while we raided theirs. But wasn't this, I reflected uneasily, as I dragged boughs across to roof our sand-pit, another thing I was supposed to have grown out of? My uncertainty, as I trod the narrow way between Kidworld and Teenland, grew as a girl of about 15, our noisy neighbour's daughter, wandered over to inspect the work. She seemed friendly enough and we were chatting in a vaguely investigative way when an older, more virile boy turned up and in a moment the two of them were play-fighting and exchanging squeals of delight. I took myself off. I had that funny feeling that was to become more familiar in the coming years.

My brother Christopher got lucky at Rheindahlen. He had reached the age when he too could expect to be sent to boarding school, presumably *my* boarding school, come the autumn. But by now the parents were not so sure. They had been impressed by his school in London, and there was a reputable alternative here too, at Queen's School. No doubt they had also taken a long, cool look at what life at the Hole had and hadn't done for me. Christopher, they thought, was less academically gifted and more practical, more down-to-earth. Chris, they thought, might follow Dad into the RAF, or at least civil aviation. Also, perhaps, although they never actually said so, they could get along fine with only one boy, but life might get a little flat with no boys at all. I think Christopher would have suffered less at the Hole than I had. He would have had me to keep an eye on things, for a start, and the boys of his year were numerous and seemed quite normal. Hole life was in any case slowly softening, like a rock bun left out in the rain. The dreadful Kate had been replaced by a gentle old buffer we called Captain Crunch, and Fanny, too, was about to abscond leaving a visibly happier, more relaxed Boss. You would never have called it comfortable but there was less brutality about as the liberalising attitudes of the Sixties filtered through to our shuttered cloister. I did not repine at Christopher's reprieve. I suspect that Dad had put his foot down. Dad liked young Chris. They drew pictures of rockets and talked about aeroplanes and cars and the RAF. Dad, especially, would have missed him.

So now I was stuck at Remlap at half-term. Those days went by agreeably enough. I cast my rod at the Pit, fishing for roach and perch; or, rather, fishing for carp but catching only tiddlers. I hated removing the hook from their little glass jaws, and feeling the pain in their accusing eyes. Alternatively I could circumnavigate the Pit in the leaky dinghy and, if it was warm enough, take a dip in the soupy water. Or I might take my net to the shallows and see what pond life I could shake out of the weeds, filling my white enamel dish with languorous leeches, scudding water beetles like animated pips, and water scorpions with their floppy nippers and fake stings. The hours I spent by the Pit drifted by in a green summer haze. One day I took a scythe to the keck (cow parsley) growing on the bank and imagined they were the French troops at Waterloo. Or I might wander down to the paper shop or the village library with Granddad, even though he had offended me by taking my kid's electric razor to his own bristly chin. "Not worth it", he had commented when I told him how much it had cost. "You *peasant*", I thought.

I drew biological pictures in the big ex-RAF ledger donated by Dad: sections of worms, guts of rotifers, cells of green algae; an imagined food-web of life in the Pit. I was discovering, partly through 'O' level biology, partly through my own casual browsing, how animals and plants work: the threnody of chemical and physiological impulses that animate matter; how each species makes good its own *ecos* or home in the world. When the time came, I intended to dissect a good many beasts, especially of the smaller sort, and take a close peer at their insides. At the same time I was absorbing just a little of the lyricism of the natural world through books, and storing up ideas against the time when I might possibly write a book myself; my own kind of book, like *My Family and other Animals* perhaps, but with added pond life.

Meanwhile it was the new year, 1966, clickety-click. I was in the fourth form now, the year we 'A' streamers were to sit 'O' levels, ten in my case, including horrible Latin. Hole life was mellowing by slow, barely perceptible degrees. The prefects were now closer to our own age and so much less scary. We sat on a separate table at mealtimes, and on chairs instead of a long bench. Our caps were now firmly off and stuffed into blazer pockets except when prefects were on the prowl, and even then we pushed them right back to show our contempt. As often as not, we put on forbidden white shirts in place of prisoner-grey. On Saturday nights we blagged our way into 'X' rated films or sipped Expresso in banned coffee bars, or even sneaked into a pub, having first posted someone to peek through the windows in case there was a teacher in there (we had already checked out, and so avoided, the known drinking holes of Boss or Crunch).

Our fourth-form classroom was high up overlooking the quad—you started at the bottom and gradually worked your way up the stairs, year by year. During the *longeurs* of French or maths I could watch Pied Wagtails going about their business on the gravel roof, hopping and dipping in the puddles. My window seat was second from the front, a safe enough place—those who rushed and shoved their way to grab a desk on the back row now found they got picked on. I was one of a quartet of class mates, all friends together; me, Woz, Stilly and Dickorum. I passed my mock 'O' levels well enough to sit for them all. All the same, and for the first time, it was tougher going. Even my beloved biology was starting to turn sour. There were no more agreeable tours round the human body, or escapes into evolution. It was back to the basics, now, a plod through cells and xylems, and doing boring things with bean plants. Chemistry, too, had suddenly become dominated by laws, of gases and volumes and pressures; in other words no more stinks and bangs. Meanwhile, physics—never a great way of spending the afternoon—had transmuted into an extra maths course, and maths itself, now that we had got on to calculus and vectors, was incomprehensible. As for Latin, our new teacher, lately transferred from some public school, and probably regretting it, was aghast at our lack of progress. We would all fail, he told us, and fail badly, which indeed, in due course, and to prove him right, we did.

'He should do well', predicted the Boss. Actually I didn't do all that well. I passed them all, except Latin, and won the history prize with my glittering 'A', but my other grades were pretty average. Based on those results I should have taken 'A' level history and English, may be with geography thrown in (no one took geography seriously). But it never seriously occurred to me to opt for anything except science. The natural world was also my world, ergo, I was a biologist, come hell or high water. But, although I did not realise it yet, I wasn't a very good scientist. Though I had been caned for it, I wasn't much interested in experimentation. Mine was the sort of mind that wonders where things come from, not how they work. I might have had an easier Sixth Form if I had opted for the arts instead. A British education forces you into such irreversible choices before you really know yourself and your capabilities. It was a bit early, I thought, and still think, to be deciding on the course of the rest of your life at the age of 15.

This time I really made an issue of it. We should, I protested, be able to take up to six 'A' levels in any damn subject we choose, and let the universities decide. Why shouldn't the school be able to accommodate freaks like me that are equally interested in guts *and* Shakespeare? And while we are on the subject, I went on, how come this school never takes the slightest interest in any of the stuff *I'm* interested in? Mushrooms, flags, fossils, moths, astronomy, Ancient Rome, orchids, stamps, calligraphy, secret codes, early mammals, the symphony, medieval armour and heraldry, classic aircraft, the complete works of Gerald Durrell and J.R.R. Tolkein, the early Flemish masters? Nothing. Not a word. How come? What the hell is *wrong* with this place? "He's an unusual personality", conceded my form master. But it made no difference: it still had to be three 'A' level subjects in either the arts or the sciences, but not both.

With the end of the fourth year came the ceremonial burning of the maroon blazer and the hated school cap. I would soon be entering the Sixth Form a year early wearing a much cooler black blazer and a spiffing long black scarf and *no bloody cap at all*. In solemn procession the symbols of our servitude were carried aloft on sticks to the awaiting bonfire. The stink of smouldering cloth was incense to our nostrils; the fragrance of slaughtered bulls at the altar of Olympus. For years afterwards I suffered a recurrent dream in which, in the process of some heroic endeavour— leading a bayonet charge, say—I would suddenly discover I was still wearing my old school cap (now how did *that* get there?). You could burn the bloody thing, you could watch it sizzle into the carbon from whence it came, but it still came sneaking back, like a thief in the night.

Life at the Hole would go on—I was inured to it—but it would henceforth be at another level: a young man in black, not a boy in red; a scholar not a pupil. There would be more freedom and even a little more money. Bring it on, I thought. Life will get better now. Won't it?

CHAPTER FIFTEEN

Butting in the Alps

The best thing about living in Germany was that we no longer had to take our holidays in Wales or Cornwall. As we knew all too well, summer holidays in England meant grey days on chilly coasts waiting for the sun. Cheap package holidays in the Mediterranean lay in the future. Air travel was still expensive and currency restrictions made life harder for the tourist abroad. But for us none of this applied. We could simply pile into the car and take off to wherever we wanted. Holidays by the Mediterranean or the Adriatic were cheaper than Bournemouth. As to where we went, I had some say, especially as my parents had no particular destination in mind. Naturally, I told them, we must go somewhere warm with interesting wild life and above all lots of butterflies. And in exchange you will get my services as a translator, though I might have exaggerated my proficiency at 'O' level French.

The Cote d'Azur, I decided, was the best place to spend Easter. As usual, Mum combed the small ads in *The Lady* and found a caravan for hire at a place called St Laurent du Var, right by the coast a couple of miles from Nice. Dad wrote to the butterfly guy at the Natural History Museum whose eventual reply was short but to the point. There is a beautiful butterfly there called *Zerynthia thais*, said T. G. Haworth, for which the museum wouldn't say no to a few more specimens. Keep an eye out for it. I certainly would for, as I discovered from my Young Naturalist book on foreign butterflies, this is a delicious looking butterfly, one which Dad instantly christened the 'Jazzy Tie' (for he thought *thais*, its Latin name, was pronounced like that). In my hard bed at the Hole I dreamed of Jazzy Ties adding their splash of the surreal to the myrtle-scented hillsides of the *Alpes Maritimes*. I longed for butterflies as a lover desires his beloved, as a barren winter land longs for spring. To my 14-year-old self, butterflies represented ecstasy, a sense of oneness with nature, or as Nabokov puts it, 'a momentary vacuum into which rushes all that I love'. Yes, I was very keen on butterflies just then.

In the Sixties, as long before, every butterfly book contained detailed advice about how to catch, kill, pin and set them, along with hints on how to find eggs or caterpillars and rear them into butterflies. And then kill them and stick them on a pin. Using one's eyes to see what others can't is pretty close to learning a magic trick. Hunting for butterflies was my gateway into proper natural history. I learned almost instinctively where to find them, and why different species preferred this place to that. And I particularly loved the variety of butterflies in Europe, far more diverse and unexpected than in England, even though it was hard to name some of them with the books available. Apart from their educational potential, butterflies satisfied the child that was still uppermost in me. They were like a kid's treasure hunt, the excitement of never quite knowing what you might find, added to the satisfaction of being able to hoard them in a collection, one that became easily the most precious of my possessions. Entomology, as we grandly called it, was interesting and absorbing, but beyond that it was thrilling. For a while, at least, both boy and man were satisfied.

My family on a butterfly outing in the wilds of Worcestershire, summer 1967: mother holding my net (she was in charge of the commissariat), younger brother wishing he was somewhere else.

You could still come across fellow collectors in the Sixties (historically women reared butterflies and men collected them). No one seemed to mind and you could wander the woods and fields with a net in your hand without embarrassment or fear of being sent on your way by some warden. You couldn't go far in a good area, such as the New Forest or the South Downs, without bumping into another addict and when you did they were usually ready for a chat. Entomology, like most hobbies, makes instant friends. It takes you to places you would otherwise not have discovered; it teaches you to see intelligently, to know where to look and what to look for. You begin to understand how a butterfly interacts with its surroundings: the way it moves through its home, the plants it seeks out, the places it chooses to lay its tiny porcelain eggs. Some butterflies, you notice, shut their wings tight. Others tuck them by their sides like a seaplane on an aircraft carrier, while others still stretch them wide and flat as if refuelling on sunshine. Every butterfly, you come to realise, is different, and not only in looks but in habits.

To begin with, and especially on those early collecting expeditions in the south of France, we approached butterflies as a stalker might view a fine stag or a fisherman a ten-pound salmon. It was all about finding a perfect specimen and securing it. My younger brother shared the passion for a while, while Dad enjoyed the experience as something he could do with his boys. To me, the pursuit of Lepidoptera in a warm climate was a kind of earthly paradise. While I day-dreamed of living butterflies, I also dreamed of dead ones, beautifully mounted and set in a cork-lined box, each one labelled with the date and place of its capture. They would remind me of those days of freedom with Dad and Chris, when nothing mattered except the pursuit of air-nymphs, sky-flakes, floating flowers.

I also liked the fact that the pursuit was not without its small dangers. Some agility was useful when hunting mountain ringlets on loose scree and broken rock, or bounding down the slope after a clouded yellow. You often returned from stalking bramble-loving hairstreaks and fritillaries with scratched arms and a hole in your net. In Germany hatchet-faced men would sometimes shake their fists and shout "*verboten*" as you hurtled past ("*verboten kaput*", we'd shout back over our shoulders). Rural farms in France seem to train their dogs to bark and snarl as the collector tiptoes past, wishing all too clearly to send him blubbing down the lane with the seat of his trousers missing, while swarms of rare butterflies stick out their long tongues and waggle their feelers at your retreating back.

The reaction to our collecting varied from place to place. In France no one cared or seemed the least bit interested. It was just another thing *les foux Anglais* did. In Germany collecting was supposedly *verboten* under federal law but we took the view that it didn't apply to foreigners like us. Once, in the former Yugoslavia, we were mistaken for Germans, and for a moment things looked very *verboten* indeed. But once they realised we were English, they were full of apologies and could not do enough for us. "Pray, take all the butterflies in my garden. Look, there is a blue one. It is for you. *Dobro*! *Dober dan*! Come again." The English were still their friends in those parts.

In England a butterfly day was always a tussle with the weather. You raced the clouds to the chalk hill or heath or sea cliff, and sat out the rain under some spreading oak. It was easier in the springtime of the Cote d'Azur. You slept in the rented caravan impatient for that pellucid moment when you awoke to sunshine slanting through the blinds. There would follow the hurried breakfast; the packing of the khaki gas-mask bag with collecting boxes; then the fast walk past bird-spun gardens and lanes lined with a foam of wild flowers to where the butterflies were playing: the golden guineas of clouded yellows and cleopatras tumbling around one another, the sapphire points of the early blues, the blurred bee-flight of marbled skippers. There was a Nabokovian ecstasy of anticipation and arrival, excitement and surprise, a kind of mind-magic.

For Dad, 'butting', as he called it, meant he could revisit his boyhood. It was healthy outdoor fun, of the sort he liked, not unlike rough shooting or fishing. He never really learned the difference between one kind and another, nor did he ever learn to set a butterfly neatly. He wasn't even that good at catching them. Naturally he preferred big, colourful species like Swallowtails and Red Admirals, and would have been as thrilled as Chris and I if we had ever managed to bag a Purple

Emperor. Little blues and skippers on the other hand excited him not at all; they all looked, and obviously were, the same. Dad's job, as he saw it, was to take the lead on our expeditions. "*Bag it!*" he would cry when some enticing specimen shot over our heads. Dad liked to think he had developed a nose for the right place. "This is the area", he would pronounce with great conviction. "*This* is the area". If nothing turned up in the next ten minutes he would change his mind. "Come on, there's bound to be some more over there". He never really understood that good things happen to those who watch and wait. Dad was a man of action and had to be constantly on the move. We would have been more successful without him, to be honest.

We spent Easter 1966 in the rented caravan at St Laurent-du-Var. It took Dad two days and two nights to get there, allowing for halts along the way. When we arrived, after negotiating a lot of hair-raising *lycettes*, it was pouring with rain and the previous occupant had failed to clean up after his stay. 'I could have done more', he admitted, candidly enough, in a hand-written note. "*J'espère qu'il fait du soleil demain*", remarked our host, M. Augusto. "*J'espère aussi*", I replied with feeling. "Ossi what?" queried Dad.

And it did. After a night of rain dawn broke with what Nabokov described as 'a long glint of dewy brilliancy'. I stepped outside blinking in the Mediterranean light. While the parents cleaned up, Chris and I wandered off to explore, nets in hand. Beneath a garden wall we found a patch of weeds that were teeming with butterflies, mostly unfamiliar kinds. One was a bit like our Orange-tip but with a ground colour of brilliant yellow, like the Provençal sun rising in saffron clouds. Another, more subtle but equally fresh and beautiful, was pure white, chequered with black and dappled beneath with an unlikely green. Not knowing their real names (which at that time were only in Latin), we made up our own: they were 'yellow orange-tips', or 'yots' for short, and 'dapples' ('Western Dappled White' is now their real name). We were still taking in this rainbow of yots and dapples when, with a sudden tigerish flash, a Swallowtail alighted with spread wings on an umbel of fennel. It was like the moment in the Wizard of Oz when everything suddenly turns into Technicolor.

By the time we returned, breathless and bedazzled, the caravan was habitable again and the parents looked happy. Later that morning we set off on our first proper butterfly hunt in Europe. "What's French for 'over there?'" asked Dad." Just shout *là-bas?*" I advised. "*Le-bas*" yelled Dad at a distant *paysan* trimming his vines, thus managing to turn a phrase meaning 'over there?' into one meaning "you're contemptible!" "*Tais-toi*" (shut up!) shouted the *paysan*, and, taking that as assent, Dad marched across his vineyard followed by his young *entomologistes* and descended into the valley beyond. "*This*", cried excited Dad, "is the area". Gosh, we might even find the Jazzy Tie there! (though we didn't). Yes, we were one happy partnership that day, explorers together, hunting butterflies when the going was good.

In the *Alpes Maritimes* there were more butterflies in early spring than in midsummer in England. We hadn't strayed very far before the Swallowtail—the 'ordinary' Swallowtail we called it now—was joined by its exotic cousin, the paler, more streamlined Scarce Swallowtail, each gorgeous hind wing tipped with orange and blue before tapering into a sword-point. They swooped like birds from the tree tops to sip nectar from flowers bordering the lane, and as they did so the sword-tails twitched dangerously. In one valley, scented with rosemary and juniper, spangled with the first flowers of Cistus, we came across the Camberwell Beauty, far from that dingy corner of South London that had lent its name to perhaps Britain's most desired species. They glided above us with scarcely a wing-beat, and for an instant you could make out the pale border beneath their dark mantle that lent them the old name of 'mourning cloaks'.

Come the summer there was another family holiday, this time on the Dalmatian coast of what was then Yugoslavia. There Chris and I 'butted' alone for a while after the parents managed to poison themselves with some local delicacy, we boys sensibly confining ourselves to the tinned food we brought with us. This experience put a damper on mother's always limited enthusiasm for hot coastlands so we decided to move inland and take a long route home stopping at likely-looking meadows in Slovenia, Austria and Bavaria. Come the following spring we were back in St Laurent, this time in a more comfortable chalet, revisiting the now familiar places between the maquis and the coast where the azure but unswimmably cold sea lapped at the shingle.

One of the butterflies we chased there was an early fritillary, freckled like a kestrel in warm golden-brown with jet-black flecks and a marbled underside, mixing tints of purple and rufous-red with spots of glinting silver. They were Weaver's Fritillaries, and they gave me my first qualms about collecting. I wasn't bothered then about conservation ethics. Nearly all the butterflies we saw were common and the few we took would make no difference. What I first noticed with this fritillary, and then with certain other butterflies, was that they dim and darken a little after dying, as though a light had gone out as life departed. In death their brilliancy and subtle interweaving of texture had somehow been transmuted into a simple pattern of brown and black. It seemed a shame. 'Sad brown' the old collectors called the colours of our more sombre butterflies, with unintentional poetic truth. Until then I had felt no great remorse at hurting the things I loved. Now, and it seemed suddenly, I saw the pity of it. Perhaps this delayed realisation was another aspect of growing up. Collecting was never quite the same again as in those dear, innocent days in the sun with little bro and my Dad.

Pinned fritillaries. I wasted a lot of my teen years doing this.

CHAPTER SIXTEEN

The Ice Box

The happiest consequence of reaching the Sixth Form was that at last I got to share a dorm with friends. There were four of us in the chilly little room above the front porch: Mich, Kosh, Bally and me. It was nicknamed the Ice Box because of the cold winds that blew in from the college campus, but it was no more frigid than the ghastly baby dorm next door, nor the big bare Eight Dorm where I had cooled my heels for the past two years. I did ask, with the growing confidence imparted by the Black Blazer, to be allowed a small electric fire on frosty nights, but Fanny wasn't having any of that: "You must be going soft, Marren". So then. Next year, when Mich and I shared a small room high up among the gabled windows, we knew better than to ask. When Boss eventually discovered us toasting our feet in front of my portable stove, he said not a word but simply added an electricity charge to the bill. He could be surprisingly subtle, sometimes, could Boss.

It was, I admit, a slight shock to find that it was young Balsdon, and not me, who was posted as dorm captain. For heaven's sake, he wasn't even in the Sixth Form! It seemed the lad had impressed Boss by walking sixty miles for charity. The whole school was out there to cheer the hero home as Bally came limping up the hill. Of course he was a mate, and decent enough to be embarrassed by this arrant favouritism, insisting that it meant nothing, Pete, *nothing*. He was right about that, but you couldn't help feeling a bit upstaged. So I rewrote the list of names on the door in alphabetical order. Bally still came first but it looked more democratic now. You couldn't have the boy feeling embarrassed all the time.

Unlike the other dorms at the Hole, the Ice Box had a sound track. We hid a record player, some tiny dancette, in a cupboard, together with a pile of paper-covered discs to play. *Good Vibrations* might have been the signature tune of the Ice Box, judging from the number of times the muffled sounds of late-period Beachboys filtered from the cupboard door. Other Ice Box favourites included the no-crap Nancy Sinatra singing *These Boots are Made for Walking* and Chuck Berry's homage to underage sex, *Sweet Little Sixteen*. My own contribution was some cheap Classics for Pleasure LPs featuring proper music by Tchaikovsky, Dvorak and Berlioz. The boys tolerated my stuff in small doses, especially the largo from the New World symphony which Mich told me had been pinched from a song called Smoky Blues. And they quite liked the Witch's Sabbath from the *Symphonie Fantastique* which I suppose they mistook for heavy metal. Every now and then the long-suffering housemaster, Captain Crunch, would potter down the corridor to tell us to pipe down. Then he would toddle off back to his flute practice, and we would turn it up again.

After a term we lost Kosh to make room for a new boy who I'll call Smyke. You'll find him extremely thick, the Boss had warned. Smyke was the forerunner, the first of a rush of knobbly oiks to arrive when our grammar school turned into a comprehensive, co-educational upper the following year. In preparation the school grounds turned into a building site as woodwork blocks and technical-drawing sheds were knocked up to accommodate the newcomers. Be nice to the new boy, the Boss beseeched us. He doesn't have your advantages; intellectual advantages, he meant, for Smyke's dad was certainly much richer than mine. Boss need not have worried: Mich and myself excepted, our black-blazered peers were all as thick as a stump in a bucket of swill. The only difference between them and Smyke was that the latter was no good at games either. He also turned out to be irritating in a variety of small ways that I have generously forgotten. He fancied himself with the ladies; perhaps that was it. There was a lot of grumbling at the time about the fallen status of the school; a widespread feeling that it had gone to the dogs. Never having been very proud of it to begin with, I didn't care much. My only goal now was to get my 'A' levels and clear off with nary a backward glance. Hole, I thought, I'm done with you.

Boss hoped to squeeze me into Oxbridge, and so help win the school a little academic lustre. In the spring of 1967 he took me to his old college, Balliol in Oxford, to meet a couple of friendly dons, along with a clever Polish boy called Big Woz (so named to distinguish him from his younger brother, my classmate, Little Woz). He hoped that I could impress them with the brilliance of my insights into the scientific method. On the way he limbered us up with science riddles. There was this truck driver, said Boss, and he had a load of live pigeons in the back. He gets stuck on a bridge, and so he climbs out and bangs on the side of the lorry to get the pigeons into the air. Why are you doing that, asks a bystander? To lighten the load, said the man. Now was he being clever or stupid? Seems sound to me, I said. Hang on, interrupted Big Woz, were the birds in a mesh cage or was it a solid floor? Was the truck airtight? Having ascertained the facts, he started expounding, most knowledgably, about Newton and the laws of momentum. Great, I thought. That's a *great* start.

After a rapid tour of the ancient stones, the quad and the leafy walk, we were taken up to some turret to meet the masters. They had put a perpetual motion machine on the coffee table and I didn't like the look of it. It had a quartet of panels painted black or white which rotated on wires on their own accord, without any apparent source of energy. Work that one out, they challenged. I hadn't a clue—I was a biologist for Chrissakes - but once again Big Woz was on to it with some plausible explanation worked up from first principles. Heat energy, was mentioned, and molecules, and—what the hell?—*photons* of light. And what are your 'A' level subjects again, they asked, turning to me. Biology, chemistry, and *what...?* "Geography", I answered with a blush. "*Geography*. Right. And what do you think is the subject that unites all sciences", was their killer follow-up. "*Maths*", said Big Woz. At this point Boss interposed. "What", he asked, ignoring my frantic hand signals, "if we put him on a crash course in maths? He can take it with the others next year". Shortly afterwards, he and the dons went off for a reunion lunch leaving Big Woz and I to find a sandwich somewhere. Let's go to the Bodleian library, I suggested. "Do you read?" asked the man at the door. Of course we could bloody well read. Why else would you visit a library? "I think he means read for a degree", suggested wise old Big Woz.

The Boss was less chatty on the way back to Loughborough. He never mentioned the interview again, but he told father later that "Peter's resistance to maths let him down. They were more interested in the other boy". As it turned out, none of my intake went on to Oxford, nor Cambridge either. Big Woz, who was not really an ancient stones man, pocketed his straight 'A's and headed for Bristol. Perhaps out of umbrage at my reception at Balliol, I put down Cambridge, not Oxford, as my first choice on the UCCA form. Oxford knew where it could stick its photons of light.

In retrospect that interview marked the point when my upward academic progress began to falter. In Big Woz language, I had rounded the parabolic curve and could see the old X-axis waiting for me right down at the bottom. This was unexpected. My row of passed 'O' levels had disguised a certain dimming of my star. I had hoped that, with the subjects that really sucked out of the way, like French and physics, and with three subjects I thought I liked, my pathway to university was secure. I was in for a shock.

Possibly my discovery of beer and the English pub had something to do with it. After four years of confinement at the Hole we were now allowed out between six and seven each night, notionally to visit the library. I was one of the few that ever did; the others would head straight for an Expresso bar and hang about in the smoky half-light hoping to pick up girls. One day I found myself with two crisp pound notes. I decided to blow them on cider. I had just turned sixteen, but I knew more about the pubs in Germany—those rustic *Kniepen* with carved wooden porches selling crispy-skinned hunks of chicken—than in England. There was a newish pub in town with coloured lights and a dance floor—clearly designed to attract underage drinkers like me— and it was to this ghastly place that I sped one evening with two chums in tow. I took the precaution of swopping my black blazer for a similar-looking charcoal-grey jacket. We had time only to wolf down a couple of pints before it was time to return for cocoa and prep. "*That was fast drinking*", commented Mich, with his habitual worldly-wise air. Yes, *he'd* enjoyed a few fast drinks in his time, had Mich.

I, unfortunately, had not. I hung up my jacket while we had our cocoa and biscuit in the dining room, and when I returned to it ten minutes later my wallet had gone. We had had thefts before in the Hole and Boss took them seriously. He had punished one boy by forbidding anyone to talk to him for a week. I stood there traumatised from a mixture of shock and cider. "Tell Boss at once", advised sensible Bally.

"Took the whole wallet, you say?" remarked Boss. "That's most unusual." Within the hour he and Crunch had interviewed the usual suspects who all denied it. They were debating what to do next when I made a sickening discovery. With all the excitements of the evening, I had overlooked the difference between a black blazer and a dark grey jacket. I was wearing the blazer. The other jacket was on the hook where I had left it, and so was my wallet with the contents hideously intact. I would far rather have lost the money. "Tell Boss at once", ordered Bally. Boss and Crunch were in solemn conference and my stammered explanation was, I think, the most embarrassing moment of my life. The masters exchanged looks. "I'll make an announcement in the morning", sighed Boss.

The story of the supposed theft had spread like lightening. Several boys had asked me about it in a self-important way, and I had told them to mind their own business. Those affronted souls now had their revenge. I hung my sorry head. "Have *you* never made a mistake?" defended loyal Bally. "Not one as bad as that!" The only thing to do in these circumstances is to eat crow and wait for it to blow over. Either that or run away to the hills disguised as a goat. A prudent boy might have viewed it as a salutary lesson in the dangers of demon drink. But I did not see it that way. The denouement was unfortunate but I had enjoyed my cider under the coloured lights. It had, during the walk back, the effect of making me feel happy, carefree, more confident and not too bad looking either, really. Witty too. More than the occasional ciggie down the old railway line, it opened up a promising new world of bars and banter, all the sweeter for being forbidden. I had fallen in love with the English pub. And that love was to be thoroughly consummated, as often as I could afford, over the coming years.

CHAPTER SEVENTEEN

Pater in filium

Our posting in Germany was expected to last the usual overseas term of two-and-a-half years. Had it done so, it would have seen me out at school. It would have seen Dad out too. Rheindahlen, he must have assumed, would be his last posting before necessarily retiring into 'Civvie Street' on his 49th birthday. But one day a letter arrived out of the blue informing him that he was 'running strongly for promotion', that is, to Squadron Leader. If accepted, it would mean he could stay in the RAF six more years until he was 55. On the other hand, it would entail cutting short his agreeable posting at Rheindahlen and moving to whatever depot or base or unit the RAF thought fit to send him. Dad needed to think about it. He had been stuck as a Flight Lieutenant for fifteen years and there had been times when he thought of breaking loose and starting a new career, in accountancy, perhaps, or supply. Perhaps wisely, he decided to stay in the RAF. And that, we soon learned, meant leaving Germany and moving to Hartlebury in Worcestershire where Squadron Leader Dad would be put in charge of a packing shed, one of several such sheds that made up Maintenance Unit 25. It was not exactly the kind of squadron Biggles would have known, but at least it was promotion.

Dad was now 47. He was no longer the gallant young officer of Hamburg and the East Riding. His hair was thinning and he would soon be resorting to dyes to disguise the strands of grey. He was still a fine figure of a man, tall and slim, dignified, always smartly turned out in a well-cut jacket, squadron tie and polished shoes. Perhaps it was only because I was growing into a languid, moody, scruffy teenager that I had begun to view him more critically. For the generational stuff had begun. Dad disliked my coming on with my flash Loughborough education. Being largely self-educated, he knew a bit about this and a bit about that, and he wasn't keen on being corrected by any son of his. He was still Dad and I was still, in his eyes, a boy, *his* boy, his 'little shaver'. Watching me grow up, tall and awkward, and increasingly independent, pissed him off. Like Dads everywhere, he found it hard to adjust to the fact that life doesn't stay still; that children grow up and turn into younger versions of their fathers. It upsets the balance of a father's family universe.

Dad, I was finding, often got upset when I was around. And when he got upset, I got upset. The whole business was very upsetting. I knew what upset me, but what was upsetting him? It was only as I was writing this, and prompted by a remark from my brother, that it struck me. I might be disappointed in him, but, equally, he was disappointed in *me*. By now I wasn't doing quite so well at school. Nor was I turning out like the officer's son he wanted and imagined. I moped about, and had my teenage tantrums, and generally failed to impress. I was, in his eyes, going off the rails a bit.

After a major falling out, we would end up staring speechlessly at one another; like a pair of bulls, Mum said. Then he would stop speaking to me for a day or two. I was no good at making up either; somehow the words got stuck in my throat. The best way of avoiding all this was to stick to neutral topics. As a family, I realised now, we didn't do interesting conversation. Once I had quite enjoyed Dad's funny little stories, his fantasies about motorway signs and farm animals, his yarns about the war and adventures with his old mate Willie. But that enchanted world had turned to chaff, and what I was hearing about instead was Dad's office routine and his daily disagreements with people I didn't know and didn't care about. To me, he was becoming a bore.

Life for Dad, or so it seemed to me, was just one bloody thing after another. He had always been an epic worrier. He worried for England. He went around with this bothered look on his face that got on your nerves. He brooded and moped, and turned whatever was irritating him over and over in his head, adding layers to it until a little molehill of trouble had turned into a festering mound.

Nor did it help that Dad was apt to screw things up. One day, soon after our return from Germany, he and I went on a weekend camping trip to the New Forest, hoping perhaps to regain some of the butterflying spirit of happier times. In our innocence of the rules we camped where we liked, were moved on to an official site, camped where we liked again, and were moved on again because, as the man pointed out, our tent was too far away from the next tent (don't you read the *rules*?). At each set-back you could sense the coiled spring in Dad's head tighten another notch. When I managed to lock us out of the car in the pouring rain the spring nearly broke. But it wasn't then but a week later that another falling-out came. Some enthusiasts we met in the Forest had given us silkmoth caterpillars to rear. Dad, typically, insisted on taking charge, but I was becoming as stubborn as he; and at length, after a lot of fuss, I told him I'd manage better on my own, thanks, and off he went and, as usual, refused to speak to me for a while. I had enough empathy with his feelings to feel miserable when I bruised them. I suppose I'd hurt his pride again. "He can't help it", said Mum, who, as usual, had a homely and straightforward explanation: "It's his service background", and, besides, "he'd do anything for you, you know". But Dad was an emotional man, and his emotions were starting to take charge of him.

Then there was the time when, at Boss's invitation, Dad came to inspect the air cadets at the school. For that purpose he got hold of an ornate parade sword which came with so many tassels and straps he needed a hand to steady it. The effect, unfortunately, seen from a distance, was as though he was holding on to his trousers to stop them falling down. If that was not bad enough, I watched Dad walk briskly up and down the ranks of cadets without saying a word to any of them, and so finishing the inspection in no time at all. He turned round to find that the other guy, a regimental colonel and friend of Boss's, had only reached his second or third cadet. There was nothing for it but to inspect them all over again, and this time more slowly. "Fastest inspection I've ever seen", remarked my neighbour, as I watched, red-faced, from the hall steps. "Isn't that your Dad?" No, I said, wrong guy (*thanks* Dad). Later, in a traffic queue on the A6 he failed to brake in time and hit the car in front. The irate driver might have said more, but then he caught sight of the sword on the back seat.

"He'd do anything for you, you know". I know, I know. He did his best. He chauffeured us on wildlife expeditions and took a fatherly interest in whatever we were doing. He got me a job in the packaging shed, and encouraged Christopher's growing interest in flying. He sold the pram dinghy to pay for my clarinet. He bought me a little Yamaha motor scooter which I promptly crashed. He could still make you smile, sometimes, with his funny remarks. But all the same I was feeling the weight of his unhappiness. What really pissed you off about Dad was that he seemed incapable of learning from experience. He seemed to think he knew everything worth knowing, yet all Dad's songs and rhymes and wise saws and opinions were rooted in the long-forgotten 1930s. The Sixties offered nothing to him but a generation of youngsters going off their heads ("damn long-haired hooligans, *put them in the army!*"). In that he was probably no different to his RAF friends and neighbours, and indeed some of them seemed to regard Dad as an unusually cultured man who could quote poetry and knew all about garden plants. But I found it impossible to talk to him about stuff that interested me. Dad might make a bit more effort, thought my 16-year-old self.

The first thing he did at Hartlebury was to take down the old sign that said 'Preservation & Packaging Section' and put up another that read: 'Preservation and Packaging *Squadron*'. One way or another, Dad was going to lead a squadron. But instead of airmen and pilots, Dad's team consisted mostly of elderly buffers and mentally subnormal work-experience youths. Although I myself worked there as a trucker's mate during the summer holidays, it was always a mystery to me what Dad actually did. He had civilians to keep accounts and foremen to lead the work crew. You occasionally glimpsed him on tours of inspection surrounded by a scrum of foremen and storemen. We humble packagers looked on uniformed officers like him as minor deities. Dad seemed to know the names of all his troops (top marks there, Dad) and addressed them respectfully, as Mr this and Mrs that. With one of them he even exchanged gardening tips. "Gardening brings you closer to Him", confided a grizzled veteran of the packing shed. "Nearer to who?" "To *Him*". "Oh, oh, I see". This was probably not what he had dreamed about, all those years ago, in the Battle of Britain, in the see-saw battles in the desert, or when peace was threatened at the time of the Berlin airlift.

It seems, though, that Dad had a second, more glamorous job that he was under orders not to talk about. He had been on a course in ciphers, and was now helping to unravel codes using a similar-looking machine to the famous German Enigma machine of World War 2. Just once he brought it home to show his younger boy (he would never have bothered showing it to me). The oil bottle alone, remembers Chris, cost £100!

Mother once remarked that Dad was never quite the same again after we left Germany. On family photographs he often looks as though he has toothache. There is strain in those middle-aged eyes. His conversation at supper time tended to revolve around some incident in the packing shed, about how he put some fellow in his place and told him what's what (or, possibly, what he might have said, had he thought of it). He could repeat an argument he had had with some recalcitrant storeman word for word, and with an intensity that not only remembered the moment but relived it. Mum pretended to listen. Her main aim these days was to avoid annoying him. Afterwards, Dad might have an incendiary word with the TV news reader: "bloody hooligans!". You wanted to put your fingers in your ears.

RAF Hartlebury where father was in charge of the 'packaging squadron'.

This normally upright man was straying a little. Dad began to fill our attic with portable items that had taken his fancy as he toured the depots: a brass propeller, a silk parachute, a bubble sextant, a regimental drum, an inflatable dinghy. They were all apparently spares that no one wanted, and would otherwise have been disposed of, so his sticky fingers could not, in his mind at least, be construed as stealing. All the same, when someone peached on him and Dad was forced to hand the item back, he made sure the sneak was moved away and out of his sight.

It is also possible that he had a clandestine fling with someone in the packing shed. There was no shortage of old girls who wouldn't have said no to sleeping with an officer. Unusually for him, Dad had begun to go out in the evening, to the pub, he said. I thought no more about it, but once Chris, riffling through his pockets for something, discovered a packet of condoms. We could surmise, therefore, that one possible cause of his evident strain was marital. But if father did occasionally get his oats elsewhere he certainly kept his secret well.

Maybe, then, the root of his problem was his family growing up and away from him. His relationship with his boys was in decline and, like many another dad, he resented it. Fathers seek to keep their sons, sons to escape their fathers. He had few friends now, and no serious interests apart from gardening. He had long been a homebody. He had been an active young man, and then a faithful parent, and now he must have felt the need for a new role to buttress his considerable sense of pride and self-respect. I don't know that he ever found it.

I don't want to give the impression that we had fallen out for good. He was, after all, the only father I had. He still made sweet little attempts to do stuff with us. Music for instance. He couldn't pretend to enjoy the horrible warblings of my clarinet but he did occasionally force himself to listen to popular classics on the radio. I remember him once telling me about a marvellous piece he had heard on the car radio. It was Grieg's Pier Gynt Suite No.1. But it was impossible to get him to listen to anything slightly longer or more demanding. He continued to buy sheets of special stamps from the Post Office, partly because he thought it might be a good investment but mainly, I think, because at that time Chris and I were still quite keen on stamps. And so, as day followed uneventful day, sometimes he was up and sometimes he was down, just as sometimes I was credit to him and at other times a disappointment. It was just life, we thought. It goes on from day to day and doesn't mean anything. *'There is no such thing as time'*, as Joyce Grenfell remembered, but only this very minute. Followed by another, and then another. We move on, into the unknown, and leave behind a void. We float like a bubble on an endless sea.

CHAPTER EIGHTEEN

Discovering Girls

When I put my head, hurriedly divested of its cap, round the door of Loughborough's newly opened discotheque, the teens were dancing. They were bouncing and twisting to the suggestive rhythm of *Bend It* by Dave Dee Dozy Beaky Mick and Tich. They were bending it, and taking it easy, showing they were liking it. To one who had only been to school dances, the rotating balls of coloured light and the girls gyrating beneath them in their short skirts looked inexpressively sexy. There's no sex like teenage sex, recalled Martin Amis in his first novel, when his memory, one presumes, was fairly fresh. It seemed to me that girls took naturally to Teenland. They were, as it were, teen professionals in a world where what mattered were attractiveness, attitude, listening to the right music, wearing the right clothes, and, generally, in the Sixties phrase, being 'with it'. I envied the ease in which they moved to the beat of Dave Dee and Co, making it up as they went along, without rules and with no shouty Mrs Robinson standing by and clapping her hands. For those of us who were without it, you sensed an exciting new world passing you by, one that you could only watch from an envious distance, from behind the walls and high windows of the Hole.

All the same, a few Hole-dwellers managed to escape into the teen world beyond the gates. Once, struck down with the flu, I shared an isolation dorm with some Sixth Formers who were boasting about their exploits with the fairer sex. One of them, when challenged, displayed by way of proof what was then called a packet-of-three. Look, he pointed out, *one missing*. I realised then that there must be girls at school who *did it*. When could I meet them? Though a missing condom was hardly convincing evidence, the very thought made me feel slightly queasy.

Until the Sixth Form I had never taken much notice of the girls in our class. I don't think anyone did. There were six or seven of them but they kept to themselves and were more or less interchangeable; a red head here, a curly mop there; one who was bossy (yeah, like *we* cared), another so rustic no one could understand a thing she said. The prettiest one was so straitlaced she objected to swearing *in Shakespeare*. "I can't say *that*", she gasped when assigned the part of Lady Macbeth during a read-through. She *definitely* didn't do it. The Sixth Form girls were different. Not only were they more self-confident, they were also prettier, friendlier and generally more amenable to the chaps—and, mostly, a year older than me. During our first chemistry practical one of them sidled over and said with a cheery smile, "isn't this *fun*?" While hastily agreeing that it was indeed great fun, oh brilliant fun, I took advantage of our proximity to take a good look at her. From a distance, for the girls normally sat in a row at the back, her long, black Sixties hair half-hid her face, and it was only up close that you could see that she was quite comely with a funny little snub nose, happy eyes, neat figure. Bit on the short side, touch of acne here and there, but well good enough for me. I was so distracted by my new friend that I failed to hear the master ordering us to hang on to whatever pungent substance we were making and gaily poured mine straight down the sink. Oops. "Hey look", I laughed. "I've gone and chucked it down the sink!" Gosh, she said, "you never!" She probably thought I was a right dork.

For a week, perhaps longer, I fancied I was in love. I turned up early and lurked around the cloakroom to snatch a brief conversation whenever she turned up for hockey practice. We chatted briefly between the grill that separated one row of coat-hooks from another. She must have known what I was up to, but she tolerated my mooching about and responded to my spoony nothings with good humour. Nothing would have come of it. She already had a boyfriend, a soccer star in the First Eleven. As I say, she was a friendly girl and she liked chaps. She was ready to accept my mooncalf adoration as a compliment so long as the situation didn't turn creepy. The experience taught me one thing. I now knew what it felt like to be in love. Up until then the love thing was strictly theoretical as far as I was concerned. I still didn't really understand the 'how' of it; I was unable to put myself in the shoes of 007 and understand how he felt when, say, Honeychile Ryder strode out of the surf with her tits out. *Now* I got it. Poor old Bond! Heh, it just creeps up on you, doesn't it? One moment you are a free man, laughing at life, and the next, blam! just pulp, with this horrible, yearning pain in your insides. Love – hard to find, harder to keep, impossible to forget. And all I had got out of it so far was a slightly better understanding of the modern novel.

Another missed Miss, perhaps a near miss, was the sister of one of my friends. She was about fifteen, I suppose, pretty well-developed for her age with mischievous black eyes, and, to my short-sighted ones, she seemed excited about something. We were alone in the house and I remember she double-dared me to do something or other, may be take my shirt off or pinch a swig of the parental whisky. But the tone of her voice seemed to suggest that it would be quite all right if I put my arms round her waist and kissed her. Having no confidence whatever with girls, I didn't risk it. Such a pity as I'm sure we could have had a lovely ten minutes together. You start to regret missed opportunities like that as you get older. For they will not come again this side of heaven.

It wasn't long, fortunately, before one actually got to touch one of these suddenly-lovely creatures. Once a year, during the run-up to Christmas, the older boys of the Hole got to host a party to which you could actually bring a girl, if you could find one. And, for those of us unable to, Boss provided a selection, volunteers from the all-girl Loughborough High School who were also boarders and so, presumably, as sex-starved as we were. For party purposes we turned the prep room into a dance floor, lined the inside wall with chairs, and—now here's a surprise—laid down some mattresses for anyone who felt the need for a little lie-down. To get things going, we also made a bowl of punch, craftily spiked with shots of vodka, to put our guests at their ease.

I am not sure what Boss had in mind when he supplied the mattresses. Was he too naïve to notice that the common room now looked like a cheap brothel in downtown Marrakesh? Perhaps he was deliberately providing us with the means to release our pent-up animal spirits, like the Festival of Saturnalia in ancient Rome when the poor and downtrodden briefly became lords of misrule. Besides, Boss's attitude towards you changed the moment you entered the Sixth. Before that he scarcely noticed you, and then, all of a sudden, you were a responsible adult who would know how to treat a girl and wouldn't dream of steering her towards the mattresses without getting at least a couple of drinks down her first.

The punch was freshly spiked when the High School girls emerged from the bus and stood around in an awkward group in the hall. They were complete strangers to us, all dolled up and scented in their best frocks. We unaccompanied chaps steeled ourselves to ask one or other of them for a dance. A top tip for nervous blokes here: *don't pitch in too soon*. It is unlikely that the boldest boy will ask the prettiest girl because, he reasons, he will have a better chance with one of more middling looks, who, he supposes, will be up for anything. Fortune favours those willing to watch and wait. It would not be altogether truthful to assert that I was the one that pursued this strategic insight most successfully. In fact I was far too shy to approach any of them, pretty or plain. But more by luck than judgement I found myself alone with some tall, slender and perfectly acceptable girl of 15 or so in a shimmery dress and called, I think, Judy (for I remember making some feeble joke afterwards about Punch and Judy). I was wearing my only casual shirt, a crimson affair, still stained with boot polish from a Bonfire Night debagging.

I had no idea how to dance but it looked easy enough. Like everyone else, I hopped from one leg to the other roughly in time to the jangling rubbish on the record player. Some older boy shouted across, "hey, well done, Clarence, you're going great guns!" Yes, I would show the fuckers. By now various couples were disappearing into the pool of darkness under the bay window. They sat up straight when the Boss came in and switched on the light, and slipped back into the shadows once he had gone and the light went off again. We must have discussed the art of seduction many times after lights out in the dorm, but in practice it seemed to come perfectly naturally. These girls were impatient to start necking. I leaned over to plant a chaste kiss on Judy's lips and to my astonishment found them slightly open. And the next moment—bloody hell—*tongues*! One of the great discoveries of the teenage male is that girls are just as keen as boys, at least some of the time. They are just a bit picky, that's all, and that's perfectly understandable. I steered her over to a vacant seat—I didn't dare suggest the mattress—for a half-hour of kissing and cuddling and, I hope, a subtle exploration of the shimmery dress and the body inside it. I don't remember a word of conversation. Then all too soon the party was over and the girls were piling back onto the bus. By the time I remembered to ask her out—to the pictures, to a pub, something, *anything*—she was gone. I never saw her again. She had wandered in and out of my life in less than three hours.

Meanwhile how had the other chaps got on? Charlie was wandering about in a daze. Occasionally he sniffed his outstretched index finger. "I got it up!" he kept saying in disbelief, "I got it up!" Whether he spoke truly, or whether he had in fact stuck his disgusting finger up his own orifice, I do not know. You could never tell with Charlie.

Kosh had invited a pretty girl he had a crush on, and to his utter shock and amazement she accepted. He was still in shock by the time of the party, and indeed all the way through it (he had been stunned by the sight of the mattresses, he told me later). Whenever the music stopped and someone changed the record you could hear him loudly and earnestly explaining the House rules while this gorgeous creature sat bolt upright next to him, as stiff and staring as a Dresden china doll. The next day another lad, fancying he had a prior claim on the lady's affections, challenged poor old Kosh to a fight. The course of true love never did run smooth.

For my part I felt it had been an interesting and enjoyable evening and something I wanted to do again sometime, in fact as soon as possible. At the next Hole party I was ready. It was another snog-fest. If anything my new girl, also from the High School—a bottomless well of talent it seemed—was even faster than the last. She was small and dark and keen and eager. I remember a close tactile exploration of her back and being defeated by the bra strap (I mean how-*do*-they-get-these-bloody-things-off?). But she too was destined to spend only the shortest possible time in my life. "Will you go out with me?" I begged between gasps for air. "Oh, I'd love to BUT…." Yeah, yeah, some stupid exam.

The last Hole party was different, for I was on duty. I had been lumbered with the job of escorting the Head Girl, Frances, there as our guest, as custom required. Probably, like Kosh with his porcelain girlfriend, I spent the evening explaining the rules. Frances was not the snogging type. I didn't fancy her in any case and it was in vain that I tried to bribe some gallant to take her off my hands. And when, after about a quart of punch, I decided that on reflection she was better than nothing, she rebuffed me. *"Ah, cummere, love, yer know yer want to…."* But no, Frances most certainly did not want to, and, besides, she had hockey practice in the morning.

CHAPTER NINETEEN

Dorms in the Attic

Towards the end of my first year in the black blazer, Boss addressed our group in the common room. "Next year you will all be in the Upper Sixth and so most of you will be house prefects", he told us. This was not news. Nearly all boys were made prefects in their final year if only to have something positive to say about them on their leaver's report. The more responsible were made *senior* prefects and allowed to stitch the school motto beneath their badge and, if they wanted to, which they didn't, wear a little tassel on their caps. A school prefect's duties were light, indeed barely noticeable, but to be a prefect at the Hole was a leaping promotion, akin to, say, one moment a choirboy, the next a bishop. No wonder this sudden access of power sometimes went to their heads. The duty prefect's whim dominated the life of the juniors during the two hours of daily prep before supper, and again as he disposed of various fag duties, as he accompanied Boss or Crunch on their routine inspections, and distributed punishments as he thought fit. In exchange for these responsibilities the prefect was allowed to go to his room whenever he liked, and, come Sunday evening, was given the run of the kitchen to cook an enormous supper of baked beans, scrambled eggs and buttered toast. By tradition anyone who had displeased us in the meantime was made to stand by the wall and watch us eat, and, if we were in the mood, to be pelted with beans.

But Boss had more to say that summer evening. "Most years", he recalled, "I have had no difficulty putting together a team to run things here. Only once did the House let me down." He paused. "But now I have another difficulty". He was, he continued in a new tone, disappointed with us. He didn't think much of us and that was the truth. He had doubts whether we up to scratch. "*So pull your socks up*", he commanded in that suddenly angry tone that was typical of the Boss. "*All of you*", he shouted, before leaving the room and slamming the door.

There was, you may be sure, some resentful muttering that night. Mich and I felt exempt; we were, after all, a year younger, and as everyone told us, over and over, A-streamers were not proper Sixth Formers, and so would not be proper prefects either. For my part, looking around me, I was ready to concede that Boss had a point. Like a harvest, a school has its bountiful summers, followed by seasons of blight, and years that the locust hath eaten. I'd say my contemporaries fell somewhere between blighted and bug-eaten. I had lived among these lads for a long time and if I were Boss I would have hesitated before putting any of them in charge of the tuck shop. Perhaps his judgement was hardest on carrot-headed Nigel King, for he was popular, played rugby for the school and had been conspicuous in the CCF. But maybe Boss had spotted a weakness, for King had a strange ambition. He wanted to be a dentist. This lone stand-out boarder in a dusty year was looking forward to spending the rest of his life in a rubber apron peering at smelly cavities before cranking up the old drill. Understandably Boss must have suspected a screw loose somewhere, though he made him Head Boy all the same. He really had little choice.

My year-and-a-bit as House prefect is perhaps the only time in my life when I have held real power. As I knew only too well, a malignant prefect could undo a boy, make his life a misery. But, just as the Sixties were ripening into a climax of free love and peace, man, so Hole discipline had softened, slowly but perceptibly. There was room for a personal interpretation of the rules. My own was to relax the prep regime, to allow the boys to talk quietly, and not to hand out punishments unless they were deserved. I was a liberal prefect. I nursed no grudge against the little kids in their maroon blazers. When I once made Head Boy King's younger brother clean my shoes for a week, he thought I was taking petty revenge. But I wasn't; he was just a cheeky little sod. On my leaver's report, Boss considered that I was 'a better prefect than he rated himself to be'. Got it wrong there, Boss. I rated myself quite highly. My way worked. There was rarely any trouble on my watch. What it seems Boss had remembered was the night when, after one of many rows with my peers, I told him I wanted to 'resign'. I wanted to make some gesture of repudiation and it was the only one

I could think of. Boss asked me to think again, and of course, I did. Generally speaking you did your best to oblige the Boss.

We prefects ate our meals isolated from the plebs under a carved wooden canopy. For years I had watched the black-blazered ones rotate around those two tables, one day at a time, with Boss fixed in pole position at one end and Crunch at the other. I had imagined that sharing a table with the Boss might be rather hard on the digestion, but in fact mealtimes usually found him in fairly good humour. God knows what we talked about. Boss was well up on current events, and his views on the economy and politics in general were usually nuanced and interesting. He might have sounded us out on various school issues, or what we thought of some school play or concert or magazine. What lodges in the mind most was Boss's habit of pronging any stray pea or scrap of bacon rind that had slipped off the plate and whipping it into his mouth. Like a heron at a pond, he'd be on it in a flash. He was a big man, the Boss, and since he ate his meals with us he must have been very hungry. We took to flicking morsels off the plate deliberately: feeding the Boss. There were no matching diversions at the Captain Crunch end. In fact I don't remember the man saying anything at all.

I shared a small room in the attic, where the prefects lived and slept, with my Jewish mate Mich. It was lit by a small dormer window through which you could crawl out onto the roof if you had a mind to, and where one year some hero hoisted the matron's knickers to the weathervane. We plastered one wall with pictures and leaflets of cameras (other, more beefy, boys preferred pin-ups, though they needed to be respectable ones, and more or less fully dressed). Another stretch of wallpaper we used for the pencilled scores of our endless games of whist and gin rummy. We got a dressing down for that. In my last few weeks I even posted up charts of how much beer we had drunk, using a mock-statistical form I dubbed the 'inebrionics'. Yes, things were getting a little lax by then.

Photography was a craze I could share with Mich. We knew all the latest SLRs (Single-Lens Reflex cameras, that is) and one of the best Saturday afternoons we ever had in Loughborough was at a big trade exhibition in town where we could try out all the latest equipment.

Mich was the real expert. Under his guidance, I fell in love with those sleek, elegant Nikon Photomics and Pentax Spotmatiks and the Minolta SR1, which sounded like a racing car. Our other shared passion was for hitch-hiking. We would sometimes thumb lifts to his place in Birmingham, and once even to mine in Hartlebury. After a while others began to notice and disapprove. Our fellow prefects found our attitude 'irresponsible', and to hear them go on you would think we had let the whole school down, not that I would have given a toss if we had. After King had buggered off back to his lair with his nose in the air, a familiar growling voice lingered outside. *"Gerra-bus yer glaikit jackies".*—*"Ah, away an' boil yer heid." "I'll gie yer a skelpit lug if ye dinnae belt it."*—*"Ah piss off Janet an tak yer tits oota ma porridge."*—*"Bolt ya rocket, ya wee sconner!"* And so forth. Yes, I was still experiencing a little local difficulty from that quarter from time to time.

Perhaps one of the things Boss had discerned about my peers was that we did not like one another very much. There were always little feuds going on. For example, one boy amused himself by pouring plaster-of-Paris into my bag, the joke being that it would swell in the rain and stick all my chemistry prep together. I retaliated by cornering him in his lair, the malignant little shit, batting him about the head for a bit and then tearing *his* homework to shreds. At that he sneaked off and persuaded the ever-obliging Jock to wreck my room (and I had more sense than to retaliate by wrecking *his*). But even for Jock belligerence had its consequences. One day I climbed the stairs to find him laid out on his bed, evidently dead drunk, with half a dozen Sixth Formers sitting on his fallen hulk like gannets on a rock. They had, it seemed, scores to settle and were settling them now while the Scotsman was safely out for the count. "Do you want to hit him?" someone asked. I hesitated, remembering, for example, the occasion when they had dumped poor old Mich in the cold bath and the over-excited Jock had punched him in the face. "No", I answered, reluctantly. "But you guys go right ahead. I'll just watch for a while."

Yet there seems to be a little chink of light, some elbow-room for redemption, in all of us. I mentioned the miracle of Charlie. In Jock's case it took the form of a girlfriend who looked older than her years and seemed to mother him. In her company, and eventually even without her, he seemed to mellow a little. At any rate, near the end of the summer term we were celebrating with a party at the pub, at the end of which he and I practically fell into each other's arms. "Yer all righ', Pete", he muttered thickly, as though, despite everything, we really loved one another like brothers. We were both drunk, and I, at least, was lying. I hated the cunt. But I had noticed that his girl was kissing anyone who professed to be a friend of the hard lad from Glasgow, and I wanted a share of the action. "She was a good kisser", I told a disgusted Mich as we lurched back to the Hole. *"Tongues and everything"*.

It was not quite my last meeting with my one-time tormentor. Later that year, after he had left to become some sort of apprentice engineer, he paid a visit to the old school. And there he spotted me, the once unbeatable top-boy of the A-stream, forced back with his tail between his legs to retake an exam. Jock threw back his bristly head and brayed like a donkey. I laughed too. After all, it was a very good joke.

CHAPTER TWENTY

Mr Henderson

I was in the black-blazered Sixth but there was still a problem, and that was compulsory games. For a month or two I took up fencing as the least worst option. Padded and masked, I pranced up and down the school hall waving my rapier about. Unfortunately you weren't allowed to swish your weapon around like Errol Flynn. The basic idea was to essay crafty prods—no lunges mind!—and subtle, dexterous flicks. It was all far too fiddley for me and so I dropped my sword—foiled again!—and took up cross-country running. The point about cross-country running—the only point—was that it was unsupervised and took you away from school. One would dash impressively across the playing field and disappear over the crest of the hill before halting abruptly and, pulling out a fag, taking a well-earned break. Then one would go bird-watching, or may be visit the chip shop, before the dash back over the finishing line and a hearty "well done, Marren" from the old fart with the whistle.

After a while I gave even that up and started to investigate the flora and fauna of local ponds instead. Inevitably someone found out and I was summoned to the Boss's office. This didn't look good. I had a heartbreaking little speech ready about the value of ecological survey, and how, after all, it *was* exercise of a sort; for you walked and may be climbed over a gate, and then you did some sweeping with the net. It's weight-training too, I insisted, lifting those buckets of pond water. *And running: you should see how fast those newts move, streaking back into the water.* Good experience of geography too, all that map-reading....

To my surprise the Boss didn't want to hear any of this rubbish. He waved my excuses away. "There's no need to sound like a tragedy queen. What did you find on your last jaunt?" "Uh?" I hadn't realise he was interested, so I gave him a brisk summary of all the flatworms, leeches and shrimps hiding out in the wetter bits of Loughborough with special reference to the palmate newt, which I considered had been under-recorded. It's in practically every pond in Charnwood Forest, I explained, for this newt is more tolerant of acidic water than the other newt, acidic because of the granite, you know. By now, Boss's fingers were rapping on the desk, his eyes glazing over. "Right. Well, I realise you don't like games—unless… perhaps you play badminton? No? Well, have a word with the biology master and we'll put your wildlife surveys on an official footing. We'll call it 'extra biology'". Was this a dream? "And take Michelson with you", he added. "He's no good either".

After that unexpected imprimatur, my playing fields were the clear pools and streams of Charnwood Forest, my goals the pencilled lists of water bugs, my trophies bottles of water fleas and hydra. I even managed to capture microscopic life, those monads and ciliates I had loved drawing as a little boy. When the combined 'A' level biology classes spent a few days studying freshwater life, I acted as, effectively, an assistant master. Hearing they were hard pressed to find a decent, accessible pond, I offered the Pit. Come the day, mother and Nanna watched giggling from the kitchen window as the biology boys and girls trooped down the path, each carrying a net or a bucket like a row of native bearers on an expedition to the interior. The masters Dupey and Warren tut-tutted like old women about the state of the steps but the girls, hockey and tennis players all, hop, skipped and jumped their way down, buckets clattering, without mishap (I'd hoped that one or two of them would fall in allowing me to spring to their rescue). As usual the Pit was swarming with beasties, and afterwards Nanna served tea and cakes under the almond tree. She and mother talked about it for weeks. Chris, who was also there, thought it was one of the funniest things he'd ever seen. I didn't get it myself. What was so funny about pond-dipping? I did that sort of thing all the time. Was anyone laughing? *I don't think so*!

One day I was in the reference section of the library poring over some wildlife tome when a white-haired old codger came over and asked me what I was doing. 'What does it look like?' I might have retorted, 'And what's it to you anyway?' But there was something about him that kept me polite. "Are you interested in wildlife?" he pursued. Uh-oh, was that wildlife or *a* wild life? "Yes", I gabbled. "I am. For instance, I collect butterflies and survey pond life, on an official basis, and I have big plans for photographing wild orchids." The old man seemed surprised. "*I*", he replied, "collect beetles and survey pond life, and last summer I spent a lot of time photographing wild orchids". I was very innocent in those days and unable to understand that the correct response to this unlikely story was to say, well, how nice, but goodness, is that the time, well, must be going, nice meeting you, goodbye. But he looked harmless—shortish, about 60, with a homely yet scholarly face and a twinkle in his eye that seemed kindly rather than sinister. As he told me about his travels around the country's top orchid spots with two companions from the Loughborough Naturalists Club I realised that here, for almost the first time in my life, I had met a fellow spirit. "Come over one evening and I'll show you my slides", he concluded, and I was so much won over that I did.

His name, I learned was Claude Henderson, and he was almost certainly the best naturalist in Loughborough. Like Darwin, his lifelong

Claude Henderson (left) and his old beetling chum Don Tozer examine a specimen.

passion was for beetles but lately he had become hooked on orchids and photography. He and his friends Peter Gamble and Michael Walpole—the Three Orchideers—had for some years past been motoring around Britain on the trail of helleborines and lady's tresses and twayblades. Henderson—he was always Mr Henderson to me—photographed his flowers in Kodachrome with an Exacta camera mounted on a heavy but wonderfully versatile Benbo tripod. I had seen very few wild orchids. I knew them only by name, but Henderson's 35mm slides were the real deal: our most exotic native flowers growing in their natural settings. His images were nicely composed and pin-sharp, and somehow sympathetic, as though he not only knew the plant but had somehow brought out the best in it. I thought it was awesome. I was, after all, talking to a man who had seen the Monkey, the Lizard, the Soldier and other fabulous flowers with his own eyes, orchids so rare you slightly doubted whether they really existed.

He kept notebooks of their expeditions with carefully drawn coloured maps on which the position of rarities was marked as though they were pirate treasure. This or that species, noted Henderson, could be found so many paces from a particular tree, or a rock shaped like a barrel, or, in one case I remember, close to three turtle-shells set into a wall. A natural copycat, I too began my own Henderson-style notebook, coloured with red dotted lines where the trail led over hill and through briars to the crossed 'X', the piratical spot where the plant hunter would get down on all fours to spot the elusive bloom.

He showed me as much as I wanted to see of his yesterday's passion: his beetles, box after box of them, every specimen neatly mounted on a square of white card with a label in Henderson's exquisite copperplate writing saying when and where the bug was captured. Most of them looked more or less the same to me, little black squiggles of former life, but the skill in which they had been coaxed into their natural posture with tweezers and a fine brush was a wonder. He was an artist with pen and paints too, producing hand-made Christmas cards painted in watercolour of favourite beetles or butterflies. I have one still, a Morpho the colour of mother-of-pearl, with the shadows of its patterned underside showing through. It was characteristic of Henderson that he would perfectly delineate these portraits but then leave a smear, perhaps a bit of the egg he'd had for breakfast, or a nicotine-stained thumbprint. In his own world he was a perfectionist, but in the one in which we all have to live, he became awkward and dysfunctional. His pal Michael Walpole, who was much more successful in the real world, referred to him as 'my dear, eccentric friend'.

He also showed me a few of the cartoons he drew purely for amusement. They were in the style of Giles, full of incidental detail, and were clearly based on his botanical experiences. Their constant feature was three elderly gents with orchids sticking out of their knapsacks and bugs clinging to their tweeds. Flower hunting is thirsty work and the trio were often depicted entering a bar with their tongues hanging out, either in anticipation of a pint or in admiration of the barmaid (another constant) and her generous décolletage.

Henderson did not much like to talk about himself, but it was clear that he had had a hard life. Though past 60, he was still working as a lab

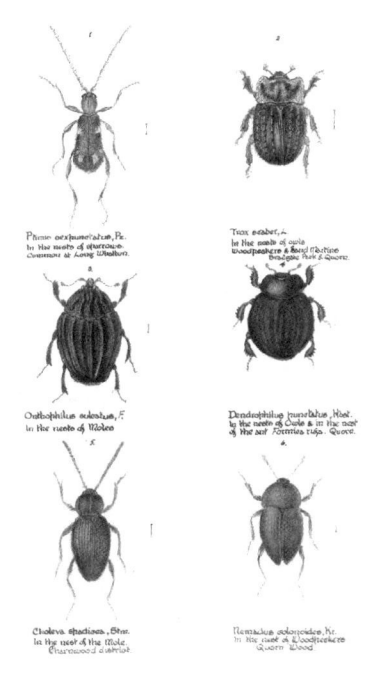

Paintings of beetles by Claude Henderson: labelled in his immaculate handwriting resembling medieval manuscript.

assistant at the College. He did not have a car; indeed he didn't know how to drive. He cycled to work and depended on the bus or friends to reach the places where the beetles lived. He was married but evidently there were no children. His wife was now handicapped, mentally and physically, obese and more or less immobile. During our slide sessions she slumped in a corner chair in their tiny parlour like a sack, occasionally making some gnomic utterance; "*no, you ain't swanking*", was one I remember. Henderson smelled pleasantly, if mustily, of dust and pipe tobacco, but more evil odours emanated from the corner chair. Once, and only once, I accepted his offer of a sandwich. When it came it smelled like the house. "Perhaps you'd rather not", murmured the kindly Henderson after I had stared at the plate unhappily for several minutes. "Come the summer we'll have some nice little expeditions together", he promised.

The parents, and still more, the Boss, seemed rather anxious when they learned I had taken up with an unknown stranger I'd met in a

Henderson's Christmas card – a hand-painted Morpho sulkowskyi.

library. Boss insisted on meeting him, and duly found him a 'charming man', on the acceptable side of oddity. So that was all right then. And so now, instead of going to the Odeon or the Barley Mow on dark Saturday evenings, I would visit Henderson's semi and see some more of his inexhaustible collection of slides—we had got on to Majorcan orchids now—and dream of the world beyond Loughborough. In the meantime I could at least tell him about French and German butterflies and present him with a little box of them in exchange for some of his duplicate slides.

Come the spring, we did go on a few 'nice little trips' in the country around Loughborough: a quarry where bee orchids grew among moss as if fresh-painted; a moist wood reeking of wild garlic with rills spangled with golden saxifrage. Later on, we hunted for orchids further afield and visited places I knew only from maps and colour slides. Henderson was a tireless correspondent, hand-writing all his letters on semi-transparent sheets, often illustrated with sketches or a little map, and all *highly secret* (once when our paths happened to cross, he did his best to pretend he didn't know me; "daft", he admitted, "but there it is"). The secret of secrets, the last circle of Bluebeard's castle, was the location of the Lady's Slipper Orchid, which came with a cat's cradle of measurements from various walls or trees. "But don't tell a soul", he cautioned, "for I'd be in the doghouse if they knew". He was right about that. Years later, when I finally paid my respects to the elusive Slipper, a bearded warden popped up from behind a wall like a Jack-in-the-box and shouted, "Who told you?"

It all came to an end in the summer of 1971. Finding myself back in Loughborough, one day, I called on my old friend. Nothing much had changed in the little back parlour. His wife was exhaling gently from her seat, and Henderson was wearing the same stained tweed jacket smelling of pipe tobacco. But he was disappointed and cross that I had failed to bring my duplicate slides with me. For my part I was starting to find it a bore. I felt I was done with orchids. By then I had botanised in the Scottish Highlands and the west of Ireland, had hung out with proper plant ecologists, and was soon to graduate in botany. Treasure hunts and Kodachrome slides seemed a bit old hat now. And so the magic departed from the back parlour leaving a lonely, dusty old man in a dirty house with his boxes and books. There were no more chatty letters on transparent paper and in fact I never saw him again.

But someone saw value in his boxes of dead insects. Claude Henderson's beetle collection and manuscript records are now in the care of Leicester Museum which has even produced a booklet about him and his fellow collectors called *The Leicester Coleopterists*. Perhaps it is only coincidence, but, to judge from his notebooks and labels, the year Henderson ceased to collect beetles was the very summer when I called on him for the last time. His orchid journeys also seem to have ceased about then. He died in 1983, aged 75. He was my first mentor in field natural history. I owe him much and maybe I should have been more grateful. But no one should expect gratitude from a teenager.

CHAPTER TWENTY-ONE

A Vast Teenage Shrug

I took my 'A' levels towards the end of summer term, 1968. Two of the three subjects posed no great difficulties. Biology had lately become dominated by a lot of yawn-enforcing stuff about processes, about the chemical pathways of photosynthesis and the progress of carbon around the ecosphere. But, still, I could do biology. And geography was simply a matter of remembering things: exports, cities, landforms. My problem was chemistry. What I had once loved—the delightful pop and whistle of reacting substances, the solemn parade of the elements, the glassworks Meccano of gas-jars and retorts—had transmuted into a dreary trudge through the seemingly endless underlying laws—one law after another, all no doubt terribly important, especially if you were a Loughborough pharmacist, but without appeal for the teenage me. The worst part, which used up three hours of valuable teen-time every week, was the practical which rarely involved anything more exciting than 'titrating' one liquid into another and measuring the difference (if you could measure boredom it would have broken the scales). I have always experienced trouble paying attention to anything that doesn't interest me, and, at seventeen, hardly anything did, except girls, cider and pond life.

Keith Carlisle, our scary, boss-eyed teacher realised at quite an early stage that I was riding to disaster, and so he bullied me at every turn. He liked to pick me out to answer some frightful question about Bolloc's Law and stared fixedly into the middle distance as I stammered my reply (with six black-blazered *girls* looking on). 'His grasp of basic knowledge is weak', pronounced Carlisle on an early report, and it went downhill from there. 'Only hard work will ensure success' (and we won't be doing any of that, will we?). Even the Boss noticed. 'Whether he makes university in 1968 or not is going to depend on the chemistry battle', he warned. On one of the many days when I couldn't be bothered—some drivel about aldehydes—and so handed in a blank exercise book, the chemistry man hit the roof. "You all did quite well", roared Carlisle, "with one exception". That was me again, and on the blank page he had written, in horrible red ink, 'unless you begin to demonstrate some interest in this subject I will not allow you to take the 'A' level exam this year'. It was bluff, of course, for he could do no such thing (I wasn't the thickest person in his class, just the laziest). All the same it came as a shock to me, the young scholar, one who had grown blasé about mounting the stage to receive his routine prize. I hated being shocked like that. It made you feel all aggrieved and annoyed. Indeed Carlisle's rebuke might well have bucked me up for a week or two before slumping back into apathy again.

As I say, seventeen is not a good time to be immersed in the study of gases. I had other things on my mind. Lanky and pimpled, I had taken to wearing cufflinks and using eau de Cologne. I grew my hair as long as I could get away with, which was not very. I drank as many pints of cider, or shots of vodka flavoured with lime, as I could afford, and read subversive books like Anthony Burgess's *A Clockwork Orange*. Once, perhaps inspired by Burgess, Mich and I discussed breaking into someone's house before realising we were both far too torpid to go through with it. I escaped school both permissively and illicitly, often on birdwatching expeditions on the back of someone's scooter, or I would bus or bike to my grandmothers where I did nothing. At a time when nearly everyone else was representing the school in the First Fifteen, or acting, or leading debates, I found myself almost completely disengaged. I was nominally in the school orchestra, playing the clarinet, but only nominally for I could not play my clarinet. Once, under pressure from the music teacher, I put together a male voice choir simply by inviting some fellow loungers to come with me. I contributed to the odd debate such as the one on arts versus science, offering my opinion that the future lay in computers and technology, and that history was dead, as well as stupid, whereat old 'Zook' Modral, who had taught history since 1066, remarked drily that "you have just made it", i.e. history. Eeh, he had a rare way with words did that Zook.

For my House, the Vikings, or Mongols, or whatever they were, I made sure I did nothing at all. I wanted my contempt for the system to show; in fact I wanted my upwardly projecting two fingers to shine in neon. So one day, when it was my turn to read the lesson—the cheek of it, a well-known atheist like me!—I felt disinclined to leave my perch in the library. Eventually someone was despatched to find me. I dragged my feet up the stairs to the room where all the Mongols stood waiting in silence. I knew this was going to be tricky. "Er, sorry", I said to the red-faced master we knew as 'Slash-house', for reasons lost in time. "It slipped my mind" (again). "Sorry?" he yelled, and you could tell he was cross. "*I'm* sorry!" (Oh, are you?). After a very angry and, I felt, unnecessarily long and loud dressing down, he ordered me to stay behind to take note of the exemplary punishment he had in mind. I think he wanted me to push a broom somewhere; in fact I think he

I wiled away the lag time during chemistry lessons by doodling, some of which turned into weird shapes like these. I considered I'd discovered a new artform: boredom made manifest; the Bored-ist school of drawing.

wanted me to push that broom *a lot*. But I was nearing the end of my time at his rotten school and it was getting a bit late for the heavy hand. After a long argument, in which I had arranged for some lads to hang about and make rude signs behind his back, Slash-house suddenly backed down. "I'll meet you halfway, Marren", he conceded. "I'll let you off punishment duty and you will agree to turn up to each and every house meeting and lend us your full support". And did I do so? Alas, no, bless you. I far was too busy doing the crossword. On my leaver's report, Slash-house, presumably remembering this incident, and considerately putting a positive gloss on it, affirmed that 'he has an independence of opinion which he is not afraid to express'. 'Express' as in 'Daily Express' presumably.

He wasn't the only master to take issue with my attitude. One day I was strolling along, hands in pockets, minding my own business, when I spotted an empty drink can in my path. Someone might trip over that, I thought, and so, with a dexterous boot, I sent it spinning away to land safely under the steps of Domestic Science. In the net! Unfortunately my goal kick had been noticed by a bad-tempered master called Stubbs. Some years earlier this man had crashed his motorbike, leaving him with a permanent limp. Probably he was jealous of my ability to do what he could not and kick a rolling tin into touch. At any rate he, too, began to shout and wave his arms and threaten me with summary discipline. So what was he going to do then? Expel me? After some argy-bargy of the 'yes, you will', 'no, I won't' kind, Keith Carlisle joined in the discussion. "You know what you must do, don't you?" he hinted, looking at me meaningfully with one eye while the other searched a corner. He meant apologise. Ah well, better an insincere *mea culpa* than press-ups at dawn. "I'm very sorry", I said humbly with what I hoped was a straight face. "What I did was wrong". To my great surprise, Stubbs suddenly became rather emotional and said, as it were man to man, "well, we'll say no more about it, then". I very nearly shed a tear. Then I went outside and gave the first crisp packet or coke bottle I found the kicking of its life.

Today when any reasonably intelligent boy or girl receives three 'A-stars' as a matter of course, they must assume that their parents must have been pretty thick to scrape their 'C's and 'D's. But, back in 1968, when exam questions were based on half-hour essays and sustained arguments rather than ticks in boxes, only the top 5% were awarded an A, irrespective of their marks. At my school it was unusual for more than one or two scholars to receive an A grade in any subject. All the same, I must admit I took it for granted that I would be one of them. May be not in disgusting chemistry, but even there I thought I could bluff my way to a 'C', say, enough anyway for a place at a decent provincial university, if not Oxbridge.

I have no memory of the 'A' level exams, which might indicate an ongoing sense of lassitude towards this culminating moment of my schooling. I had no sense of coming disaster. Predictably enough, chemistry had been a crock, and my answers mere guesswork, but, I hoped they were *inspired* guesswork. After all, I told myself, the thing about chemistry is that there is only one *possible* answer. Chemical reactions can only go one way, and you can more or less work out where from first principles. Unfortunately, it seems I didn't know any principles, first or otherwise. My feelings after the last wretched paper was finished were overwhelmingly of relief. That's it; it's all over; no more school, no more Hole. Thank God Almighty, free at last!

I wandered out of the exam hall, absentmindedly taking with me the number of my table. 'Zook' Modral came running up. "You boy". "Do you mean me?" I had spoken my last 'Sir' at this dump. "My number!" shouted Zook. "Oh, do you mean this?" I said holding up his little tag between finger and thumb. "What did you want it for anyway?" he wanted to know. I had no idea. There had been a time when I was terrified of this old skull-face. Now I shrugged my shoulders with a nonchalant teenage air that I knew would annoy him most horribly, and drawled, "I dunno, souvenir, may be?" He glared at me speechlessly for a moment with frazzling eyes. "You're round the bend, boy" he barked. "What?" "*You're round the bend*". I kept on smiling. Piss off, Zook. None of them bothered me anymore.

Six weeks later, safe at home in Hartlebury, the brown envelope arrived. One reads these things like a book review: a first, quick glance from the corner of one's eye. Expectant parents clustered near. I snapped open the folded paper. B for biology. A bit disappointing, that, but it hadn't felt like an A. B for geography, ditto. Ah well. Not Cambridge then. But for chemistry there was not one letter but four: 'O ORD'. For a moment I didn't take it in; the only relevant letter was 'D', could that be it? Then I remembered. The examiners marked near-misses with a compensating 'O' level. It meant I had nearly scraped a pass, but that I had nevertheless failed. Carlisle had been right; I had fucked up my chances of university that year. Maybe I could still have got into some technical college or poly, but that would have been a sad end for the Boss's one-time Oxbridge hope. I was still seventeen, a year ahead of other university entrants. I could afford a gap year and, besides, it would provide a space for all those natural history adventures I had promised myself.

Dad took charge. There was nothing for it, he said, but for me to return to the Hole and retake my missing 'A' level. Er, *Da-ad*? There were alternatives; I could have taken the bus to a crammer somewhere. But the parents were insistent that I should return to the same school for one last term of chemistry and titrations, and jolly well pass this time. I shrugged my teenage shoulders. Dad wrote to Boss, who agreed to have me back and hold my room. I could of course have stayed at Remlap and taken the bus to Loughborough, but by now I thought the Hole offered more fun than life with the gramps. I would have money in my pocket thanks to my holiday job, and plenty of time to idle about town spending it. So teenage Pete agreed to become 'Marren' again for one last term, to redeem his honour with a second run at the lists, and this time, as Boss put it, in his headmasterly way, 'to pass, and pass well'.

CHAPTER TWENTY-TWO

Farewell to the Hole

Keith Carlisle was magnanimous about being proved right. "You nearly proved me wrong!" he exclaimed, cordially enough, as though there was an offhand merit in getting an 'O-ORD' instead of a straight 'F'. But he spoiled it by adding that "this time round, it could be an 'A'!" Oh no it bloody well couldn't. Danger: threat of hard work ahead! Carlisle clearly had in mind some serious grafting from the failed 'A'-leveller. He expected me to attend every chemistry lesson and in the meantime to think deeply about ketones and carbon chains and so forth. For my still abundant spare time he had arranged a little *divertissement* in biology. They had just acquired an instrument called a freezing microtome, with which you could cut thin sections of tissue for staining and examination with the microscope. I was to become the master of the microtome. All this threatened to make my last term at Loughborough unutterably tedious.

I checked out the biology, and it was as bad as it sounded. I was determined to spend as little time as possible in my despised school. There was a group of reprobates I used to hang out with called the King Club, which awarded a bum-shaped mark or 'scrote' every time one slacked off games or lessons. I doubt if anyone won more scrotes than I did that term. I entered and left school as I pleased, rarely attended house meetings or morning assembly, and, even when there, was far more likely to be found with my feet up in the library or senior common room than in the lab. To underline my semi-detached status, I tore the badge from my blazer. I spent a lot of time idling about town, reading books and newspapers, drinking coffee in bars, and heading off to the cinema on wet afternoons after a sandwich lunch in the pub. I was, I considered, here for one reason only and that was to get fucking chemistry out of the way; a minimum grade would do. I felt in limbo, a prolonged, eerie void between school and university, and, up to a point, between boyhood and man's estate. I used to dream about it. Where, thought my dream self, where the hell am I? How did I get here? Where's the exit?

When, late in the day, Carlisle discovered the full extent of my slacking he threw a wobbly. It was the worst wobbly he had ever thrown, and his high, furious voice could be heard from one end of school to the other. I remember one boy emerging from a nearby classroom looking stunned. "What the hell was *that*?" There was no doubt that I had deceived him, and that his anger was justified, but being full of teen angst and self-pity, I was in no mood to listen. By the time I had returned from a long walk, a drink, and a lot of cigarettes, Carlisle had calmed down. Evidently he and Boss had had words and decided it was all spilt milk now. Carlisle actually apologised for losing his rag. "I expect I deserved it", I answered, anxious to adapt to the forgiving mood. "Yes, you did, but even so…" replied the chastened master. I was leaving in a few weeks. None of it mattered so long as I could scrape a 'C' or so in his filthy subject. Working the microtome was his fucking idea, I reflected. It would not have helped me pass an exam. It was just work for work's sake, the Loughborough way of using you up.

This was not only an idle term but a rather lonely one. Most of my few friends had moved on. Mich was retaking his missing 'A' levels in Birmingham, and, by the sound of it, making up for lost time as far as sex and drugs and rock 'n' roll was concerned. Other pals had sailed through to various colleges; we had been one of the Boss's better years, with nineteen boys and girls entering university and another seventeen heading for polytechnics. All my old enemies at the Hole were gone; the bullies, the sneaks, the all-round crap-tossers, all embarking on their several destinies. The lads in charge now were easy enough to get on with. I shared my old dorm with a boy called Jackson, generally known for some reason as 'Strap'. Strap had been at the Hole for ages but had always kept a low profile. His great friend was a younger boy called Jones. They did everything together, like twins. I liked Strap. He was friendly and normal and cool, and obviously undamaged by Hole-dwelling. Sharing the dorm next to the box room with my old mate Kosh was a certain Haycock, noted for the large collection of soft porn which he kept hidden in a suitcase in the box room. We were treated to seedy lightshows where he kept up a running commentary: "Here is titivating Tiffany from Woking, 35D-23-36. Tiffany is a policeman's daughter and I bet you'd like to take down *her* particulars. *Now, salivating Samantha, 34B-24-35 from Hull, likes to peruse music shops. She particularly enjoys a rewarding poke in the country section…*" Haycock joined the army and rose to become a lieutenant-colonel and intelligence chief in Northern Ireland, so there must have been a hard core inside all that soft-core.

Another top-floor character was Gibbon—'Gibbo' or 'Gibby'—who, naturally enough, was a bit of a monkey. Gibby kept us amused with his scrapes. Once, while pulling on his clothes at speed with the breakfast bell jangling, he yanked up his zip unaware that his little old man was peeping out. Gibby had no intention of letting a little thing like that get in the way of his morning porridge. Somehow he slipped into his place on the Boss's table without anyone noticing his pink impediment. For twenty minutes he sat there taking part in the necessarily polite conversation while wrestling with the recalcitrant zip under the table. "Are you all right, boy?" questioned the Boss. "Oh yes, Sir, just a groin injury, Sir, from a rugby tackle". "Ah. See matron if symptoms persist".

On another occasion, possibly after the school dance, when we were most of us taking it in turns to throw up in the bog, trust Gibby to go one better. From the shadows of his dorm came a merry cry: "*Gibby's shat himself!*"

The Hole was no longer the hard place it had been on that distant day when I watched the white Morris disappear down the drive. A new and unfamiliar quality had entered our austere domain. It was kindness. The smaller boys were positively mothered by our new matron. All of a sudden they were allowed to grow their hair long, and she even called them by their *Christian names* for Christ's sake. Of course we old-timers didn't care for that at all. Once, when we gathered in my room to enjoy a long moon about favouritism and falling standards, we made jolly sure the window was open so the new housemaster would hear us. Sure enough, he soon appeared at the door, prepared to have a reasonable conversation with us about the new lovey-dovey Hole his matron-wife was trying to build. For my part I quite welcomed the new atmosphere and thought it well worth the irritating simper on the faces of matron's favourites. Bullying still went on, of course, and it sometimes fell to me to have a quiet word with the victim, as one (as Boss so annoyingly put it) 'who has also suffered'. Boss himself had mellowed to the extent of occasionally inviting favoured ones into his inner sanctum to watch an educational film on telly or to talk about old times. He was looking forward to moving to a new home in Charnwood Forest with his post-Fanny lady love, and to retirement. He invited me to come and stay for a weekend sometime. I wish I had, now, though I never did. It was hard to imagine a relaxing weekend with the Boss.

For a week or two before the chemistry retake I did my best to cram up on chemical facts. Far too late I realised that some of this stuff was not actually all that bad, and that most of my trouble had been self-inflicted. If, instead of striking attitudes, I had done a modicum of work, I could have been at university now, punting my girl down the river, or laughing about town with some fine fellows before heading up the quad to smoke a few joints. Well, it was all too late now. I sat my retakes in the echoing hall with a few other rejects and slunk out feeling I'd probably failed again.

One of my last memories of school was of taking part in a production of *Amahl and the Night Visitors*. I was a shepherd, with false whiskers, heavy make-up and a woolly hat which some of the girls thought made me look rather saucy. Realising that these girls were, after all, really rather easy to pull, so long as you had a bit of attitude and wore a silly hat, was another discovery I made too late. Amahl was a happy production right up to the day of the performance. We shepherds and shepherdesses lined up in the foyer and entered the hall in groups singing lustily about Emily and Bartholomew and how their sheep were getting on. Suddenly I spotted my old nemesis Slash-house staring at me from the back row, and for a moment I dried. "*Go on, Marren*", he hissed. Feeling a little thrown by the encounter, I tottered on to the stage and promptly knocked over a cardboard palm, nearly clouting young Amahl and scattering the night visitors. At that very moment I was meant to sing my only solo line which was: "Oh look! Oh look!"

For the rest it was one last, extended goodbye to the life I had known. The lads were good enough to chuck me into a cold bath that last morning. I was touched by their gesture. Unpopular guys never got chucked into baths. Boss shook my hand and expressed the hope I would get through this time—and that was that. Suddenly they were all gone and young Pete (at last, no longer 'Marren') was left all alone. I thought I would be overjoyed to be leaving the Hole at last, having rehearsed this moment in my mind for years. But, as I watched Kosh and the others disappear down the path in their dark winter coats and long black-and-yellow scarves, I felt something else, and quite unexpectedly: sadness at losing old friends, a kind of emptiness at leaving the old life behind; and, beyond that, regret for all the time I had wasted during the past few years, failing to fulfil my potential, disappointing everyone that cared about me. I watched it all drift away from the gable window of the Sixth Form bathroom, still tingling from my bath. And then, inside the hour, there was the car, a different one, but with the same old Dad inside, and this time I wasn't coming back.

Drinking cider with Kosh outside the Blackbird, Loughborough 1968.

The school liked to round things off with a leaver's report designed to put the best possible construction on one's school 'career'. In my case there was no need for the generous space allocated for games and other out-of-school activities. Boss didn't mince his words. Games, he wrote, 'held no interest for him'. But he built up the biology, judging me 'fanatically keen' on all pursuits involving the study of plant and animal life, adding that I had 'a first class brain' even if I didn't always use it. As for the bit about 'personal qualities', he admitted that I had become rather reserved and distrustful, traits, he might have added, that I had acquired at his institution. On the whole I was not, he implied, a successful product of the system. But, he went on, with would-be generosity, I was basically a decent enough chap when you got to know me, trustworthy, well-meaning and so forth. Even Slash-house managed to find a positive gloss to put on my undisguised hostility to his Mongol hordes (I had forgotten that he would have a hand in this farewell charter). My fine bearing, he claimed, had 'contributed to the tone of the house'. I had a good chuckle over that.

The Boss's valediction, that I was 'potentially a lone wolf', was less amusing. Though prescient enough, Boss was never one for nuance. A career spent speeding rustic trogs on their way to Loughborough institutions had blunted his critical faculties. It's more complicated than that, I saw myself saying, while shoving him against the wall. Before they dumped me at your boarding school, my days were happy and carefree. They were filled with sunshine. It was your school that fucked me up, Boss. You *knew* my parents had made a mistake, even if they didn't. Christ, I could have got better exam results at home. But, I had to concede, letting go of his lapels, in the end it was no one's fault but my own. Having accepted the Hole and the modest local grammar out of a kid's mistaken sense of honour, coupled with sheer irresolution, I might at least have tried to make the most of my situation. Face it, I had screwed up my schooling.

The time of the Hole as a boarding school for boys was nearly up. Come autumn 1971, the boys moved out to Charnwood Hall, near Woodhouse Eaves, accompanied by matron and all her little charges. The regime there was described to me many years later as 'hearty'—

ha-ha-ha-hearty. The Hole became a boarding school for girls, and it was thus that I found it when, happening to be in Loughborough one day, with time on my hands, I decided to knock on the old front door. I would, my guide assured me, find it much changed. Well, yes and no. The old broken beds had been replaced with wooden bunks and colourful duvets. The dorms were now heated and the Boss's old hall was a common room. There was even a phone booth. The girls could dress as they liked at weekends, wear make-up, and go home when they pleased. The atmosphere was less Tom Brown and more that of a community centre. On the other hand the place was still badly in need of a makeover; there was the same air of shabbiness; the paint flaking, the brasses dull, the wallpaper grubby and fading. The porridge, one guessed, tasted much the same. Some of the girls were quite pretty but they avoided my eye. They looked like frightened hares. I was an old man to them now.

The school, meanwhile, had become a 'community college', that is, an upper school for Sixth Formers. There were hideous new buildings all over the place. The long-awaited swimming pool had been installed. There were now blocks where Loughborough lads could learn drama and office management, on how to organise a race. The blackboards were now white boards, and covered in graffiti. The school, I read from the brochure, was a place where 'all members of the community can be involved in their own education'. You would probably need to spend some time there to find out what that meant. I never had any sense of being 'involved' in my education. It was simply imposed on us, like the Rules of the Hole.

In 1997, the school was given yet another change of clothes and turned into a sports college. Instead of aspirant engineers and teachers, it now turns out would-be athletes and their trainers, bound for what is now Loughborough University. Their leavers report has even more space for games, I guess.

Boss retired in 1970. He played more bridge, and stood as a Liberal candidate for Blaby against Nigel Lawson in the February 1974 general election. Although he lost (he hadn't a hope), he garnered a respectable 14,500 votes. At some point his health went into decline. Around 1980,

I spotted a piece in the *Leicester Mercury* about some old boy reunion at the College. Some of the teachers, like Zook Modral and Mrs Park, were still recognisable, indeed hardly changed—Zook was born old—but Boss seemed to have shrunk inside his own skin. He had obviously had a stroke, was trying to smile, and you wished he hadn't. Two years later he was dead. He is hardly mentioned in what passes for the school history, unlike his predecessor, Eggs, who became a local institution. But then, the Boss was never a Midlander. Loughborough looks after its own.

Keith Carlisle landed the headship of a comprehensive in Sussex; he retired in 1989 by which time that school, too, had become a 'community college'. I found two references to him on Friends Reunited. One remembered him as 'easily the scariest teacher in the school'. But the second brought a smile of empathy from this ex-pupil. For it seems Carlisle shared my old Hole nickname of 'Clarence'. In his case it was a reference to Clarence the Cross-eyed Lion in some forgotten film of the 1960s. And his deputy was a Mrs Slaughter (you couldn't make it up). *Pax domine vobiscum.* It is all over now, a small wave in the ocean of time, one that takes its brief sparkle from the overhead sun and then is over and gone beyond recall.

The End

(Of Part Two)

PART THREE

Nothing happens unless first we dream.

Carl Sandburg, American poet

CHAPTER ONE

A Trail of Flowers

It felt like starting again, but this time as a grown-up. I had taken my last school exam for good or ill. I had said goodbye to friends I would probably never see again. I had come home. And now I was alone, a short-sighted, insecure, rather vacant teenage beanpole. I had no job. I had no car. Of course I had no girlfriend, but beyond that I had no friends at all, or at any rate none nearby. It was New Year 1969 and I had nothing to do. There were seven months of limbo to fill before university. I did not even know for certain that I would be going to university, although I was fairly sure that some place, somewhere, would take me even if I fluffed chemistry again. I had just turned 18 but I did not feel like an adult; rather I felt robbed of my boyhood. Those far-off misty vales were where I wanted to be, with their simplicity and reassurance and endless promise. Reality, by contrast, seemed indigent and empty. For the immediate future, I had only one fixed idea and that was to save enough money to buy a camera, after which I intended to find and photograph as many wild flowers, and particularly wild orchids, as possible. That, at any rate, seemed an attainable goal. I had dreamt about botanical rambles for a long time. Now I planned, with my family's help, a whole summer of expeditions.

But that was later. For now it was mid-winter. What to do, what to do? I spent a lot of time in my den, the long bedroom overlooking the green space beyond the garden with its swings, sometimes occupied by a pretty teenage girl who used to sit there staring into space (I could get a fairly good view of her with my X30 telescope). I lounged dreamily amid the trophies of my life: my slowly expanding natural history library, my cages of chrysalids and caterpillars, my pile of classical music LPs, my cabinet of pinned butterflies with a copy of Mayfair hidden in the nineteenth drawer. I drew maps of where to find rare orchids. I drew pictures of mushrooms for a projected book. Then I got bored with all that and threw them away. I didn't know what the hell to do.

Fortunately Dad did. The previous summer he had found a holiday job for me at his RAF packing 'squadron' a mile down the leafy Worcestershire lane. I had been the driver's mate, sitting alongside Alec McGinty in the lorry. At each stop I shifted loads of aircraft spares from the back of the lorry while Alec, clearly fatigued by the short drive, took a break for a ciggie and the Mirror crossword. That had been a boy's job, but now there was another boy in place to do it, a cheerful, popular, local lad. But he was of no account and, once again, Dad, or rather one of his storemen acting on his orders, told the boy to make way for the officer's son. I had returned. The packers failed to appreciate such blatant nepotism. It wasn't my job; it was that other boy's job. What business was it of mine to march in here and kick him out? But what they thought was neither here nor there. I was the son of the boss, and I turned a deaf ear to the mumblings and mutterings among the packing crates.

At seven on the dot each weekday morning, father would leave a cup of tea by my bed. Half an hour later, while it was still dark, I started my little Yamaha scooter, with its L-plates fore and aft. A couple of miles down the lane was the hangar, now home to Dad's Preservation & Packaging Squadron. There, after another cup of tea with a cheerful old lady called Joan and her decrepit admirer, I loaded up the lorry to begin the morning round to the outlying depots. At mid-day I rode the scooter home for the deliberately stodgy lunch mother cooked for her working lad, followed by a repeat journey around the hangars and sheds, loading and unloading, and so home for tea at four. So keen was I on earning enough slaves wages to buy a camera that I sometimes stayed on overtime, gluing labels to crates or whatever other little tasks the foreman could dream up for me. Being the officer's boy, I could have as much overtime as I jolly well wanted.

One day Dad's main man came in with news. "Good news, Peter", he sang. Your headmaster has phoned to say you've got a C in chemistry and that that should be enough for what you want. He was right. It wasn't a *good* grade but it was enough. Good enough for Exeter anyway—a fasionable university that specialised in Oxbridge rejects like me. Phew! It was a relief to know that this lorry-loading life wasn't going to go on for ever. Come the autumn I would, after all, be leaving home again to read for a combined honours degree in zoology and geology—the best outcome I could manage with my dud 'A' level in geography. I had no interest at all in rocks and strata, but, I reasoned, once you're in, you're in. Then I would drop the rocks like a stone. Very devious and cunning, I thought.

A few days later, the man came over again with some more news. Less good this time. I'm very sorry, he said, but a situation has arisen. They need a man over at A-Site and I'm going to have to send *you*. Hard luck, and all that, but its last-in, first-out, I'm afraid. So it's you. This was a crappy turn of events. Even Dad could do nothing about it. And so my ousted rival was beckoned back from some outhouse with many a back-slap and solemnly shaken hand, to take his rightful place by the side of Alec McGinty. And I took myself off to the other place.

Our workplace, Maintenance Unit No. 25 ('25 MU') at RAF Hartlebury, was due to close in three years' time. As part of the winding-down process it was proposed to remove aircraft parts and other materials from outlying depots and store them in a central location to be called 'High Density'. No one was keen to release anyone for this task, however vital to long-term strategy, and few of Dad's squadron of packers were physically up to it in any case. Only I fitted the bill, especially as there was no union to look after *my* interests and rights. Me, and another newbie, a retired maths teacher called Bill.

Bill was all right. In fact Bill was a plus. He looked a bit like old Jock Chalmers, the demon French teacher, with his stocky build, short bristly hair and little round specs, but he was intelligent, which made a pleasant change at 25 MU, and could be quite amusing. I forget why he had ended up skivvying in an RAF shed, but it seemed that he had had to retire from schoolteaching early and unexpectedly, and there had been some sort of domestic upset followed by a nervous breakdown. Perhaps his wife had run off with the milkman. Bill seemed resigned to whatever fate had in store for him. Our work, though sometimes physically demanding, left us free to talk about all sorts of things as we lifted trays full of nuts and bolts from the shelves and packed them into trollies: the day's headlines, the state of England's youth (we broadly agreed about that), the foibles of our fellow workers. When the time came he even took a headmasterly interest in my natural history outings, and insisted on seeing all my orchid snaps. Bill was all right. Just now and again something would upset him, and then he would have to sit down, wheezing heavily. At such moments, I discovered, it was best to leave him be and take an unscheduled tea break.

And so time went by, and my account slowly rose until I had saved enough to take the bus to Worcester and, on Henderson's earnest advice, buy myself a single-lens-reflex camera, a Practica Nova with a non-standard f2.8 Tessar lens. As more money came in, I added a simple tripod, an exposure meter, a flash-gun, some extension tubes, a stiff leather camera bag and a wooden box for 35mm slides that smelt curiously of bananas. With the means of turning dreams into reality within my grasp at last, I loaded up the Practica with a test film and wandered about Hartlebury Common taking pictures of anything that caught my fancy. They included my first photograph of a rare wild flower, a wild tulip, as shiny yellow as the morning sun that peeped over the wall of the ruined rectory. The pictures were all rubbish, but I put that down to the limitations of commercial processing.

At last it was orchid time. Claude Henderson was spending a few days on the downs near Dover, and, by way of bait, he had offered to show me where all the rarities grew, including that dream-flower, *Orchis simia*, The Monkey. At that time we owned a caravan, and so it was a straightforward matter of persuading the parents to take a break during Christopher's half-term holiday and, like Gloucester in *King Lear*, make our way to Dover. I took their compliance for granted. After all, I reasoned, they had nothing better to do. So Dad limbered up the caravan, mother packed it with provisions, plastic plates and a pressure cooker, and I wound the first colour film into the Praktica, or at least I thought I had. We camped at a place called St Margaret's-at-Cliffe and prepared to meet the orchids.

When I described my first encounter with a rare wild flower in the opening page of my book, *Britain's Rare Flowers*, I let the genius, Vladimir Nabokov, speak for me: this was 'ecstasy, and behind the ecstasy something else…It is like a momentary vacuum into which rushes all that I love. A oneness with sun and stone. A thrill of gratitude… to a lucky mortal'. Yes, I felt one lucky mortal that morning on the white cliffs with the blue sea beyond and a hovercraft rumbling gently into port. It is not often one gets the chance for some self-quotation, so kindly humour me a little. This is also from *Rare Flowers*:

'I had impressed upon my mother that the flower we were seeking was so very special that if we found it we should stay absolutely calm, otherwise someone might spot us, come over, and pick it… We did not really expect to find it, though it had been a good morning so far, with Nottingham Catchfly, Wild Cabbage and other good things on the cliffs above the beach. But without much searching, there all of a sudden it was, a little group of Early Spiders perched close to the cliff edge where white chalk showed through the turf. Forgetful now of any prowling pickers, I roared with delight, waved my arms about (or so it was claimed) and fell to my knees… It was a transcendent moment in which wild flowers, chalk cliffs and the colours, sounds and scents of nature seemed to imprint themselves in my bones… Later I showed them to Claude Henderson. He looked down at the diminutive flowers for a moment and then looked me in the eye. "Were you a bit disappointed?" he suggested, gently.'

Was it really like that? Probably. More or less. That moment became a bright pebble in the memory, polished so many times that it is hard to know now what was real and what has been refracted through the mind. It was certainly a pleasant surprise. Spider orchids normally flower early in the year and I was not really expecting to see them at the end of May, yet here they were, fresh as paint, brown as felt, with shiny blue-grey lines, and bulging in a delightfully spider-like way. They were as common as daisies in some places, especially on the broken, trampled, rabbit-chewed ground where the grass was sugared with chalk dust. I blew half a roll of Kodachrome on them. "That's right", said wise old Henderson. "However good it looks, always come up on the other side and take another… I know, I know, advice from an old campaigner". The flowers looked brilliant, the light was perfect and this photography lark was, I thought, a piece of cake.

Father was our chauffeur that week. Henderson, of course, had no car, and we were obliged to bring his pungent wife with us, hunched like a sack in the back. One day we made a pilgrimage to the secret site where the Monkey Orchid grows, but this was a late spring and they had barely begun to flower inside their little cages of chicken-wire. We had better luck with the luscious Lady Orchid which bloomed in plenty at a magic place called Yocklett's Bank where singing nightingales almost drowned conversation. So too at Queendown Warren where the Lady was joined by the Man, the Fly and what used to be called the Egg Orchid, until some dullard re-named it the Large White Helleborine. I had imagined these encounters for a long time and the orchids did not disappoint. We were a long time setting up tripods, waiting for the wind to stop fanning the flowers, and fiddling about with extension tubes and flash guns. It was, I fear, rather a strain for poor, impatient Dad, who was clearly less than totally thrilled by the flowers, and whose nerves were plainly fraying. "I think he gets a little *confused*, you know, your father", whispered Henderson, as Dad crashed the gears again after taking another wrong turning. And when I unilaterally invited my old friend to supper with us in the caravan, Dad nearly had a fit. "You'll get inviting them for supper! What will your Ma say? What will she *say*", he wailed after we had dropped them off at their farm-house. Mother of course, took it in her stride. A few more spuds, a little less pressure-cooked chicken each, and the catering was sorted. Not for Dad, though. All evening he fumed at the rashness and caprice of his eldest son.

Dad, probably, was happy to get back to Hartlebury and the packing shed. I had originally planned a diversion to the Isle of Wight where I thought we might bag a few Glanville Fritillaries and tour the special flowers of the island before heading back. A deep depression from the mid-Atlantic, matching the one Dad had begun to suffer, put paid to that. But I had another trip with Henderson to look forward to in which an obliging friend had offered to drive us all the way to a secret chalk-pit near Mildenhall in Suffolk to photograph The Soldier. In the meantime there were the first lot of images to look forward to, and I reckoned they would be brilliant.

The processed film fell with a thud on the doormat. I ripped open the plastic boxes, watched by mother who was taking a maternal interest in the proceedings. The first was a blank. So was the second, oh and the third. After the fourth or fifth I got it. They were all duds. I had somehow managed to wind the film on backwards, or maybe it hadn't wound on at all. There was a silence which Mum felt the need to fill. "Why don't you get a *sensible* hobby?" were her words. Mother often made crass remarks like this when she was upset. She mentioned some strapping young neighbour who played tennis or bowls and always had a *terrific* time. No, I wouldn't be playing bowls. He could keep his fucking tennis. I would get over this thing. I accepted that some people get the lemons and others the pips. Life is a lesson, a learning curve, a sense of continuous striving. Some things take a little time. I would learn.

I took more care when it came to the Soldier Orchid. Perhaps this time I let Henderson show me how to fit the film. "You can tell when it's taken by the tug you feel on the wind-on", he admonished. "Here, try it on mine". By such gradual degrees I came to master the intricacies of focus, shutter speed and flash distance, and when it was the turn of the Soldier Orchids to parade in their plastic box the results were not half bad. It's all about finding the right flower, Henderson explained. Not the biggest or the best group, necessarily, but the *right* one. Experienced photographers can spot the best one more or less at a glance, but anyone else would see just a bunch of similar-seeming flowers. The Monkey and the Soldier marked the start of a lifelong quest to see and photograph all the native wild flowers in their natural setting. The Soldier is a stately plant with a spike of rosine-purple florets, each one a little dangling military man in his red coat and coal-scuttle helmet. Jocelyn Brooke based his best-known book on this half-exotic, half-comic species. As for me, so for him, it was more than just another flower. It had come to symbolise both the frailty and resilience of the natural world. The Soldier had died out and then returned, miraculously, to flourish in this tiny pit in the middle of the woods, now imprisoned inside a tall fence to keep out the likes of me (fat chance). I might not have gone as far as Brooke in also seeing in it all the masculine virtues that the man felt he lacked and wanted to possess. 'I was timid, a coward at games, terrified of the aggressively masculine, totemist life of the boys at school; yet I secretly desired, above all things, to be like other people. These ideas had somehow become incarnated in *Orchis militaris*.' I felt more secure in my sexual orientation than Brooke, but, yes, I had been there and, yes, I knew how he felt.

The trail of flowers took up most of my weekends that summer. I persuaded the family to take the caravan to the Gower (Fen Orchid!) and picnic on Painswick Beacon, where, as luck would have it, the dainty Musk Orchid was coming into flower just as the dusky Bird's-nest Orchid was going to seed in the woods nearby. Both smelt of vanilla and honey. I made a solo trip to Newborough Warren in Anglesey to find and photograph Dune Helleborine—and to be evicted by the filthy Forestry Commission for my pains—followed by a long walk

Soldier Orchids in Suffolk. My first successful flower portrait. Shame about the distracting tree, though.

with Henderson in the Derbyshire dales in search of its prettier cousin, the Dark-red Helleborine. Come August, I persuaded the family to tow the caravan all the way to Killin in Perthshire to enable me to climb the hill of my dreams, Ben Lawers, and its wealth of alpine flowers. Orchids were the focus of most of these trips, but inevitably things that were not orchids crowded in; birds, for instance, and, beyond the species-spotting, the overwhelming beauty and wonder of wild Britain; windy dunes and tidal saltings, fragrant downland and sepulchrous beechwoods, Highland cattle up to their hocks in rushes and heather. I learned, without consciously learning, which flowers grew where and what differentiated a good spot from a dull one. Perhaps I felt that most strongly on the cliffs of Ben Lawers where a patch no larger than our garden could contain half a dozen distinct habitats: flushes dotted with yellow and white saxifrage, windswept rocks crowned with cushion plants and mosses; cracks and ledges containing botanical treasures exquisite enough to bring a tear to the eye. With the help of Hugh Lang, a Scottish botanist I met among the hills, I even began to tackle alpine sedges, which, we agreed, are the very best kind of sedge.

By the end of summer the slide box that still smelt of bananas was full. I had walked or waded or clambered through most of the natural habitats Britain had to offer, and, although I had not yet achieved my goal of ticking off all the wild orchids, I had seen more than two-thirds of them. I had also seen enough nature reserves to understand a little of the philosophy behind those uninformative signs surmounted by the cast-iron crown of Government. I was about to go to university to read zoology and geology, but it began to dawn on me that what most interested now wasn't animals but plants and vegetation; in other words, botany.

I was looking forward to leaving home again and beginning the great new adventure of university, which, I hoped, would combine freedom with genuine intellectual stimulation. I felt ready for that. I was heading, I wrote pompously to my grandmother, towards the frontier of knowledge. I would learn how beasts and plants worked from the inside out. Whether I was equally ready for the opportunities for a busy social life, I was much less sure. My wanderings down the primrose path might have stoked my inner world but it had done little to encourage the more outgoing spirit of a normal teenager. I shook hands with my workmate Bill at 25MU. The family saw me off at the station. On the way to Exeter I got into conversation in fractured French with a foreign girl on the seat opposite. "*Oui*", I agreed in best 'O' level, *le soleil* most definitely *brille fort, aujourd'hui*. Outwardly I might have looked relaxed and optimistic as the long train drew into Exeter St Davids. But inwardly I knew that, natural history aside, this was one poor, fucked-up boy feeling alone in the world.

The Ghost. Claude Henderson photographed this Ghost Orchid by flashlight in a wood near Henley in 1971. It vanished from those parts in the 1980s and has only been seen once in the past thirty years. For we plant hunters it has become the Grail. See p.356.

CHAPTER TWO

Not the Place's Fault

Exeter was only my third choice of university, and so an admission of failure; of my inability to find anywhere better. Yet I was excited at the prospect. I had always had a thing about Devon, glorious Devon, fairest of counties, home of heroes.

> *When Adam and Eve were dispossessed*
> *Of the Garden hard by Heaven*
> *They planted another one down in the west*
> *'Twas Devon, 'twas Devon, glorious Devon.*

Devon, glorious Devon, I thought, I'm ready to enjoy you. After seven years of Loughborough and seven months stuck in an RAF Maintenance Unit, I was at last in a decent bit of Britain. I knew all the words of the Devon song (it was one of Dad's). *The maids are fair as the*

Exeter University campus at about the time I was there. Note the horrible way we looked then with our long hair and bell-bottomed trousers.

apple bud/ and the men are men indeed". Please, for once, don't shit on my dreams. I don't want shit on my dreams.

"You will meet lots of interesting new people", promised Mum. Yeah, I'd heard that before, and now, in my insecure teens, I found the thought more discomforting than exciting. Years without close friends at home had turned me into an intensely shy person who found communication with strangers a nervous strain. As mother would have put it, I was unsure of myself, a bit like she had been. My social skills were close to zero. I was far too timid and on the defensive to make friends easily. I was also rather irritable. I was capable of responding to overtures of friendship from others, so long as the other person seemed interesting and personable, and not intimidating, and with nothing to take an immediate dislike to, such as a slovenly accent or a supercilious expression or any kind of smell. But I was wary of seeming too eager to please in case I got snubbed. Like Dad, I didn't care for that. You needed to be constantly on your guard to avoid exposing yourself to a slight. Unlike Dad, I also feared bores. And I was soon bored out of my mind unless conversation took an interesting turn. I could bear a lot, I considered, thinking of the past six years, but not boredom. O! let me not be bored, not bored, sweet heaven; Keep me in temper; I would not be bored! The trouble with other people was that you had to listen to their views and opinions, which were quite often, I thought, unoriginal, ill-thought-out, badly expressed and humourless. And were supposed to remember their names next time you met. It was hard work, this socialising. Dad had the knack of remembering conversations that impressed him and could often quote them word for word. I found I had usually forgotten what someone had said within ten minutes, even assuming I was paying attention. Maybe I was too busy concentrating on what I was going to say next. I was, I thought, becoming a bit of a cynic. Or possibly a stoic, one or the other. It all depended on what sort of attitude I was striking that day.

If 1950 was a pretty crappy time to be born, the end of the Sixties was, at least for some of us, a rather trying time to grow up. All the mature certainties were fading away and in their place came a vacuous 'yoof' culture where people said 'peace man' and affected silly, faux-left-wing attitudes. They also looked terrible with their long hair and patched, bell-bottomed jeans. Students ate out in cheap Chinese restaurants with flock wallpaper, and drank keg beer and liebfraumilch. And the music they listened to had taken a down-turn. The backbeat, rhythm-based melodies I grew up with had been replaced by guitar-hero screech. Perhaps it sounded better after a few joints, just as Mahler generally hits home after a stiff gin or two, but my naturalist's ears shrank from the bedlam of manic drummers and stoned guitarists. At parties I could never hear a word, which was awkward if a pretty girl was apparently talking to you and all you could see was her mouth opening and closing like a goldfish. Fortunately there was a solution, and that was to avoid parties. All things considered I had the makings of quite a boring person.

But at least one old friend was a fellow fresher that year. Boss had told me that my school mate Dick Oram would be sharing my geology course. Dick and I had rubbed along pretty well. I had been to his house. We had sat at the same school dinner table and chummily side-by-side in class. Admittedly our paths had diverged since then for, unlike me, Oram was good at games. By joining the elite first rugby fifteen as a prop forward, he had entered a privileged set of boys who were rather offhand with those of lesser caste. Even so, I was bucked up by the prospect of an old chum to share in the great adventure of university, so much so that when asked if I was willing to share a room in Halls, I ticked the box. Obviously they would put old schoolmates together.

Come the day I found that I wasn't sharing a room with a blast from the past but a total stranger. He was a sullen looking bloke, aggressively working class, good-looking in a rock-star sort of way, with a long nose and a mod haircut. Oh great, I thought, here we go again: bad-luck Barry, born under the wrong star-sign, jinxed by the Scales. Being middle-class and British, I tried to make the best of things. "Hello", I said, coming forward with outstretched hand, "I'm Peter, who are you?" Perhaps it was his northern accent, but all I heard was a mumble, followed by what sounded like "Unk".

"Unk?"

"Me name's Clunk, thanks".

"Clunk? Excuse me, but did you say *Clunk*?" Clunk? What kind of name was that? What sort of person would be called Clunk? Something about his manner made it questionable whether we would totally hit it off.

With a sense that someone had made a mistake, and that it was probably me, I went around the halls checking the lists to find out where Dickoram had got to. Is there an Oram in the house? "Don't think so", they said. "Old flame is she?" I was about to say, no, she's a he, but on second thoughts, I said, yeah, old flame, that's right, that's what she is, a real hottie. When I eventually spotted the absent Dick at the student's union, he was friendly enough but not, as in my sad case, overjoyed. He, it seemed, was in his element already. He had grown his hair long, wore bell bottomed jeans and a frilly shirt, and had obviously brought his laid-back, rugby charisma with him. Only once did he deign to visit my room. Clunk was in, and to my astonishment they greeted one another with relaxed, open-handed banter, as though they had known one another for years; indeed, as though it had been Clunk, and not I, who had marked up his Latin homework and swapped knock-knock jokes during RE. I could hardly believe my ears. "Hi, how's it goin'?" "Great, man. Hey, nice shirt!" "Thanks. Enjoying yourself?" "Yeah, it's cool." "Great innit". "Peace man". "Anyone want to see my stamp collection?" came a reedy voice from the annex. I might not have used those exact words, but I was certainly feeling left out. Why did everyone find it easy to make friends except me?

I did make a few, mostly low-status nerds and geeks. The high point of the week was a fresher's fair in which student societies competed to pull in the newbies. Some of them were political. The Fabians were sober and wore red ties, and you knew instinctively that their meetings would be like dragging a dead donkey up the tarry shingle. The Trots or revolutionary socialists looked a better bet, with their wholehearted support for the IRA and refusal to live in halls, but I suspected they were in fact embittered and madly jealous of anyone who didn't drop their aitches. There were queues at the rugby and rowing booths, and no one at all at the various Christian sects who wore their fake Jesus-grins behind piles of pamphlets and Bibles. I chose climbing and diving, both activities which, I thought, would be useful accomplishments to life as an adventure naturalist. Of course I also joined the camera club. Pushing through the throng I eventually found a Bird Club represented by two beanpoles in specs called Brian and Mike. Brian has since reminded me of my embarrassing words of greeting: "At last, a worthwhile club to join! *Put me down, gentlemen*". The Bird Club, it turned out, had a membership of about twelve (thirteen now), but it organised outings to Stoke Woods and the Exe Estuary and even weekends away to more distant, bird-haunted shores and islands. Its full title, explained Brian, was the Bird Club and Natural History Society, although no members had so far expressed an interest in Natural History. Apart from Mike, that is, who claimed to be interested in snails. Mike was one of those people who always did the opposite to everyone else, not that anyone really noticed or cared.

Clunk and I shared a second floor room in one of three identical concrete shoe-boxes that made up Birks Halls, one of the university's two main halls of residence (and yes, yes, a lot of us *were* berks). The rooms were Spartan but newish and of reasonable size. The main downside was a horribly steep hill to climb to reach the campus. There were washing machines and drying rooms, a couple of baths on each floor and a pay phone at the bottom of each flight of bare concrete stairs. At one end stood a central block with a small library, a comfy lounge and a refectory where you lined up to pile stuff on your plate. On the day of my arrival it was eggs, beans, sausages and chips. "Very poor stuff today", said the chap opposite, "it's normally better than this". With memories of the Hole still recent, I thought it was OK—it was the sort of nursery food I used to enjoy at my grandmother's.

Every now and then we dined more formally in the hall when you were expected to wear your shorty undergrad's gown. The strain of dressing up obviously told on some of the gowned diners for the moment the master had left a food fight would generally start. Once I made the mistake of sharing the same table as some meek, short-haired church-goers in their blazers and college ties (maybe, I might have thought, I could be as happy as them if I believed their load of old rubbish). The plates had hardly been removed before we became the focus of a fusillade of buns and cheese rinds. I decided to get the hell out of there, which was just as well because someone, some revolutionary atheist, had taken what you could call the nuclear option. He had unleashed the bread sauce. The way to throw bread sauce is to swing the sauce-boat in an arc, like bowling, but without letting go. Gravity does the rest. The sauce shucks free of its moorings to whiz through the air in a gooey lump, changing shape as it goes, at one moment like a thunder cloud, the next like an octopus trailing quivering tentacles of dough. The Christians were like rabbits caught in the lights. Open-mouthed they stared as their doom approached. A moment later a tsunami of slop hit their table and gowns and blazers vanished behind a huge explosion of dough. The whole hall erupted. When the mist had cleared you could see that the martyrs were still in their seats, dripping with sauce, pretending that nothing had happened. All you could make out was their eyes peeping out through the dough, and their fixed toothy smiles. May be they were turning their cheeks for the next volley, which was custard.

I told myself I was not going to be intimidated by university. It was, after all, not unlike the Sixth Form, though they now called you by your first name and classes were now called lectures. Exeter was then a relatively small campus university of about 3,000 students, distributed among various red-brick and concrete buildings set in a former park. There were enough places in halls for students to live on the campus for two years out of three, if they wanted to. There was a sufficiency of common rooms and bookshops and coffee bars. When the weather permitted, you could lounge on the union terrace in the sunshine and watch the student world go by, with its mini-skirted girls and raffish late-Sixties lads. There was a theatre, a cinema and plenty of libraries. While there was no pressing need to go anywhere else, the seaside at Exmouth or Dawlish was only a twenty-minute train ride away. In the other direction, you could cadge a lift to scrumpy-toting country inns tucked away in places called Clyst Coddlescombe and Munchimcobleigh. As campuses go, you could do worse.

I learned how to rock climb, and, while I was never one of the top guys, and always second on the rope, I was good enough to a loop a one-handed bowline round my waist and manage climbs graded as 'difficult' (which in climbing parlance means 'easy'. Actual difficult is 'severe'). I'm not such a spaz, I thought to myself. It's only *competitive* sports I can't abide. I also learned to dive to third-class standard and handle what was then called an aqualung. For a short time I even joined the choir and was there roaring heartily in the bass section for the university's famous performance of Beethoven's Choral Symphony. When in funds I shifted a certain amount of cider and beer and nasty cheap wine. I did all these things but during that first year I often felt alone in the crowd, as if surrounded by an invisible bubble. Some folk have the gift of social adhesion; wherever they go stout chaps and pretty girls just stick to them. I felt more like a paramagnet, the one that repels so powerfully that bits of iron go scittering away and fall off the table. Once, some geologists spotted me being sick in the shrubbery near Northcote Theatre. "Hey, who's that there in the bushes? Look, it's Pete. Are you all right, mate?" "Yes, yes", I slurred, wiping my chin. "Just enjoying a quiet night out". I wasn't going to be cowed by new experiences.

I was though. I was hopelessly out of my depth. My way of responding was to retreat once again into my private world. In my head, at least, England was still a green and pleasant land full of retreats where a chap could dream. I might, I considered, have been a monk. But I would rather have been a knight. I was reading T.H. White's *Once and Future King* and imagined myself on a boar hunt, or in the tiltyard, jousting for the hand of that popular but inaccessible girl in the physio lab. I went so far as to book riding lessons, although they didn't last long; ignoring my cries of giddyup, my nag stopped to enjoy a leisurely lunch of long grass before looking up and—hey, wait for me!—galloping off after the rest of the pack, bouncing its rider like a rubber ball ("whoa, whoa, Christ, where's the brake?"). I tottered home with a bruised arse and decided you can keep the Middle Ages.

Sometimes, ignoring the hubbub around me, I took refuge in drawing or making stupid lists of flora and fauna. It was at such a moment when, deep in my counter-universe, two girls came over, and, in the relaxed and friendly way some girls have, asked me what I was doing. One of them was called Dee, a Welsh girl from the valleys, very left-wing or so I'd been told, and maternal in her ways, no doubt with a soft spot for waifs and strays. "What are you doing, now?" She was taking a companionable interest in my work. Startled, I looked up, and then down, and realised that, Rain Man-like, I'd been writing out the Latin names of sea-anemones. This autistic tendency is not something you necessarily want the world to know about. "It's just a little list. It's nothing." "Why then are you doing it?" she persisted. "Because I feel like it", I snapped, embarrassed. "Oh", and she pulled a face as if to say, "that's me telt, then". I went back to my pathetic list and she didn't speak to me again for at least a year.

One day Clunk put up an inflammatory poster on the wall opposite our shared wash-basin. It was called 'Climax' and consisted of nothing but the close up of the face of a dark-haired girl with her eyes shut and her mouth wide open, threaded with harp-strings of saliva. Clearly Clunk wanted us to know how well he was getting on with the ladies. The poster was in the best possible taste of course, in monochrome, beautifully shot on grainy film, but even so you didn't necessarily want to see it in your shaving mirror first thing in the morning. Clunk's girls had caused me enough grief already. There was, for instance, the time when he brought one back to the room late at night and I had to pretend to be asleep. "Is he really asleep?" she kept asking. "Oh, yeah, he's always out like a light". "Are you sure?" To help him out I might at this point have obliged him with a snore. There was more embarrassment when he caught me inspecting a sex magazine he had left lying about. It was called *Forum*, and the lead article, I remember, was written in an austere style, halfway between an Airfix manual and the *Journal of Zoology*. It was about a sex position I had never heard of called '69'. We were advised, I remember, to take this thing easy, one step at a time, as it was 'inclined to be an overwhelming experience'. Then, as I say, Clunk came in and caught me, red-handed and red-faced, before I could scuttle back to my annex. "Heh, heh, just checking out your magazine". Clunk said nothing but shot me a sour look as he consigned his filth to a drawer.

"We have different lifestyles, you and me", he pointed out one day. That was certainly true, and I liked his lifestyle much more than mine. He read *Forum*, I read *History of the English-speaking Peoples*. He hung out with classy chicks and sports dudes, I went bird-watching with Brian and Mike. Sharing the same space as Clunk, I thought, is making me miserable. Fortunately Clunk was on to it. "I've arranged a room swap", he said offhandedly. "Another guy is coming in here; I got you a single room in Raddon." Which was obviously good news, though I would rather he had asked me first. Still, I reflected, as the poster girl made me nick my chin again, this is no place for a thinking man like me.

CHAPTER THREE

Failing to Impress

As I say, the great thing about Exeter was its location. The city itself is nothing special: a typical West Country town, blitzed by the Luftwaffe and wrecked by postwar planners, it is full of shopping malls and their monstrous car parks. Only the cathedral close, which the Germans neglected to bomb, has anything to offer the civilised visitor. Fortunately, decent countryside lay within reach. I took it for granted that my course would include lots of field excursions across the county, from its high moors to its wide estuary and seaside rock pools. Devon, I found, was full of wonderful wild places: Dartmoor's quaking bogs and woods of twisted, mossy oaks, Berry Head's rock gardens of rare flowers, Dawlish Warren with its shorebirds and unique wild crocus, and the miles and miles of crazy cliff near Axmouth where a large chunk of the county had slid into the sea. What kind of biology course would turn its back on places like that? Moreover, I'd heard that the two newly-appointed professors of biological sciences were both outdoors men. John Webster, the senior of the two, was a mycologist and a great believer in working from fresh material wherever possible. Many of the plant diseases we studied were from his garden which he maintained as a kind of devil's domain: apple trees crabbed by brackets and cankers, mildewed cabbages and blighted leeks, poisonous toadstools on the sickly lawn. He was also deeply interested in some odd aquatic funguses whose spores could be found in the foam of streams, and were shaped like anchors, caltrops, sputniks. That sounded good, and so did David Nichols, the youngish zoology prof, who was a marine biologist and a qualified diver. With Nichols at the helm, I imagined not only cheery explorations of rock pools and caves but dives to sample the deep stuff, or may be trailing a hook on a fishing boat with the sporting chance of pulling in a shark. Their predecessor, a decent old stick called Harvey, had not only founded the Lundy Field Society but had written the (not very good) New Naturalist volume on Dartmoor. As for geology, if they did not use Lyme Regis regularly and often as a source of rocks and fossils there was something wrong somewhere. That's what I thought about that.

The geology course did indeed entail a certain amount of delving about among the rocks. With our hammers, we gave the strata a good bashing perhaps once a fortnight and got to know the make-up of South Devon fairly well. Biology, though, fell well short of my hopes. I make no bones about it, it was a terrific disappointment. There were field excursions to come but for the time being our bottoms were stuck fast to the hard wooden benches of Hatherley lecture theatre. The first-year course turned out to be an expanded version of 'A' level but developed in ways that were not to my liking. What seems to have happened was this. The vogue in the 1960s was for what they called production ecology. Essentially this envisaged species as units in a continuous flow of energy, originating from the sun and handed down in parcels along the food-chain until it reached top carnivores like me. The amount of

My Prof: John Webster. Actually he was a bit younger than this when I knew him.

living material (biomass) produced by the transformed solar energy was called production, and the quantity of growth within a unit area was called the standing crop. The details are far too boring to discuss here, but in essence the system managed to reduce the natural world and all its wonders to the home economics of a field of wheat. With models like this, they claimed, it was possible to measure everything without knowing anything at all about nature. It was a case of maths conquering the world, including the natural world. To turn theory into practice, scientists in the Lake District had bought a wood and were steadily stripping it down to its component parts, chopping up all the trees and weighing each leaf, twig, acorn, root and worm. They were obviously out of their minds. I sat on my hands as equations covered the board, determined not to understand any of it.

It seemed a rather odd way to begin three years of natural science, this deep-end dive into hardcore bio-maths. But some expendable old buffer had been on a course and returned reborn with his head full of little arrows circling wildly round and round, and numbers cascading down all over the place. Grasp how energy is dispersed through living systems and you have grasped the fundamentals of life, he claimed by way of squiggles of chalk with Greek letters attached. I imagine that the Profs, mycological Webster and submariner Nichols, might have had their doubts about letting him loose among the freshers, but they were new here, keen to try something different, and so they let him have his way.

As the lectures grew ever more abstract, I began to think I had made a seriously bad choice. I saw now why those dons at Balliol had been so keen on my taking Advanced-level maths. The natural world, I was learning, is maths in motion. Trees are nature's way of processing numbers. Badgers trundle through the woods shedding equations and algebraic constructions. Life itself was a gigantic computer distributing weighable amounts of energy hither and thither along 'pathways', and then recycling it by way of some heavy number crunching in the basement.

After a while I gave up attending lectures. As Einstein must have discovered, as he groped for a theory that would explain everything, the closer you get to fundamentals the harder they are for any normal mind to grasp. But if this was real biology I was a tadpole. At the end of the first term we were tested to see how thoroughly we had mastered it all. I didn't know the answers. I didn't even understand the questions. They might as well have been written in a foreign language. Still, I managed to scrape 28%. I noticed with interest that several of my classmates scored even less.

We had all been assigned a tutor although Exeter tutorials were perfunctory and infrequent. I was part of a small group assigned to a rather weary old plant pathologist. Too ancient to give lectures, he turned up at the university now and again to tend his pot plants in the greenhouse. I have no idea what we talked about. After the first-term exam fiasco, it was me that insisted on having it out with him, not the other way around. I wanted to tell him that this course stunk. "Eh, what", replied my tutor, thinking of his pots. "My test result", I said, louder. "The bio-maths? The energy stuff? The one we all failed? The guy with 28%?" "Ah, the test…" He looked out at the trees. There were lots of trees on the campus. Some of them probably had interesting pathologies, mildews, whatever. "The test you say?" A couple of birds flew by. A cloud floated past from one side of the window to the other. "Ah, yes, your marks, not very good, I see". Another minute or two passed, and a car rumbled up the drive. "Well, I'll be off then", I said. "Ah, ah, yes, goodbye", replied my tutor still gazing out of the window. I legged it down the corridor. Exeter tutorials might not be Oxbridge exactly, I thought, but at least they don't seem to hold things against you.

Fortunately there were occasional reminders that living things did exist. David Nichols led a couple of extra-curricular trips to the shore at low tide. It was a mild thrill to find that all this stuff I had known since I was a child was fit for a university course. I was back on Blackrock Sands again, gazing at cushion stars and sea anemones, watching the prawns dart in and out of the weed. In the pools nearest the sea lurked gorgeous dahlia anemones, exquisite yet deadly nests of amethyst and carnelian sunk in brown and white gravel. I still have a photograph of the scene, which came out in a weird blue light, of girls in tight, cut-off jeans bending over rock pools with chaps grinning from their vantage points on barnacled rocks. Nichols seemed to find shore life wonderful even after years of tutoring; his post-retirement lectures focussed on the patterns and colours of nature. I wish I'd seen more of him.

Prof. Webster seemed onside too, despite his hauteur and obvious disapproval of long hair and student scruffiness. His departmental year had begun with a fungus foray. Hitherto all my forays had only one forayer—me. Now I found that others, including the Prof., shared my love of toadstools, brackets, stinkhorns and puffballs. I liked the ambience of the communal foray, the brollies and mackintoshes, the happy chatter of adults on an outing, the rich red earth and dank, woody smells of Devon in autumn, the funguses piling up in the baskets, some for studying back at the lab, others on their way to the frying pan.

And then there was Michael Proctor. Michael taught ecology and plant anatomy. When I first met him he was giving a talk on flower photography to the Camera Club. Michael's beautiful, technically perfect images of nature in close-up made me realise how far I lagged behind with the Practica, but something about his name seemed familiar. It came to me while I was having a word with him afterwards. "You must be M. C. F. Proctor!" I exclaimed, for this was the name which often appeared under pictures in my favourite botanical books. It was indeed he. He was about 40 then, lean and neat, with a long tanned face and the expression of a kindly mammal, a sort of Uncle Badger, with his warm, slightly crooked smile and intelligent, interested eyes. His voice I recognised as quintessential Fifties Oxbridge—still using words like ra-*ther* and *frightfully* which had died out everywhere else. Michael was one of a brilliant generation of biologists that emerged from Cambridge Botany School in the post-war years; he was altogether my idea of a proper botanist. He knew the names of every flower, moss, lichen and seaweed, and all about them. He also knew about them in their natural context as *vegetation*. He had revised the classic account of natural habitats, *Britain's Green Mantle* by Sir Arthur Tansley, the man who invented the science of plant ecology. Michael even knew about nature conservation, having briefly worked for the Nature Conservancy in Wales before finding it too bureaucratic by half and turning to an academic career instead. He remained at Exeter to the end of his life. To say that Michael was a moss-gatherer was to state the case quite literally for he was indeed a gatherer of mosses and had conducted all kinds of abstruse experiments to show how these things can survive on next to nothing. In fact, as I came to know him better, I realised that Michael knew pretty well everything worth knowing in the botany line. In his zeal for photography and orchids he bore some resemblance to my old mentor, Henderson, but Michael's engagement with science was also fully modern and embraced cutting edge stuff like gas chromatography, pollen analysis and molecular taxonomy. His wizardry in the field was matched by technical know-how in the lab. I began to think I had met my first genius.

The rest of that first year at Exeter is a blur in the memory. Something had poleaxed me for sure. I particularly didn't enjoy the practicals. For instance we spent a lot of time pithing frogs. There seemed to be a limitless supply of these unfortunate creatures. They were brought to you in a plastic bin by the lab assistant, alive and croaking, and before conducting your ghastly experiment, you first had to knock them on the head. This was the 'pithing'. Having very little brain frogs are peculiarly hard to kill. What you had to do first was stun the animal by picking it up by the hind legs and slamming it hard against the bench. After which you picked up a scalpel, stuck it between the eyes and, by jiggering the blade to and fro, scrambled the nerve centres. This is harder to do than it sounds because, of course, frogs are slippery and understandably eager to escape. And when they did, the experiment was put on hold while white-coated students scampered about after their runaway amphibians among the briefcases and lab stools.

In the geology theatre the animals were all safely dead and turned to stone. There were no dinosaurs, alas; the only critters on offer were nondescript ones like corals and graptolites. Fossils are simply a means to an end, we learned, which is to find out how old the rock is. Our lecturer in palaeontology was a shy man who was said to get all confused and embarrassed when talking about the sex lives of ancient sea-creatures. Once he took us to Lyme Regis to bash fossils out of the bluish, fine-grained rocks piled up on the shore. You could hardly move there without stepping on a long-dead creature: pens of ebony that once belonged to cuttlefish, curly-whirly lamp-shells and endless ammonites, one the size of a cartwheel. I brought my haul back to my room and started scrubbing them in the sink, only to find the fossils disappearing as the stone dissolved back into the mud from whence it came. After all, I might have reflected, what are rocks but petrified mud? How interesting is that?

Rocks are a minority pursuit, and for once I found myself among the majority. On the whole, geology and I did not get on. It seemed to be just one bloody rock after another. After a while you found yourself turning into a rigid, rock-like state yourself as some old fool droned on and on about unconformities and anticlines. I had planned to bail out of the whole rotten subject as soon as I could, but unfortunately there were exams to get through first. Some universities threw you out if you failed the first-year paper. Exeter was more liberal—in fact it was almost impossible to get fired—but the faculty was certainly capable of kicking you out of the honours course and onto an ignominious pass degree if you failed to make the grade. I squeaked through, just. I failed one geology paper and was forced to retake it during the long vac. But this failing contained a silver lining. It meant I could offer a plausible reason for dropping rocks, on the grounds that I was no good at them. It proved surprisingly difficult to convince the geology prof. that I wanted out. What, not interested in rocks? Over and over he told me about his terrible sense of disappointment and how my desertion was hurting him personally. I didn't care; I was determined to go and I had the lousy marks to back me up.

Meanwhile I was also having second thoughts about my main subject, zoology. It wasn't just the poor froggies. It was dawning on me that my interests were tending away from lab animals and their smelly innards and towards plants and fungi and their place in the countryside. Before the second year was upon us we were presented with three alternative syllabuses. The choice lay between zoology, botany and biology, the latter being a sort of pick 'n' mix from both courses. The botany syllabus looked the best bet to me, on the whole. All right, it contained more than its share of physiology and plant breeding and tough calls of that sort, but it also included Webster's star course on fungi, as well as a primrose path through all the plants from seaweed to ferns to orchids. The lecturers were better too. I was sorry to lose David Nichols and Robin Wootton's courses on entomology and fossils, but on the other hand I could look forward to Michael Proctor on plant ecology and Brian Ivimey-Cook on seaweeds and plankton, as well as an attractive-sounding field course in Western Ireland. I liked drawing things from the microscope, which was Prof. Webster's speciality. And, I'd decided, I'd far rather section a plant stem than pith another frog or weigh out more dollops of dung (and that was another thing—plants don't crap). "Are you quite sure, this time?" asked genial David Nichols. "Sure you won't change your mind again and ask to do maybe social sciences or modern music?" Anyone would think he was sorry to lose me. No, I replied, it's plants for me. I'm a botany guy. It's gardens for me, not zoos. I've really made the right choice this time. *Definitely*. Probably.

Washington Singer laboratories look like one of our less comfortable prisons but it was apparently the last word in lab architecture when it was built back in 1931.

CHAPTER FOUR

Wordplay

Privacy, oh blessed privacy. My first solo room in halls; no more Clunk, no more voices whispering, "is he awake?", no more nervous shaving under the closed eyes of the ecstasy girl. My new room looked out over the roof of a lower shoebox and on towards Exeter St Davids where the freight trains trundled and jolted into the night. Strains of Led Zeppelin drifted from the window downstairs. It was too late now to dream of Oxford quads and spires; of lunching with poets and dining with dons; of late night port in ivied turrets. If I was to become a full-time nature guy, and I really couldn't think of anyone else I wanted to be, I needed a degree in biology. And since it was becoming increasingly clear that I wasn't very good at biology, a minor university was all that I could reasonably have aspired to. It might, I consoled myself, have been worse. Exeter was all right. My room was warm and comfortable; meals were regular and adequate. It was better than the Hole. I had enough money for my modest needs, just. And slowly the course was picking up; there were islets of pleasure in the ocean of disappointment. And soon it would be spring.

I had a lot of botanical excursions lined up for the summer. I intended to combine climbing with flower-finding in the Avon Gorge and in the cliffs around Torbay. I would take full advantage of the departmental trips on offer, to Berry Head, Braunton Burrows and the wooded cleaves of Dartmoor. I would nudge the Bird Club in the direction of other good spots. I thought at one time it might even be interesting to take a good look at seaweeds with the university diving club.

And I would be doing another round of wild orchids, with a fellow addict, a postgrad called Keith Fry, who, moreover, offered transport in the form of an old, pale-green Ford Anglia called Clarissa. Michael Proctor, too, did everything he could to encourage a fellow photographer. Early on he invited Keith and me to his home for an evening of botanical chat over the slide projector. He was of course polite and positive about our amateurish snaps, suggesting a bit less of the flash here, may be a better angle there, but on one or two shots his eyes narrowed. "What a funny looking thing", he remarked as I got to a puzzling marsh orchid I had photographed on a trip to Anglesey. He got a book out and checked off the features. "Irish Marsh Orchid, *Dactylorhiza kerryensis*," he said. "That's what you've got there, I'd say." It was, it seemed, a new British record. The book came out again when I showed another odd orchid, neither one thing nor the other. "That's surely a hybrid!" he exclaimed. I had, it seems, casually photographed an unrecorded cross between the Large White and Sword-leaved Helleborine, and very pretty it was too, with flowers like broken eggs with the yolk showing through. I should have written up these discoveries for a journal. But for that a repeat visit would be necessary, as well as a trawl through the literature, so I never did and someone else got all the glory. What a pity. It would have been good to have a couple of peer-reviewed papers to flash at a career interview, showing initiative and all that.

My close-up of a then unknown hybrid orchid Cephalanthera × schulzei.

Come the day, towards the end of May, Keith, I and Keith's lovely fiancée Angie, who had just finished her finals, piled into Clarissa for the long journey through the night for a weekend's orchid-hunting in Kent. With Keith's eccentric aunt putting us up, we made a repeat tour of the county's hot spots, finding The Monkey again and in full bloom this time (but missing its hybrid, the Monkey-Man cross, known in the trade as the Missing-link Orchid). In the process we even bumped into Claude Henderson, on a trip of his own with a Loughborough chum. He seemed less than pleased to see me and I was too stupid to understand why: that he was embarrassed at having revealed orchid localities to me. Please yourself, was my attitude. May be we *won't* go plant-hunting again. On your way, old man. We spread our tripods for orchids and other rare flowers all over southern England that summer. We even came within a whisker of finding the Ghost Orchid, the most elusive of them all, the one that flowers only once in a blue moon. Someone, possibly Henderson again, had marked the spot where it had

Down in the wet, photographing Bog Orchid in the New Forest in summer 1970, Clarissa the Car in the background.

flowered most recently with a wooden stake, as though the orchid was a vampire (and, if plants could be vampires, it would certainly be a good candidate). But all that remained of the Ghost were a couple of dried stems which might, I suppose, have been something else.

Plant-hunting continued into the long vac. I persuaded my long-suffering family to drag the caravan back to the Gower coast for a short break, and got Dad to chauffeur me to the New Forest and the Purbeck heaths. Memories of those excursions remain like strips of coloured celluloid in the monochrome of my university days: the golden samphires and rock sea-lavenders on the cliffs near Worm's Head; the marsh gentians blooming among the flowering heather; Clarissa parked by the shallow, weedy waters of Hatchet Pond with Keith curled up in the wet trying to photograph the midget Bog Orchid. By the end of summer 1970, I had satiated a pent-up passion. Too bad seeing England's native flora in its natural setting wouldn't help me to a botany degree.

There was a lot to write up. I did so in no great style in a standard A4 student's folder, listing the stuff we had found with a general impression of the scene. Michael Proctor had lent us his Cambridge notebooks so I could see how it was done, even though I could never match his scientific insights. It was some time later, but as a logical extension to this slight journal, that I began to record my impressions of life in general. My diary became a running commentary on what had happened that day, what I had seen and heard, people I had met, books I had read; plus an Eeyorish rant about rubbish lecturers and yobbish fellow students. It might, I suppose, have been a reaction against our itinerant life as a family, when each new posting was preceded by a mass throw-out. Hardly a single document or exercise book had survived from my schooldays. Into the bin go yesterday's memories, while you pack for the next move. Diaries represent a form of stability. Humans, like other animals, appreciate a bit of regularity in their lives.

The great diary, in effect the chronicle of my life, began when, alone in my room late at night, bored, still wide awake, I needed something to do. I'd written up a short account of some botanical trip and, not wishing to stop just yet, continued with a recent visit to Stockbridge Down. That led to another account of some recent birding with Brian and Mike, and, by degrees it turned into a diary as though keeping a regular journal was the most natural thing to do. Over the rest of the term, page followed page about birds and bees, unavailable girls, parties avoided, the unacceptable racket of my neighbour's hi-fi, the beautiful melodies on my own. This is the raw stuff of history, I thought. They are going to love this in about two hundred years' time. I could imagine someone basing a thesis on it: *Marren: A Naturalist's Tale, a searing indictment of late-twentieth-century education.*

Forty years on, that diary fills five fat loose-leaf volumes, hundreds of pages, hundreds of thousands of words. I need a narrative; it helps me get along. Besides, I quite liked writing. I should perhaps mention that I was by now fairly well-read, for a scientist. I had devoured the entire corpus of work by George Orwell, most of Evelyn Waugh, and I knew large chunks of Shakespeare more or less by heart. Even back at the Hole, I had always enjoyed the English lessons of 'Twitch' Griffin, probably the nicest teacher in the school, if not the world. Through him I had managed to absorb not only the rudiments of grammar but, more importantly, the realisation that words can be fun; that, when deployed with sufficient cunning, they can transform dull, quotidian reality into a fireworks display of insight and wit. I was beginning to feel lost to science. Perhaps, then, it was my despair at the reality of academia that roused the dormant beast which had last raised its head in Twitch's poetry class.

Unfortunately I have no Exeter diary to help me now. Some years later I re-read it and, filled with shame and disgust, threw it away. I remember odd bits—lame attempts to be funny, would-be world-weary aphorisms, tilting at forgotten windmills. It was all rubbish. All that survives are some plain tales of field excursions, with lists of plant and animal species attached, to which I sometimes added a bit of clever-dickery or a cynical aside. Reading again them now, I note my inability then to create the simplest kind of word picture. My field excursions are full of arthritic phrases like: 'The orchids were exceedingly local'… 'the butterflies were found to be common'… 'this was unfortunate as in the light of better knowledge'… Evidently my style had not progressed much since those school essays on What I Did In My Holidays. Was this shrivelled stuff really what I was like then? True, science writing, so we were taught, should eschew any personal element; should stick to objective facts and their elucidation. No flowery phrases: that was 'art', and if that was your game you were on the wrong side of the campus. All the same, it seemed to me that we were missing something. What we were missing was the human factor—the experience of life itself.

Of course, teen kids think mainly of themselves and their appetites. They are quite right to live for the day. Energy and high spirits were what you had then and raw experience is what they brought you. I wish now I had acquired more of it while I had the chance. I spent far too much teen-time curled up with a book. Even when I wasn't reading or writing, I was probably drawing. Such creativity as I had was lavished on posters for the Bird Club. A typical design might include a tempting bird, an avocet perhaps, or a peregrine, along with some fancy lettering and a stout birder with gigantic binos clearly having the time of his life. Judging from the paucity of newbies on our outings these efforts were a complete waste of time. I remember one meeting when no one turned up at all. This probably did not bother Brian and Mike who were far too busy recording the birds of South Devon to run a social club. But it bothered me. It made me wonder, yet again, whether my natural tendencies were cutting me off from life.

Is it nature that makes us crabby or were we born that way? In his study of the tribe, *Birders*, Mark Cocker presents them as single-minded, highly competitive and almost entirely male. It's a form of collecting, he suggests; their 'specimens' are ticks on lists, although behind each tick there is a memory, an indelible image, perhaps also an anecdote. But birding can easily become a way of avoiding a normal life. My own vocation of natural-history writing is, or can be, a similar form of life avoidance. Given my time again, by some benign fairy, I might do it all differently. Writing could wait. So could orchids and avocets. Instead I would dive into whatever university had to offer, gain some much-needed social confidence, and come out of it feeling I'd used my time well. Too late you realise that university life back then was a golden age when no one worried much about debt and we could take it for granted that there was some fine job waiting for *this* graduate. Perhaps I could have pretended to be a socialist, grow a thoughtful Marxist beard and chase those dreamy girls in the arts. For the birds and butterflies of South Devon are still available, while young love, passionate engagement with causes, and the sheer exhilaration of youth have all gone forever. At the time youth seems eternal; and then one morning you look in the mirror and those sad eyes look back and tell you otherwise. It's over mate. It's all over, and you were never really there. You fucked it up, you twat. Alas, alas.

CHAPTER FIVE

Finding a Direction

The lecture theatre was three-quarters empty now. Only three students, including me, had opted for the botany course, joined by another dozen who, unable to make up their minds, had plumped for the pick 'n' mix biology option. My fellow botanists were Mick, who was chiefly interested in biochemistry and so hardly counted, and Dee, the Welsh girl who had made friendly overtures to me and been rebuffed for her pains. Mick was a brash Cockney loud-boy who seemed to have grown up faster than most of us; half-way through the course he was marched to the altar and by the final year he was a daddy. He certainly used his time. He was all right when you got to know him. Dee was sweet, broad-minded, and, as far as botanical preferences went, unaligned. She was paying for university herself, and lived on some farm in the Devon outback, with a mature student called Mark, where chickens ran through the rooms and hot water was available only now and again. She thought anyone who lived in Halls was a sissy. As my brother Chris commented after meeting her: "hmm, tough chick!"

I lived in halls. We had the option of staying in Birks Hall a second year, and, with no alternative plans, I took it. It saved a lot of time over meals and so on, and left you with drinking money so long as you didn't waste it on books. I supplemented my income by taking holiday jobs, apple picking in the summer, the Andover Post Office over Christmas. In this second year, I had some friendly, easy-going neighbours in halls. Chris Johnson was long-haired, dreamy and, with his beaky nose and soulful eyes, attractive to a certain kind of girl. He was keen on falconry. Once we went hawking near Exmouth and I remember Chris's goshawk, a moody bird, much given to sulks and 'bates', sticking its talons into a screaming baby rabbit, and then, with the wriggling beast in its clutches, crouching there, spread-winged and pop-eyed, clearly unsure what to do next. Chris had to take a knife to the poor bunny. This, I thought, is worse than pithing frogs. A few rooms along was

Tony Barton, who spent most of his time painting model soldiers. He still does, professionally now, and very good they look. Even back then he seemed to live in a bygone age. Naturally he was in the Sealed Knot, the Civil War re-enactment society, an officer in Lilburne's regiment, a notoriously bolshie crew who wore rugby shirts under their buffcoats. Tony taught me to fight with a sabre, blade to blade. Up and down the corridor and on to the stairwell we went, cutting and slashing like Errol Flynn in *Elizabeth and Essex*. With him, I also learned how to shoulder and push a pike. Knotties love a good scrimmage and parading about the town as though they own the place, and requesting long-suffering bar-maids to draw a stoop of ale, I prithee.

I cannot remember whether my closest second-year chum, John, had any eccentric hobbies. He did manage, once, to nurse a pair of oiled guillemots back to health with the most extraordinary devotion, and might have made a good vet or zoo-keeper. He didn't have a girlfriend either, and so was usually available for a pub crawl or an evening in the union bar, called the Ram (short for Ramshackle, apparently). Time passed in a pleasant enough way, with students' chatter over coffee or beer, or visiting pubs out on the moors, or, back in the halls, drinking horrible, vinegary bottles of Hirondelle and Lutomer. I was starting to enjoy myself. I felt more at home now, with the paradoxical effect that I felt less at home when I was home. With a nod to Charles Dickens, I now referred to the parents as The Elderly Pees.

Late teens are a time of peculiar intensity. No doubt evolution has equipped the maturing human male with the capacity to fall in love at the bat of a woman's eyes—in order to bring on the babies as soon as possible. Of course it helps that most young men have nothing much going on inside their heads and so are the fall-guys to any passing whim or fad. Having no girl to swoon over, I tended to fall in love with things. Nature was of course the focus of my principal love; it was, I liked to think, the only good and noble thing about me. By comparison everything else—one's passing taste for the early Dutch Masters, my singing in the bass section, my feats at the end of a climber's rope—were mere pastimes, passing fancies, jolly wheezes. Another fancy that came and went was for Merry England, although in practical terms it amounted to little more than a few, farcical riding lessons and my nose in a book. No sane person, I knew, would really enjoy living in the fourteenth century—the cold, the dripping roof, the rotten food, the violence, the plague, the endless kow-towing to the toffs. Life as a monk—my likely vocation—would have been especially awful; shagging the odd nun or midnight visits to the abbot's beer barrel being the highlights. But all the same, it drew you in, from a safe distance. All this reading and imagining—for you make your own pictures with good history in your lap—might in other circumstances have led me to write a comic novel—The Adventures of Petroc, the Bad Monk, perhaps. But it would not have occurred to me then, and it was too much effort in any case.

The Middle Ages also contributed to my brief, and, considering what had gone before, unlikely, flirtation with religion. These were the days when the followers of Billy Graham, the loud-mouthed American, were targeting university campuses. I went along to one of their meetings—for, after all, we were always checking out the latest thing, whether a revue, or a band, or an arty film. In my naivety I found this Yankee brand of Christianity, based on enthusiasm and shared experience, much more lively and, in a way, more convincing than those desolate Sunday mornings at the Hole. The missionary guy was witty and positive, and sold the gospel as a kind of drug. A dose of Good News would help you through troubled times, he promised; it would fix those feelings of depression and loneliness. It could hold your hand and whisper sweet consolations during biochemistry; hell, it could probably get you a decent degree too, and a nice, clean girl to accompany you to church. OK, I decided, I'll give it a whirl. For perhaps a week I wandered the campus with a holy expression—a kind of fish-eyed smile—and contemplated eternal things. I might even have binned my stash of girly magazines. Returning home that weekend, I told the Aged Pees about my conversion; that their eldest was a reformed man now, and no swearing please, in my presence. Mother rolled her eyes and Dad was of the view that I would be striking another, and quite different, attitude next week. He was right, of course. It wasn't long before I recalled that 'god' was an invention, and that, even if he did exist, we wouldn't get on. A night or two later a bunch of Christians came tapping on the door to share some more Good News and perhaps to discuss the colour problem. "Bugger off", I shouted through the door as I leafed through my new copy of Penthouse.

Nature conservation was a more lasting influence; indeed it grew to be the biggest, most enduring thing in my life. Even in 1970, even in Devon, one did not have to look far to see that the landscape was changing in ways that did not bode well for the skylarks and bees. It was no longer possible to be interested in wildlife without worrying about the rate at which it was disappearing. For instance, the modern way to look after a wood was to chop the whole thing down and replant the ground with dense ranks of deep-shading conifers, all lined up with military precision, crops of arboreal plastic obliterating everything that had ever flourished there. Similarly the best way to farm efficiently was now to dust the fields with DDT, which, being a persistent sort of chemical, stuck around in the food-chain until it had poisoned pretty well everything, from bugs to peregrines. Instead of working with nature we were wiping it out. Meanwhile the uneven bits of land that previous generations had left alone—the wet hollows, the steep banks, all those little scraps of wild—were being ironed out to create level runways for the combine harvester. And we were paying for it all with taxes. The only safe place for wildlife, it seemed, was on a nature reserve, and even they were not as safe as they seemed. The thing I cared about most in all the world was being comprehensibly, insensibly, trashed.

Nature conservation was not part of the botany course. I occasionally managed to squeeze it in during tutorials, though Mick in particular would always dismiss the subject as trivial. It was rubbish because conservation, in his opinion, wasn't science; it was more of a value judgement, and we didn't do those. It was perhaps no accident that the only text book on the subject, Dudley Stamp's *Nature Conservation in Britain*, was written by a geographer. Conservation could be seen less as biology and more as a form of land-use. A few people were doing their best to turn it into a science of sorts, but their work had not yet penetrated as far as Exeter. Even Michael Proctor found it a bit of a bore.

But I didn't. Once a subject really interests me I find I master the essentials fairly quickly. I had been around Britain a bit and seen some of our remaining wild places for myself. I harboured no illusions that I, or anyone else, was going to make any difference to the on-going rape of the natural world. My fascination for conservation was partly temperamental—I tend to prefer the old and tested; distrust the new—but it also offered a way into nature as a career. So when I met a chap called David Alexander, who had formed a university Conservation Corps, I said, count me in. One of our first outings was to Yarner Wood on the edge of Dartmoor, an oakwood famous for its nesting Pied Flycatchers. It was winter and the flycatchers were far away, in Africa somewhere, but the dark season is in fact the busiest in the wood's calendar, the time when forest workers are out in all weathers cutting bushes and chopping trees and mending fences. I remember being surprised that all this was really necessary in a nature reserve—wasn't it supposed to be reserved for nature? The bearded warden explained all about it over mugs of soup drunk with mittened fingers. Forget about wilderness, he said, there's not one wood in England that hasn't been worked over and over, since the dawn of history. It's the job of a wood to provide, well, wood. But so long as you don't fell it all at once the wildlife adapts to what we do, and even thrives. And then, by way of putting his words into practice, he handed out the axes and billhooks and saws and we got to work cutting down the trees, in this case unwanted sycamores. If we just left this wood to develop naturally, he said, we'd end up with one great big useless thicket and no flycatchers. So get chopping.

I was pleasantly impressed by all this. I imagined the life of a nature warden, living in a lonely shack in the middle of the woods, dedicated to keeping green a few last acres of old England—a highly romanticised view, needless to say. The job held just the right combination of dedication, vision and science to appeal to me. Of course I could never have become one. The routine of power-tool maintenance and log-stacking and—I would discover—form-filling—would have driven me mad in no time at all. But I felt an affinity with the warden and his young assistant, and I liked the way they set about things. I learned that nature reserves are as 'managed' as any other patch of land, only with this difference—that the work aims to maximise, not minimise, the wildlife. More or less from that moment, I had no doubt about what I wanted to do with my life, and that was to join the Nature Conservancy. I had heard about another Conservancy post called a warden-naturalist, which involved keeping an eye on things, getting to know the county's wildlife better than anyone else, and defending it as and when necessary. That, I thought, is more up my street: the local nature bloke. Yes, that was what I wanted: to be the county naturalist, the rover with a mission, Mister Green.

Conservation seemed to be catching on, just then, even in the Bird Club. Brian wanted to make a serious contribution to bird monitoring and came up with a plan to count the nesting sea-birds on Lundy. This would entail camping out on the island for several days and scanning every inch of rock and cliff, perhaps even a certain amount of scrambling and boating. I was up for it. This was surely the sort of thing that nature blokes did: keeping an eye on the birds so that you noticed if their numbers were starting to fall, or if, for whatever reason, they failed to raise their usual brood. It meant getting to know the birds, too, lounging about on their rocks, and jabbering at one another whilst Dad brings in the fish.

Four of us set out on the big adventure. I brought along the little green pup tent that Dad had bought with cornflake coupons. It didn't last the first night. After a blustery day on the cliffs, we retired under canvas after a few well-earned pints at the Puffin bar. I remember getting up at dawn for a pee and startling a Sika deer intrigued by the newcomers in its bosky habitat. Then the storm blew up. Rain galloped off the canvas; puddles leaked through tied door flaps and soaked into the bags. It soon looked as though we had chosen to camp in the middle of a pond. So, packing up our gear, we squelched over to see the aged patriarch Felix Gade, a kind of local Prospero who more or less ruled the isle. He kindly let us castaways use a barn. Over the next few days we counted guillemots and razorbills and kittiwakes and puffins. On the last day, while the chaps finished off, I conducted my own survey of a plant called the Lundy Cabbage. Although it looks too much like oil-seed rape to attract any attention, this is in fact one of the rarest flowers in the world, for it is found nowhere else except on Lundy. Presumably some ancestral cabbage had colonised these rocks and evolved in isolation to produce something unique and perfectly attuned to a life overlooking the Bristol Channel. I seem to have been the first person to have shown any interest in the Lundy Cabbage since its discovery, back in the 1930s. My subsequent article in the *Bulletin* of the Lundy Field Society became my first published paper based on original research, the very modest base for umpteen subsequent surveys. For conservationists are slightly more interested in Lundy Cabbage now.

It was while wandering about looking for cabbages that I underwent the only mystical experience of my life. I remember searching for an ancient enclosure called the Friar's Garden—a misnomer for Lundy never had any friars, nor many gardens either. All I knew was that it lay close by Parson's Well, but that was no help because I couldn't find the well either. And then, as I was pacing the ground looking for the faint shadows that mark an ancient field system, I distinctly heard the faint sound of tinkling bells. Aha, I thought, I'm thinking about friars and parsons so my mind has come up with a spontaneous peal of fairy bells. So I stopped and listened but it wasn't certain whether the chimes, which seemed to be getting louder, came from inside me, like a sudden tinnitus, or were out there on the wind, may be behind, may be in front, no wait a minute, they are everywhere. For perhaps thirty seconds the sky rang with phantom bells and then, all of a sudden, they stopped and all I could hear was the wind running through the grass. Am I, I thought, am I going to tell the chaps about this (one of whom was an archaeologist and might have had a few suggestions)? Once, on a lone walk in the Derbyshire dales, I heard cows humming a surprisingly tuneful dirge as they lay chewing the cud among the buttercups. Then, as now, with the mystery of the bells of Lundy, I decided that this is the sort of thing you should probably keep to yourself.

I loved everything about Lundy: the wonderful formations of its weathered granite, variously shaped like cheeses, slippers, the profile of an ancient knight; the sonorous gullies loud with the call of gulls (and the odd grey seal hauled up below); the rock where the grass grows so thick you can bounce on it; the stupendous cauldron in the cliffs with the sea boiling and spouting far below. I made sure I had an excuse to return there next year, now with a grant from the Lundy Field Society to study the rhododendron problem (another paper!). Lundy's magic gave me a lifelong love of islands, especially British islands, and for a time I tried to spend at least a few days on a different one every year. The actor Richard Burton was of the opinion that islands are prisons; he could not look at the sea for a minute without wishing for wings. For me they are the opposite: the siren song of the sea, the smile on the brow of the waters, summer isles of Eden beckoning from the shore. Britain is surrounded with islands like a string of precious pearls, and some of them are hardly ever visited except by naturalists. Yet even in such company, Lundy is peerless. It is for me the perfect island, the right size, without tarmac or traffic, and yet with sufficient amenities to sustain the island man. When I die you can scatter my ashes on Lundy. The perfect place does exist and it's here.

Auk counting team on Lundy: from left, Reg Harding, Brian Gregory, John Aylett.

CHAPTER SIX

Falling for a Welsh Girl

Towards the end of the summer term Michael Proctor asked me whether I would be interested in a job over the long vac. The Nature Conservancy wanted someone to set up a monitoring experiment at Wistman's Wood in the middle of Dartmoor. This wood is, or was, one of the weirdest places in England. Trees, it is generally agreed, grow upright with roots at the bottom and twigs at the top. But not here. At Wistman's—a ghostly name for a spooky place—they grew more or less horizontally, coiling like pythons in and out of moss-covered boulders, so you are never quite sure whether a particular bit is a root or a trunk or a branch. Time was when the only way to penetrate this elfin wood of criss-cross timbers was to crawl in on hands and knees. But lately the trees had started to grow up in the normal way. Wistman's Wood, it seemed, was slowly turning from something unusual into something comparatively ordinary. Today we would probably blame climate change. Back then it was a mystery. The Nature Conservancy wanted me to produce a sort of map against which future change could be measured.

I had already been to Wistman's Wood and enjoyed its creepy atmosphere. It sounded a fairly tough assignment, and promised to be lonely work, but I was so eager to join the Nature Conservancy after graduating that I thought it might be prudent to show willing. I had a motor scooter, and was confident the Aged Ps would lend me the caravan. So, I said, all right, I'll do it. Then Dee, who was listening from across the bench, piped up and said she would like to do it too. It sounded like a job for two people, she pointed out.

I had seen quite a lot of Dee that year. We had become friends and she had even invited me to her place in South Wales during the long vac. Jolly nice of her, I remember writing rather snootily in my diary, but of course *quite out of the question*. Why was it out of the question? Why? I liked her and she seemed to like me. She was on the pretty side of plain, about five-foot two, usually dressed casually in jumpers and jeans, with an oval, happy, young-working-mum sort of face, shortish curly hair; neat figure, nice round bum, infectious Welsh laugh. She was only two months older than me, but about five years up in terms of experience. She had a pretty wit, and kept me entertained with hot gossip about our fellow biologists, which was often surprisingly *Seventies*. Half of them were on drugs and some seemed to have eventful sex lives. There was, for instance, the tough boy and louche girl who came to an *arrangement* on every last Friday in the month. Or the earnest young woman who seemed to be quiet and retiring but who had apparently experienced *six* orgasms during one presumably frenzied evening with her chap. "Poor girl", commented Dee. Poor? It sounded all right to me. "No, I mean, you know, that she was *count-ing*. One, two, three it is, ah, *duw, duw*, there's goes another one, you see, *four* isn't it…" I wondered how she knew all this but I did get the impression that Dee was quite interested in sex.

What I couldn't work out was the nature of her relationship with this chap, Mark. A mature student of conventionally left-wing views, he seemed to be her regular man and they even lived together, although, insisted Dee, nothing *went on*. I gathered it was more a brother and sister thing. I knew Mark had occasional flings with socialist sisters, including the daughter of the president of Malta. It sounded pretty rum to me, but it was 1971, after all, and experimental lifestyles were in full swing. There was another bloke in Dee's life too, an even older guy working for a pharmaceutical company who she rejoined during vacations. Theirs was a long-term relationship, apparently, and what went on in term time didn't seem to count. Dee seemed to have a complicated love life. Still, it was none of my business; she was just a friend. But I did begin to wonder how we would get along, cooped together in the parents' caravan in the middle of Dartmoor.

At the start of the long vac we all set off in a couple of minibuses to Western Ireland for the field course under the tutelage of Michael Proctor. I was looking forward to it: new flowers, the eternal rockscape of the Burren, the bogs and bens of Connemara. We were lucky with the weather. In a normal year it might rain three days out of four but we experienced hardly a drop in the whole fortnight. I was young and eager and among friends. Proctor kept us busy by day. We mapped the Burren's amazing shrinking lakes, known as turloughs, and painted dots on the wings of burnet moths to see how many there were ('the size of the population'), and recorded 'transects' of seaweeds from high to low tide. We made longer excursions over limestone pavements and the boggy lakeland on the other side of the bay. After long, hot days in the sun, we dug ticks from one another's legs and backs, and smeared cream on our bites. And then went to the little bar behind the grocer's shop in Kinvara to drink Guinness and play cards.

One day we climbed the Twelve Bens of Connemara and witnessed the eerie spectacle of a Brocken Spectre, a projection of a shadowy figure haloed by a rainbow on a roof of mist. When you wave at him he waves back, for the joke is that the 'ghost' is you, projected into the sky by a trick of the light. By then we were late for our lift home, lost in the mist, and I volunteered to go ahead and inform the driver. I ran down that mountain like a hare, skinny and half-naked, with the sun on my brow and the wind in my hair, leaping over rocks, splashing through the pools, as if Cuchullain the mighty and all the hounds of Munster were on my heels. I was fit then, lean and light with springy heels and

Michael Proctor's botany team surveying a turlough (a temporary lake) in the Burren, Ireland, July 1971.

knotty, tireless legs. It was for this that I was born, I thought. I was, I considered, right in my element.

On our local walks, sometimes a barely-seen shadowy figure would follow us. Once we set an ambush for him, whoever he was, but he spotted us in time and turned back. Then one day—it might have been the second or third of our stay—I was about to turn in to my bunk in the caravan when I heard a quiet call from the scented dusk. "Fancy a walk?" suggested Dee.

We set off down the track that led towards the massive roll of Mullaghmore, the heart of the Burren, an ocean swell frozen in stone. Once we were out of sight of the village we found a soft grassy knoll strewn, like Titania's bed, with bedstraw and eyebright, and were soon necking as though it was the most natural thing in the world to do. After a bit, I sat up and said something like, "look here, Dee, this is going to be a bit awkward, isn't it, Mark being here and all. What will he say?" She seemed surprised. He wouldn't say much, and, besides, there was no reason for him to be told. We would carry on as before. "But the caravan, Dee, what about the caravan on Dartmoor? How will he feel about us being together for weeks on end? He is going to suspect hanky-panky, Dee, he really is." "Why, what do you think we are going to get up to in the caravan?" She had me there. I knew what I intended to happen in the caravan, but these were deep and uncertain waters and I wasn't sure what to say. "Why?" she said suddenly, "don't you fancy me, then?" "Of course I fancy you" (how I hated that phrase, so *pleb*). "I think you're lovely. I just can't believe my luck, that's all". "Well, you might as well believe it".

And so a, to me, bizarre relationship developed: colleagues by day, friends by evening and lovers by night. Those warm, windless nights lying with Dee on the banks of the Burren were, I thought, deeply romantic. I was learning about love, in my selfish male way, putting my own feelings under the microscope but not really having a clue about hers. If Kingsley Amis was right, that without a woman you are living only half a life, then Dee had just doubled the stakes. And for a while I did feel twice the man I was. It is astonishing how a girl can make you feel so much more male, so much less disconnected, dried-up, ugly. It was that epiphany that was driving me now, in the first flush of discovery. Every time she grabbed my hand, or put her arms round my waist, or darted a kiss on my cheek when no one was looking, felt thrillingly intimate, like a secret, shared language. I'm sure everyone knew; even Michael Proctor had begun to give me funny looks. But they were English gentlemen—not everything had died out in the Sixties—and nothing was said, or at least, not to us.

Even then I was aware of the potentially negative side of a relationship. Since those early days at the Hole I had done my best to keep my feelings under control. Officer's boys don't smile for the cameras. Officer's boys don't cry. Dee made me cry all right, but not yet. For the time being I felt fully alive, enough to recognise now that my first year at Exeter had been a kind of denial, a retreat from reality, a half-life, may be a quarter-life. For now my cup seemed full. There is a price to pay for love, or what one imagines to be love, notably in the realisation of how much more complicated life becomes when there are two of you, of the endless compromises and boring discussions in which the question of feelings enter quite often. But there was also an inner glow inside my twenty-year-old self as we drove back through Ireland with Dee sitting beside me, secretly squeezing my hand.

We had arranged to meet at Dee's digs, which she still shared with Mark, before setting off with our backpacks and scooters to Dartmoor. The parents had of course lent us the caravan, which they left clean and fully stocked, parked at the top of a lane by a farm at Two Bridges. The job would take about a month, I reckoned. But Dee was in no hurry to start. Conveniently, Mark was working nights so we had the days to ourselves—and soon the nights too, after the latter was banished to the spare room to avoid waking us up. He seemed to accept the situation with equanimity—not that I ever discussed it with him. I suppose something like it might have happened before. May be I was Dee's vacation project. As I say, the whole thing was beyond my understanding. I learned that Dee was a good cook, in the Welsh way of making a little go a long way. I discovered that she liked 1930s films, especially musicals, and (with touches of her own) could do an old Jessie Matthews number called 'Over my shoulder goes one care'. She had obviously done a lot of babysitting, with a fund of bedtime stories as well as the ability to do cutesy drawings of bunnies and little girls and flowers to keep the kids happy. She was self-reliant, mercurial, very Welsh with her fast talking and gestures, and, in some way that is hard to put into words, maternal. That was what everyone said about Dee. She was good with kids and *motherly*. She'd make a lovely Mum, would Dee.

We had taken steps to ensure there was no danger of my becoming a less-than-lovely Dad. Like every spotty teen, I had often wondered what sex would be like. There was no visible, explicit sex then, certainly not on TV, nor even in girly mags where all traces of body-hair were still solicitously airbrushed away. The only places where you could see a man and woman actually at it were in so-called sex manuals where the pictures seemed designed to make the whole business as unappealing as possible (for one thing, the partners were always turned away from the leering reader). In the event, of course, nature takes hold and some deep genetic memory whips the chap on to a conclusion without pausing to consider the means, the ins and the outs, so to speak. "I don't know what books you've been reading", murmured Dee. "Erm." (One does not, does one, wish one's lady to know about the educational material one keeps at the top of the cupboard). "Well, what was it like? Did you enjoy yourself?" "Oh, yes, yes". Not much, the first time, to be honest. It was self-conscious and rather awkward. Far too much all at once. "I expect I'll get used to it", I blurted out without thinking, whereat Dee burst into tears.

A tramp wandering over the moor a few days later might have seen the little caravan rocking pleasantly at midnight, a sign that one was getting used to it. I lived for those nights snuggled up in the double bag. As for daytime, thank God she was there to keep me company. Each morning we set off for the elfin wood, leaving the scooters behind a wall and trudging off across the moor to the tangled oaks on the skyline. No wood-elf would have envied our task, setting up our tapes and making compass bearings before recording every damn plant or moss or rock, from the top to the bottom, and then going along a bit and starting all over again. Each time we finished a 'transect' we painted a red spot on the stone wall below so that some lucky chap could repeat the work in a few years' time. When all that was done we started mapping the position of every tree within a fenced-off part of the wood, set aside for experimental purposes. I did most of the identification, Dee the surveying and note-taking. While we marched, or munched our lunchtime sandwiches, and noticed, wearily, how much there was left to do, Dee told stories. Her favourite author was Scott Fitzgerald, and when it was my turn to read her copy of *This Side of Paradise* I wondered when the story would ever get going, and eventually found out that it didn't. At the end, around page 400, the protagonist laments, 'I know myself and that is all'. Yeah, and a bit too much, I thought, you boring wimp. "Great book", I said, handing it back. "I knew you'd like it", she said, fishing in her bag and handing me *The Great Gatsby*.

And so the summer rolled on. Wistman's Wood was duly mapped and Dee went off on holiday to Italy while I returned home to Andover to pick apples. How dull home seemed now. How eagerly I ticked off each day until her return. We had arranged to share a seaside flat at Dawlish. I was, under Dee's tuition, shedding my boyhood skin. Like the guy in Dee's boring novels, I was becoming a man, a man in *lurve*. I might even, I thought, attain a taste for Scott Fitzgerald.

The caravan on Dartmoor where we lived during the Wistman's Wood survey, summer 1971.

CHAPTER SEVEN

As a Moth to the Flame

Do you sense the inevitable: the car crash waiting just down the road? The decision to share one's life with someone you love, or think you do, is perhaps the greatest you ever make, but we had done it casually without much discussion. It was the Seventies, after all. Yeah, why not? She had moved into a two-bedroom flat in Dawlish earlier that summer, and so it was just a matter of the discarded suitor leaving by the door marked exit and Peter entering in triumph through the other. Tough luck on Mark, of course, but all's fair in love and war. But I lacked the experience for a step like this. It is experience that eventually turns us into pessimists. "Always expect the worst", says my brother Chris, "and you'll never be disappointed". But I was flowing over with expectation, and besides, my senses were bedazzled. I was drawn to that flat in Dawlish by the flames of romantic illusion and sexual desire as

Dawlish—England's Riviera—the quintessential seaside town. The arrow marks the approximate position of our flat.

eagerly and helplessly as a moth. How trivial and pathetic my life in halls seemed now. Welcome to the grand adventure of real life! This new term was going to *rock*.

It took me a while to find the place, a first-floor flat in a pre-war villa a few hundred yards back from the sea-front. And when I did, Dee had company. Some former suitor, some deluded mooncalf, some berk with a past, had come a-calling. Dee took him out for a walk, back to the station I supposed. They were gone some time, and when at last she returned, breathless and starry-eyed, she was carrying something. "Look what he gave me". It was a melon. A bit simple is he, I wondered, a bit gone in the head? "No, don't you understand? It means 'I'm not wanking any more, baby'". "What?" "Apparently some of them do it with a melon. It's very realistic, they say". "WHAT??!" "Anyway, come to bed".

We went to bed but we didn't do much except talk. Dee had a sick hamster. It was only September but the place already felt cold and damp. She said the best place for the poor little mite was in bed with us, cage and all. Cradling a cup of cocoa she told me all about her holiday in Italy. It had been a disaster, so awful she had had a nervous breakdown. She showed me the pictures, and she certainly looked pasty-faced and unwell. She had a headache that night, and the next morning, and the one after that. May be she caught it off the hamster. Then Mark came to call. To my surprise, Dee didn't turn him away; in fact they went off for a walk on which, once again, I wasn't invited. After a while she came back on her own. "He wants to move in. I told him to go home".

Soon enough I learned that love is not all necking in an earthly paradise, or even joyously coupling in a caravan in the middle of the moor. Love was a challenge, or, rather, an endlessly repeated set of challenges. One of them was waiting outside the phone box on cold wet nights while Dee made her daily call to Mum, to her best friend, to half the bloody Rhondda by the sound of it. Love was the tedium of housework, of shopping, and washing the pots and pans after our frugal supper. Dee joked that she would have to brick me up, I took so long about it. Love was also pigeon shit on the washing. There was a machine in the scullery but in the dank seaside air the clothes refused to dry properly, and in the meantime the pigeons came and did what pigeons do. And drying skirts and towels on the radiator made the flat damper than ever. And damp makes you bad-tempered. "Oh, you're always complaining you are", said Dee. "Used to it comfy, were you? Did Mum do all that for you?"

Another thing I had not considered was that, with digs in Dawlish, one would be marooned on the campus all day long. I was used to going back to halls after a lecture, making a coffee, putting one's feet up, listening to a record, reading a magazine. Now there was an endless hanging about, in coffee bars, in common rooms, in libraries. We had to be up early to catch the train in time for the rash of nine-o'-clock lectures that term. Which we rarely managed for, as I was learning, everything takes three times as long when there are two of you. "Oh, here come the Dawlish lot", they would chorus as we piled in late after trekking up the hill from the station. "Nearly time to go home then." "Do come in", Michael Proctor would murmur with icy sarcasm. "We're getting along nicely. Ah, Peter, how awfully nice to see you smiling". Ah, God, I was getting fed up and the term had barely started.

"They're living together!" It was a change to be up there in the gossip, along with the Friday girl and the orgasm fiend. Dee had made an effort to smarten me up. "You're to stop carrying that bag. It looks stupid". What my dear old duffle bag, my shoulder-companion, my bulky friend? "It looks stupid. Now put on this shirt. Yes, that's a bit more you isn't it?" "It's a bit brighter than I'd normally wear." "You'll get used to it. And get rid of those vests. And as for those…*what* am I going to do with you". Dee cast her critical eye over my friends and found them wanting. My old orchid-hunting pal Keith, for instance, had come round to show me an ingenious shooting stock he had rigged up on his camera, and was eager to tell me all about it. Dee listened to the flow of technicalities for a minute or two before making an excuse and bounding for the door. *Rude-ish*, I thought. As for the Bird Club, Dee came along to one outing, just one, and discomforted Brian and Mike with a stream of suggestions: Bird Club raffles, dances, tea parties, buttered scones. She could make the scones. Brian's face was a study in scorn and disbelief.

As for *Dee*'s friends... I spent an uneasy twenty minutes sitting silent on the bed while she chewed the fat with her best friend Caroline. The latter's glance at me said it all. *What* has she picked up this time? *That's* not going to last.

"She thinks *Mark*'s a creep", she said afterwards, leaving it unsaid what she thought of me. In the caravan we had both practiced forgiveness (and I'd be the first to concede that she practiced it better than me), but patience was wearing thin. Our frequent flare-ups were a symptom of an underlying malaise, a growing disaffection, fault lines developing in a romance turned brittle. Of course we had had rows in the caravan too. There was that time, for instance, on a day off from the wood, when I couldn't stand it a moment longer and stalked out over the moor while she tidied the caravan with, I imagine, many a bump and a bang. But then the world had left us alone, and now it was lapping at the walls. "Mark thinks you're odd", she said. "How odd? I thought you told me Mark thinks I'm great". "He did think that and now he thinks you're odd". "Well who bloody cares what Mark thinks? Do *you* think I'm 'odd'?" "Well... you're hard to live with". "You lived with me in the caravan". "Yes, but that was different". "Why? I loved you then and I love you now". "No you don't, you're just infatuated with me". One could have replied, I suppose, that love and infatuation are much the same thing; that love is a form of madness—*I'm* mad about *you*. But you learn never to tackle a girl on the subject of love. They *know*. They are the professionals here; we the amateurs, the bumblers, the oafs in the haystack.

She was much too strong for me. It was her life I was sharing, not the other way round. She nagged and I protested and whined. The bickering came to a head one day in Bristol. It had started reasonably well. We enjoyed a short walk in the park and a Chinese lunch that Dee insisted on paying for, as a treat, and then we went shopping. Something she said, some remark or other, some word or gesture, tripped my switch. I can't stand this any moment longer, I spluttered, this ridiculous, this... this... *thing*, and off I went. I went on walking, propelled by burning, pent-up resentment and self-pity. I thought, I can't turn round now, I'd look a *fool*. Dee called after me but I had become blind and deaf to everything except my own spleen. There was a very angry and tearful reunion in the flat that night. I was banished to the cot in the spare room where I dare say I blubbed into my pillow (it was damp already). How did Philip Larkin put it? 'She had staked out a large claim in my pesky emotions and when she withdraws I feel nearly half my feelings drawn after her, as if some Friday-night poulterer were drawing my liver and lites'. Yes, that sort of thing. God help us, you thought, is this what real life is like—tattered cockerel versus bristling hen?

As the dénouement drew nigh, Mark's visits grew more frequent. The two of them shared some bond compared with which my *grand passion* seemed no more than a mild diversion. It was obviously time to bail out of the wreck, to flee from the burning building, before they kicked me out. But for some reason, perhaps a lingering hope that I could win her back, possibly just sheer inertia, I remained there, like a bit of grit, for several more weeks. One of the things that kept me flitting round the light, the poor, singed moth with its blind bug eyes, was Dee's own irresolution. Now and again, usually after a night out, she would press me a kiss as sweet as cinnamon, and I would run my hands over her body to remind myself of what it had been like. Once we even had a play-wrestle which she seemed to enjoy. Sitting up and tidying her disordered hair, she murmured, "We should have done *that* in the caravan".

More often she behaved as though she could hardly stand the sight of me. When her pals called round the conversation usually tended towards politics. Dee was fashionably left-wing and had once been something of an activist; she claimed to have thrown ink over Ted Heath. I tended to bite my tongue when they discussed the coming revolution but the conclusion was always the same: "you aren't like us" (unlike, for instance, Mark. Mark was 'like us'; Mark was what she liked). I was still the son of my dad and secretly wished that things had stayed the way they were in, say, 1958. I was certainly not looking forward to *their* utopia, a future of union power, free tuition and two-bob packets of hash at Woolworths. While more dynamic spirits argued and laughed together I shrivelled into my shell and felt my crippling shyness, partly cast off in my second year at Exeter, reassert itself. I didn't belong here, in this classless *milieu*. I wanted to be on my own island again.

And so I cleared off. As Mark (triumphant Mark) put it during our last supper, in his insufferable high-pitched squeak, if it hadn't been you, it would have been us ('us!'). Dee said nothing. I packed my books, my dive-gear and the rags of our still unfinished Wistman's Wood report. Sending them on in a van, I tramped down to Dawlish station in the rain—the place where we had had such fun a month earlier dodging the waves as they crashed over the sea wall. After an unsuccessful search for digs in town I found a place in Duryard Halls on the edge of the campus, the halls where J. K. Rowling lived, a few years later, although they bear no resemblance whatever to Hogwarts. And so I dragged my sorry ass back to the single room with its narrow bunk, its shelf and plain table, its student's cupboard and single-barred electric fire. Not far away the freight trains clanked and jolted, and the familiar strains of Led Zeppelin issued from an open window. I'm back where I started, I thought, luxuriating in the warmth and the sudden rush of privacy. It's not much but I'm *safe* here.

And so life resumed without my love. And all this time I bet you've been wondering. You've been asking yourselves: *did the hamster live?* Or was our sacrifice all in vain? Yes it lived. Later Dee bought it a mate. Once, when I happened to drop by, the pair of them were at it, the hamsters I mean, shagging their little hearts out on the carpet. I watched them nostalgically. The lucky little bastard.

CHAPTER EIGHT

On the Anvil

The trouble with me, I thought, is that I never seem to like what I've got. When I was on my own I wanted company. When I had it I longed for solitude. Maybe I just wasn't a social being. It was hard, I was finding, to reconcile the inner child with the burdens of growing up. The loving-boyfriend role had been a real strain, while the mere notion of being a hubbie, and then a dad, struck me as appalling. How does anyone ever manage it? All I'd got out of love so far was a broken heart. I felt like so much flotsam—bones, guts, skin—washed ashore after a storm. And that creep, that so-called friend, that fucking traitor, had taken my rightful place, or something like it, at the side of my lovely Dee ("he doesn't get what you got", insisted Dee. Well I bloody well hoped not). As Aristotle, or possibly some other guy, reminded us, there are no words so sad as those that say 'might have been'. Although 'I screwed it up' seemed to fit my case just as well. A proper sort of chap would have shrugged the thing off and found someone else, someone *better*, pronto. Me, I felt I'd had the stuffing knocked out of me. I just felt like moping for a bit.

I divided my lost Exeter diary into sections with titles borrowed from the poets. 'The Hollow Mask of Mirth' (Auden) was one, and there was also something from *Purgatorio*, about those poor saps that carry rocks on their backs. The present chapter, I remember, was called 'On the Anvil', a title borrowed from Churchill's *History of the English-Speaking Peoples*. In the hands of the great man it was about the hammering out of English law and constitution, the forging of the Parliamentary system and the government machine. In my case it was the tough story of a sad kid turning painfully into a man. I had carried my bleeding heart back into halls and was free to carry on where I had left off six months ago. The kid still in me would have sneaked back to Dawlish at night and smashed their fucking windows. The adolescent simply went on brooding: Prometheus on his rock, Siegfried in the ring of fire; I knew all the myths and a fat lot of good they had done me. Finally the pair of us, child and man, got together and decided on a course of action. What we did was to paint a picture. It was a free rendition of Goya's 'Pilgrimage of San Isidro', about a bunch of blind men singing in the dark. This, I thought, was the *romantic* solution. The finished picture, done in poster paint, mostly black and yellow, on a large sheet of cartridge paper pinned on a board, was dark and threatening, and terribly gloomy. It hung in the parents' dining room for ages. "Our son did that", they exclaimed proudly. You would watch the guest's faces and see in their eyes the expression forming that said: "you've got a bloody peculiar son, mate".

Relations with mother and father had been another casualty of the Dee imbroglio. They hadn't said much about my plans, or at least not to my face. They had met her and seemed to like her, but I suspect that Mum, at least, disapproved of her son's latest venture and, being a mother, instinctively resented it. I had not helped matters by crowing about my new life and deciding to remove *all* my books, thank you very much, and thanks for having me. Their reaction was to let Chris move into my old quarters and turf out all my stuff into a smaller corner room.

Dee had been aghast at my little library, the Classics paperbacks, my Chrétien de Troyes, my *Greek Myths*, the precious volumes of Dante. All these books, exclaimed Dee, and *nothing to read*! My literary tastes, she thought, were weird. They weren't weird to me, but that is what the solitude does to you—you never realise how peculiar you are. Once, as we trudged over the moor for another day in the fairy wood, I recited selections from *Henry V* in what I hoped was a passable parody of Larry Olivier. I remember Dee's discouraging response: "That's the first time you've ever been really boring". Not the last though. She felt the same about my lullaby in the style of Paul Robeson and my stories from Chaucer. It's only when you get to know someone well that you start to find corners of strangeness, furtive and solitary hobbies, traits of peculiarity that you'd rather weren't there. She had started to find mine. The trouble from my point of view was that the things that interested me—a pretty good range I felt—didn't seem to interest anyone else, and certainly not Dee. My amusements, it was starting to dawn on me, were forming the groundwork for a solo existence. Well, I couldn't help it. I didn't want to be normal, at least not Exeter-normal (and definitely not Loughborough-normal). I might have been more at home at Oxford, dreaming amongst the spires, among my own kind discussing Arthurian legends in the senior common room. 'Might have been', again. More shreds of Led thudded behind the wall. Shut up, *shut the fuck up*!

I was still at Dawlish with Dee when I celebrated my 21st birthday, but put that word 'celebrated' in quotation marks, and maybe '21st' and 'birthday' too. It was a non-event. Dee came home—she had been away somewhere the previous night—with a superior bottle of wine and a bag of goodies. I think there were even candles on the table. That was nice of her but I don't think either of us enjoyed it much. My day had already been blighted by an uncharacteristically curt and bad-tempered letter from my mother. She had wanted to know *at once* whether my present had arrived safely and when I forgot to tell her (the phone box was some distance away and it was raining) her resentment boiled over. Dee remarked that if *her* Mam had spoken to her like that she'd have been *devastated*. What they had sent me was a crate full of diving gear. I never told them this but it was all crap. Dad had ordered the stuff from some catalogue. The aqualung was a cheap thing made of cast-iron which rusted in salt water and, besides, you needed so many weights to stop it floating that your belt hung down towards your knees. Iron bollocks, it looked like. When I gave the awful thing away to a friend he nearly drowned. It was a bad call. I should never have asked Dad to get me anything that required knowledge. I should have asked for money, like everyone else. Damn, damn, DAMN.

While all these crappy things were going on, I hardly spared a thought for the botany. The previous year I had been so entranced by Ivimey-Cook's short course on the algae that I started a new masterwork. It was to be 'The Concise British Alga', designed as a companion to Keble Martin's famous flora, and in the same format. To complete it I would have had to live alone in some lighthouse painting nothing but highly magnified pond slime for about ten years. That would have been great. I got as far as illustrating a couple of plates in drawing ink and crayon before jacking it in. The finals were just over the horizon now, and we were turning into the final lap: good stuff too, mostly, like plant evolution and angiosperms, things we might usefully have learned at the start instead of now, at the end, when it was getting a bit late.

Of course my former friends shared the same lectures and I could hardly avoid their company. Seeing Dee every day, arriving later than ever from the Dawlish train, irritated my tender scars; it made me miserable. Pretending nothing had happened seemed as false as open enmity. One cold day, I remember, Dee swept past in a long violet maxicoat without, I thought, favouring me with so much as a glance. That was worth a page or two in the old diary; a fairly intensive curdling of bile. Obviously I was getting paranoid. I was behaving like a little boy who'd had his sweeties taken away. Dee was present on parade again during the long weekend in the Easter vac when the three of us went down to the seaside to study seaweeds. Oh God, make her go away! I ought to have enjoyed this outing but during the journeys in the minivan I pretended to be immersed in a book.

There was one ray of light in this dismal term. Someone, probably Michael Proctor again, had told me of a special M.Sc. course in nature conservation based at University College London. Set up ten years earlier as a mere diploma, it was designed first and foremost to teach aspirant young conservationists the basics of ecology, land-use and conservation: a bit of biology, a bit of geography, a bit of social planning, and a whole lot of travelling to research labs, nature reserves, farms, even nuclear power stations. As Michael pointed out, you'll probably need a postgrad qualification and a bit of experience to join the Nature Conservancy as a scientist. Although there were alternatives—there were, for instance, Masters courses in ecology at Bangor and Aberdeen—he thought this one offered the best career choice for me.

I applied and got an interview. There were three of them there, three men in their thirties and forties, obviously mates, bunched together in a cubbyhole of an office, just above the entrance hall where the corpse of the college founder, Jeremy Bentham, mouldered away quietly in his Sunday best. For a change I felt fairly confident and relaxed. I could tell this trio about the seabird count on Lundy and my wood-chopping at Yarner Wood, not to mention the sacrifice of my long vac measuring trees on Dartmoor. When the oldest of the three, a good-humoured, long-haired Liverpudlian called O'Connor, summed up our 'discussion' with many a technical phrase—it was 'empirical' this and 'deductive' that—I just nodded wisely. They offered me a place. A studentship from the Natural Environment Research Council would be mine, too, if I could manage to get a first or even a second, even a *lower* second. That was a bit of luck. "Hopefully it's in the bag", I said to Michael, as we walked the Devon coast one day. "Make sure you get that second", he replied. "I will, surely?" "Just make sure. Leave nothing to chance. Don't think you're outstanding or anything", he added, "because you aren't".

Things were looking up socially too. I was scrambling out of my self-dug pit. There was a girl or two involved. In the lab a red-haired girl kept coming over to borrow a scalpel, suggest a coffee, make conversation. She was hot, or so they said. Go for it, mate, go get her. I hesitated, and of course you should never do that or you will spend the rest of your life regretting it. As I have. Damn, damn, *damn*. When I last saw her she was wrapped around some long-haired oaf, sharing, no doubt, her heat. She would have made me happy for a week or two, I'm sure, before she found out how boring I was.

Dee, on the other hand, was showing signs of stress. One day we met by accident on the campus, said hi, and went for a short walk in the greening park. It was the first time I had been alone with her since Dawlish. She was worried about work. She thought she was bound to fail, get a pass degree, be turned down by the college she had set her heart on. She was so worried, she told me, that her hair was turning grey. "Bloody hell! Anything I can do?" "Oh, would you? Do you mean it?" She suggested bringing work over to my place so we could revise together. Over a few days I gave her a crash course on the bits of botany I thought I knew about, such as the differences between one kind of flower and another. But that wasn't what she needed. What she craved was reassurance, a sympathetic shoulder to lean on (so Mark was no good at that, eh?). For my part I was relieved that we seemed to be ending up as friends, the way we had begun, and that she would have some small reason to think well of me. I still 'fancied' her too; a pity there was no time to start over. She took me to lunch by way of a thank you. A shame Mark had to be there, and in no good mood it seemed, but what the hell. It was all coming to an end anyhow. None of it mattered now.

Image of a broken heart: blind men singing in the dark. A free rendering of Goya's Pilgrimage of San Isidro *by P. Marren, artist.*

CHAPTER NINE

Finals

It should have been my best year and I blew it. If I'd spent my time chasing girls, going to parties, getting drunk, it would at least have given me something to remember when I exited through the door marked 'fail'. Or alternatively I might have tried to become a better climber or diver or singer. Or even (and here's a novel idea) worked harder at getting a good degree. But I spent far too much of it living aimlessly, moping about. And then I wasted the Devon spring in a panic-stricken attempt to make up for three years of, at best, intermittent work.

For the penultimate term we had to choose a project. Maybe 'choose' is not quite the right word here. There were only three of us and so tidy-minded Professor Webster wanted us to share the same subject, and that, he informed us, would be plant viruses. There were all kinds of reasons why I didn't want to work on viruses, the main one being that viruses suck. Viruses are utterly dreary. They are not even proper plants, for heaven's sake. I want out, I moaned. Let me do something else. Please god, not viruses.

All right, said John Webster. What he found for me was, in effect, a ringside seat in the Prof.'s current research. It was about some unusual micro-fungi called aquatic hyphomycetes, or Ingoldian fungi, after their discoverer, Webster's friend and mentor, Terence Ingold. Although to the naked eye they look like nothing more than fluff, these moulds are noted for their strange spores, shaped like anchors or TV aerials or bananas. Webster isolated them by bottling up samples of foam from brooks and streams and then passing them through a filter. Then you took a look at the tiny sputniks embedded in the filter paper and tried to identify them and, in my case, count and measure them.

The work was fiddly and time-consuming, and, to be honest, not a lot of fun. Working nimbly with lab equipment was another area in which I revealed a stunning lack of talent. I kept a disastrous bench. My clumsy sausage fingers spilled filters and solutions, knocked stuff over and smudged the slides. Only my blood-stained drawings were passable. One day the Prof. came over and, having run a practiced eye down my list of measurements, scribbled the word 'significant'. Academically it was probably my proudest moment at Exeter. Quite without deductive intent I had helped to demonstrate that, the faster the current, the longer were these sputnik points, these draglines attached to the spores. In other words I had unknowingly worked out what these funny, spiky points were *for*. They were to catch on to leaves and other debris as the spores swirled downstream. And the faster the current, the longer the anchor lines needed to be. Q.E.D, and now it's proven, let's go home. Perhaps it earned me a few marks as the final reckoning approached. All the same I do not envy the life of the experimental biologist, all this patient, weary work to prove some tiny, insignificant point. It certainly isn't for everybody. In fact I'm surprised it suits anybody.

As the finals drew near I began to sweat. I hadn't done nearly enough to do well. Large chunks of the course were still more or less incomprehensible. I used to have recurrent nightmares about entering an exam hall and reading a paper that might as well have been written in Chinese for all the sense it made. I decided to mug up on at least one subject so that I would be able to shine in something. The subject I chose, bizarrely, was plant pathology, the diseases of crops and plants. I got hold of an advanced textbook and read through every line, making copious notes on the hideous cankers and blights of horticulture—a chamber of plant horrors: mildews, rusts, scabs, rots. It was a complete waste of time. As it turned out, no one was interested in what I knew about mildews.

Come the dread day, we entered the echoing hall. Vast it seemed, vast and silent and oppressive. There was a susurrus of movement as papers were turned over and forty pairs of eyes took in the ghastly things printed on them. I remember practically being sick over mine. I have kept my degree papers, six in all; four three-hour long knowledge tests and two three-hour practicals. Time has hardly mellowed the disbelief, followed by anger and then despair, that I felt then.

It wasn't fair. There was hardly anything here that interested me in the slightest. If I hadn't known it before I realised it now: modern botany was less (far less) about flowers and fungi and more about smelly biochemicals and disgusting molecules. One fairly typical question asked us to write an hour's worth of hot science on something none of us had ever heard of called an episome. Even the lone mycological question was gibberish: *'Discuss the mechanisms which promote outbreeding in fungi.'* Answer, according to Wikipedia: *'In fungi highly polymorphic mating-type loci mediate mating through complementary interactions between molecules encoded or regulated by different mating-type haplotypes'*. Great.

This should suit biochemical Mick down to the ground, I thought, though I noticed he wasn't looking too happy either. It took me ten minutes to search out any possible Peter questions. Where were they? Where? What had they got against me? How did they think I was going to get to do a Masters like this? I should have gone to Bristol, Southampton, anywhere but fucking Exeter, those (and here I quote from the remark I made on my exam paper) BLOODY ROTTEN STINKING PITILESS BASTARDS.

I thought I'd be lucky to scrape a 2.2. I hated this kind of science, requiring a maths brain, a narrow, focused mind for data and processes. I hadn't got one of those, you see. I had no problem with knowledge. I liked knowledge. Knowledge came easily. But without a deductive understanding of the scientific method, knowledge alone was proving useless. Perhaps I redeemed myself somewhat with the big three-hour essay. From a prick-shrivelling list of options I chose to discourse on what were then called the blue-green algae. With the *Observer's Book of Pond Life* coming to the rescue, I poured out pretty well everything I knew about these humble blobs of matter, pointing out that, since they lack a cell nucleus, they could not truthfully be called 'algae' or indeed plants. They were bacteria with added chlorophyll. Perhaps I picked up a mark or two there for today everyone agrees with me; they are indeed not plants and therefore not botany either. They have been demoted to germs and are studied by white-coated geeks in hospitals.

By the time we reached the last practical, I think we were all feeling the strain. We discussed whether to make a formal complaint about the unreasonable nature of our exam compared with those that had gone before. But, as Mick and Dee pointed out, that would be a hard argument to sustain, and besides, it might not have been as bad for others as it was for me. That last practical was a joke. Mick was feeling jittery after the Prof. had bawled him out for lounging against some apparatus. "What's this?" someone hissed. "I dunno, maybe it's another fucking enzyme." "What have you got for question 10?" "I've got 'episome'?" "Yeah, there seem to be a lot of them about this year" "It's a vintage year for episomes". "Episomes are the in-thing". "Episomes are great!" The examiner, a young man in a lab-coat, looked up and stared hard, but we ignored him. "What about question 7?" "Allosteric enzyme?" "I'm going to put episome again". "Yeah, when in doubt…" I imagine we all got more or less the same marks.

The last stage of the ordeal was the *viva voce* from a visiting senior academic. We got Dr Donald Pigott, a Cambridge ecologist and friend of Michael Proctor's. The interview was a formality: the results were already typed out ready for pinning on the board. It was just an opportunity to look back over the past three years and for the man to tell you where you did good, or, alternatively, where you fucked up. You fucked up on continuous assessment, he told me. "I see several zeros here. Pity… Michael tells me you're an ecologist", he went on. "So why didn't you answer the ecology question?" " Because I found in it a dangerous ambiguity", I replied. "I like knowing what it is I'm being asked to do". Pigott shook his head. "And you're keen on mycology, I hear. The same question applies. Why didn't you pick that one?" Because the shit-face that set that hate-question was intent on ruining my life for me, was my sturdy rejoinder. Pigott obviously found me a queer study. "What a pity", he repeated, pulling a face. "Anyway, good luck!"

We had only ten minutes to wait before finding out what he meant. The door opened and the Prof. emerged with a piece of paper. He pinned it impassively to the notice board before disappearing wordlessly back into his office. "They're all the same", shouted Dee as she led the rush. All 2.2s, all lower seconds. Of the thirty-odd of us in biological sciences, only one, a quiet girl in zoology, had managed a first. We digested the result in our different ways. Dee, who had expected a third, was "so happy". She was dancing down the corridor. Mick, who needed a 2.1 for a place on a postgrad course, looked crushed. And I? I was somewhere between the two, relieved rather than proud. A 2.2 was enough to qualify for my advanced course studentship but hardly a cause for wild celebration. I'd squeaked through again. Pigott had been hinting that if I'd worked a bit harder, if I'd had answered the right questions, if I wasn't such an idle bugger and bloody fool, I'd have walked a 2.1. I might even have had it in me to get a first, if I'd really knuckled down, if I'd used my head a bit more, if I'd put in the course work, if I wasn't such a schmuck. Ah well. In the event it made no difference. I was where I wanted to be, with hope if not honour.

That was the beginning of June. The year still had three weeks to run, weeks of beach parties or prom dances or balmy evenings in the beer garden. I went birdwatching. I also began recording plants around Exeter for Ivimey-Cook's Devon flora but soon gave up out of boredom and restlessness. I walked over Exmoor and traced the River Ex back to its source. I walked parts of the south Devon coast. I walked all over the place. I was marking time, you see, before the long vac, which was going to be more eventful. I'd arranged to go with Proctor and the second years to the Swiss Alps, notionally as a demonstrator. I'd also landed a grant from the Lundy Field Society, enough to give me two more weeks camping on the island. And shortly after that I would be off with the UCL conservation course to learn about nature conservation at Monks Wood Field Station. Things had come together after all. It felt like walking out into the open air, the fresh wind blowing over the moor, the spray rising to greet the cliffs. For those who had made the most of their time at Exeter these were sweet-sad days. I merely felt liberated.

It only remained to get the degree ceremony out of the way. We waited in our silk-lined, sky-blue hoods and hired graduate's gowns while speeches were made to the greater glory of the University. Then we mounted the stage one by one to receive our scrolls. The red-robed Chancellor and his minions certified that I had fulfilled the requirements of the Ordinances and Regulations (uh?) and by the authority of the Senate had been admitted to the degree of Bachelor of Science, second class. The name and subject had been added to the allotted space with a typewriter. The scroll looked a bit cheap to me. It might have been nice, for instance, if they had printed the college arms in colour. I bet you get a better scroll at Oxbridge. Seated on my left, and looking very fetching in her academic rig, was Dee. She needed to dash off somewhere immediately afterwards. "*Cofion cynnes*", I said, squeezing her arm as we got up to leave. It was one of the Welsh phrases she had taught me, meaning 'warm memories', or, more loosely, 'goodbye'. She was in a hurry, and if she said anything in reply I didn't catch it. I never saw her again.

Graduation Day – me standing gawkily in the puddle with my second-class degree.

Afterwards I donned my mortarboard and stood in a puddle outside the Student's Union while the parents struggled with the Practica. I had declined to have the shot done professionally, which was a shame since the light was poor and father misjudged the exposure. Glasses of cheap wine were dispensed from a plastic tray. Once again I felt a twinge of envy for those Oxbridge scholars in their fur-clipped gowns sipping Bolly among the dreaming spires. "Well, Peter", beamed Michael Proctor, "what does it feel like to have a degree". I bet he says that to all the newbie graduates. Oh, great, I said shortly, and introduced the parents. We've heard so much about you, they said, and, we will miss him, said Michael (yeah, yeah), and then we stood awkwardly, wondering what to say next. "Well, good luck", said Michael. Good luck, said Brian Ivimey-Cook. Good luck, said the Prof. Goodbye, I said. Thanks for having me. And, I told them, I know what an episome is now. And with that we piled into the Toyota and set off on the long road home.

CHAPTER TEN

In Which Our Hero Sets Forth

That might seem an inconsequential note on which to end. The conclusion of a story is supposed to bring resolution of some kind, for example of how one has learnt from bitter experience the way to a better, happier, more fulfilled life. But real life, honestly told, is never quite so neat; there are few genuine beginnings and ends, birth and death being the main ones. For most of the time we just bump along: babyhood, school, job, marriage, babies (or not), promotion (or not), retirement, old age. For me Graduation Day marked none of those things. I was merely heading on for more of the same: another university, another hall of residence, another academic journey, another set of exam papers. The location would change, but hardly the circumstances. Eventually, of course, all this bloody learning, this eternal dislocation, this unsteady, jolting ride in a second-class carriage, would reach its due destination in the form of a job, and that job would have to be in nature conservation because nothing else would do. It might happen next year, or the year after, or some years hence if I managed things right (for I didn't want a full-time job just yet). In fact it happened four years later when the 1976 summer of drought turned into a winter of ice and snow and I rode the night train north to Inverness to begin my new life as an 'assistant regional officer' in the Nature Conservancy ('North-East Scotland Region'). In between lay limbo years: a master's degree in London, a trail of short-term jobs, an aborted PhD on alpine plants, before the job advert, the interview and the letter of acceptance.

All the same one thing really had ended and that was my childhood. I had broken out of that bubble at last. I had entered man's estate: I had a degree; I had left home and I had known a woman. Innocence lasted longer then, and my sense of being, if no longer a child, then at least emotionally subadult, had taken me into my 20s. Until I went to Exeter I had hardly begun to live like a teenager, let alone as a young man. I had a now-distant memory of the games we played as boys, of roaming and small adventures, and finding out about things for myself instead of as part of a class. I remembered the security of a loving home and what it meant when that was removed. At the Hole I had learned how to cope with fear, loneliness and discomfort, at some cost, no doubt, to the sunnier side of my disposition. Books and the natural world came to mean more than games and gangs, yet this inward vision had the paradoxical and ultimately rewarding effect of turning my thoughts outward, away from the sordid realities of the present and out into the air where galaxies whirled like pinwheels and miracles of small life lurked in every mill-pool and stream. I discovered that you can make a land inside your head and explore it, even dwell inside it. Or you could liken this interior place to a smart-phone which you stock with favourite things: poems, songs, pictures. At the Hole I used to dream about a warm, comfortable room with a fire in the grate and a soft chair where I could curl up with a book of my choice. All alone where no one could bother me. That was what I wanted then above all things. I liked being alone, or, at any rate, I thought I did until I got lonely.

For a writer, a solitary disposition is not just an advantage but an absolute necessity. Writing is solo, inward work, alone in the swivel seat behind the desk by the big window. My kind of writing consists in essence of exploring a subject and then ordering it into a narrative with as much skill and panache as one can muster. Each book is the product of an interior journey; one which, even when you know the ultimate destination, can take you to unexpected places, unscheduled little halts. That may be one reason why one can write a narrative of a hundred thousand words without losing one's mind. What I did not fully realise when I set out on the book you hold in your hand is that the past, anyone's past, is made up of stories, chains of events that, in hindsight at least, seem to say something, to go somewhere, even when you failed to notice it at the time. I never expected to enjoy writing about my time at the Hole, but the words materialised as though they had lain in storage all this time, neatly laid out, all packed and sealed and ready for opening. It seems to me now that at least two things define my era and set it apart from childhood today: the freedom to roam and the enforced discipline of boarding: opposed sunshine and shadow. No doubt it is better today, when no one roams, and children cannot be slippered and beaten and caned, but at any rate today's boys and girls will have a different story to tell.

Some of the characters in my drama have departed the stage never to be seen again. Dee went to a teacher's training college in Wolverhampton; we lost touch after a year or two. My birding friend Brian joined the teaching staff of a private school where he formed another bird club but eventually discovered that plants are just as interesting as birds. 'Bally' followed his parents down-under, went native and became a free-lance photographer, filming outdoor escapades around the world. 'Mich', after working in his father's business for a while, set up his own computer company. 'Kosh', as I say, did rather well at propping up failing companies and putting them back on their feet. Most other Hole contemporaries seem to have vanished into the mists of the world never to be seen again.

My grandmother, dear Nanna, lived to the ripe old age of 93. After Grampa Redvers' death she struggled on alone at Remlap for another decade until the day she slipped and broke her leg. After that it had to be the care home in Sileby. She did not die so much as fade away. Anaemia runs in our female line, the Y-chromosome of the Palmers, and in her last days she resembled nothing so much as a gentle, patient ghost. The vicar described her as a 'dear old thing', which she was. They are all dead now, those once numerous uncles and great-aunts and great-grandads I knew as a child but could never work out who was who. Our family is shaped like an inverted tree with a mass of Palmers and Keelings above but just the four of us, two pairs of siblings, sitting in the grass beneath the boughs. From village homes bursting with brothers and sisters and uncles and aunts we have arrived at last with me in one house and Chris in another, just up the road, each alone like peas in a tin whistle.

Younger brother Chris, always the apple of his father's eye, did what Dad could not and learned to fly. After gaining his commercial pilot's licence at Hamble he joined a small airline, Air Anglia, based in Scotland, where for a time he was my neighbour in the village of Aboyne, chosen in his case for its proximity to a nearby gliding club, in mine for its anglophile and bio-diverse ambience. Eventually he landed a better-paid job in Cathay Pacific where he is now a senior captain and lives in a bigger house than any of his ancestors; and where, once again, I find myself his neighbour. He has become the father of two little Marrens, my nephews Ben and George, the first bearing our Grandad's name of Redvers, the second that of my mother's brother, our dear old Uncle George. Chris is now divorced. I have no genetic ambitions. I am the last and least productive of my line. I have no desire to help populate the world.

My father enjoyed a long retirement from the RAF, although 'enjoy' is just a turn of phrase, is it not? After I left home for the last time, in the fall of 1969, I saw him mainly during vacations and not always then. Some while ago I made a compendium of Dad-entries in my diary and many of them have a characteristic flavour: 'My new home: Dad Takes Charge'; 'Kids tell police Dad threatened them with a gun' (he hadn't but that didn't stop them); 'Dad outsings the carol singers'; 'Dad mistakes the smoke alarm for a mouse'; 'Dad walks into a wall—blames the wall'. Several entries say: 'Dad crashes the car'. Several more are to do with our nervousness at letting him loose with the chain-saw. After Chris and I moved to Ramsbury, he often used to come round to perform what he called 'little jobs' around the house and garden; more often than, frankly speaking, we wished for. I regret to say I sometimes used to hide as he peered through the glass, or nipped out round the back when his car nosed through the gate. The reason was that communication—you could hardly call it conversation—with our deaf and increasingly confused father could quickly turn surreal. From Dad's point of view we were the ones who were a little slow on the uptake.

The best of Dad was his eagerness to get involved in everything we did. Until his eyesight failed he read everything I wrote. Once, when he got wind that I was intending to write a little book about the Battle of Hastings, he turned hastily to the relevant passage in Churchill's *History of the English-Speaking Peoples* to acquaint himself with the details. Then he rang me up. "It's a marvellous story! You must read it". He insisted that I mention the feigned retreat, and the arrow that hit King Harold in the eye, and did I know that Duke William was a bastard? And of course everything Churchill had written was unarguably correct because

Churchill was advised by *historians*—and in Dad's view historians had a hotline with the Almighty. This was Dad, and he was trying to help. Dads like to help, seldom asking themselves whether their help is actually wanted or needed. It's the Dad-gene at work.

I am not sure exactly when he lost the plot altogether; it might have been the Christmas when his presents consisted of: a child's clockwork dinosaur, a packet of Bassett's liquorice allsorts and a video of *Sanders of the River*. Almost to the end of his days Dad kept physically trim by walking and swimming. His problems lay above the neck: in deafness, then near-blindness; then a slow but steady decline in his mental faculties. His memory went, and he started imagining things that were real only to him. He sometimes seemed to be in the grip of an obsession, often, seemingly, about the injustices and indignities he suffered as a child. He grew paranoid. Without warning his anger would blaze up and he would start shouting. The doctor was called in, but Dad refused to cooperate. "There's absolutely nothing wrong with *me*" (there might, he implied, be something wrong with the *doctor*). In the end, for the safety of my poor mother, I had to get him sectioned. He was taken away in a police car and, after futile efforts by psychiatrists to discover the cause of his sudden rages, there was nothing for it but to lock him away in the EMI ('Elderly Mentally Ill') ward of a care home. I was there when he died, aged 93, having no idea at all about what was happening to him. The last sentient emotion to leave him was anger; it was anger, the doctor said, that was keeping him alive. But there was a moment near the end when he suddenly seemed to notice mother and me, and his expression softened. He managed to say, "you two…" I think he wanted to say: "you two can go home now". He died on Easter Sunday, at peace at last. The hospital wing was named after Saturn, the bringer of old age, but the room where he died was called Sunbeam.

They say that childhood never really ends until your father has gone. For with his passing go the ties that had their origin in the cradle. 'What was silent in the father', said Nietzsche, 'speaks in the son.' Perhaps it is a reaction to the Dad within us, this eternal genetic armlock, which has made my brother and me chary about being too open with our feelings. We hold it in, like true sons of wartime England; we don't like it when people talk about their 'passion', as though surrendering self-control is the right way for a man to behave. In our day, it was thought better, more *British*, to keep a lid on things; better the head than the heart. Half the troubles of the world are caused by idiots who count excitement above intelligence.

My mother died on 6th September 2015. She, too, had just turned 93. The old person's friend, pneumonia, got her in the end. She passed away as quietly and uncomplainingly as she had lived. I think she was ready to go. Her ashes, and Dad's, are buried in the same grave in the churchyard in Ramsbury, by a sunny wall bright with flowers.

And now this really is the end. It would be foolish to say I have no regrets. My story is full of them. If I had been more receptive to good advice and influence, if I had been more determined to join in, and been less wayward and antipathetic, if I had pulled myself together and not given in to idleness and self-indulgence, if I had made more of my opportunities... But I am not going there. I made my choices with a free will and I'll stick with them now. I was lucky to be born with a kind of inward vision to compensate for the lousiness of my outward eyesight. I was lucky to feel that, wherever my young life took me, there was always a sense that I belonged to the natural world and it to me. And because I cared so much about it, as much as my own life, it was always odds on that I would find a way of turning nature and its conservation into a way of life. I acquired some sense of purpose there. In retrospect my career in the Nature Conservancy, and subsequently as a nature writer, was implicit from the start. It was the compass bearing which prevented my childhood from becoming a mere random set of events, and turned it into a story. For it is surely through stories that we make sense of the world and of our own small lives within it. What redeemed me was nature.

Omega et alpha. The end and the beginning.

Acknowledgements

This memoir represents what I remember about my childhood and teens. My late mother and father recalled details of their childhoods for me, and also of the first few years of my own. My brother Christopher read the first two parts in an early handwritten draft with a spirit of good-humoured tolerance; and he put me right on certain details, especially about aeroplanes. My dear late mother read the early chapters and was astonished at what I could remember although she remembered it too.

My schoolfriends Philip Balsdon and Simon Khosla shared with me some of their own experiences of Hole-dwelling. Michael Proctor kindly read the university section and I much valued his comments. With her expertise in ancestor-hunting, Niki Salfranc provided valuable leads on my father's family. With her eternal generosity, Libby Ingalls read the whole lot and her enthusiasm was hugely encouraging. Sue Everett gave me some advice about publishing which I took, and it turned out to be very good advice indeed. Mike McCarthy and Dick Seamons read extracts and made encouraging remarks. From the bottom of my heart I thank them all.

I could not have self-published this memoir without the design flair and technical expertise of Peter Creed of the Naturebureau. I also thank Barbara Creed for designing the beautiful jacket and Aurea Paquete who had the unenviable job of placing the images from my changeable notes. And finally I thank Bernard Mercer and Anneli Meeder of the Natural History Book Service for their kind help with storage and distribution.

This memoir is dedicated to my nephews Ben and George, the latest Marrens. They inherit a very different England to the one I knew. I hope my version of a lost world will interest them as they enter their own teens, and won't horrify them too much.